Reading the Qurʾān in Latin Christendom, 1140–1560

MATERIAL TEXTS

Series Editors

A complete list of books in the series
is available from the publisher.

Reading the Qurʾān in Latin Christendom, 1140–1560

Thomas E. Burman

PENN

University of Pennsylvania Press
Philadelphia

Printed in the United States of America on acid-free paper

10 9 8 7 6 5 4 3 2 1

First paperback edition 2009

Published by
University of Pennsylvania Press
Philadelphia, Pennsylvania 19104-4112

A Cataloging-in-Publication is available from the Library of Congress

ISBN 978-0-8122-2062-9

Contents

A Note on Matters of Form

Where I have quoted directly from medieval Latin manuscripts—this occurs mostly in the notes—I have in general maintained whatever punctuation, or lack of it, those manuscripts offer, and I have followed their spelling as well. When quoting Arabic in transliteration, both in the notes and in the text, I have largely followed the system for Romanization developed by the Library of Congress. Some Arabic terms and names that are used widely now in English I have normally used in the text without the full complement of diacritical marks (*hadith* and *Muhammad*, for example, rather than *ḥadīth* and *Muḥammad*). The name of the holy book that is the focus of this study, however, I have set out, as is commonly done these days, in diacritical fullness: *Qurʾān*. Because I believe it to be one of the better manuscripts of Mark of Toledo's thirteenth-century Latin translation of the Qurʾān, I have typically quoted that translation using Turin, Biblioteca Nazionale Universitaria, MS F. V. 35, despite the fact that it is a late fifteenth- or early sixteenth-century manuscript. Though I make no mention of this in the notes themselves, I have generally compared its version of the passages I quote with the two earliest manuscripts and have found that it nearly always is in agreement with them.

Introduction
Qurʾān Translation, Qurʾān Manuscripts, and Qurʾān Reading in Latin Christendom

The Qurʾān was a best seller in medieval and early modern Europe. Like the *Communist Manifesto* or *Das Kapital*, texts that were read by all sorts of non- and anti- and pro-communist inhabitants of the Western democracies during the Cold War, the Qurʾān was a book that, because of the way it informed a vast, competing, dangerous, and deeply attractive civilization, demanded to be read by Christian Europeans across the whole period from the mid-twelfth to the mid-sixteenth century. It was translated into Latin at least three times in this period—four times if we count a partial version. Some forty Latin and Arabic manuscripts of the Qurʾān that we know to have been read by Latin-Christian scholars have survived to this day, as well as one partial and two complete sixteenth-century printed editions, numbers that suggest a wide readership indeed.[1]

But though Islam's holy book found many readers in Latin Europe, Qurʾān study was not an identifiable scholarly discipline in medieval Christendom in the way that, say, biblical study was.[2] Though in the thirteenth century the Dominican order clearly encouraged some of its members to study Arabic and, presumably, the Qurʾān in its specialized language schools for missionaries,[3] the Qurʾān was not a text that anyone normally lectured on in the schools or universities. Lacking any consistent institutional framework in which to flourish, Qurʾān reading in medieval Europe left behind few traces of itself in some ways. For example, we have scarcely any information regarding specific groups of scholars who shared an interest in Qurʾān study, and little evidence that would allow us to reconstruct the chains of scholarly affiliation through which the Qurʾān circulated and along which ideas about how it ought to be read were passed. This lack, of course, is not at all surprising, since Qurʾān reading—even widespread

Qur'ān reading—could only be pursued at the edges of the main scholarly and intellectual traditions of Latin Christendom.[4]

But while many aspects of Latin Qur'ān reading remain hidden from us, there is still much that can be learned about how Latin-Christian intellectuals reacted when they opened the Qur'ān's pages. This is so in part because so many of them, after doing so, wrote down what they thought about both it and the religion it inspired in treatises attacking Islam and defending Christianity, treatises that have survived in large numbers down to the present. While there is relatively little modern scholarly work based on this body of literature that focuses directly and exclusively on Latin-Christian study of the Qur'ān,[5] the topic receives frequent, usually indirect, attention in a number of works that address the broader Christian understanding of Islam and Muhammad. Of these, none has been more influential—and deservedly so—than Norman Daniel's *Islam and the West: The Making of an Image*, originally published in 1960, but reissued in an expanded second edition in 1993 just before the author's death. Written in elegant prose and informed by a nuanced and careful reading of a vast number of Latin treatises against Islam, Daniel's book makes overwhelmingly clear the processes by which Latin clerics turned to largely authentic sources of information about Islam (including Latin versions of the Qur'ān) and collectively constructed an image of it that, while clearly identifiable as somehow Islamic (with Islam portrayed as strictly monotheistic, Muhammad as merely a prophet, and the basic practices of Islam more or less correctly sketched out), was nevertheless designed for the needs of Christian polemic and apologetic: Muhammad was a lecherous warmonger; Islam is a bellicose and promiscuous religion; the Qur'ān is a fraudulent pseudoscripture compiled from scraps of the Jewish and Christian Bibles combined with the epileptic ravings of Islam's false prophet.

In describing all this in rich and judiciously chosen detail, Daniel also tells us much about the Latin-Christian interaction with the Qur'ān itself. We see Latin intellectuals reading it closely to find passages that, for example, could be used to refute the Muslim claim that Christians had corrupted their scriptures by smuggling in Trinitarian notions and excising prophecies of Muhammad's coming. One Christian polemicist did this by taking "three texts from súrah V, which 'introduces the Lord, saying about Jesus, *We gave him,* that is, Jesus, *the Gospel, in which there is direction and light.*' But God, he argued, could not have said that there was guidance and light in the Gospel if it were corrupt."[6] Daniel likewise introduces us to Christian Qur'ān readers attending to such matters as the surah titles, which in their unexpected specificity—"The Ant," "The Spider," "Smoke"—always struck Western readers as odd.[7] A substantial section of the book allows us to watch Latin scholars combing through the many Qur'ānic verses that deal with Jesus and Mary. "Quite the most remarkable" of these readers, Daniel tells us, was William of Tripoli, a thirteenth-century Dominican who knew Arabic well and wrote an influential treatise on Islam in which he quoted a long sequence of Qur'ānic verses, all carefully translated into Latin, at one point even having "recourse to the [Muslim] commentators on the Qur'án." William was, in Daniel's view, unique: "This careful distinction between the commentators and the Qur'án is part of Tripoli's very rare respect for the text."[8] Rare it might have been; yet Daniel also makes us aware of William's fellow Dominican, Riccoldo da Monte di Croce, doing much the same thing,[9] and points out that Richard Fitzralph, non-Arabist though he was, took great pleasure in being able to quote directly from the Qur'ān. Indeed Fitzralph, Daniel tells us, worked "over [Robert of] Ketton's paraphrased Qur'ān with a scholarly care and attention to the letter which he was unable to give to the Arabic."[10]

While Daniel's great work focuses, as its title suggests, on the development of an overall Western image of Islam, and therefore dwells more on the formation of Latin-Christian ideas about Islam than on the actual act of Latin Qur'ān reading, his readers inevitably gather a great deal of insight into the dynamics of Qur'ān study in the medieval West. We come away with a vivid impression of Latin intellectuals aggressively analyzing the text, searching out its internal inconsistencies, its peculiarities, its departures from the biblical narrative.

But while much has been learned in the work of Daniel and others[11]—and doubtless much more can be learned—about Qur'ān reading in Europe based on the many Christian anti-Islamic treatises that survive from the medieval and early modern period, these polemical sources in themselves present interpretive difficulties that historians have not generally faced up to. "Polemical roles," as Thomas F. Glick has recently put it, "are tightly scripted":[12] each side in the literature of religious disputation tries inevitably to depict the other in the worst light possible, searching out the most damaging arguments against its religious adversary, formulating the harshest black-and-white assertions concerning the relationship of one religion to the other. These tightly scripted rules force polemicists to stay strictly on task, allowing them little opportunity to reveal other dimensions of their interaction with either the religious beliefs—or sacred texts—of the other. More seriously still, these rules consistently suppress the expression of any sense of ambivalence, any complexity of attitude about the religiously other. As a result, in a peculiar (yet somehow just) reversal, while diminishing the objects of their polemical attacks by forcing them into narrow and misleading categories, the authors of such tracts end up diminishing themselves: they come to seem rather small to us, tediously preoccupied with the narrowest doctrinal concerns. Thus Ibn Ḥazm of Cordoba (994–1064), one of the most learned and persistent critics of Jewish and Christian belief in the medieval Arab-Islamic world, gives the impression in his famous polemical works that he had no interest in Jewish belief and practice beyond what could be usefully deployed in arguing against Judaism.[13] We begin to feel, upon reading such works, that their authors learned about the religions that they attacked on a strictly "need-to-know basis," as Jeremy Cohen has so aptly put it, being entirely satisfied with the minimum necessary for polemic.[14] Yet Ibn Ḥazm, one of the greatest intellectuals of the medieval Islamic tradition, wrote in a number of other genres besides interreligious polemic, and his views on Judaism seem much different, his tone much more irenic when he discusses Jews in his legal works.[15]

If there is a single weakness in Norman Daniel's magnificent treatment of how Latin Christians came to conceive of Islam, it is the failure to account for this built-in deficiency in polemical literature. While we are occasionally treated to arresting portrayals of Latin scholars sifting through the Qurʾānic text, we learn virtually nothing of—because polemical treatises offer scarcely any evidence of—the reading strategies that these scholars employed to understand what this difficult text meant or to find the Qurʾānic passages that were of use to them. More seriously, Daniel's analysis of these first Latin readers of the Qurʾān overwhelmingly emphasizes a sort of collective incapacity to step outside a polemical frame of reference: "For a Latin it was an impossible imaginative effort" to understand how Muslims could view Jesus and Abraham as Muslims; "they could not imagine Scriptural stories in forms other than those in which the [biblical] Scriptures recounted them"; "[t]hey could not think themselves, even for the purposes of argument, into a position that was not based upon [the Bible]"; "[n]o medieval author could see any concept of God that was not Trinitarian as other than wholly defective"; "[t]he frontier that divided the mental attitudes of Christians and Muslims was emphatically defined and crossed with the greatest difficulty"; for "[a]t that time in Europe too great an effort was required to understand the unfamiliar."[16]

What Daniel's focus on polemical sources did not allow him to see is that this inability to move beyond a polemical engagement with the Qurʾān might have been a feature more of those polemical sources as a genre than of the men who wrote them. He took the constricted engagement with Islam and the Qurʾān that his sources revealed to him to be a result not of the tight-scriptedness of religious polemic in general but of the moral and intellectual deficiencies of Latin-Christian intellectuals. In this he was not by any means unusual. Glick has argued that most modern scholars have assumed that medieval polemicists were displaying the full scope of their personalities and abilities in the tracts that they wrote, and that, moreover, "religious ideology [was] the immediate context" of all interaction among people of different religions, so that "all such interaction was hostile."[17]

This book, in building on the irreplaceable work of Norman Daniel and many others, is an attempt to get around both the limitations of the polemical sources and the narrow view of the human personality that they engender, by examining Latin-Christian readers of the Qurʾān as they are revealed in a different and largely unexplored set of sources: the Latin translations of the Qurʾān and the many manuscripts in which they and the original Arabic version circulated in Latin Europe between the mid-twelfth and mid-sixteenth century. If we wish to get a glimpse of Latin-Christian scholars with the Qurʾān open in front of them at moments when they are not actively intent on producing arguments for Christianity and against Islam—if we hope to catch sight of them when they have not forced themselves into the narrow roles that polemical scripting requires—then these sources are our best hope.[18] Making our way through the Latin versions of the Qurʾān side by side with the Arabic text allows us to see how at least a handful of translators attempted to reckon with a difficult text written in a difficult language. While translation can, at times, be a vehicle for ideological polemic,[19] in general translating a text and attacking it are rather different things. Watching a Latin-Christian scholar making the Arabic of the Qurʾān speak in Latin, therefore, allows us to witness a very different sort of engagement with the text. Such Latin Qurʾāns, moreover, survive in dozens of manuscripts spread throughout Europe. As medievalists have long known, and as scholars of other periods have recently begun to realize, the specific material form in which texts exist can tell illuminating stories about how they were read.[20] Paying attention to the other works that were bound together with the Qurʾān in medieval manuscripts and early printed editions, to the study aids and commentaries that later readers affixed to it, and to the intriguing messages that the layout of the text on the page communicates: all this allows us to get some sense of how manuscript makers read the Qurʾānic text themselves and how they thought other readers would want to engage it. Finally, by taking notice of the things that later readers scribbled in the margins of their versions of the Qur'ān, it is possible for us to get a sense of the immediate and somewhat unformed reactions to it of Latin intellectuals.

Such an approach to understanding Latin-Christian Qur'ān reading—through how it was translated and how it circulated in Christian Europe in manuscript and printed form—will, I argue in this book, substantially modify the way we think about how Latin readers reacted to Islam's holy book.[21] Not only will it enable us to sketch the contours of how an academic study that lacked clear disciplinary status and an institutional home actually operated,[22] but this approach will also allow us to see that Latin-Christian interactions with the Qur'ān were a good deal more complex than we have long thought. It is true, as this book will show in some detail, that these unexplored sources testify to the ubiquity of polemical Qur'ān reading—Christian Europeans, it seems, were often thinking about polemic even when they were not actively writing it. But if the history of interreligious and intercultural contacts throughout the world "has a moral," as Anthony Grafton has remarked, "it is surely that no one likes anybody else very much."[23] Discovering this is not, therefore, all that surprising. More intriguing and, I think, more worthy of dwelling on at length are the reading approaches, the philological tools, and the textual concerns that worked in tandem with these polemical concerns. While usually invoked in service of polemic, these other approaches, tools, and concerns sometimes served other, very different purposes and even diverted the attention of polemicists away from their narrowly conceived goals. Any serious study of these Qur'ān readers, therefore, must, as Grafton argues, pay as much attention to these other scholarly tools and methods as it does "to the general human prejudices" that so often inform the study of other peoples' holy books.[24] And this book will attempt to do so. It will argue as one of its main theses, in fact, that Christian Qur'ān reading in this long period is characterized as much by what I will be calling philology—the laborious study of the meaning of Arabic words and grammar, of the historic Muslim understanding of the Qur'ān, and of its textual problems in both Arabic and Latin translation[25]—as it is by polemic; that these two modes of reading often existed side by side in the mind of the same reader; and that while philology was typically undertaken in the service of polemic (one has to understand a text in order to attack it), it also existed here and there quite independently.[26]

But I will also be arguing that there is a second kind of complexity that characterizes Latin-Christian Qur'ān reading. Alongside the complexity of reading practice—polemical and philological reading interacting with each other in intricate ways—I will be suggesting that we also find a complexity of attitudes toward the Qurʾān and of ways of experiencing it as a text and object. As far as I can tell, all the Qurʾān readers on which this book focuses considered it to a be false antiscripture. Yet there is plenty of evidence that they were nevertheless capable of viewing it and experiencing it in quite other ways at the same time. Most Europeans in this period, for example, read the Qurʾān in Robert of Ketton's much (and not entirely deservedly) maligned Latin paraphrase of the mid-twelfth century. While Robert had nothing good to say about Islam itself, he nevertheless chose a notably elevated register of Latin in which to present its holy book to his readers. As a result, while those readers probably also would have said nothing kind about Islam if pointedly asked, they nevertheless encountered the Qurʾān in the dress of elaborate, periodic Latin prose of the sort that contemporary rhetorical manuals recommended for important documents. Robert's own complex, even ambivalent interaction with the text—translating what he considered the fraudulent holy book of a "death-dealing" religion into elegant Latin—therefore created a text that his readers likewise viewed as evil but necessarily experienced as having some sort of prestige and high status.[27] A somewhat different set of complex attitudes is revealed in a handful of manuscripts from the end of the period in question. In these cases, the Qurʾān was given the form of an expensive collector's book meant for a wealthy aristocrat's library. The names of these collectors, illuminated in gold leaf on the frontispieces of such manscripts, instruct us that, in addition to understanding that the Qurʾān was a fake holy book, such consumers could view it at the same time as a desirable and exotic object useful for impressing one's wealthy friends.

The rapidly growing body of scholarship on the history of reading[28] has argued that ways of reading which historians and literary scholars have long thought to be antithetical to each other frequently existed side by side in the same period, even in the same reader. So we find, for example, that what we usually think of as humanist approaches to Latin texts were current among mid-fourteenth-century scholastics[29] and that in Renaissance France, rather than repudiating the typical medieval allegorization of Ovid, Renaissance readers actually mixed it with humanist ways of reading.[30] Any history of the "complex and protean enterprise" of reading, Anthony Grafton has further observed, must therefore "eschew grand theses and rapid transitions and accept the possibility of paradox and contradiction."[31] In a very real sense, I will be arguing that even though the Qurʾān was the holy book of Christendom's feared and powerful rival, Qur'ān reading in the Latin West was often just as complex and protean, just as frequently the site of paradox and apparent contradiction, as the reading of any other text, and that in its history, though there is a discernible but gradual evolution, there are no rapid transitions.

The present volume can be thought of as consisting of two parts. In Chapters 1 and 2 I will explore what can be learned about Qurʾān reading in Europe from looking closely at the handful of known Latin translators as they worked. In Chapter 1 I will argue that, while we might expect Christian translators to manipulate the Qurʾānic text as they put it into Latin, making it seem as shockingly wrongheaded and as fully un-Christian as possible, we actually have little evidence that they did so. In fact, watching the translators as they work allows us to see in a particularly vivid way that Latin readers certainly could engage the Qurʾānic text—at least when they were actually translating it—without polemical preoccupations overwhelmingly shaping their reactions. What we see here, indeed, is rather thoroughgoing philology. What they produced was by no means always good, but the problems with their translations have much less to do with intentional distortion of the Qurʾān than with varying philological ability. In Chapter 2 I will suggest that the most striking aspect of this philological approach to the Qurʾān on the part of its translators is the frequency with which they turn directly to Muslim sources to inform themselves about its meaning. Their Latin versions, and especially that first translation by Robert of Ketton, are frequently shaped by—indeed, they often incorporate directly—the views of Muslim Qurʾān commentators on difficult passages. In turning thus to Muslim authorities, these Christian translators, I will argue, actually approach reading the Qur'ān much as medieval Muslim translators of the Qur'ān did, for if we look at these Latin versions of the Qur'ān side by side with late medieval Castilian versions made by Iberian Muslims, we cannot help but notice that all these translators—both Christian and Muslim—freely turn to authoritative Muslim exegetical sources and interpolate words and phrases from them into their translations. In all this these translators anticipate, moreover, the reading approaches of still later Latin Qurʾān translators, such as Germanus of Silesia and, especially, Ludovico Marracci, among whom more modern approaches to Western Qurʾān study are generally thought to have developed.

Chapters 3 through 6 form the second major part of the book, each of them dwelling at some length on the complex frames into which these Latin versions of the Qurʾān, as well as in some cases the Arabic original, were inserted in the manuscripts in which they circulated. It is here, in the messages sent by the other books with which the Qur'ān was typically bound, by the commentaries through which it was explicated, and by the illuminations that accompanied it, that we really see the deployment of a thoroughly polemical way of reading the text. Indeed, the Qur'ān rarely ever circulated in Western Europe without such a polemical frame hedging it in and instructing its readers on the properly Christian way to understand it. Yet these frames that surrounded the Qur'ān and attempted to control how it was understood actually are much more than merely polemical tools, though it is that dimension that most obviously strikes the eye of a reader. From the very beginning, these framing devices were often shot through with philological concerns as well. The complicated apparatus of other works, marginal commentaries, and study aids that typically accompanied the Qur'ān, therefore, often turns out to be at once polemical and philological in its goals and procedures. Indeed, some of the later frames for the Qur'ān embody far more philology than polemic—at least on the surface—and a proper understanding of them requires us to see them as serving both functions. And these chapters will do so. In Chapter 3 I will analyze the deeply polemical and deeply philological frame constructed for the original manuscript of Robert of Ketton's widely read Latin Qur'ān; Chapter 4 will recount some of the variations in that frame as Robert's version was copied over and over in the twenty-five-odd manuscripts that preserve it; Chapter 5 will examine the much less abundant manuscript traditions of the Latin Qur'āns of Mark of Toledo (fl. 1193–1216) and Flavius Mithridates (fl. 1475–85); while Chapter 6 will discuss at length the two surviving manuscripts of the remarkable bilingual Qur'ān produced in 1518 under the auspices of Cardinal Egidio da Viterbo. In considering both the polemical and philological dimensions of the frames that surrounded the Qur'ān, I will also be discussing in these chapters the ways in which they help us to gain insight into the complex attitudes that Latin readers expressed regarding the Qur'ān, for it is often in these framing devices that we are able to catch glimpses of the Qur'ān being seen not just as a book to be attacked polemically, or analyzed philologically, but as an object to adorn one's book collection or even as a textbook on the basis of which to undertake Christian theological reflection.

In the conclusion I will attempt to draw together the various strands of this argument and to suggest some broader conclusions by reflecting on a rather different sort of source, written soon after the fall of Constantinople. In the later 1450s the Spanish theologian Juan de Segovia, in sponsoring and cocreating a new trilingual edition of the Qurʾān (in Arabic, Castilian, and Latin), read the Qurʾān with nearly obsessive intensity and left behind a lengthy description of that experience—the only narrative account of Latin-Christian Qurʾān reading from this period that I know to have survived. I will suggest that Juan's narration of his own encounter with the Qurʾān turns out to encapsulate many of the main features of Latin Qurʾān reading in the four centuries that this book discusses, and therefore obliges us to revise our understanding of the evolution of Qurʾānic and Islamic studies in the West.

I have elected in this book, perhaps rashly, to take on a broad period of history—the four centuries from the mid-twelfth century, when the Qurʾān first circulated in Latin, to the mid-sixteenth century, when it was first printed. I have done so in part because, like many contemporary scholars, I am anxious to examine the ways in which the high Middle Ages and what has traditionally been called the Renaissance and Reformation can fruitfully be seen as one coherent era unified by profound continuities, despite the real differences that separated the age of Aquinas from that of Luther. But this approach is also, and perhaps more truly, simply a result of where the sources themselves led me: when I began collecting microfilms of Qurʾān manuscripts that circulated in Western Europe, I found myself as fascinated by the stories that the sixteenth-century codices had to tell as I was by those of the twelfth and thirteenth centuries.

Yet while I have cast my net broadly, there are many issues that I have not addressed here. Lack of necesssary linguistic skill has prevented me from exploring the shape of Qurʾān study in Byzantium, where the Qurʾān certainly also circulated and was read by Christian scholars.[32] Moreover, those familiar with the study of Islam in the medieval West will find that the key figures—Peter the Venerable, Ramon Llull, Ramon Martí, Riccoldo da Monte di Croce, Nicholas of Cusa, Alonso de Espina[33]—play almost no role here, for by turning my attention away from the standard polemical and apologetic sources, I have necessarily turned my attention away from these seminal Latin-Christian students of Islam. Though I have been able to make valuable use of a certain amount of Latin marginalia jotted in copies of the Qurʾān that circulated in Europe, I have in many ways only scratched the surface of this abundant but difficult-to-use source.[34] Nor have I examined Qurʾān reading in Christian Europe as it appears in vernacular sources, such as the first Italian version of the Qurʾān printed in 1547.[35] There is much more that can be learned about Christendom's engagement with Islam's scriptures, therefore, not only from further study of the sources that will preoccupy us in this book but also from what I suspect will be the enormously fruitful results of relating these sources to the many others that I have just mentioned. Though I am convinced that the overall argument I am making here is fundamentally sound, I am certain that I have not said the last word.

Chapter 1

Translation, Philology, and Latin Style

In taking up their task, Latin-Christian Qurʾān translators had to find a way to make the Latin language utter the meaning of what is, as Qurʾānic verse 12:2 declares, a self-consciously Arabic book: "We have revealed it as an Arabic Qurʾān so that you perhaps will understand."[1] And not just Arabic, but "clear Arabic" (16:103) miraculously spoken by God through Gabriel directly to Muhammad. But while the Qurʾān's Arabic seemed miraculous to Muslims—both then and now—it was not miraculously clear in any simple way. Like all great holy books, the Qurʾān is, in fact, quite a difficult book in some ways. The reader, whether Muslim or not, must reckon with anachronistic language (anachronistic even to early Muslims), ellipticism, and allusion to stories and events that are not completely told within the text itself. From the earliest period of Islam, one of the most common things that Muslims have done as they have tried to adhere faithfully to the Qurʾān is to talk about what, after all, it means.

It was no small task, then, to find the Latin that could make this inimitable Arabic, this clear yet difficult Arabic, somehow speak to European audiences. In trying their hand at it, the four Latin Qurʾān translators that we know of before 1560 had to engage the Qurʾānic text very differently than did their contemporaries who wrote polemical treatises against Islam. The latter could, in the age-old manner of religious disputation, focus on a handful of Qurʾānic verses that could serve as useful proof texts, the rest of the book remaining largely irrelevant. Qurʾān translators, on the other hand, even those whose translations were specifically intended for use by polemicists and apologists, had to come to grips with the whole text. Flavius Mithridates, as we will see, translated only two surahs of the Qurʾān. Yet even he had to contend with extended portions of Qurʾānic narrative containing here and there the sort of proof texts that interested the disputatious but consisting for the most part of material irrelevant to polemic though not infrequently difficult to translate.

By examining how these four translators went about this task, therefore, we are able to watch as at least a few premodern European readers make their way systematically through Islam's complex holy book, reading each word and pondering its meaning, not—at least while they are preoccupied with translation—looking nervously here and there for the best ammunition to use against Muslims. What we will see as we watch this process is that these translators are not always very successful (at least one fails spectacularly), but that they are, nevertheless, primarily reading the Qurʾānic texts as philologists and not as polemicists. They are attentive, that is, to the minutiae of linguistic and textual interpretation—what does this word mean? how should one translate this nonstandard construction?—not to the matters at issue in religious disputation. It is true that we will come across evidence from time to time of translators momentarily adopting the mode of the polemicist, choosing a Latin word or formulation that makes the Qurʾān and Islam look misguided or heretical from the Christian point of view. But one cannot read through these translations without noticing how rare such tendentious translation is. As we will see, some of these translators were quite hostile to Islam, and we have no evidence that any were Islamophiles. When they were working as translators, however, the philological tasks that this role imposed pushed whatever polemical urges they had to the periphery. Working out how to make this difficult Arabic book speak in Latin was burden enough.

In addition to revealing philologists at work on the Qurʾānic text, this examination of the methods of Latin Qurʾān translators suggests something else as well. Translators always have to make choices about how they are going to carry out their task. Should the translated text follow the original as closely as possible, maintaining its word order, perpetuating its idiomatic qualities? Or should one attempt only to translate the sense, adopting the word order and ways of speaking characteristic of Latin? A quick glance through these surviving translations makes clear that, while the former approach—translating word for word—was by far the more common, the latter approach produced the version of the Qurʾān that was by far the most widely read in Latin Christendom. And not only was the most read version of the Qurʾān—Robert of Ketton's twelfth-century *Lex Mahumet*—translated according to the sense, rather than the word, but its translator actually went even further, inserting the Qurʾānic text into a kind of Latin style that was usually reserved for high-status, prestigious texts. It is not easy to determine why Robert of Ketton did this or what he meant to communicate by it. Yet this approach to translation made for an intriguingly complex way of experiencing the Qurʾān on the part of his readers. They were taking up an heretical pseudoscripture, or so they were told by the marginal notes and accompanying works that typically were bound with his version (as we will see in later chapters), yet its heretical ideas spoke to them in the elegant, elevated Latin of high culture.

Translators

To see all this, however, more must be said about these four translators and what led them to take up this difficult task. Three of the translators, Robert of Ketton, Mark of Toledo, and Flavius Mithridates, left us prefaces to their translations, though these are not particularly informative in many ways: like many premodern translators, they tell us virtually nothing about their translation methods. In addition to these prefaces, however, certain other information can be gleaned about these scholars that can give us some sense of how they each approached the Qur'ān. The translators sort themselves into two quite distinct groups—distinct in time and in intellectual and cultural context. Robert of Ketton (fl. 1136–57) and Mark of Toledo (fl. 1193–1216), creators of complete Latin Qur'ān translations, were both closely connected with one of the most important developments in medieval Latin-Christian intellectual history: the translation into Latin of the great works of Arabic science and philosophy.[2] Both Robert and Mark had been possessed by the twelfth- and thirteenth-century rationalist spirit that undergirded the Renaissance of the twelfth century and the Scholastic period, and, as we will see, they showed themselves far more loyal to that cause than to engagement with Islam as a religion. They made Qur'ān translations because wealthy and persuasive patrons made it worthwhile for them to set aside temporarily their enduring scientific interests. Having finished their Latin Qur'āns both returned to their first loves.

The second two Qur'ān translations were undertaken within the very different humanist world of the late fifteenth and early sixteenth centuries. Though we know almost nothing about the actual translator of the complete Latin Qur'ān of 1518, a shadowy figure named Iohannes Gabriel Terrolensis, we know a great deal about his famous patron, Egidio da Viterbo (1469–1532) and are fairly well informed about his contemporary Flavius Mithridates (fl. 1475–85), the translator of an extended portion of the Qur'ān. Like many other humanists in this period, they were both deeply involved in the study of Semitic languages. The study of Arabic (and Aramaic as well) was for them, as for other like-minded intellectuals—

especially the so-called biblical humanists who applied humanist methods of textual study to the Bible itself—a necessary part of mastering Hebrew.[3] Something else connected them and other contemporaries as well: they were keenly interested in Kabbalah. In the period of these latter two translators, a number of Christian intellectuals had begun to create a Christian Kabbalah, which saw in the theosophy of Jewish Kabbalah striking confirmation of Christian belief in the Trinity and Incarnation.[4] As we will see here and in later chapters, there are intriguing connections between Qurʾān study in this period and Christian kabbalism.

In 1142 Peter the Venerable, the powerful abbot of Cluny, came to Spain and, during his inspection of a number of Cluniac daughter monasteries, gathered together a group of Arabic-to-Latin translators and set them to work making Latin versions of a series of Muslim religious works. His plan was to provide Christian scholars with a body of authentic Islamic texts on the basis of which they could both understand Islam and refute its claims. Over the following few years Peter's translating team created Latin versions of *The Apology of al-Kindī*, a widely read Arabic defense of Christianity written by an anonymous Middle Eastern Christian, and a series of somewhat peculiar collections of Islamic Tradition, as well as the Qurʾān.[5] Robert of Ketton, an English member of Peter's translation team, perhaps with the assistance of an almost completely unknown Muslim named Muhammad, was the translator of the centerpiece of Peter's collection, the Latin Qurʾān which bore the title *Lex Mahumet pseudoprophete—The Religion of Muhammad the Pseudo-prophet.* Robert of Ketton's translation would go on to become the most widely read Latin version of Islam's holy book. It survives in some twenty-five medieval and early modern manuscripts and would be printed in editions of 1543 and 1550. When European Christians read the Qurʾān any time between the mid-twelfth and late seventeenth century, they usually read Robert's version.

Robert had come to Spain in the 1130s, drawn there by the hope of finding and studying Greco-Arabic science and mathematics. He traveled widely in Spain and England as he pursued his scientific interests and an ecclesiastical career, in both of which his Qurʾān translation, completed between 1141 and 1143, was an anomalous interruption.[6] To his translation Robert of Ketton affixed a preface in the form of a letter to Peter the Venerable, written—as was the custom of the genre—in remarkably elegant and complex prose.[7] Not surprisingly, he has nasty things to say here about the Islamic religion: it is a "death-dealing religion" (*lex letifera*) and the enemy of Christianity. In making his translation, Robert tells us, he has most diligently opened the ways and entrances for Peter's rejoinder to Islam, for he had seen how passionately Peter "thirsted to make fertile the sterile . . . swamp of the Saracen sect . . . and to destroy its ramparts altogether."[8] But Robert's surprising conclusion to this preface undermines the sense of polemical zeal that he otherwise communicates here. In a rising celebration of astronomy, Robert promises to Peter the Venerable a gift embracing the science that, "according to number and proportion and measure, entirely reveals all the heavenly orbits and their quantities . . . , and their effects and natures . . . to those who most diligently seek, leaning now on probable and sometimes on necessary arguments."[9] This concluding sentence would have been more suitable in a treatise on the astrolabe than in this introduction to a Latin Qur'ān, and its presence suggests that Robert was, all things considered, more interested in science than in Islam's holy book—"fanatical," as Dorothee Metlitzki said of him, "only on request."[10] After finishing his translation in 1143 Robert went back to translating scientific works and never, so far as we know, interested himself in the Qur'ān or anti-Islamic polemic again.

About his method Robert gives only a few hints.[11] His goal, he tells us, was to provide the raw material, what he called "the stones and wood," so that Peter could create from them his refutation of the Qur'ān as a "most beautiful and spacious edifice, interconnected and indissoluble." He claims, moreover, that he did so without excerpting or altering anything "in regard to sense (*sensibiliter*), except only for the purpose of understanding."[12] Robert never intended, then, to provide a word-for-word translation. Indeed he was, as scholars have been pointing out for five hundred years—usually with disgust—an extravagant and energetic paraphraser.[13] With this one adverb, *sensibiliter*, he openly announces to his readers that what follows is an attempt to translate the Qur'ān according to sense. We will see in the next chapter the remarkable lengths to which Robert often went to determine what Muslims thought was the sense of their holy book.

There is, finally, another term that may help us understand Robert's translating methods: *Latinitas*. A word often used in this period to mean "Latin Civilization,"[14] *Latinitas* is the only word that Robert uses to describe the culture that he is part of and for which he is making his Latin Qur'ān. "All Latin Civilization (*Latinitas*)," he says, "oppressed by the . . . inconveniences of ignorance and negligence, has allowed itself to ignore and fail to drive away the cause of its enemies."[15] It is striking that in his introduction to a Qur'ān translation made explicitly for Christian apologetic purposes he chooses a linguistic-cultural term, rather than a religious term (such as

Christianitas—"Christendom"), to identify his civilization. We shall see that Robert's translation, which aimed to provide the unexcerpted *sense* of the Qurʾān's meaning, also aimed to do so in an elevated Latin style suitable for someone who saw himself primarily as a citizen of "Latin Civilization."

In 1210 or 1211, three generations after Robert completed his Latin Qurʾān, Mark of Toledo was similarly persuaded to set aside scientific study in order to produce a Latin version of the Qurʾān for a powerful patron. Mark, a native of Iberia, probably learned Arabic growing up in that still highly Arab land. He was best known for medical translation.[16] It was the powerful archbishop of Toledo, Rodrigo Jiménez de Rada, together with his archdeacon, Mauricius, who set Mark to work on a new translation—Robert's translation, though made in Spain, had been diffused from Cluny and was apparently not available in Spain at this point.[17] As Lucy Pick has shown, Rodrigo's activities as archbishop were informed by a theology of Spanish Christian society which both made a place for Jews and Muslims within it and yet justified the dominance over them of the Christian church in general and of the archbishop of Toledo in particular.[18] Rodrigo's commissioning of a Qurʾān translation was just one aspect of the most striking initiative to arise from this vision: his mobilization of arms and opinion before and during the great campaign of Las Navas de Tolosa, which, in 1212, saw the combined armies of the Spanish kingdoms destroy the army of the Almohad dynasty that ruled Islamic Spain and which opened the way for the dramatic Christian conquests in the following four decades. Rodrigo wanted to subject Iberian Muslims to his overarching authority; for this a Latin Qurʾān was a necessity.

Mark says nothing kind about Islam in the preface to his Latin Qurʾān. Much of it, in fact, is dedicated to a polemical biography of Muhammad and an account of the expansion of Islam.[19] It is only after all this that Mark describes the genesis of his Qurʾān translation, and this he locates entirely within Spanish-Christian concerns about Islam. Archbishop Rodrigo, Mark tells us, "had recognized that [the see of Toledo] was infested with enemies of the cross . . . . for in places where suffragan bishops were at one time offering holy sacrifices to Jesus Christ, now the pseudoprophet is extolled in name."[20] For this reason Rodrigo took great care to see that the book which contained Muhammad's "sacrilegious principles" (*sacrilega instituta*) and "monstrous precepts" (*enormia precepta*) should be translated and put in the hands of orthodox Christian believers.[21] He had real hope for conversion too, or so Mark says: Rodrigo and Mauricius, his archdeacon, commissioned the translation so that "confused by the Christians, some Muslims might be drawn from the detestable principles of Muhammad into Catholic faith."[22]

Mark's hostility to Islam here is unstinting,[23] though other than translating some short treatises by Ibn Tūmart, he also never again concerned himself with Islamic literature.[24] Mark's Latin Qur'ān, usually titled *Liber Alchorani* (*The Book of the Qur'ān*), was known among later Latin Christians, though not nearly so widely as Robert's version. It survives in seven medieval manuscripts, one of them fragmentary.[25]

In the second half of the fifteenth century, Qur'ān translation entered its second phase, the earliest surviving product of which is the translation of two surahs of the Qur'ān completed in 1480 or 1481 by a somewhat shadowy figure usually known as Flavius Mithridates.[26] A Sicilian-Jewish convert to Christianity (in about 1470) he referred to himself by various names after his conversion—Guillelmus Siculus ("William the Sicilian"), Guillelmus Raymundus de Montecathero, or later by the adopted classicizing name, Flavius Mithridates, at times combining all these into the impressive Flavius Guillelmus Raymundus Mithridates. Famous for his knowledge of Semitic languages, Mithridates eventually was ordained and, in 1477, found his way to Rome where he remained for some years.

Mithridates' high standing at the papal court is indicated by the fact that on Good Friday of 1481 he preached a "Sermon on the Passion of Christ" before Pope Sixtus IV, a sermon that drew upon a wide range of unusual sources—including the Talmud and, strikingly enough, even the Qur'ān.[27] By 1485–86 Mithridates was in Perugia and Fratta, where he was the teacher of Pico della Mirandola in matters kabbalistic and made for him Latin translations of a series of Aramaic and Hebrew kabbalistic texts. While he translated other Hebrew, Greek, and Arabic works into Latin, these kabbalistic texts, some thirty-five hundred folios in length, represent the main body of his translation work and had an enormous influence on the development of Christian Kabbalah.[28]

While the passages of the Qur'ān that Mithridates quoted in his sermon before Sixtus IV (4:157 and 5:46–47) were not drawn from the two Qur'ānic surahs—twenty-one and twenty-two—that he translated and published, they may have been by-products of the larger Qur'ānic project that, though he never finished it, he was working on in the later 1470s and early 1480s. For, as he tells us in a short preface to his translation addressed to Federigo da Montefeltro, Duke of Urbino (1444–82), who had requested that he undertake the project, Mithridates was planning a polyglot Qur'ān: it was to be "translated from Arabic into the Latin language, then into Hebrew, and afterward into Chaldean and Syriac."[29] I will say more about the significance of this polyglot project in a later chapter. Suffice it to say here that Mithridates just barely got this project off the ground before moving on to other things. In a manuscript of 1480 or 1481[30] he set out his translation of the two surahs, with the Arabic originals on facing pages. No evidence of any Hebrew, Syriac, or Aramaic versions survives, nor of any translation whatsoever of the rest of the Qurʾān, though there are, as we will see, interesting signs that Mithridates was reading the Qurʾān alongside certain kabbalistic texts. While Bobzin has observed that long-term influences of Mithridates' Qurʾān translation are difficult to determine,[31] it is suggestive that his version of the two surahs exists in at least six manuscripts—by no means an insignificant number.[32] Someone was certainly interested in it. Whether it was actually much read is, as we will see later, another question.

What Mithridates achieved only partially—a bilingual Qurʾān—another and more famous Renaissance humanist and kabbalist, Egidio da Viterbo (1469–1532), accomplished in its entirety, though in the role of patron rather than translator. Of the translator of Egidio's Latin Qurʾān we know nothing other than his name: Iohannes Gabriel Terrolensis. Though Egidio left little to posterity in the form of published works, he was one of the leading intellectual and ecclesiastical figures of the age.[33] He was widely admired for his learned, biblical scholar's knowledge of Latin, Greek, and Hebrew. [34] François Secret, the leading modern scholar of Christian Kabbalah, remarked that "he knew all the Hebraists" of his day and observed that his work, all of which remained unpublished at his death, represents "the most remarkable effort in assimilating the Kabbalah within the world of Christian humanists."[35] He was one of the most admired preachers of the period[36] and was tapped to give the opening oration at the Fifth Lateran Council in 1512. Having served as Prior General of the Augustinian Hermits, an order he had joined in 1503, he was named cardinal in 1517 and eventually was a serious candidate for the papal throne. He was an energetic supporter of church reform and had been heavily involved in the reform of his own order.[37]

Egidio cultivated an interest in Semitic studies. He composed a lexicon of Hebrew and Aramaic which contains some hundred and twenty citations of the Qurʾān. His library included a *Table of the Alphabet in the Qurʾān in the Spanish Language*, and he was later said by Johann Albrecht von Widmanstetter to be the only man in Europe to have a competent knowledge of Arabic.[38] In 1518, soon after becoming cardinal, he was sent to Spain as a papal legate and, like Peter the Venerable before him, seized on the opportunity that a visit to Iberia presented to further his investigations into Islam. There he commissioned a new, complete translation of the Qur'ān, engaging the services of the native Spaniard Iohannes Gabriel Terrolensis, who completed it that year. No preface tells us about Egidio's (or Iohannes's) motives in making this translation or sheds any light on the translation principles that informed it. Egidio had been involved in religious apologetic and polemic—he had, for example, written a treatise against the Jews only a year earlier, in 1517—and he may have had such plans in mind here as well. But he also was deeply influenced by Ficino and Pico and, like them, was, as John O'Malley put it, "able to discover Christian truth in authors and systems which fell outside the limits of institutional Christianity."[39] Though we cannot be sure, this disposition may also have had something to do with his Qur'ān project. In Chapter 6 we will see that though the edition and translation that he commissioned no longer survives in its original form, we can be certain of many of its features. It is striking that, as Flavius Mithridates had done, Egidio presented the Latin version and the Arabic original side by side, and in this way clearly encouraged philological investigation: facing page translations are there, after all, to help one wrestle with linguistic problems. I will suggest later that there may well be polemical concerns beneath this extraordinarily philological surface, but in all its outward features, Egidio's edition and translation of the Qur'ān is a supremely philological tool and was, as later marginalia in one of its manuscripts make clear, read very much in that fashion by at least one sixteenth-century scholar.

Translation as Philology

When we turn now to look at these translators as Qur'ān readers, what we see primarily—I want to emphasize—is philology. They were all Christians, of course, so, not surprisingly, we do find here and there that these translators have wittingly or unwittingly distorted the Qur'ānic text so as to make it and Islam look silly or barbaric. Yet such tendentious translation is really rather rare. They do make plenty of mistakes, but these mistakes are overwhelmingly the mistakes of translators grappling honestly with the text. Nor do we have to ascribe to them particularly high-minded motives for this. For one thing, there was already plenty of material in the Qur'ān that Latin-Christian polemicists had been able to exploit to put Islam in a bad light without manipulating the text. For another, good, convincing apologetic and polemic—of the sort that Peter the Venerable and Rodrigo Jiménez de Rada wanted to develop—required sound translation if it were to be convincing to Muslims. At any rate, these translators, at least when they were translating, did not primarily approach the Qurʾānic text as polemicists attacking another religion's holy book: they read it largely as philologists trying to make their way through a difficult text.

This is a simple—perhaps even obvious—point, but one worth lingering over, and it comes out especially clearly in the case of three translators who produced word-for-word Latin versions of the Qurʾān: Mark of Toledo, Flavius Mithridates, and Iohannes Gabriel Terrolensis. While Robert of Ketton, the zealous paraphraser, also—as I will argue at length in the next chapter—read the Qurʾān largely in a philological mode, it is in the work of these verbatim translators that we are able to observe philological Qurʾān reading in its most elemental form on the part of Latin-Christian scholars. To watch them make their way through the Qurʾānic text, finding Latin words to express its Arabic, is to watch Christian scholars who otherwise seem to have had no love of Islam nevertheless putting aside the powerful compulsion to attack the text in favor of a quite laborious lexical and grammatical analysis of it.

We can see this by looking at even a relatively short passage. The first five verses of the Surah (22) of the Ḥajj occur right in the center of the Qurʾān and read as follows in a close English translation:

(1) O mankind, fear your Lord. The earthquake of the hour is a tremendous thing; (2) on the day you see it, each nursing mother will forget the nursling, and each pregnant mother will give birth to her pregnancy, and you will see mankind drunk when they are not drunk. But the punishment of God is hard. (3) And among mankind is one who disputes about God without knowledge and follows every defiant Satan. (4) It is prescribed for him that whoever follows him, he will lead astray, and guide him into flaming punishment. (5) O mankind, if you are in doubt about the resurrection, then [remember], we have created you from earth, and then from a drop, and then from a blood clot, then from a morsel of flesh formed and formless, so that we may make clear to you; and we make what we want to dwell in the womb until an appointed date, and then we bring you forth as a baby, then that you reach your maturity. And among you is one who dies, and among you is one who will be brought back to the basest of lifespans so that he knows nothing after he had known something. And you will see the earth lifeless, but when we have sent down upon it water it quivers and swells and sprouts forth every joyous pair.

Mark of Toledo's verbatim approach to translation is apparent from the first line of this passage,[40] his thirteenth-century version typically consisting of Latin words set forth in much the same order as the Arabic words that they translate. Most of the time, moreover, his Latin version is perfectly adequate, as in the first verse: *O vos homines creatorem timete quia terre motus hore est magnum quid* ("O you men, fear the creator, for the earthquake of the hour is a great thing"). Now it is true that his translation is marred here and there by obvious misunderstandings of the words he is translating,[41] but his attention to the most basic linguistic details of the Arabic before him is palpable. This is particularly noticeable in the obvious Arabicisms in his Latin. The beginning of verse 3 reads in Arabic, *min al-nās man yujādilu*, literally, "from among mankind is one who disputes." Mark, trying to match this common Arabic construction as closely as he can, writes *quidam hominum disputabunt* ("Certain of men will dispute"), rather than the normal Latin *quidam disputabunt* ("Certain ones will dispute"), and similar Arabicisms appear elsewhere in his version.[42] Sometimes, in fact, his intense focus on the meaning of each word as he encounters it leads him to misunderstand the larger meaning of what he is translating. He fumbles here, for example, a very common usage, the so-called *waw* of accompanying circumstance, in verse 2: *uidebitis . . . homines inebriatos*, he writes, *nec erunt inebriati* ("you will see men drunk and they will be not drunk"). The *wa-* that he translated here as *nec* ("and . . . not") should really be "when," as it was understood in the Arabic ("and you will see men drunk *when* they are not drunk"). And sometimes his clinging to the Arabic phraseology culminates in Latin that is grammatically allowable but must nevertheless have been hard to understand, as at the beginning of verse 4 where Mark has *Et scriptum est super ipsum* ("and it was written above him"). This is an overfaithful version of the Arabic's *kutiba ʿalayhi* ("it is written upon him," meaning "it is prescribed for him").

So this is hardly a perfect translation, but Mark's preoccupation with issues of philology—what does this word mean? what Latin words best communicate both the meaning and the form of the Arabic words?—is obvious. As he puzzles through the Arabic in front of him, moreover, Mark does not hesitate, even in this short passage, to depart from the strict verbatim approach he generally follows elsewhere if he thinks that clarity requires it. So in the phrase I just mentioned he gives us *ipsum* ("the same [person]") where the Arabic had simply "him" (*-hi*) in order to make clearer to the reader that the person in question is the Satan referred to in the immediately previous verse. For clarity's sake as well he indulges in a rare paraphrase in verse 2. The Qurʾān says here that "you will see each nursing mother forget her nursling." The verb that I have translated "forget" here is *tadhhalu*, which can mean either "to be stunned" or "to forget." To get across this range of meaning, Mark, with real insight, wrote *uidebitis lactatricem stupefacere et obliuiscere quem lactauit* ("you will see the nursing mother be stunned and forget the one she nurses").

Indeed sometimes we cannot help but be impressed by the results. Verse 5—the long discussion of the process of human development from the womb to the grave—presented several difficulties, not the least of which was the peculiar phrase "and we have created you . . . from a morsel of flesh formed and formless" (*muḍghatin mukhallaqatin wa-ghayr mukhallaqatin*). What "formed and unformed" meant here was, as any perusal of Arabic Qurʾān commentaries makes clear, a matter of real debate among Muslims, but it is striking to notice that Mark's solution, that it meant "consolidated and unconsolidated flesh" (*carne consolidata et non consolidata*), fits very well within the range of meanings that Muslim exegetes themselves offered.[43]

Mark of Toledo, as we have seen, had nothing kind to say about Islam in the polemical preface to his Qurʾān translation. Yet when we watch him translate this passage, we see a man in whom the thousand philological problems presented by Arabic-to-Latin translation have pushed aside all polemical and apologetic concerns. When he reads as a translator, he reads philologically.

Much the same thing can be said of the shadowy Iohannes Gabriel Terrolensis, who translated the Qurʾān for Egidio da Viterbo three hundred years later. Iohannes' translation of this passage[44] follows the Arabic of the Qurʾān every bit as closely as Mark's did, as his Latin version of verse 3 demonstrates: *et ex hominibus sunt qui disputant de deo absque scientia et sequuntur omnem diabolum maledictum* ("and from among men are those who dispute about God without knowledge and follow every cursed devil"). Indeed the first few words here—"and from among men are those who dispute"—echo the characteristic Arabic *min-man* construction much as Mark's *quidam hominum* ("certain of men") did. Iohannes's Latin, like Mark's, therefore, came to be shaped by distinctively Arabic ways of speaking. And like Mark's translation again, there are a number of problems here. Somehow out of the Arabic *sukārá* ("drunk") he got *uiduos* ("widowers"): "you will see humans as widowed and they will not be widowed," he writes in verse 2, this translation also failing, just as Mark's had done, to capture fully the sense of the Arabic *waw* of accompanying circumstance ("you will see mankind drunk *when* they are not drunk"). Iohannes' version of those puzzling words in verse 5, "we will create you . . . from a morsel of flesh formed and formless," is not nearly as effective as Mark's. Where the latter had "from consolidated and unconsolidated flesh," Iohannes gives us "from a piece creatable and un-creatable." This translation fails to convey to us that this is a piece of *flesh* (*muḍghah*) even as its "creatable and un-creatable" (*creabili et increabili*) does not communicate the completed action implied in the corresponding Arabic passive participles (*mukhallaqatin wa-ghayr mukhallaqatin*). But just as often, Iohannes's version is as sound as Mark's. His "on the day in which you will see each nurse abandon what she suckles" (*in die quo uidebitis relinquere quamcumque nutricem quod lactet*) captures the beginning of verse 2 with all the directness of the Arabic original.

We know nothing at all about Iohannes Gabriel Terrolensis's views on Islam—or on anything else for that matter, so little do we know about him. He may well have been a Muslim convert to Christianity and may thus have had unusual knowledge of the Qurʾān and, perhaps, real sympathies for his previous religion and its scripture.[45] At any rate, his translation of this passage is, like Mark's, primarily the work of a linguist preoccupied with pressing and difficult linguistic problems, not a polemicist concentrating on attacking what he is reading. We follow his eyes and brain, as we did Mark's, as they read each Arabic word, thinking through the manifold issues of case ending and conjugation; of pronoun reference (who is the "him" in "it was written above him" in verse 4?); of verbal tense, mood, and aspect; of Arabic morphology (what is the meaning of the second form passive participles—*mukhallaqatin*—in verse 5?); and syntactic coordination (how do the two clauses of verse 1, joined by a simple *inna* in Arabic, relate to each other?). His answers to these questions are not always right, but these are the questions—philological ones all of them—that he is intent upon answering; and when he gets them wrong, his mistakes are the result of insufficient learning, not whatever hostility toward the Qurʾānic text he may have had.

The work of the third of these verbatim Qurʾān translators—Flavius Mithridates, who completed his Latin version of two Qurʾānic surahs a generation before Iohannes gave us his complete Latin Qurʾān—in one way seems to argue against the case I have been making, for he seems not to care about careful philology at all.[46] Like Mark of Toledo and Iohannes Gabriel, Flavius Mithridates follows the Arabic syntax closely as he translates, but where their versions were marred from time to time by smallish errors, his is riddled with serious mistakes. In verse 2 of this passage, for example, he writes that on that terrible day, "Men will seem drunk, and why are they drunk?" Not only has he changed the active verb of the first clause to the passive, but he also wrongly reads the negative particle *mā* as an interrogative meaning "why." In verse 4 he reads the verb *WLY* V, here meaning something like "to take for a friend,"[47] as some form of the root *WLD*, meaning, in general "to give birth," and does not know what to do with the following verb, *yuḍillu*, "he will mislead," all this yielding, "It is written above him from when he was born, that he was most wickedly born" (*scriptum est . . . super eo a quando natus est. quod pessime natus est*). The Qur'ān says in verse 5 that "among you is one who will be brought to the basest of lifespans," having lived, that is, to the point of decrepitude and senility. Here Mithridates writes that "a certain one is brought back to earth" (*quidam ad terram reuertitur*), mistaking *ardhal*, "the basest," for *arḍ*, meaning "earth."

Errors on this scale show up throughout Mithridates' translation. The end of verse 34, which tells us that God is one, "so submit to him, and give good news to the humble" (*fa-la-hu aslimū wa-bashshir al-mukhbitīn*), Mithridates presents as "so announce [this] through messengers" (*et nunciate per nuncios*).[48] And the problems are just as severe in the previous surah. At verse 21:7 he misreads the Arabic *nūḥī*, "we inspired," as *Nūḥ*, "Noah," writing that "we sent before you Noah" (*missimus ante te noe*) where we should have "we sent before you none but men whom we inspired" (*Wa-mā arsalnā qablaka illá rijāl nūḥī . . .*).[49] Verse 35 is doubly garbled: "Death will taste every soul and they will be corrupted, and we will repay to you good things or bad things because of [your] merits, and to us you will return" (*Omnes animas gustabit mors. et corrumpentur: et reddemus uobis pro meritis bona uel mala: et ad nos revertemini*). He has confused subject and object in the first clause (all souls will taste death in the Arabic, not the other way round: *kull nafs dhā'iqat al-mawt*), and he has misrepresented the second: "we will try you with evil and good" (*wa-nablūkum bi-al-sharr wa-al-khayr*).[50]

Still, Mithridates does show a real feel for Arabic sometimes. He works hard at clarifying the relationships between clauses, for example. He is sensitive to the fact that *wa-*, "and," must often be translated as "for indeed," or "namely," and so gives us the occasional *enim* as a translation.[51] Despite his many failings, he not infrequently captures the Arabic meaning in particularly apt Latin. At the fourth verse of surah 21 he translates *ʿalīm*, "the knower," as *scientiam omnium habens*, "the one having knowledge of all things," which is particularly appropriate since God is what is being described in this passage, and the word certainly does mean "omniscient."[52]

Despite successes of this kind, it is tempting to conclude, with Giorgio Levi della Vida, that Mithridates' "knowledge of [the Arabic] language was far from perfect,"[53] and that the manifold errors of his translation are simply the result of insufficient learning of the sort that Guillaume Postel (d. 1581) also manifested a few generations later when he attempted to translate a number of passages of the Qur'ān for use in his *De orbis terrae concordia*.[54] Nevertheless we will see in a later chapter that there are compelling reasons to think that Mithridates knew far more Arabic, and far more about the Qur'ān, than this sloppy translation suggests. In working out an explanation for why a learned linguist like Mithridates would let such shabby work appear under his name we will come up against one of the most intriguing aspects of Qur'ān reading in the late fifteenth and early sixteenth centuries.[55]

Translation as Polemic?

Neither Mark of Toledo nor Iohannes Gabriel Terrolensis was a great translator, as we have seen, and Mithridates' version of surahs 21 and 22 is so defective as to be virtually useless, but neither they nor Robert of Ketton, whose very different translation methods we will consider presently, are anything like wholesale polemical distorters of the Qur'ānic text. Such tendentious translation, we should not forget, was certainly not unknown. James Hankins, for example, has shown that as a translator, Leonardo Bruni took the route of "selection, bowdlerization, and suppression" in order to make Plato seem more acceptable to Christian readers.[56] There are, moreover, passages that seem ripe for such polemical distortion. Verse 2:25, for example—the passage that tells how the righteous shall have paradise—caught the eye of many a Christian polemicist. It was the first of the many verses of the Qur'ān that described what medieval Christians disdainfully viewed as the carnal Islamic heaven, and was often the first verse to which Qur'ān readers added marginal notes as they read.[57] The standard Latin gloss on Robert of Ketton's Latin Qur'ān called on Christian readers to "Note that he [i.e., Muhammad] everywhere promises such a paradise, manifestly of carnal delights, which was another heresy earlier,"[58] and later polemical writers often gave their imaginations free rein on this subject, depicting the Islamic paradise in prurient and orgiastic images.[59] The Latin translators will have none of this, however, all of them translating this verse rather soberly.[60] Robert of Ketton's version had it that "they will possess the sweetest waters and various fruits and variegated produce and most becoming and pure women."[61] Mark of Toledo's translation relates that "those who will believe and who do good things" will have "paradises under which rivers will flow. As quickly as food from the fruits is collected for them, they will say 'it was collected for us before,' . . . and they will have in them chaste wives."[62] Egidio da Viterbo's version is similar: "those who have believed and done good works" will have "paradises under which rivers flow: and whenever they will be nourished with the nourishment of their trees, they will say, 'this is that by which we were nourished before' . . . they will have clean women."[63]

If we look elsewhere in their translations, we typically find the same thing—that passages lending themselves to polemical or apologetic distortion are nevertheless typically translated carefully and soberly. In 2:87 the Qur'ān recounts earlier revelations: "We gave Moses the Book, and we sent after him [other] messengers; and we gave Jesus son of Mary clear signs and upheld him with the holy spirit." The Qur'ān actually speaks frequently of this "holy spirit" (*rūḥ al-qudus*), sometimes, as here, as a divine helper for Jesus, sometimes identifying this holy spirit with Jesus. In conjunction with passages that describe Jesus as God's "word" (most famously in 4:171), such verses were typically used by Christian apologists to construct Trinitarian arguments on the basis of which apologists could then triumphantly claim that the Qur'ān actually validates this most difficult of Christian doctrines.[64] Yet there is no effort on behalf of the Qur'ān translators to distort 2:87 in favor of this Trinitarian interpretation. Robert of Ketton is particularly restrained, writing that "A book" had been given "to Moses and other prophets afterward, and likewise to Christ son of Mary, for whom the divine spirit was present as help and testimony."[65] It would have been perfectly legitimate to translate the key phrase, *rūḥ al-qudus*, as *spiritus sanctus*, the Latin-Christian term for "holy spirit," for this is essentially what the Arabic means. It is, in fact, the term that Arab Christians have traditionally used for the third person of the Trinity, and it is how the term is often translated in modern English versions of the Qur'ān.[66] But Robert here uses a notably less Trinitarian locution: "divine spirit" (*spiritus diuinus*). Mark of Toledo's verbatim translation actually has a slightly more Trinitarian feel, but there is no undue distortion of the text: "And we already gave Moses a book, and sent after him prophets, and we gave to Jesus son of Mary proofs and supported him with the holy spirit."[67] The version in Egidio's bilingual Qur'ān is very similar to Mark's.[68]

Nor did these three translators attempt to de-emphasize the aggresively anti-incarnational language of another famous passage, surah 112. Here Muhammad is called upon to "(1) Say: he is one God, (2) the everlasting God. (3) He does not beget, and he is not begotten. (4) And there is not to him any equal." Muslims understood (and understand) these verses to reject any notion that God has offspring. Indeed one Muslim commentator asserted specifically that verse 3 is "a denial of the Christians."[69] Robert of Ketton, however, does not soften this anti-incarnationalism in the least—in his version God is described as He "Who did not beget, and Who was not begotten, and He has not anyone similar to Him."[70] Mark of Toledo is no less direct: "He did not beget, and was not begotten, and nothing is similar to Him."[71] Iohannes Gabriel Terrolensis' version is equally uncompromising.[72]

It would be foolish to imagine that the Christian beliefs of these translators would never intrude into their work. In fact, we will see below a case in which Robert translates the word *jinn*, a term for the spiritual beings that Islam believes can be either good or evil, as "demon" in a context where this mistranslation seems willfully damaging to the Prophet's religion, and we will come across other examples from time to time as well.[73] Indeed, Norman Daniel opined that Robert of Ketton "was always liable to heighten or exaggerate a harmless text in order to give it a nasty or licentious ring, or to prefer an improbable but unpleasant interpretation of the meaning to a likely but normal one."[74] Yet it is worth pointing out that one of the few passages that Daniel singled out as exemplifying this tendency may not have been as gratuitously polemical as he imagined. At verse 12:31 the Qur'ān tells us that upon seeing Joseph certain women of Egypt "exalted him" (*akbarnahu*). Robert gives us this translation: "when they saw him, they all menstruated."[75] Daniel concedes that the verb could have this meaning, but to translate it thus, in his view, is far-fetched in the extreme: "Ketton deformed it to make it repulsive to decent readers."[76] That may well be true, but if so, he deformed it in a way that Muslim Qur'ān interpreters had also already deformed it, for many commentators had suggested explicitly that *akbarna* should, in fact, be understood to mean "they menstruated" (*ḥiḍna*). It is true that this seems to be a minority opinion that al-Ṭabarī and Ibn ʿAṭīyah find doubtful, but other commentators are more welcoming.[77]

We will see later that such influence of Muslim Qur'ān exegesis on the Latin Qur'ān translators was surprisingly widespread. The important thing here is to notice that, while Robert probably was polemically distorting this passage, albeit in accordance with an accepted Muslim interpretation, such obviously polemical reworkings of the text on the part of these translators are strikingly few in number. Indeed, Daniel stressed elsewhere that both Robert of Ketton and Mark of Toledo felt that they visibly had to "disown" their largely unpolemical translations by writing unrelentingly hostile prefaces to them. Ketton's version, he observed, "does not look careless or shoddy . . . . any analysis of the text" suggesting, in fact, that "each omission and elision . . . is deliberate," intended "just as he claimed . . . to make it intelligible . . . to the reader, not to make it seem more evil than he already thought it."[78] Gilbert Dahan has recently shown that the Christian-produced Latin translations of Talmudic extracts made in the thirteenth century, while by no means always correct, were nevertheless also relatively faithful versions of these Jewish texts, polemic playing only a rare, "secondary" role in the translation process itself, even though these extracts were emphatically intended for polemical and apologetic purposes.[79] The Latin Qur'ān translations embody almost exactly the same features.

What is noticeable about these premodern Qur'ān translators, therefore, is not that they pour their efforts into distorting the Qur'ān to make it suit Christian expectations, but rather that they go to such great lengths to get across what they (often mistakenly) see as the meaning of the text. Daniel was doubtless correct that when it came to writing polemical treatises, Latin-Christians found that "[t]he frontier that divided the mental attitudes of Christians and Muslims was emphatically defined and crossed with great difficulty."[80] But when we look on as Latin Christians translate the Qur'ān, rather than attack it, we find that they cross these boundaries in surprisingly effective ways, struggling with the meaning of Islam's holy book in a thousand minute and recondite ways, directing their effort at translating its basic meaning, even the obviously anti-Christian meaning of surah 112.

Robert of Ketton: Translation, Paraphrase, and the Elevated Style

Robert of Ketton's Latin Qur'ān, by far the most widely read of the four translations, resembles the others in many ways. His work is informed by extensive philological investigation—even more so, in reality, than any of the others, as the following chapter will make clear. While it is by no means flawless,[81] it shows, as we have just seen, relatively few signs of obvious polemical distortion. The only remaining task for this chapter is to reflect on the one notably unusual thing about his translation: its ambitious, paraphrasing approach. Robert has been notorious for this from the fifteenth century down to our own day, critics assuming that because his version is a paraphrase it must necessarily be less reliable than the word-for-word translations we have just examined.[82] But during these six hundred years of hand-wringing no one has asked what the consequences of this approach might have been for his later readers. To answer this question we must pay close attention to the surprising Latin style of the result.

There is no denying that Robert often reworked the Qurʾānic text with astonishing ambition, as his version of 2:23–28 makes all too clear. In a close English translation, this passage reads as follows:

(23) and if you are in doubt about what we have revealed to our servant, then produce a surah the like of it, and call your witnesses other than God, if you are truthful. (24) But if you do not do it, and you will not do it, then fear the fire whose fuel is humankind and stones, which is prepared for unbelievers. (25) And give good news to those who believe and do good works, that for them are the gardens under which flow rivers; whenever they are granted provision of fruit from them, they say, 'this is that of which we were given provision previously,' and it is given to them in resemblance of it; and for them are pure companions there, and there they are ever abiding. (26) God does not blush to coin a parable even of a gnat or what is beyond it. As for those who believe, well they know that it is the truth from their lord, and as for those who disbelieve, well they say, 'what does God mean by this parable?' He guides many astray through it, and he guides many aright; and he guides astray only the iniquitous. (27) Those who break the covenant of God after agreeing upon it, and who sever what God orders to be joined, and who become corrupt on the earth, these are those who are lost. (28) How do you disbelieve in God? When you were dead, he gave you life, and then he will cause you to die, and then he will give life to you and then to him you will return.

Robert gives us this version:

(23) huncque librum ueracem esse penitus credite: uel consimilem simul omnes manum conferentes. si possibile sit: perficite. testibusque firmate. (24–25) Sin autem: ignem gehennę malos puniturum pertimescentes. deum paradiso bonos inducturum. ubi dulcissimas aquas. pomaque multimoda. fructusque varios. et decentissimas ac mundissimas mulieres. omnemque bonum in eternum possidebunt: predicate. (26–27) Prauos autem et incredulos. culicibus uel huiusmodi comparare: deus nequaquam erubescet. Multis itaque bonis recto calle gradientibus. cum mali plures. ipsique soli mentientes deo. nefanda et a deo prohibita. sicque sibi flagicio sunt. gerentes. perniciosam sectam exequantur: deum prece quare non flectitis? (28) Hic namque uos ad uitam de non esse deducens: mortem inducet. et ad se uos resurgere faciet.[83]

[(23) Believe deeply that this book is true, or, with all lending a hand at once, complete—if it is possible—one resembling it, and vouch for it with witnesses. (24–25) But if not, then fearing the fire of Gehenna about to punish the evil, announce that God will lead the good into paradise where they will possess the sweetest waters and variegated fruits and various produce and most proper and most clean women and every good in eternity. (26–27) God by no means will blush to compare the depraved and unbelieving to gnats or such like. With, therefore, many good people walking by the straight path, why do you not make God turn [to you] by prayer, since many bad people, lying to God alone, follow the pernicious sect, doing things unspeakable to and prohibited by God, and so are a disgrace to themselves? (28) For he, drawing you out of nonbeing into life, will bring on death, and will make you rise up to him.]

This is thoroughgoing paraphrase from start to finish. The first verse's "if-then" construction—"If you are in doubt . . . , then produce a surah the like of it"—Robert has recast as a dual command: "Believe . . . that this book is true, or . . . complete . . . one resembling it." He has left out the question that begins the last verse ("How do you disbelieve in God?"). In between, he has collapsed two pairs of verses into single sentences. Verse 24's "But if you do not do it, and you will not do it," he curtly renders "But if not," and then takes the imperative "then fear the fire" and reworks it as a participial phrase, "fearing the fire of Gehenna," which itself he annexes to the imperative of verse 25: "announce that God will lead the good into paradise." After conveying quite clearly the first part of verse 26 ("God by no means will blush to compare the depraved . . . to gnats . . ."), he then, flummoxed perhaps by troublesome grammar here, translates the remainder of that verse and all the following in a way that only vaguely relates to the Arabic original.[84]

This is just the sort of thing that Robert's scholarly readers over the centuries have loved to condemn in him. Juan de Segovia, who in his preface to his own lost Qurʾān translation wrote the first, longest, and fairest critique of Robert's Latin Qurʾān, summarized Robert's faults as a translator as follows: he moved what was at the beginning of many passages to the end, and vice versa; he altered the meaning of Qurʾānic terms; he often left out what was explicitly in the text, and included what was only implicit in the text.[85] Nearly every one of these sins appears in the above passage. It is easy to see why, therefore, David Colville, a Scottish-Catholic Orientalist of the early seventeenth century, would say of Robert's version that in it "you will scarcely find one line that squares with the text."[86] Such criticisms have continued to the present.[87] It is also true, however, that this particular passage of Robert's translation is not entirely representative. While he paraphrases throughout—what Bobzin insightfully described as translation by "new composition"[88]—there are not many places in his *Lex Mahumet* where the Latin version and the Arabic original are as far apart as they are here in 2:26–27. Yet even though his version of verses 22:1–5 conforms more closely to the Arabic syntax, Robert of Ketton is still the paraphraser when he comes to that passage,[89] and his zeal for paraphrasing never flags: we still find him adjusting and reworking when he arrives at the final verses of Islam's holy book.[90]

But while many scholars have mentioned Robert's paraphrasing ways, no one has discussed what, I suspect, is really a much more interesting question: what is the character of the resulting Latin text? What I want to suggest in the remaining pages of this chapter is that what Robert was producing with this energetic recomposition was a Latin Qur'ān that conformed, intriguingly enough, to the contemporary canons of good style, what modern scholars have called "the elevated style." When Latin readers read Robert's translation, therefore, they encountered a document whose style bespoke prestige and cultural validity, even though—as we will see in later chapters—the standard notes that surrounded it and the supplementary works that accompanied it instructed them to read it as an heretical pseudoscripture.

If we shift our gaze away from Robert's departures from the Qur'ān's Arabic word order and toward the character of the Latin text that emerged as a result, it becomes clear that Robert was systematically employing Latin compositional techniques that were recommended in his age in such widely read rhetorical manuals as the pseudo-Ciceronian *Rhetorica ad Herrenium*.[91] In verses 2:21–29,[92] for example, we cannot help noticing that Robert has built symmetry into his text by the use of syntactically parallel clauses, a common practice among cultivated authors in this period.[93] He casts verses 21 through 25 as three long sentences built around a series of clauses most of whose main verbs are in the imperative and placed at the end: *(21–22) Omnes igitur homines Deum . . . inuocantes: <u>timete</u>. eique nullum existere parem <u>firmate</u>.* (23) *huncque librum . . . penitus <u>credite</u>: uel consimilem . . . omnes manum conferentes . . . <u>proficite</u>. testibusque <u>firmate</u>.* (24–25) *Sin autem: ignem gehennę malos puniturum pertimescentes. deum paradiso bonos inducturum . . . <u>predicate</u>.* Moreover, within this series of parallel imperative clauses, Robert adds another symmetrical element—repeated present participles (*inuocantes, conferentes, pertimescentes*). Verse 26 contains another notable parallelism (*<u>deo nefanda</u> et a <u>deo prohibita</u> . . . gerentes*), as do the following two verses with their alternating present participles and third-person verbs: *Hic . . . uos ad vitam . . . deducens: mortem* inducet . . . *qui mundanis peractis ascendens: septem celos omnium sciens.* disposuit.

The first five verses of Robert's version of the Surah (22) of the Ḥajj embody similar techniques. Here Robert employs the technique known as hyperbaton, the separation of words that normally belong together, a literary figure that the highly inflected Latin language facilitates: *deus malum inferet grauissimum* (verse 2), and, even more notably, *et erit quidam mortis iuri suppositus* (verse 5). He builds in parallelism as well—*quando nutrix suum alumpnum renuet. pregnans aborsum faciet* (verse 2)—in one case even incorporating a further literary figure, the repetition of a word at the beginning of successive clauses, a technique called anaphora by ancient rhetoricians: *et erit quidam mortis iuri suppositus. quidam autem ad uitam peiorem deductus* (verse 5), this first clause containing, as we have just seen, hyperbaton as well.[94]

Robert was still drawing on such techniques at the end of his Latin Qur'ān, perhaps nowhere more strikingly than in his version of the hundredth surah, the Surah of the Runners:

(1) Quando strepitum hanelo pectore emiserunt equi. (2) et ex suorum pedum ictibus ignis e lapidibus excussus. (4) et e terra puluis eleuatus. (3–5) mane preda facta contigit: (7–8) homo bonorum atque diuitiarum studiosus. (6) deo nequaquam inde gratiam seu gloriam: persoluit. (8–9) Nonne cogitauit quod deus homines e foueis suscitaturus: (10–11) illis suscitatis omnia facta sua reuelabit.[95]

[(1) When horses emitted a rumbling groan from the panting chest, (2) and fire was struck forth from the stones from the blows of their feet, (4) and dust was raised up from the earth, (3–5) morning broke when the plundering was done. (7–8) Man, zealous for goods and wealth, (6) by no means offered God thanks and glory afterward. (8–9) Did he not think that God, who will raise all men from graves, (10–11) will reveal to those arisen all their acts?]

These remarkable lines are constructed around some of the same techniques that Robert used in the previous passages. The use of parallelism is particularly clear, the verses as a whole being reworked into three sentences, each ending in parallel third-person verbs. The second of these sentences, moreover, incorporates the symmetrical pairing of *gratiam seu gloriam: persoluit* (verse 6), a certainly gratuitous addition by Robert, the Arabic here reading simply, "A man is ungrateful to his Lord" (*Inna al-insān li-rabbihi la-kanūdun*). In the last line Robert introduces still another figure, what Latin writers called *traductio*, the use of the same word in different cases to make for eloquence: *deus homines e foueis suscitaturus*: (10–11) *illis suscitatis omnia facta sua reuelabit*.[96]

There can be little doubt, therefore, that the Latin prose into which Robert of Ketton inserted the Qur'ān has the "sonorous, sermonlike style" associated with elevated prose in this period.[97] Robert's Latin has, in fact, at least one somewhat unusual feature that may well have made it seem even more majestic. Where other twelfth-century prose writers preferred to place main verbs early in the sentence, the remaining clauses and phrases elaborating on that core idea, Robert clearly preferred to put the essential meaning of the sentence at the very end by placing the main verb last or nearly last. In Cicero's prose, suspense is the key element, the essential meaning of the sentence being held in reserve until the very end, the complex, interwoven clauses and phrases that precede it creating a sort of dramatic lead-up to the main clause.[98] Robert of Ketton's sentences typically have much the same movement, he perhaps intentionally imitating the great Roman orator in the same way as did other writers of the age such as Meinhard of Bamberg (d. 1088) and John of Salisbury (d. 1180).[99]

Writers contemporary with Robert, such as Peter the Venerable, recognized that an elevated style of this sort was not suitable for all occasions or all audiences, and were quite willing to adopt a less solemn tone in other circumstances.[100] Indeed translators throughout history, such as Jerome, have recognized that different kinds of texts can require very different translation methods.[101] Robert likewise appears to have believed that the Qur'ān required a different Latin style than scientific treatises did, for, while he also tended to rework the Arabic syntax in his scientific translations, his paraphrasing of the Qur'ān seems notably more ambitious. He appears, therefore, to have singled out Islam's holy book for a particularly elevated Latin style.[102] Indeed, it looks very much as if he were aiming, in his Qur'ān translation, at a Latin style that translation theorists might describe as "functionally equivalent" to the Arabic style of the Qur'ān.[103] With its unusual rhymed prose, often containing intriguing rhythmical patterns, Qur'ānic style was seen not only as inimitable but as profoundly suited to its solemn and elevated theme.[104] That Robert was trying to give his Latin Qur'ān some of the same solemn feel of the Arabic original comes out all the more strikingly if we look again at the other Qur'ān translators. While Mark of Toledo in one case adopts a peculiar classicism (*Avernus* for *al-sa'īr*, "fire"),[105] his version otherwise has little of the parallelism, balanced phrasing, or elegant figures such as *traductio* that we find so often in Robert's Latin.

Unlike our other three translators, then, Robert wrote his Latin Qur'ān in the elevated Latin style admired in his day.[106] This fact, moreover, was not lost on at least one of his medieval readers. In the midst of his searching critique of Robert of Ketton's Latin Qur'ān, Juan de Segovia observed that Robert was "a splendid rhetorician and poet," as one could plainly see from the preface to his Qur'ān translation, and that Robert's Latin Qur'ān was translated according to "his mode of eloquence."[107] We will never know how Robert himself would have explained or justified the choices he made as translator. What is certain is that most of Christendom, not only through the mid-sixteenth century, but down to the beginning of the eighteenth, encountered the sacred scripture of Islam in the form of this Latin Qur'ān produced by "a splendid rhetorician and poet."[108] For these many later students of Islam, therefore, to read the Qur'ān was to read an ecclesiastically condemned book written in culturally validating language. It was the pseudo-scripture of a false prophet, and, at the same time, a Latin text that inspired admiration.

But Juan de Segovia was not merely impressed with Robert of Ketton's abilities as rhetor and poet; he also, despite all his criticisms of Robert's translation method, conceded that Robert had added no fabrications to his Latin Qur'ān and had suppressed nothing essential. "In fact," he observed, "almost the whole substance of the Qur'ān is found in that same translation."[109] While modern scholars have generally been contemptuous of Robert's achievement, a few have made much the same concession.[110] That Robert achieved so much arises from another central aspect of his translation method, one that he shared with Mark of Toledo and Iohannes Gabriel Terrolensis as well: in order to understand the complicated Arabic text in front of them as they translated, all three of these translators—but especially Robert—turned directly to sources of Islamic Qur'ān exegesis to help resolve textual problems. In doing so, as we will see in the next chapter, these translators anticipated by hundreds of years the scholarly approaches of those seventeenth-century European Orientalists among whom modern, western Qur'ān scholarship has long been thought to have begun.

Chapter 2

Latin-Christian Qur'ān Translators, Muslim Qur'ān Exegesis

There is no clearer sign of the potential difficulties for the Qur'ān's translators than the existence in the Islamic world of a whole genre of lexicons of the so-called "strange" or "foreign" words in the Qur'ān. For as Muslims realized early on, there were a number of words in their sacred text that were not part of ordinary Arabic discourse, some of them deriving from rare Arabic or Semitic roots, some of them traceable to even more exotic languages, such as Persian.[1] For a medieval Latin translator such "strange" Qur'ānic terms must have been maddening. What was one to do, for example, with the peculiar terms *jibt* and *ṭāghūt* in verse 4:51: "Have you not seen those who were given a portion of the Book? They believe in *jibt* and *ṭāghūt* and they say to those who disbelieve: 'these are more rightly guided along the way than those who believe.'" These words were rare enough that the lexicons of the Qur'ān's foreign vocabulary regularly discussed them,[2] as did the more typical Arabic commentaries on the Qur'ān. The twelfth-century Andalusī commentator Ibn ʿAṭīyah, for example, set forth a typical range of views on their meaning: some early Muslims said that they were both idols (*ṣanamān*) of the Arab tribe Quraysh; others said they were particular men whom some of the Children of Israel had believed in and followed; some suggested that *jibt* meant "sorcery" (*siḥr*) while *ṭāghūt* referred to Satan; still others considered that the former meant "soothsayer" (*kāhin*) while the latter meant "sorcerer" (*sāḥir*).[3]

While these two words—whatever they meant exactly—did turn up occasionally in later Arabic texts,[4] they were hardly commonplace Arabic terms, which makes it particularly striking when we turn to Robert of Ketton's Latin version of the Qur'ān and find that he provides us with a translation of them that clearly reflects what commentators like Ibn ʿAṭīyah said about them. *Magos et idola credentes*, "sorcerers and believers in idols," Robert wrote, suggesting something else about how he, as translator, read the Qur'ān.[5] No amount of study of Arabic morphology and grammar was much help here. To get these terms right Robert needed to tap into a body of traditional Muslim ideas about what the Qur'ānic text meant: he had to turn to Muslims themselves. Somehow Robert managed this, finding out that these two perplexing words were thought by many Muslims to refer to sorcerers and idol worshippers. And Robert did this over and over in his Qur'ān translation, as indeed did Mark of Toledo and Iohannes Gabriel Terrolensis. Repeatedly we find that, faced with the sort of difficulties that the "strange" words of the Qur'ān presented, these three translators turned to Arab-Muslim authorities themselves for guidance. Their Latin translations, as a consequence, were palpably shaped by the views of Muslim scholars. Translating the Qur'ān between 1140 and 1560, therefore, not only meant engaging the Qur'ānic text itself; it also often meant being drawn into the vast body of Arabic Qur'ān commentary and exegesis, as if by its tremendous gravitational pull. I will say more later about why this should not surprise us. Suffice it to say here that just as medieval Latin-Christian Biblical commentators on the book of Ruth found themselves relying heavily on Jewish exegesis because of the peculiar difficulties presented by that book,[6] so Latin-Christian Qur'ān translators, faced with a range of difficult Qur'ānic passages, likewise took the path of least resistance: they turned directly to the Qur'ānic commentaries or to learned Muslim scholars for explanation. This requires us, moreover, as I will suggest at the end of the chapter, to recognize that the distance between these Latin-Christian translators and both contemporary Muslim Qur'ān readers and later European scholars of the Qur'ān is not nearly as great as we might imagine.

This dependence of Latin Qur'ān translators on Islamic Qur'ān interpretation is clearest in the case of Robert of Ketton, whom we find incorporating material from the Islamic exegetical tradition throughout his translation. In fact, it shows up in the passage (22:1–5) over which I compared the methods of the four Qur'ān translators in the last chapter. Most notably, Robert added the qualification that the "earthquake of the hour" described in 22:1 will occur on the "day of resurrection" (*die resurrectionis*).[7] Though there was disagreement about its exact timing, there was agreement among Muslim commentators that this earthquake would occur in conjunction with the *yawm al-qiyāmah* ("the day of resurrection"), just as Robert insisted.[8] Verse 5 likewise contains an adjustment based on Islamic exegesis. Here, in the midst of the long description of God's creation of individual humans from conception to death, Robert wrote that "a certain man will be soon (*cito*) placed under the jurisdiction of death,"[9] whereas the Qur'ān simply says, "and among you is he who will be made to die" (*wa-minkum man yutawaffá*). Qur'ānic commentators, however, did in fact insist that this phrase referred to those who die young. As al-Ṭabarsī put it, "that is, he will die in the state of his minority or youth"[10]—he will die "soon," then, just as Robert specified.

These examples from 22:1–5 are by no means unusual. The influences of Islamic Qur'ān exegesis can be found throughout Robert's Latin Qur'ān. Sometimes this reliance is rather subtle. Verse 2:192, for example, is part of a set of verses about Jihād, verse 191 being one of the most important Qur'ānic passages for elaborating the doctrine of religiously justified war.[11] "But if they desist," 2:192 says, "then God is forgiving and merciful." In Robert's version these few words—there are but six in Arabic—become an eleven-word Latin sentence: "To enemies just as to others returning to God He, the righteous one, offers pardon."[12] There are echoes here of how the commentators explain this verse, for like Robert, they also assume that these people whom God will forgive have not only desisted from armed struggle against Islam, but have also "returned" to right belief in God. Al-Ṭabarsī, for example, says that the phrase "But if they desist" means "they refrain from their unbelief through turning away from it," and al-Bayḍāwī and Ibn Kathīr have similar views.[13]

But in many cases, Robert's reliance on the Muslim exegetical tradition could not be clearer. Earlier in the second surah, for example, Robert demonstrates that he knew the standard Islamic interpretation of the key Qur'ānic term *furqān*, a word that, among other things was commonly used as an alternative name for the Qur'ān itself. In verse 2:53, God calls on his faithful to remember "when we gave Moses the Book and the *furqān*." In Robert's version the *furqān* becomes *boni malique discretum*, "the discerner of good and evil," a formulation that closely resembles what commentators commonly said about the term.[14] Al-Ṭabarī, for example, explained that "by the *furqān* [God] means the act of deciding between truth and untruth," quoting many hadiths in support of this view.[15] Ibn Kathīr put forward the same interpretation, but also suggested that the *furqān* was "what distinguishes (*yafruqu*) between guidance and error."[16] Robert's "discerner between good and evil" fits nicely within this range of meanings.

Nine verses later, in 2:62, Robert comes across the troublesome word *Ṣābi'ūn* ("Sabaeans"): "those who believe, and those who are Jews, and Christians, and Sabeaens . . . surely their reward is with their Lord." This verse as a whole inspired an enormous amount of Muslim commentary on several issues,[17] among them the identity of the *Ṣābi'ūn* (sing. *Ṣābi'*) mentioned here. While there was considerable disagreement about which actual group of people this verse referred to,[18] there was wide agreement on the term's literal meaning. A *Ṣābiʾ*, as al-Ṭabarī put it, was someone who "invents a religion other than his [own] religion," for "anyone who departs from the religion to which he had adhered and [then] joins another is called a *Ṣābiʾ* by the Arabs."[19] In essence, Robert translates the phrase by boldly inserting this definition right into his text: "All who live uprightly," his version reads, "the Jew or the Christian or *he who, having abandoned his [own] religion, proceeds into another* . . . will doubtlessly obtain divine love."[20] A similarly striking insertion of exegetical material occurs at verse 2:255, where the Qurʾān, in the midst of a ringing celebration of God's omniscience and omnipotence, says that "His throne encompasses the heavens and the earth." This sentence presented difficulties for Muslim commentators who were hard-pressed to explain in what sense God's throne (*kursī*) could be said to contain the cosmos. One strategy was to argue that "throne" was being used as a metaphor (*majāz*), as al-Bayḍāwī put it, "for [God]'s knowledge or his dominion."[21] Muslim commentators commonly said, therefore, that the throne in this verse "is the knowledge of God," a hadith from Ibn ʿAbbās normally being cited as justification.[22] In his Latin version Robert once again replaces a difficult word—"throne"—with a standard Muslim gloss of it, giving us *cuius sapientia celum et terram comprehendens*: "whose knowledge comprehends heaven and earth."[23]

Moving to other parts of Robert's *Lex Mahumet*, we find much the same thing. His versions of two verses of the Surah of the Ḥajj, 22:28 and 22:36, also incorporate exegetical material. Both passages concern the pilgrimage to Mecca, the readers being told in the former verse that "they will witness things that are beneficial to them, and they will recite the name of God on the understood days (*ayyām maʿlūmāt*) over the grazing beast (*bahīmat al-anʿām*) which [God] bestowed upon them." As in other passages informed by Islamic commentary, Robert's version is more specific than the original Arabic text. He writes: "let them come in order that in testifying they might see something profitable for themselves, and, while naming God, *they might sacrifice animals* on the determined days."[24] That the recitation of God's name will occur in conjunction with the sacrificing of these animals is not mentioned in the Qurʾānic Arabic at all; yet this information is widely available in Qurʾānic commentaries, for such sacrifices did take place during the Pilgrimage,[25] and the commentators make clear that the reciting of God's name as described here is connected with those sacrifices. Al-Ṭabarsī, for example, observed that the reciting of God's name occurs during "the sacrificing and butchering" of these animals,[26] while Ibn Kathīr concisely explained that this passage refers to "the recitation of God['s name] at the sacrificing" of animals.[27] When much the same events are described again just eight verses later (22:36), Robert's translation again reflects the traditional interpretation.[28]

Robert was just as likely to turn to commentaries when he came to the short surahs at the end of the Qur'ān. In Sūrat al-Fīl (the Surah [105] of the Elephant), he encountered an allusion to the campaign of the Abyssinian ruler of the Yemen against Mecca in the year of Muhammad's birth. God thwarted the designs of these attackers, the surah tells us, by sending against them something called *ṭayr abābīl.* The first word was clear enough: it means "birds." But the second term is problematic in the extreme. This is its only appearance in the Qur'ān, and it is, moreover, of foreign derivation,[29] making it a particular challenge to the commentators. Generally, though, exegetes explained that it meant, as al-Ṭabarsī put it, "groups in dispersal, troop upon troop" (*jamāʿāt fī tafriqah zumratan zumratan*), so that the two-word phrase meant something like "flocks [of birds] following one after the other" (*aqāṭīʿ yatbaʿu baʿḍuhā baʿḍan*).[30] Robert captures this interpretation nicely: *inmittens illis uolucrum multimodarum cohortes quam plurimas*, that is, "sending on them as many companies as possible of various flying things."[31]

Robert's Latin Qur'ān, then, is clearly and extensively informed by how Muslim commentators understood the Qur'ānic text, but his is not the only version that demonstrates this sort of influence. Mark of Toledo's translation of seventy years later is likewise shaped by Muslim exegesis, though these influences are much less frequent. There are, in fact, passages in Mark's version that suffer badly from his lack of awareness of the traditional exegesis. At the verse I just discussed, for example, where Robert had learned rightly that the *ṭayr abābīl* were understood to be many companies of "various flying things," Mark misstepped badly, assuming that the second word was the name of a famous city, writing "[God] sent over them birds of Babylon."[32] Nevertheless, from time to time Mark also turned to sources of traditional Qur'ān exegesis. Like Robert, he had learned the received meaning of the term *furqān*, for in his version of 2:53 he both transliterates it—*folcanum*—and inserts a gloss that explains it: *id est distinctum inter bonum et malum*, "that is, the distinction between good and evil," which effectively follows the Islamic interpretation.

In the Surah of the Ḥajj, Mark at one point inserts into his translation a phrase that Muslim commentators suggested should be understood as linking two clauses that seem otherwise incompatible. Verses 22:19–21 describe certain punishments of the unbelievers in the next world. Mark's version of 22:22 then tells us that "as soon as they will have desired to leave behind the anguish, they will be guided back to it, and they will say to them, 'taste the torment of fire.'"[33] This, as usual for Mark, follows the Arabic of the Qur'ān quite closely, except that the phrase "and they will say to them" (*dicentque eis*) does not appear in the Qur'ānic text at all, the command to "taste the punishment of fire" following immediately upon the first clause of the verse. Strikingly enough, however, the Muslim commentators all insist that the phrase "and it is said to them" (*wa-yuqālu lahum*) must be understood between the first clause and the second.[34] Mark's verb is, unlike the Arabic, in the active rather than passive voice,[35] but it does get across just what the commentators suggested as the proper interpretation.

Near the end of the Qur'ān, we again find Mark demonstrating awareness of traditional Islamic exegesis in his translation of the Surah of Abundance. Here (108:2) the Qur'ān calls on the believer to "Pray to your Lord and sacrifice (to him)." But while the second verb of this verse normally did mean "to sacrifice," Qur'ānic commentators often proposed that it might mean something else. One hadith suggested that it could mean "placing his right hand on the middle of the left forearm, and then placing them both on his breast,"[36] this meaning apparently arising from the fact that a noun from the same root, *naḥr*, means "chest, breast." Mark's version incorporated this view: *leua manus supra pectus* ("lay [your] hands over the breast").[37]

The Latin Qur'ān commissioned three hundred years later by Egidio da Viterbo and translated by Iohannes Gabriel Terrolensis was also influenced by traditional Qur'ān exegesis, not as frequently as Robert of Ketton's version, but far more often than Mark of Toledo's. Its version of verse 2:36, for example, tells how, after being cast out of Paradise, Adam and Eve were to dwell on earth where they would "have a dwelling on earth and good things for a fixed time *or up until death* (my italics)."[38] This follows the Arabic closely except for the final phrase, which is a clear addition to the Qur'ānic text. It does, however, restate a common explanation for what the immediately preceding phrase (*ilá ḥīn / pro tempore determinato*) means. In Arabic as in Latin these words mean something like "for a certain period of time," but Qur'ānic commentators suggested that they meant something more specific: "until death," or "until the hour of resurrection."[39] Mark's "or up until death" is clearly based on the former widely held Islamic view.

A similar insertion happens at 2:58, where Muslim believers are asked to remember when God told the followers of Moses, upon arriving at Jerusalem, to "enter the gate in prostration, and say, 'ḥiṭṭatun!'" On its own, this last puzzling term means either "alleviation" or "humiliation," and while there were a range of interpretations of its use here as an exclamation, the preferred explanation depended on etymology. The root *ḤṬṬ* means, among other things, "to take on a burden," so this exclamation could mean, the commentator al-Ṭabarī observed, "God has taken over the burden from you of your sins" (*ḥaṭṭa Allāh ʿanka khaṭāyāka*).[40] Egidio's version interpolates this interpretation right into the text: *et ingredimini per portam prostrati et dicite, 'aufer nostras culpas'* ("and enter through the gate in prostration and say, 'take away our sins'").[41]

The first verse of surah 17, which contains the Qurʾānic basis for Muhammad's famous night journey into heaven, explains how God carried his servant to the "most distant place of worship" (*al-masjid al-aqṣá*). Iohannes had learned that this phrase was always taken to refer to Jerusalem,[42] and translated it, therefore, as *templum Hierusalem*.[43] A similarly curt statement at the beginning of surah 54 led to consultation of exegetical sources as well. Verse 1 says simply that "The hour approaches and the moon is divided," the verses immediately following doing nothing to clarify this statement. Most commentators, however, saw the first half of the verse as a reference to the hour of judgment. Al-Ṭabarī, for example, said that the phrase "the hour is near" meant that "the hour in which the resurrection would occur was near," and that this verse was consequently "a warning from God to his servants of the proximity of the resurrection and the nearness of the destruction of the world."[44] Aware of this view, Egidio's translator wrote *appropinquata est hora* iudicii *et frangetur luna*, "The hour *of judgment* has been brought near and the moon will be broken."[45]

Each of these three Latin Qurʾān translators, then, periodically turned to sources of Muslim Qurʾān commentary as he translated, consulting Muslim books or Muslim scholars on the meaning of the Muslim scripture. At some points of the Qurʾānic text we can watch as more than one of them turns to such exegetical sources to resolve the same problems. This happens most often at passages containing some particularly difficult term or usage, the sort of problematic words that figured in the lexicons of "strange" words of the Qurʾān that I mentioned at the outset of this chapter. The beginning of surah 37 is a vivid example. It begins with the phrase *Wa-al-ṣāffāt ṣaffan*, "By those arranged in ranks," there once again being little in the context of the passage to explain what this meant. Muslim commentators naturally had to provide some clarification, and the normal view that they advanced was that by those arranged in ranks "[God] means *angels*," as al-Rāghib al-Iṣbahānī (d. 1108), author of a widely read lexicon of difficult Qur'ānic terms put it.[46] All three of these translators have learned this somehow, Robert writing, "By a row of *angels* in heaven," Mark, "By holy orders of *angels*," and Iohannes, "By *angels* set in order" (my italics).[47]

Another famously difficult passage occurs at verse 83:7. Here evildoers are warned about the coming judgment, for "the record of the immoral, verily, is in *sijjīn*." Now although the immediately following verses state clearly that the unusual word *sijjīn* referred to a written record ("And what will make you know what *sijjīn* is? It is a written record [*kitāb marqūm*]." [vv. 8–9]), and although commentators often pointed this out, it was nevertheless also commonly asserted that it was located in the "the seventh earth,"[48] this being, in Qur'ānic cosmology, the lowest point on earth corresponding to "the seventh heaven," the highest place in heaven.[49] Robert and Mark both follow this Islamic interpretive tradition. Mark translates *sijjīn* as *abbyssus*,[50] while Robert, even more impressively, manages to capture the complex view offered in many exegetical works: "The book of them, marked with their evils, is concealed in the lowest of earths."[51]

In this case Mark drew upon the exegetical tradition just as Robert did, but Robert's paraphrasing style allowed him to incorporate more of the explanatory material. This sort of thing happens elsewhere. In the second-to-last verse of the Surah (96) of the Blood Clot, the translators came across the puzzling word *al-zabāniyah*. The larger passage in which it occurs describes how God will deal with the one who denies him: "(14) Does he not know that God sees? (15) On the contrary, if he does not refrain, then we will seize him by the forelock, . . . (17) Then let him call his council. (18) We will call *al-zabāniyah*." The root in *ZBN* did exist in Arabic[52] but this particular form was unusual enough that Qur'ānic commentators felt obliged to explain it to Muslim readers. They often suggested that it here meant the same thing as the common root *DFʿ*—"to push away, drive back."[53] Ibn Qutaybah, for example, argued that the role of these "pushers" in 96:18 must be "to push the inhabitants of the fire into it."[54] Robert captures this view with precision: "I ordered him to be taken away by the helpers who will guide him to the fire."[55] Mark, drawing on simpler interpretations that said that the *zabāniyah* were "the angels of punishment"[56] or the "angels in charge of (hell)fire,"[57] concisely rendered the passage this way: "I will call guardians" (*ego conuocabo satellites*).[58]

In the mid-fifteenth century, Juan de Segovia both commissioned and helped produce a new Latin translation of the Qur'ān, which was then inserted into a manuscript containing both the Arabic original and a literal Castilian version from which his Latin version is, in part, derived. While that trilingual edition of the Qurʾān has, sadly, been lost,[59] his preface to it survives—as we will see at some length in the conclusion to this book. Among the many fascinating aspects of this rambling text are his insightful comments on Robert of Ketton's translation, which he had studied closely. While he found much to criticize in Robert's Latin Qurʾān,[60] Juan also, uniquely among the many critics of Robert over the centuries, recognized, as we have, that Robert's version was heavily influenced by Islamic exegetical sources of some sort: "in many passages," Juan wrote, "just as one commenting, [Robert] explicates the Muslim meaning, though it scarcely is available in the literal Arabic."[61] This intriguing observation could be made equally of Mark of Toledo and Iohannes Gabriel. They also often "explicate the Muslim meaning" even though that meaning "is scarcely visible at first glance in the literal Arabic." Indeed, the interpretation that, say, the *zabāniyah* of 96:18 are guardians of hell is an interpretation that is strictly "not available in the literal Arabic" of the Qurʾān: our three translators could only have learned of it by consulting sources of Islamic Qurʾān exegesis.

We should not be surprised that this is so. Both the nature of the Qurʾānic text and scholarship and the nature of Latin-Christian culture converged to make this necessarily the case. Though revealed in "clear Arabic," the Qurʾān is not an easy text, and around it there had grown a huge tradition of exegetical scholarship that addressed its difficulties in minute detail. Faced with such troubling problems as the meaning of *al-zabāniyah*, nothing could be more normal than to turn for clarification to Qurʾānic commentaries or directly to Muslim scholars. Gerard Wiegers has convincingly argued, moreover, that Qurʾānic commentaries circulated widely among the Mudejars—the subject Muslim population of Christian Spain—even in the fifteenth century.[62] They were doubtless in even wider circulation in the twelfth and thirteenth centuries. These commentaries circulated among learned Muslim scholars who, even in the late fifteenth century, could be found in surprisingly large numbers in Christian Spain, as Mark Meyerson has shown.[63] Finding either written Qurʾānic commentaries or learned Muslim informants, or both, would have posed few problems for Latin-Christian translators in need of help. And doing so was by no means a uniquely Latin-Christian act. Muslim readers of the Bible, such as ʿAlī ibn Rabbān (810–c. 865) and al-Maqdisī (fl. 966), consulted Christian and Jewish biblical commentators to help them understand an equally difficult book.[64]

But turning to sources of Islamic Qur'ān exegesis would have been a natural act not only because the difficulties of the Qur'ān almost demanded it; it was natural also because these Latin translators had been taught not merely to read texts together with authoritative commentaries on them, but, in fact, to view the boundaries between text and commentary less rigidly than modern readers would. Writing commentaries was an essential part of scholarly education in the Latin West throughout the whole period in question,[65] and one read the canonical texts together with nearly canonical commentaries on them: the Bible together with the *Glossa ordinaria*, or, later, the *Postillae* of Nicholas of Lyra; Virgil alongside Servius's commentary; Aristotle in conjunction with the brilliant commentaries of the Arab Muslim Ibn Rushd (Averroes). This "hermeneutical" nature of medieval culture brought with it a tendency to conflate text and commentary. Martin Irvine has written that "the divisions between text and commentary . . . were not clearly defined . . . and it is clear that for a medieval reader everything on a page—layout, changes in script, glosses, construe marks, corrections . . . was experienced as an integral feature of the system of meaning that constituted the book."[66] Though he was speaking of the early Middle Ages, the same could be said of later medieval culture.

One sign that this is so is that the actual practices of medieval translators were often shaped by such a way of reading.[67] Notker the German "recognized no distinction" between text and later commentary in his early eleventh-century translation of Martianus Capella's *On the Marriage of Mercury and Philosophy*, for his German version of that Latin work "incorporates and restates glosses and commentaries that pertain to the text." Likewise Jean de Meung's thirteenth-century translation of Boethius' *Consolation of Philosophy* is decisively molded by an earlier medieval commentary on that work.[68] Similar things happened among Renaissance humanists: Lorenzo Valla incorporated early glosses on Thucydides into his Latin translation of *The Peloponnesian War*.[69] Translation and textual interpretation were, in fact, seen as so closely related that the same verb—*interpretor*—was often used to describe both acts. Not infrequently they were identified with each other.[70] That we should see Latin Qur'ān translators consulting the Islamic exegetical tradition and including material from it directly in their translations should surprise us not at all, therefore. In many ways, this was simply standard procedure.

That these translators should have done so inevitably raises two further interesting but (at this point, at least) largely unanswerable questions. First, how exactly did they draw on such sources—by reading Qur'ānic commentaries directly, by consulting Muslim informants, or both? And second, whether they consulted informants or learned directly from Qurʾānic commentaries, on which written sources was their knowledge based? Leaving aside Iohannes Gabriel Terrolensis for the moment, it must be said with regard to the first question that we are profoundly lacking in clear evidence one way or the other. There are vague references to an otherwise unknown Muslim named Muhammad whom Peter the Venerable hired to be part of his translation team, and whom some scholars have suggested must have helped Robert translate the Qurʾān.[71] This is certainly a possibility, as is the consultation of similar informants by the other translators. There are examples throughout the medieval period of Latin-Christian translators turning to informants from other religious traditions to help them understand scriptural texts. Jerome consulted a Jewish rabbi while preparing the Vulgate;[72] Theodulf of Orléans was helped by Jews or converted Jews in his Biblical scholarship in the ninth century;[73] Andrew of St. Victor, and a number of other Christian Hebraists in the high Middle Ages, discussed the *Hebraica veritas* of the Old Testament with rabbis;[74] Martin Luther, like Jerome before him, turned to rabbis as he created his German Bible.[75] Robert and Mark, living in the still heavily Arab-Muslim world of medieval Spain, would likely have had little trouble finding Muslims learned enough to explain difficult Qurʾānic passages.[76]

Yet the extensive influence of Islamic exegesis on their translations is not, by itself, clear proof that these translators learned what they knew of Islamic exegesis solely from consulting informants. It is, in fact, clear that, at a later date, Latin-Christian readers were fully capable of using written Arabic commentaries without any oral discussions with Muslim scholars. In the early seventeenth century, Sir John Selden, the great benefactor of the Bodleian Library in Oxford and an energetic Orientalist and humanist,[77] owned a copy of the sixteenth-century Latin edition of Robert of Ketton's Latin Qurʾān, which he annotated as he read. When Selden's Latin notes are examined in any detail, it quickly becomes obvious that he was—remarkably enough—reading Robert's Latin paraphrase of the Qurʾān with copies of more than one Qurʾānic commentary at his elbow, and was using the Qurʾānic commentaries to help him understand the text. At 3:123, for example where, as Robert translated it, God "furnished victory in Badr" (*victoriam in Badar praebuimus*),[78] Selden has written in the margin that Badr is "between Mecca and Medina" (*inter mecham et medinam*). Since Badr is a relatively obscure place in Arabia, it is hardly surprising that the Arabic Qurʾānic commentaries also tell their readers where it is, and they do so just as Selden himself did later, by telling us that *Badr mā bayna Makkah wa-al-Madīnah*, "Badr is what is between Mecca and Medina."[79] John Selden, therefore, has pretty clearly taken this information from some Arabic Quʾrān commentary, this conclusion being confirmed by the immediately following marginal note: "On this [place] see also Mahumed ben Achmet, p. 86, in the middle" (*De ea item vide Mahumed Ben Achmet, p. 86 in medio*).[80] *Mahumed ben Achmet* is without doubt a reference to ʿAbd Allāh *Muḥammad ibn Aḥmad* al-Anṣārī al-Qurṭubī, the author of an important thirteenth-century Andalusī commentary who likewise tells us much about Badr and its location.[81] And these references to Qurʾānic commentaries, together with page numbers, continue for many pages in his copy of Robert's *Lex Mahumet*. Working in early seventeenth-century England, John Selden had no opportunity to consult Muslim informants. He had no trouble, however, turning to Qurʾānic commentaries, several of which he possessed in his large library.

As we will see later in this chapter, moreover, by late in the seventeenth century the herculean work of Ludovico Marracci (d. 1700), whose edition of the Qurʾān with Latin translation and extensive notes based directly on a range of Qurʾānic commentators, makes abundantly clear that Latin-Christian scholars did not need Muslim informants in order to have intimate knowledge of traditional Qurʾānic exegesis.[82] The unfortunately little-known contemporary work of Germanus of Silesia (d. 1670), who, working at El Escorial, produced a similar edition of the Qurʾānic text which was never published, suggests the same thing.[83] Neither scholar could easily have turned to Muslim informants. Assuming that Robert of Ketton, Mark of Toledo, and Iohannes Gabriel Terrolensis did know Arabic modestly well—and it certainly seems likely that one could learn Arabic in twelfth-, thirteenth-, or fifteenth-century Spain at least as effectively as one could in seventeenth-century Britain or Italy—there is every reason to assume that they could have used Qurʾānic commentaries as effectively as did John Selden or Ludovico Marracci.

More research on the translations themselves may yield clearer answers on whether they consulted informants or turned to Arabic commentaries or both, but for the moment we must be satisfied with agnosticism on this question. And the same holds true regarding the question of which written sources their knowledge was ultimately based on, at least as far as Robert of Ketton and Mark of Toledo are concerned. In the case of certain Christian Hebraists, scholars have been able to identify the written sources from which their knowledge of Jewish biblical exegesis is derived, even though they gained this knowledge through the mediation of informants.[84] This is not true—in the current state of research at least—for Robert and Mark. As the endnotes to this chapter make clear, in every case where I have been able to show that one of them included information from the tradition of Islamic exegesis in his translation, I have been able to find more than one written source containing that information. It is, in fact, characteristic of the Qurʾānic commentaries that they repeat a great deal of what can be found in other commentaries.[85] Short of an explicit statement about which commentary or commentaries were the ultimate sources, scholars will be very hard pressed to identify definitively which commentators were most influential.

In regard to both questions, Egidio's translation, made by a man who may well have been a Muslim convert to Christianity, is different. As we will see in a later chapter, the notes that occupied the fourth column of the original manuscript, now lost, of that edition were overwhelmingly based on Arabic commentaries, particularly al-Zamakhsharī, and they are cited by name.[86] This would suggest that the Islamic exegetical influences on the translation itself derived from those commentators as well. It likewise suggests that Egidio's translator, Iohannes Gabriel Terrolensis, did not work with informants.

But what of Flavius Mithridates? We have already seen that his fifteenth-century translation is seriously flawed, though, as we will see in a later chapter, there exists other evidence that Mithridates had real familiarity—at least at some point in his life—with Arabic Qurʾān commentators. What is clear is that he did not consult them much as he completed his Qurʾān translation. It is true that two or three passages in Flavius Mithridates' translation do bespeak some awareness of Islamic exegesis. At 22:5, for example, the word *baʿth* occurs, literally meaning "resurrection." Mithridates translates it, however, as *emissio de sepulchris*, "sending forth from the graves."[87] This closely echoes what commentaries often say at this point, al-Ṭabarī, for example, paraphrasing it thus: "if you are in doubt about our power to raise you from your graves" (*min qubūrikum).* Later, at 22:48, Mithridates adds similar specificity to the Qurʾānic text. Where the Arabic says, "Then I took it (i.e., a certain city)" (*thumma akhadhtuhā*), Mithridates writes, "Then we will take them in destruction" (*tum recipiemus eas in perditione*).[88] His change of the object from singular to plural is hard to explain, but what is particularly interesting is that his elaboration—that God will take it/them "in destruction"—parallels what commentators say here. Al-Ṭabarī says that the phrase "I took it" means "then I seized it with punishment," and that the following phrase, "and to me is the destiny" (*al-maṣīr*) means "to me is the destiny of them after the destruction (*halāk*) of them."[89]

But over against these few signs of Mithridates' familiarity with Islamic Qurʾān exegesis are countless examples of complete ignorance or neglect of it. In immediate proximity to both the foregoing examples, we find catastrophic errors that are hard to imagine in a translator at home with how Muslims understand their book. At the beginning of verse 22:5, in the very clause where he had rightly translated "resurrection" as "sending forth from the graves," Mithridates bungles the phrase "if you are in doubt" (*in kuntum fī rayb*), giving us nearly its opposite: "since there is in you understanding" (*cum fuerit in uos intellectus*).[90] Qurʾānic commentators often went to some length to explain what *rayb* meant (indicating, perhaps, that it was relatively unusual to Arabic speakers too). Al-Ṭabarī and al-Ṭabarsī, for example, both paraphrase this verse, substituting the common word *shakk*, "doubt," for *rayb*.[91] Mithridates' translation here can hardly be the work of someone consulting Qurʾānic commentaries or Muslim scholars. Similarly for 22:48: while he somehow came to understand that God would take these cities "in destruction" as the commentaries specified, Mithridates completely misunderstands the first half of the verse. Where the Arabic text reads "Many a city on which I was merciful when it was sinful!" he writes "For that reason, the cities which are full of them are sinners."[92] It is difficult to conceive of how anyone consulting Qurʾānic commentaries on this verse could have come up with such an inept Latin version.

Though Mithridates' translation shows little dependence on sources of Islamic Qurʾān exegesis, Robert of Ketton, Mark of Toledo, and Iohannes Gabriel Terrolensis turned to such sources relatively frequently. This fact collapses much of the distance that we might assume separates their way of reading the text from the way that Muslims read the text themselves, and from the way that later and supposedly more sophisticated European scholars read the text. In fact, if we compare how Robert, Mark, and Iohannes handled the Qurʾānic text with how Spanish-Muslim translators in the high Middle Ages did so, and with how the European Orientalists who have long been thought to be the first systematic, philological readers of the Qurʾān dealt with it, we find surprising similarities.

We have an abundance of relevant evidence regarding how Spanish Muslims translated the Qurʾān, because by the late fifteenth and early sixteenth centuries there was a "proliferation of versions" of the Qurʾān in Castilian made by Muslims themselves.[93] As Consuelo López-Morillas has shown, these usually anonymous Spanish-Muslim translators often did just what Robert, Mark, and Iohannes did: they likewise found themselves incorporating background information, glosses, and interpretations from Arabic Qur'ān commentaries into their translations.[94] No more vivid evidence of this can be found than a precious codex produced in 1606 and preserved now at the Public Library of Toledo. A copy of the complete Qur'ānic text in Castilian, this manuscript (MS 235) is presently at the center of a debate relevant to this study in another way.[95] Gerard Wiegers has argued that it is a copy of none other than Iça of Segovia's literal Castilian translation produced, as we will see later in this book, for Juan de Segovia's fifteenth-century trilingual Qur'ān, which has long been thought to have disappeared.[96] Consuelo López-Morillas has recently raised serious doubts about this conclusion without, however, denying it outright,[97] and for the moment the intriguing suggestion that MS 235 is Iça's lost Castilian Qur'ān, and thus valuable further evidence about Juan de Segovia's trilingual Qur'ān, must remain no more than a possibility. But whether or not the translation was made by Iça or some other Castilian Muslim, what is valuable for us at the moment is the way in which it exemplifies how similar the approaches of Latin-Christian and Spanish-Muslim Qur'ān translators were.

Whoever made this translation not only frequently imported exegetical material from Qur'ānic commentaries into it, but went out of his way to make clear to readers which was which. At least that is what we find in the copy of his work in MS 235, for here the copyist carefully wrote anything extracted from such commentaries in bright red ink, rather than the muted brown of the rest of the text, or, in the later parts of the manuscript, placed such material between red slash marks. If we read this manuscript alongside, say, Robert of Ketton's Latin Qur'ān, we find that at many places where the Castilian translation has bright red ink or red slash marks, Robert has also imported material from the Islamic exegetical tradition. Verse 2:28 is a striking example. Here the Qur'ān asks how humans could continue to disbelieve in God, "for when you were dead, he gave you life, and then he will cause you to die, and then he will give you life, and then to him you will be returned." With its puzzling assertion that God brought humans initially into life from a state of death, this verse inspired a great deal of exegetical comment, and the Muslim translator of Toledo MS 235 has made a small adjustment that reflects one interpretation: "'¿Cómo descreéis con Allah?' Y érades *esperma* muerta y os rebibcó . . .": "How do you disbelieve in God, and you were dead sperm, and [He] revived you . . ."[98] The word "esperma" appears in red letters in the manuscript to signal to us that it has been imported from the exegetical tradition, and indeed the view that the Qur'ānic Arabic's "when you were dead" refers to when humans were sperm in the loins of their ancestors was widely advocated in the commentaries.[99] But there were other interpretations, including that it meant "You *were nothing*; then [God] created you," as an oft-quoted hadith had it.[100] Al-Zamakhsharī (1075–1144) actually asserted that when the Qur'ān said "when you were dead" it "refers to the *nonexistence* of life" (*yuqālu dhālika li-ʿādim al-ḥayāh*), while Ibn Kathīr argued that this clause meant "when you were *non-existent*, he drew you into existence" (*ay wa-qad kuntum ʿadaman fa-akhrajakum ilá al-wujūd*).[101] Robert's elegant paraphrase incorporates this latter interpretation: "For he, *drawing you out of nonbeing* into life, will bring on death, and will make you rise up to him" (my italics).[102] His insertion of explanatory material from the Arabic exegetical tradition is not highlighted in red ink as the Muslim translator's was, but it is clear that, when reading the Qur'ān as translators, both Robert, a Latin Christian, and the anonymous Spanish Muslim did much the same thing: faced with the same puzzling verse they turned to sources of Islamic exegesis.

There are many other examples. Like Robert, the Castilian translator turned to commentaries at verse 2:62. Robert had translated the problematic term *Ṣābi'ūn* by interpolating the common exegetical definition of the term—"[those] who, having abandoned [their] own religion, proceed into another."[103] The Muslim translator initially simply wrote the difficult term in Roman script—*açcabines*—but then added an explanatory clause identifying them as "those who worship the *almalaques*," another transliterated term meaning "angels" (from the Arabic *al-malā'ikah*).[104] The view that the *Ṣābi'ūn* worshipped angels was also an idea commonly advanced in exegetical works.[105]

At other points, not only do Robert and the Muslim translator turn to exegetical sources; they come away from them with the same answers. Verses 2:229–30 form part of a lengthy discussion of Islamic marriage and divorce law, the former verse beginning with the statement "When the pronouncement of divorce is made twice, then retain her with equity, or divorce her in charity," meaning that until the divorce has been pronounced publicly three times it is not binding and the husband may take the wife back. The rest of the verse then discusses related issues, after which verse 230 begins: "If he divorce her, then she is not lawful to him again until she has married another husband," the verse going on to stipulate that after she has been divorced from that second husband, "it is no sin for both of them [i. e. the original couple] if they return to each other." Now Qurʾānic commentators normally explained that verse 230 referred to "the third pronouncement of divorce," as al-Ṭabarsī put it,[106] so that phrase meant, "If he pronounce the divorce *a third time*" then the further stipulations come into play. In his version Robert of Ketton studiously incorporated the commentators' view, writing that "those who have been abandoned *a third time* by no means [may return to their husbands] until they have married other husbands and been abandoned by them."[107] The Muslim translator of the text in MS 235 takes much the same approach: "Pues si la attalacará *terçera vegada*, pues no es halel a él después hasta que ella case con marido fuera dél"("Then if he divorce her *a third time*, then she is not permitted to him afterward until she marry another husband besides him").[108] Once again we have Muslim Arabic words absorbed into the Castilian (*attalacará* from *al-ṭalāq*, meaning "divorce," and *halel* from *ḥalāl*, meaning "allowed"), but the Islamic exegesis is concisely included here just as in Robert's version.

What is true of Robert of Ketton's Latin Qurʾān is also true of the other two complete Latin versions, for they likewise often parallel the Castilian-Muslim translation,[109] and these similarities continue throughout the Qurʾānic text, as their translations of the first verse of Sūrat al-ʿĀdiyāt make clear. Here at nearly the end of the Qurʾān, all were faced yet again with one of the "strange" terms of the Qurʾān, the word *al-ʿādiyāt*, which gives the surah its name, the Surah (100) of the Runners. The first short verse reads, "By the runners snorting (*ḍabḥan*)," with no hint about what or who was doing the running. Qurʾānic commentaries and lexicons, however, explained that these "runners" were either camels or, more often, horses.[110] All these translators amplify and clarify this concise verse using one of these interpretations. For Robert the "runners snorting" are "horses" who "emitted snorting from the panting chest;"[111] for Mark they are "swift horses" (*equi veloces*);[112] Egidio has them as "running camels" (*camelos currentes*);[113] while in the Castilian-Muslim version they are "caballos resoflantes quando corren" ("horses exhaling when they run").[114]

At many points, therefore, all these medieval and early modern Qurʾān translators, whether Christian or Muslim, found themselves drawn into the Islamic exegetical tradition and compelled to incorporate its teachings into their translations. The distance here between reading the Qurʾān as a Christian translator and reading it as a Muslim translator has become small indeed. This is not to say, of course, that the Christian and Muslim had identical experiences of the text otherwise. For the Muslim translator to have included so much Arabic in transliteration is but one of many signs that reading the Qurʾānic text from within the Muslim community, even as a translator, was very different from reading it from without. Indeed, reading the Qurʾān as a believing Muslim—saying parts of it in daily prayers, hearing it chanted beautifully in mosques, attempting to conform one's life to it—and reading it as a Christian commissioned to create a Latin version of it were in many ways, of course, entirely different things. It nevertheless cannot be denied that Latin-Christian intellectuals were quite capable of an essentially philological reading of the Qurʾānic text, of the sort that Muslims frequently undertook. And just as, for Muslims, such a philological reading was by no means the only way to experience the revelation sent down to Muhammad, so the translator's philology was not the only way that Christians read this text. But it was one way, and they could be surprisingly good at it.

Good enough, in fact, that we must recognize that the divide between them and later European scholars of Islam is not so broad as has been assumed. Modern scholars have generally argued that sometime in the seventeenth or eighteenth century a radical change happened in how Europeans read the Qurʾān. Ludovico Marracci's great *Alcorani textus universus*, with its careful edition of the Arabic text together with a literal Latin translation, is sometimes singled out as the initiator of this new period of western scholarship.[115] There is no disputing the towering achievement of Marracci, but the evidence presented in this chapter should be sufficient to make clear that while there was an important evolution in how the Qurʾān was read—something I will say more about not only in this, but in later chapters as well—there was nothing like a radical revolution in European scholarship on Islam's holy text. Indeed, if we examine the reading practices of the likes of Marracci, we cannot help but notice the impressive continuities that link them to their medieval Qurʾān-translating forebears.

Indeed, Marracci was not nearly as innovative as most have thought, even if we set aside Robert of Ketton and other medieval Quʾrān translators, for Marracci's magnificent work was actually anticipated by a few decades by the remarkably similar, but never published, work of Dominicus Germanus of Silesia.[116] An Observant Franciscan, Germanus had traveled widely in the Middle East as a missionary and had learned Arabic, Persian, and Turkish, but then spent the remaining eighteen years of his life at the great royal monastery of El Escorial in Spain. Germanus passed much of that time working on his new edition and translation of the Qurʾān, dying in 1670, just a year after he finished his Qurʾān project. The manuscript of it remained in El Escorial and was never published,[117] though a second copy of it found its way to Montpellier.[118]

The author of the only detailed study of Germanus' Qur'ān edition wrote, more than a century ago, that Germanus was "the first European who attempted, and . . . accomplished . . . the difficult task of making the basic book of Muslim beliefs be understood with precision."[119] Although in light of the evidence advanced in this chapter this seems a rather excessive judgment, there is no doubting the admirable thoroughness of Germanus's philology. The format of his Qur'ān edition is actually very similar to that of Marracci's printed volumes, and incarnates the same vast erudition. In the enormous autograph manuscript—528 folios[120]—Germanus divided the Qur'ān into a sequence of short, successive portions that he first presented for the reader in a literal Latin translation. Each of these is followed by a "scholium" that discusses various aspects of it—everything from the occasion of revelation to difficult terminology—these scholia also often including polemical or apologetic observations. The sources for the nonpolemical material in the scholia are standard Islamic exegetical authorities, which Germanus often mentions by name in the margins, not infrequently in Arabic script. So that his readers will have some understanding of who these scholars are, he includes a descriptive list of the "classic expositors" at the beginning of his edition—al-Kāshānī, for example, is identified here as a "Mystical and tropological expositor, a notable philosopher and metaphysician."[121] This list of Qur'ānic commentators is preceded by a similar list of the "chief disciples [of Muhammad] whom the commentators or elders . . . cite," these being the companions of the Prophet on whose authority the Traditions are related that the commentators so often draw on.[122]

"I judged," Germanus said in a preface to this work, "that I would not have spent my leisure and my study badly, if I will have attempted a translation of the Qur'ān, not from dictionaries and lexicons, but according to the opinion and declaration of the disciples of the author himself, or others contemporary with them or near to them in age, and of the native expositors of the Qur'ān itself."[123] The results of this effort are impressive. His version of surah 108 is a good example. He first gives the surah title in Arabic and Latin (*Sūrat al-Kawthar De amne paradiseo*), and then translates it literally, with his explanatory insertions underlined:

> In the name of God, the mercifying, the merciful. (1) We at any rate have given you the paradisial river which runs perpetually, that is, your memory in this and the next world will never die out. (2) Obediently, therefore, pray to your lord and sacri-

fice [to him] the first fruits of your fields. (3) But he who pursues you in hate will not leave any memory after himself, that is offspring or any good work worthy of memory.[124]

While Germanus called his Latin translation the *Literal Interpretation of the Qur'ān*,[125] this version of surah 108 is not literal in any simple way, for he has amplified the text of this short and concise surah at a number of points—and not just those underlined—by the inclusion of material from those "native expositors" of the Qur'ān. The "paradisial river," for example, translates the single word *al-kawthar*. Another of the "unusual words" of the Qur'ān, *al-kawthar*, which meant something like "abundance," was explained in a variety of ways by commentators, but the interpretation that it was a river in paradise was one of the most common.[126] That it stood metaphorically for Muhammad's renown in this world and the next was also commonly asserted.[127] Likewise, verse 3 literally reads, "For the hater of you will be cut off" (*Inna shāni'aka huwa al-abtar*). The specification that what he [that is, one of Muhammad's enemies] will be cut off from is offspring and good memory is, again, based on Islamic exegesis.[128]

After this amplifying translation, Germanus describes, in the scholium to this section, what Muslim scholars call the "occasion of revelation" of this surah—the circumstances of Muhammad's life, that is, in which this piece of the Qur'ān was revealed. "They say," Germanus observes, "that a male child had been born to Muhammad, [and] he named him Ibrahīm," but this child "died while still an infant." But Muhammad, he continues, did not suffer as much from the death of the child as from the joyfulness (*laetitia*) of his enemies, whom Germanus mentions by name, and who told the people of Mecca that "now our Muhammad despairs, deceived of any hope of posterity, because he begets no male child after this." This surah, then, was meant, Germanus notes, to console Muhammad by making clear that his memory would be immortal, not through a male child "but through the multiplying of his faithful."[129] Like his amplifications in the translation itself, this scholium is based on traditions commonly cited in the commentaries to explain the occasion of this surah's revelation.[130]

Now there are real advances here over the work of the medieval Latin Qur'ān translators, who, for example, with the exception of Iohannes Gabriel Terrolensis in the early sixteenth century, never make clear to us what sources they are drawing upon for their knowledge of Islamic Qur'ān exegesis. But all this should not blind us to the similarities between how Dominicus Germanus and, for example, Robert of Ketton actually approached this passage as translators. Robert's twelfth-century paraphrase does not amplify the text as fully as Germanus's does, but it nevertheless clarifies the text notably, drawing on the same kinds of exegetical sources: "In the name of God, the righteous, the merciful. (1) I have now prepared for you a spring in paradise. (2) Therefore pour out prayer before God, and sacrifice to him humbly. (3) For your enemy will lack helpers and offspring."[131] Like Germanus, Robert inserts the common explanation of *al-kawthar* as "a river in paradise" directly into his translation. Like him also, Robert replaces the vague statement that Muhammad's enemy would be "cut off" (*al-abtar*) with the exegetes' elaboration that he will be lacking "offspring."

Both Germanus and Robert were, then—to use the former's words—"attempting a translation" based on "the native expositors" of the Qurʾān.[132] This is an equally apt description for what Marracci essays in his work published in 1698. Like Germanus, Marraci divides the Qurʾānic text into manageable sections, but these he presents to the reader in both a fully vocalized Arabic edition and a careful Latin translation. A series of notes follows that explain difficult morphological, grammatical, and interpretive problems, and a second set of notes, called *refutationes* or *refutata*, then systematically disputes the Qurʾān's doctrines. Once again, there are clear improvements over the scholarship of Latin Qurʾān translators between 1140 and 1560. Marracci is zealous about naming his exegetical sources, often quoting them in Arabic and then translating them into Latin.[133] He aims, in fact, at a comprehensiveness like that of ample Arabic commentaries, discussing, typically, the occasion of revelation, the merit for the believer in reciting each surah, the number of verses, whether each surah is Meccan or Medinan, as well as the difficult interpretive problems posed by rare words or unclear allusions.[134] We have nothing approaching this in the period treated in this book until Egidio's bilingual Qurʾān of 1518.

Yet Marracci's approach to Qurʾān scholarship simply builds on the philological way of reading that the medieval translators adopted. Like them, he periodically inserts Islamic exegetical material directly into his Latin version. Where all three translators, as well as the Castilian-Muslim translator of MS 235, made clear that the "Runners snorting" of 100:1 were either horses or camels, so also does Marracci: *Per equos concitatos cum fremitu anhelanti*, "By swift horses with a panting roar."[135] Though he does not do so here, he normally places such amplifications in italics or both italics and brackets to make clear that they are additions. Thus in the following verse, he clarifies the equally puzzling *fa-al-mūriyāt qadḥan* ("and [by] the kindlers sparking") by writing "et *per equos* incutientes *pedes ad silices* cum excusione ignis," meaning "and *by horses* striking their *hooves on pebbles* with a sending forth of fire." These insertions are based on a widely cited view that the "kindlers sparking" here are precisely those same charging beasts described in the previous verse who "kindle fire with their hooves when they travel over rocks and gravelly earth," as al-Ṭabarsī put it.[136] Like Robert of Ketton, who also inserted this interpretation into his version of the verse—"[When] fire is struck forth from the blows of their feet[137]—Marracci has clarified by amplification, but he has alerted his readers to this by the use of italics.[138]

More frequently, however, Marracci illuminates the Qurʾānic text, not by amplifying insertions, but by commentary in his attached notes. His version of the first five verses of surah 77 is a good example. Here is another concise and allusive surah that begins with God swearing by various objects. As in the case of 100:1–2, it poses difficult interpretive problems: "(1) By those sent out (*al-mursalāt*) with a mane (*ʿurfan*), (2) and those that blow with a blowing, (3) and those that spread with a spreading, (4) and those that divide by a division, (5) and those that bring forth a remembrance." Here Marracci attempts to capture in his Latin version the literal meaning of these compact phrases, as in verse 2: *Et [per] spirantes validè impetuosè spirando*, "and [by] things blowing vehemently, impetuously with a blowing."[139] It is only in the notes that, working verse by verse, he presents the Muslim interpreters' views. Verse 1, he observes, "certainly [means], 'by intelligences, or angels' . . . Thus al-Zamakhsharī, who explains" that these are—and here he quotes him in Arabic first, and then Latin—"orders of angels, whom God sends with his commands."[140] Often he provides more than one explanation, as at verse 3, where he points out that one commentator (al-Suyūṭī, d. 1505) believed that the "things spreading with a spreading" were winds, while another (al-Zamakhsharī) thought that they were angels, just as in verse 1.[141] But where he finds universal agreement, he signals this too, as at verse 5, where he says of "those bringing forth a remembrance" that "all agree with (al-Suyūṭī)" that here are to be understood—and again he quotes first in Arabic, then in a close Latin translation—"angels, who descend with the revelation to the prophets and messengers, so that they will announce the same revelation to the nations."[142]

This is thorough exegesis. Yet when Robert of Ketton translated the same passage more than five hundred years earlier, his concerns were in many ways the same, though presented to the reader in a different way. Like Marracci, he went to some trouble to clarify what these curt phrases were thought to mean. "(1) By the efficacious *angels* of a legation," he writes,

"(2–3) and by *dry and rainy winds*, (4–5) and by *spirits* who will separate *licit and illicit things, and bear correcting and instructing divine commands to the prophets* . . ." (my italics).[143] The italicized words here are insertions based on Islamic exegesis. That "those sent out" in verse 1 are angels, that the "spreaders" of verse 3 are winds, and that "those bringing forth a remembrance" in verse 5 are angels who bring the revelation to the prophets—all these are interpretations that we have already seen. But it was also widely held by Muslim commentators that the "blowers" of verse 2 were also winds, as Robert indicates, and that "those that divide" in verse 4 were angels as well. Al-Qurṭubī, for example, relates that the former were often thought to be winds, while the latter were angels who, as Robert insisted, distinguish between truth and untruth and "what is permitted (*al-ḥalāl*) and what is forbidden (*al-ḥarām*)."[144]

Despite the differences in how their work appears on the page, all these translators, therefore—to quote Germanus once more—"attempted a translation of the Qurʾān" in reliance on the views of its "native expositors."[145] This forces us to recognize, I suggest, that there was no abrupt change in the later seventeenth century in how Latin Qurʾān translators read that text. For every translator from 1140 to 1698, the task was primarily a philological one—a task concerned with understanding what the often difficult words, constructions, and allusions of the Qurʾān were thought to mean, a task pursued through repeated interrogation of the Islamic tradition of Qurʾān interpretation itself. The distance between Dominicus Germanus and Ludovico Marracci on the one hand, and Robert of Ketton and Mark of Toledo on the other, is diminished even further if we bear in mind that for all of them, this philological reading necessary for translating the Qurʾānic text was intimately connected to very different polemical ways of reading. In the case of Robert and Mark, the connection runs through their patrons, who paid for their work in order to further their own polemical projects. For Germanus and Marracci, however, despite the splendid philological apparatus of their Latin Qurʾāns, the connection subsists precisely in the remarkable editions that they produced, for alongside their literal translations and erudite notes, there are, as we have seen, frequent arguments in favor of Christian belief and against Qurʾānic and Islamic ideas in the former's scholia and the latter's *refutationes*. Philology and polemic existed side by side and often in the minds of the same readers throughout this whole period.

If the distance between medieval Qurʾān translators and seventeenth-century Qurʾān translators is narrower than scholars have assumed, therefore, then the distance between them and translators of our own time is also narrower than we might imagine. Modern translators, for example, have puzzled over what to do with the compressed images at the beginning of surah 51, the Surah of the Scatterers. Here the Qurʾān, in another of the so-called oath-saying passages, represents God swearing by vividly described phenomena: "(1) By those that scatter with a scattering, (2) and those that carry a burden, (3) and those that flow with ease, (4) and those that distribute by command." As in so many other cases, it was left to later exegetes to work out exactly what was being described in these vivid images, and a consensus view emerged: "those that scatter" were winds; "those that carry a burden," were clouds; "those that flow with ease" were ships sailing on the sea; and "those that distribute by command" were angels.[146] Modern Qurʾān translators have worked this interpretation into the very language of their versions. N. J. Dawood, for example, gives us this: "By the dust-scattering *winds* and the heavily-laden *clouds*; by the swiftly-gliding *ships*, and by the *angels* who deal out blessings to all men (*my italics*),"[147] and Muhammad Marmaduke Pickthall's version of seventy-five years ago is quite similar.[148] But we can go all the way back to Robert, Mark, and Iohannes Gabriel Terrolensis to find the same procedure, Mark giving us, for example, *[P]er ventos afferentes pluuiam et nubes eam concipientes et naues currentes et angelos sanctos* . . . , "By *winds* bearing rain, and *clouds* conceiving it, and *ships* sailing quickly, and holy *angels* . . . ," and the other two doing likewise.[149] That does not mean that these translators were somehow modern scholars occupying a medieval past, but it does mean that the practical constraints of translating a given text can work in very similar ways across enormous spans of time, people as different as Robert and Mark and modern Muslims all finding themselves forced to adopt the same methods to deal with the same textual problems.

Yet we should not imagine that it is only in the rather rare pursuit of Qurʾān translation that such a philological reading of that text could flourish within Latin Christendom. As we move on now to consider the complex packaging in which these Latin versions of the Qurʾān were presented to their readers, we will certainly find that a set of polemical concerns—the desire to attack the Qurʾān as a fraud, the desire to use it to argue for Christian belief—clearly informs, and often dominates, Christian Qurʾān reading. But we will also find that such polemical reading rarely existed independently of some amount of philology, for the lexical, grammatical, and interpretive problems that preoccupied Qurʾān translators turn out to have been very much on the minds of many other Latin-Christians who took up Islam's holy book as well.

Chapter 3

Polemic, Philology, and Scholastic Reading in the Earliest Manuscript of Robert of Ketton's Latin Qurʾān

The oldest physical form in which Robert of Ketton's Latin Qurʾān and the rest of Peter the Venerable's anthology of Islamic works survives is a mid-twelfth-century codex now part of the National Library of France (MS Arsenal 1162). Browsing through the pages of Robert's translation as it appears here, what strikes one is not so much the text itself, as all the stuff that surrounds it. Abundant notes, written in a careful hand, litter the margins of many folios. They thunder with hostility: their favorite noun seems to be *mendax* ("liar"), the preferred adjective *stultissimus* ("extremely stupid"). In place of the Qurʾān's usual surah titles, someone has concocted a series of mocking rubrics: "Surah Thirty-One, Enveloped in Absurd Lies and the Characteristic Repetition of Incantations."[1] The bright red ink of these vicious titles has also been employed on folio 11 to draw a portrait of Muhammad "under the form," the library's modern catalogue succinctly informs us, "of a monstrous fish with a human head," probably meant to make Christian readers imagine Muhammad as a seductive and dangerous siren of false doctrine (see figure 1).[2] Standing before and after Robert's Qurʾān translation are the other works whose translation Peter also commissioned, including a handful of quirky collections of Islamic tradition, which must have struck Latin-Christian readers as both fictitious and perverse, and a widely read Arab-Christian attack on Islam.[3]

In this valuable manuscript—which, as Fernando González Muñoz has recently argued, almost certainly represents the original assemblage, done either in Spain or at Cluny, of the Toledan collection out of what had clearly been separate gatherings containing copies of its constituent works[4]—Robert's Latin Qurʾān finds itself, therefore, encircled within a hedge of marginal notes and jarring rubrics, hostile illustration and polemical accompanying works, all shedding light both on how the compilers of

Figure 1. Paris, BnF, MS Arsenal 1162, fol. 11ra. Muhammad depicted as a monstrous man-fish. By permission of the Bibliothèque nationale de France.

this manuscript read the Qur'ān and how they thought other readers ought to and would read it. The clear Arabic of the Qur'ān has not only been translated into Latin, therefore; it has also been placed within a frame intended to make it easier to understand and to control how it is understood. In this it is like all books in all ages. As medievalists have long understood, and as scholars of later European history have been discovering in the last few decades as well,[5] the particular, concrete form of a book is in itself valuable evidence of how the text within it was read. Paying heed to how expensively manufactured a book is, to what illustrations grace its pages, to what prefatory materials precede and what accompanying works and appendices follow it, to what glosses occupy its margins—all this opens a broad window on how texts were used and understood in the past. Moreover, since these framing devices change over time, new readers with new concerns creating new forms in which to insert the texts of interest to them,[6] paying close attention to this evolution is a powerful method for examining how readers' approaches to texts change over time.

Having examined the process of translating the Arabic Qurʾān into Latin in the previous two chapters, I will devote the present and the following three chapters to the frames into which Latin Qurʾāns found themselves inserted between the mid-twelfth and mid-sixteenth centuries. In doing so, these chapters will attempt to tease out the ways in which specific framing devices shed light on how the Qurʾān was read in Latin Christendom. There is no mistaking at least part of what this first frame for Robert's Latin Qurʾān was intended to do: as John Tolan has so felicitously put it, the many hostile notes added in its margins were intended to instruct Latin-Christian readers on "where to be shocked" by the Qurʾān's contents. They were there to insure that Latin readers understood the text in a suitably anti-Islamic way.[7] Indeed, it is here in these notes and hostile surah rubrics—and not, as we have seen, in the translation process itself—that we truly see for the first time an intentional and systematically polemical reading of the Qurʾān on the part of Latin-Christian scholars. The erudite linguistic analysis of the text required of Qurʾān translators has here given way to aggressive religious disputation.

Yet if we occupied ourselves solely with the polemical dimensions of this first Latin Qurʾān's frame, we would miss much of what is most interesting about how Islam's holy book was being presented to readers here. For even the polemical reading that these Latin annotations urge is more complex than first meets the eye. Along with their mean-spirited and repeated attacks on Muhammad and Islam, these notes also energetically continue and encourage something very like that philological reading that Robert used when he translated the text. They do so because even a hostile reading of the Latin Qurʾān required a surprising amount of sophisticated textual interpretation and linguistic analysis.

The larger purposes of all this become particularly clear, however, when we reflect on other aspects of the frame into which this text has been inserted. For in addition to being translated into Latin and surrounded by marginal annotations and supplementary works, the Latin Qur'ān has here been presented to its earliest readers within a very specific sort of manuscript design—that which was characteristic of the books produced for the new scholastic intellectuals of the twelfth-century Renaissance. The manuscript makers, for example, subdivided the Qur'ān into easily digestible chunks, marked off from each other by vivid paragraph marks and colored initials, and in doing so created a text that, as Hugh of St. Victor (d. 1142) recommended, could be read, remembered, and evaluated more easily.[8] Given the same form as those many other scholastic textbooks, the Qur'ān could "be subjected to the same procedures of analysis and debate" as they were, thereby allowing it to be drawn into the grand project of the scholastic movement: "to stabilize, make accessible, and defend," as Richard Southern put it, "an orthodox Christian view of the world against the attacks of heretics within, and unbelievers . . . outside" of Latin Christendom.[9] Seeing this earliest manuscript of Robert's Latin Qur'ān as a scholastic textbook helps make sense of both the polemical and the philological dimensions of the frame that surrounds it—both were typical concerns of scholastic readers and essential to the movement's larger goals.

Yet this manuscript's scholastic qualities entailed an important irony. To fit the Qur'ān out in this way meant to control (or attempt to control) how it was read. Yet it also meant granting it, almost necessarily, a kind of authority and prestige. Properly surrounded by a Latin-Christian commentary and given the physical form recommended by contemporary Latin intellectuals, the Qur'ān became one of the canonical textbooks on the basis of which proper Christian doctrine could be established. The heretical scripture of Christendom's principal rival thus became an authoritative source of arguments against that very rival. The surprising authoritativeness thereby granted to the Qur'ān—an authoritativeness that intriguingly parallels the elevated Latin style of Robert's translation—is nowhere more apparent than in the visual similarities between this manuscript and exactly contemporary glossed Bibles.

To read Robert's Latin Qur'ān as it appeared in Arsenal MS 1162 was, therefore, an impressively complicated act: the reader was introduced to Islam's holy book along *both* polemical and philological lines, all in service of the scholastic goal of clarifying and defending Christian belief and practice; moreover, he held in his hand a book that not only was written in elegant twelfth-century prose but looked and operated ever so much like a contemporary Christian scholar's Bible.

Annotations, Polemic, and Philology

Perhaps the most basic decision regarding how Robert's Latin Qur'ān was to be laid out in manuscript form concerned all the material that Robert had inserted into his translation from the Islamic exegetical tradition. It had become, one might say, something of an "amplified" translation of the Qur'ān, a translation whose difficult parts and elliptical passages often had been filled out by material drawn ultimately from Arabic Qur'ān commentaries. Neither he nor those who later assembled the Arsenal manuscript, however, contrived any device whereby these interpolations could be signaled to readers. Such devices—the use of brackets, or underlining, for example—were adopted by later Qur'ān translators who, as many did, otherwise used Robert's approach. But from the very earliest manuscript of Robert's version on, these insertions in the text were concealed entirely from later readers, what was Qur'ānic text in the strict sense and what really had been taken from Islamic exegetical sources appearing as a textual whole. Later readers, of course, then treated whatever they found as a single Qur'ānic text.[10]

In this, Robert's *Lex Mahumet* resembles a nearly contemporary and profoundly influential work of biblical scholarship, Peter Comestor's *Scholastic History.* Written in the 1160s or 1170s, Comestor's seminal work was a massive biblical paraphrase that, like Robert's Latin Qur'ān, was frequently filled out by material drawn from a wide range of commentaries and other exegetical works. Comestor's paraphrase went on to become a standard university text, but eventually also found itself translated into a variety of vernacular languages, so that it functioned as a key source of lay knowledge of the scriptures.[11] The interpolated passages in this widely read text are, to be sure, much more extensive than those in Robert's Latin Qur'ān, but in each case both original text and inserted exegetical material are presented to the reader as one text, as can be seen in the earliest manuscript of the *Scholastic History*, a codex now in Paris, dating from 1183, as well as in later copies.[12] This is by no means the only time that we will find Latin Christians approaching the Qur'ān in ways that, consciously or unconsciously, are reminiscent of how they have been handling the biblical text.

But while the designers of Arsenal MS 1162 concealed the authoritative views of Muslim scholars on the meaning of the Qur'ānic text within Robert's paraphrase, they intrusively presented the authoritative views on the Qur'ān of another community—Latin Christendom—in the very frame created for Robert's *Lex Mahumet.* Nowhere is this more tediously obvious than in the polemical rubrics, some examples of which we have already seen, that have been added to the beginning of many surahs.[13] Within the Islamic world, each Qur'ānic surah came to bear a title derived from an unusual incident or reference in it, hence the Surah (22) of the Ḥajj, the Surah (50) of [the Letter] Q, or the Surah (72) of the Jinn.[14] In this first manuscript of Robert's Qur'ān, this system has been almost entirely overthrown. While the Latin titles of the first two surahs essentially replicate the traditional Islamic names,[15] the great majority of surahs have either no title at all or are preceded by new titles which appear, in fact, to have been something of an afterthought for the makers of the manuscript, for they often are too long for the space available for them and have to be inserted in smaller script or allowed to spill over into the margins.[16]

The titles are always written in vivid red ink, as at the beginning of what Robert presented as the eleventh surah:[17] "Here he says—as he often does—that the Jews did not kill Christ, but rather someone otherwise unknown but similar to him, and that God has no son, among the typical insanities."[18] Like this rubric, some of the rubrics purport to describe as well as denounce the surah's contents, but many others amount to little but name calling: *Azoara XXX. III. vana. stulta et impia* ("Surah Thirty-Three, Vain, Stupid, and Impious").[19] Why many surahs have these rubrics while others lack them is not clear, though the fact that the last thirty-eight surahs have no polemical titles suggests that the length of the surah had at least something to do with it: as the surahs became shorter and shorter toward the end of the Qur'ān, it apparently began to seem less and less necessary to remind readers of how "most full of vanity"[20] they were. But not a few longer surahs early in the Qur'ān also lack polemical rubrics.[21]

Yet these hostile surah rubrics ultimately make a much smaller impact on the mind of the reader of this Latin Qur'ān manuscript than do the copious notes written in the margins and between the lines of many of its folios. Written in a relatively careful hand, these annotations are not the casual jottings of some later reader, but rather are clearly intended as a kind of study aid for readers of this manuscript. On the one hand, they are simply an extension of the polemical rubrics, the same vocabulary of disgust and derision being employed in both. A note between the two columns of text on folio 27r, apparently responding to the Qur'ānic account of Moses upbraiding his people for worshipping the calf in 2:52–55, which is just to the left, is emblematic: *Nota ridiculum mendacium*, "note the ridiculous lie."[22] The tone of this note sounds throughout many of these annotations, though played in a number of variations. That the Qur'ān is a tissue of fabulous fictions is constantly urged: "A most stupid fable follows about God and Adam and the angels and the Devil, and I do not know where he found it."[23] Here Muhammad is implicitly identified as the author of these fictions, something that the reader is constantly reminded of. "Here he boasts," we are instructed at 2:23, "as if no human being could make such a book."[24] Since a great deal of the Qur'ān retells stories already familiar to Christian readers, the annotations accuse Muhammad of theft. Thus at 3:75, where Robert has translated the term *qinṭār*, a term here meaning something like "a great amount of wealth," with the rather suitable, but very biblical, phrase "talent of gold" (*auri talentum*), a note complains that "he steals this from the Gospel."[25] But not only is Muhammad portrayed as a writer of scandalous fictions and a plagiarizer. He wasn't even very good at it: "Note how stupidly and how often he repeats this just as many other things" says a gloss next to 2:115, "not having anything else that he might say."[26] That Muhammad often seemed to contradict himself the notes frequently point out to the same end.[27]

Sometimes the marginalia attack the text itself, directly, with no reference to Muhammad's role in revelation. A description of an aspect of Islamic divorce law at 2:230 is simply condemned as a *lex turpissima*, "a most foul law."[28] That God is often portrayed in the Qur'ān, especially in later surahs, as swearing by the dawn, or clouds, or charging horses, seems laughable to the author of these notes, and so at surah 75, which begins "By the Day of Resurrection" (*Per diem seculi futuri* in Robert's paraphrase), he wrote, "Again how stupid the oath is by which he makes God swear."[29] Sometimes he simply jotted down a marginal reminder in the form of a *Nota* ("Notice!") with no other comment. But even these are often implicit attacks on the content of the Qur'ān. Many of the last fifteen verses of surah 55 concern the Islamic paradise, described in all its vivid richness. The five repetitions of *Nota* here clearly call on readers to bear in mind the contrast between the supposedly carnal nature of the Islamic afterlife and the putatively more spiritual nature of the Christian one.[30] The spirit of these notes is captured nowhere better than in an exasperated comment near the end: "Notice the stupidity everywhere!"[31]

It is clear enough, then, that these notes were devised in order to insure that Latin-Christian readers would recognize "where to be shocked [and] what to find ridiculous" in the Qur'ān.[32] There is, in fact, a noticeable tension between the restrained character of Robert's translation—a translation informed by Islamic Qur'ān exegesis, a translation which plays up neither the potentially Christian interpretations of some Qur'ānic passages nor the vivid anti-Trinitarianism of others, a translation in which words such as *stultus* and *fabula* scarcely play a role—and the stridency of the marginal annotations. In this tension can be grasped the wide gulf that separated the philological reading of Qur'ān translators from the hostile reading of anti-Islamic polemicists. In this tension as well can be grasped the important fact that both sorts of reading could exist even in the middle twelfth century, could exist even within the same circle of scholars, and maybe even, as we will see when we take up the question of who, after all, wrote these notes, within the same man.

Yet these marginally shouted insults should not deafen our ears to the fact that these many notes are actually rather more complicated than they seem at first reading, something Marie-Thérèse d'Alverny briefly suggested more than a half century ago. While many of the notes indeed "censured" the Qur'ānic text, others, she pointed out, translated words that had been transliterated in the Latin version, and others gave geographic, linguistic, and historical information. Above all, many of the notes provided "doctrinal explanations which indicate a rather profound knowledge of the theology of Islam."[33] One note, for example, which d'Alverny transcribed in its entirety in a famous article, explained the "beautiful names" of God that Islamic tradition identifies; another note provided an alternative translation of the short first surah; still others carefully point out biblical parallels to the Qur'ānic text. There are some errors—such as in the note that gives a mistaken etymology for the word "surah"—but in general, she observed, these notes are often "inspired by Arab sources."[34]

In looking now in some detail at these notes, we will find that d'Alverny's largely intuitive conclusion was entirely correct. Like Robert's translation itself, these notes are often based on the Islamic exegetical tradition, to which their author or authors turn for the same reason that Robert did: to help clarify a difficult text. And just as Robert's careful philological reading of the Qur'ān as he translated it directly served the needs of Peter the Venerable's polemical program, so polemic and philology continue to be linked in these notes. But now the linkage is even more overt—hostile notes and philological notes appear side by side, or, not infrequently, polemic and philology flow into each other in the very same note.

Many of the notes, in fact, are quite simply corrections to this fair copy of Robert's Latin Qur'ān, someone having read carefully through the whole of it and inserted necessary emendations, usually interlinearly.[35] In the first verse of the Surah (3) of the Family of ʿImrān, for example, the text originally referred to the God who is *uiuus et altissimus preter non est alius*. Very clearly a *quem* is missing before *non*, and an annotator has duly inserted one, so that now the text speaks of a God who is "living and most high beside *whom* there is no other."[36] There are many other similar examples,[37] and for our purposes what is interesting about these corrections is the attitude that they express toward the text. The Qur'ān was thought to deserve vitriolic denunciation, as we have seen, but it was also considered worthy of careful correction, if only so that it could be more efficiently denounced. That, for some medieval Latin-Christians, reading the Qur'ān thus meant systematically correcting its text is demonstrated by an impressive amount of evidence that we will examine in Chapters 4 and 5 as well.

A number of other notes are simply explanations or paraphrases of passages that, in Robert's version at least, were not seen to be sufficiently clear. Partway through verse 6:92, for example, where Robert's translation reads, "But indeed he did not explain his precepts to you or your ancestors before you," an interlinear note identifies the person in question as Moses (*id est Moÿses*), something that the annotator grasped from the context, that prophet figuring in the narrative a few lines above.[38] There is nothing hostile about this—no complaints that this is a "vain" or "most ridiculous" statement. This is simply textual clarification, and a number of other notes similarly clear up ambiguities, without explicitly attacking the text.[39]

Many notes of this kind clearly derive, as d'Alverny suggested, from extensive knowledge of Islamic belief, practice, and Qur'ānic interpretation. A large minority of these are what might be termed "reader-orientation" notes that explain the conventions of Qur'ānic narrative, for example, or the terms used for divisions of the Qur'ānic text. An interlinear note above verse 3:31 explains that the statement that "those who love God should follow me" (*deum diligentes me sequantur*) is in the "voice of Muhammad" (*vox Mahumet*), this being an entirely correct clarification of Robert's paraphrase, which fails here to make clear that the bulk of this verse is something that Muhammad is supposed to preach to his people.[40] Here the annotator must have known the relevant Arabic text, which does indeed begin—as Robert's version does not—with that oft-repeated Qur'ānic command to Muhammad to "Say" what follows.[41]

As puzzling to Latin readers as the Qur'ān's frequent, and often unsignaled, changes of narrative voice would have been a series of terms and conventions associated with the Qur'ānic text, and these also the Arsenal's marginalia attempt to explain. Next to the first use of the term "surah" (*azoara* in Robert's transliteration of the Arabic *al-sūrah*), the annotator explains that "what we call chapter in Latin, they call *azoara*."[42] That the

Qur'ān itself—like many of its constituent surahs—could be known by other names is also clarified in the notes. Where Robert transliterated the word *al-furqān* (meaning "criterion," but used frequently as an alternative name for the revelation to Muhammad) a note explains that "it is the same as the Qur'ān."[43] On more than one occasion, the marginalia remind readers that the "men of the book" (*homines legum*) mentioned in the Qur'ān are Jews and Christians.[44]

Some of these reader-orientation notes attempt to acquaint Latin Qur'ān students with the broader background of Islamic history and belief as well. To remind Latin-Christians of the ethnic and linguistic connections of the Arab people, a note near the beginning of Robert's translation points out that "It is to be known that the Arabic language has the greatest kinship with Hebrew," and explains that they therefore write letters from right to left rather than left to right.[45] The note that carefully explains the "beautiful names" that Muslims ascribe to God fills the margin as well as parts of the right and left margins of one of the early manuscripts that contains it.[46]

While many of these notes designed to make Latin readers feel at home with the textual conventions of the Qur'ān are physically quite distinct from the hostile notes I have already described, not infrequently the one sort of note flows into the other, philology and polemic linked together in the same marginal comment. A note at verses 2:136–39 is a good example. "The voice as if of those who profess him," the comment reads, next to this passage in which the narrative voice seems to shift back and forth between God and contemporaries of Muhammad, "and he does this often, changing persons in speech, in order that he appear to speak like a prophet."[47] The observation that the Qur'ānic text often "chang[es] persons in speech" is quite correct, but this instructive textual observation is immediately drawn into one of the polemical concerns of these notes—to demonstrate that the Qur'ān is Muhammad's own composition, not God's transcendent revelation.[48]

Moreover, some of these reader-orientation notes seem to have been written not just in rather detailed awareness of Islamic beliefs and practices, but with specific knowledge of how Qur'ānic commentators interpreted particular verses. Next to the beginning of the first surah, for example, which was called the "Chapter of the Mother of the Book" in Robert's version, we are told that "He calls this short, first chapter 'the mother of the book' because from it the whole religion takes its origin and foundation, and it is the beginning and sum of all their prayers."[49] This is very much the kind of thing that Muslim commentators on the names of the first surah say. Al-Suyūṭī, for example, pointed out that in Arabic the phrase "mother of something" refers to the origin of a thing. The first surah is, in fact, "the origin of the Qurʾān because of its encompassing of all the intentions of the Qurʾān and because of what it contains in the way of sciences and wisdoms."[50]

The same kind of awareness of the standard exegesis of particular verses of the Qurʾān can be seen in many notes that, rather than orienting the reader in general, are more directly concerned with explicating the text of the Qurʾān.[51] The final verse of the short first surah refers to the "path of those upon whom you have bestowed favor, not the path of those who have received your anger, nor those who have gone astray." In Robert's concise version, these last two categories of sinners have become simply "the enemies" (*hostes*) and "those in error" (*erroneos*). We cannot be sure what the marginalia in the Arsenal manuscript consisted of here, since the first folio of Robert's translation has gone missing in this manuscript, but it seems almost certain that there were, first of all, interlinear notes above both terms—"scilicet iudeos," respectively, and "scilicet christianos"—[52] the same interpretation appearing in marginal notes: "He calls Jews 'enemies of God' because they wanted to hang Christ [on the cross] who was the greatest prophet, living ever without sin, the most just, and the one born of the Virgin without guilt."[53] "He calls Christians 'those in error' both because they [i.e., Muslims] consider that they worship three gods, and [because they consider that they worship] images."[54] That these two terms referred to Jews and Christians respectively was indeed a nearly standard view among Muslim commentators.[55]

A comment on the immediately following passage, the first verse of the second surah, also depends on standard Islamic exegesis. Like many surahs, this one begins with what are known as "mysterious letters"—a group of Arabic letters, that is, that do not form a word, but seem to be initials standing for other words. While there is no agreement, among either Muslim or non-Muslim scholars, about what these letters mean, there has been enormous discussion of them from the earliest Islamic periods, especially in commentaries on the Qurʾān.[56] That discussion spilled over into the annotations on Robert's Latin Qurʾān, for in certain early manuscripts three peculiar letters—they are neither quite Roman characters nor Arabic, but look respectively like a "B," a "d," and an "l" in one manuscript, and like an "S," an "a," and a "Z" in another[57]—are written at the very beginning of the Surah of the Cow. Above each of these letters is an interlinear note: "*mim*, that is 'king'," over the first, "*lem*, that is 'wise'," over the second, and "*elif*, that is 'God'," over the third.[58] Now while they are in the opposite order from how they appear in Arabic Qurʾān manuscripts, Arabic and Latin being written in opposite directions, these are precisely the three "mysterious letters"—*alif* ("A"), *lām* ("L"), *mīm* ("M")—that appear at the beginning of this surah. A more extensive marginal note provides further background on what these letters were thought to mean. Muhammad begins the surah with these letters, we are told, "because *alif* is among them first both in the order of the letters [of the alphabet] and in the name of God [i.e., "Allāh"]; the majesty of God is designated through the *lām*, the ruling power through the *mīm*."[59] While the interlinear notes and this marginal note disagree regarding the meaning of the *lām*, they are both quite similar to what one finds in Qurʾānic commentaries on this passage. Al-Ṭabarī, for example, quotes a tradition that says that the *alif* does stand for "Allah," while the *lām* is for *laṭīf*, meaning a range of things—"gentle," "benign," but also "subtle" or "knowledgeable of hidden matters," and in this sense "wise" (*sapiens*) as in the Latin notes. The *mīm* means *majīd*, "glorious" or "majestic," much as the marginal (rather than the interlinear) note explains it: "majesty" (*maiestas*).[60]

No more concise evidence of the dependence of these annotations on Islamic Qurʾān exegesis can be found than an interlinear note on 2:72–73—an explanatory comment that also illuminates the continuities between the philological reading of Robert as he translated and of the annotators as they attempted to clarify his Latin Qurʾān. Robert's own translation of this rather difficult passage had already been decisively influenced by Islamic exegesis. The Arabic original asks the Children of Israel to remember when they had killed someone and fallen into disagreement about it, so that God, in order to resolve the dispute, had said—in a particularly problematic phrase—"hit him [*or* it] with some [*or* part] of it [*or* him]." Robert had learned from Islamic sources that this passage was clarified by assuming that the first pronoun referred to the dead person (*nafs*) mentioned in 2:72, even though that pronoun, -*hu*, is in the wrong gender, *nafs* being feminine, while -*hu* is masculine. The second pronoun, though feminine, could not now be understood as referring to *nafs*, the dead person, though at first sight it would seem to, but must be understood, Muslim commentators said, as referring back to the "cow" (*baqarah*) mentioned in earlier verses, 2:67–71. Thus these troublesome words must be understood to mean something like "hit the dead man with a part of the cow."[61] This was to be done so that the dead man would, the commentators went on to say, "be brought back to life and then tell . . . Moses . . . , and those who disputed concerning it, who his killer was."[62] Robert's highly compact paraphrase incorporates all these insights from the commentators: "When someone, at God's bidding and with his approval, will have desired to bring to light an unknown murderer, let him touch the dead man with some small part of the cow; thus revived he [i.e., the formerly dead man] will give information about what really happened."[63] But there was one question that this text raised that Robert did not answer in his translation, even though the commentators generally addressed it: what part of the cow, after all, was used to strike the dead man? Al-Zamakhsharī observed that there was disagreement about this, "for it is said [that it was] its tongue, and it is said its right leg, and it is said the base of its tail, and it is said the bone which lies near the cartilage and is the base of the ear," and so on.[64] So engaging was this question that the views of Islamic commentators urged their way into the annotations on Robert's Latin Qurʾān, for in an interlinear note we are told that the dead man was struck *cum cauda secundum quosdam. cum crure secundum alios* ("with the tail according to some, with the leg according to others").[65]

Here an interlinear note offered Latin readers the same information typically supplied by Muslim exegetes in their Arabic commentaries on this verse, and similar examples abound in these Latin annotations. This is particularly noticeable in the notes that translate or explain the Arabic words that Robert had transliterated rather than translated. When a marginal note on 4:60 points out that the *Theut* mentioned here was "an idol of the ancient idolatry of the Arabs,"[66] it reproduces one of the views of Muslim commentators on this word (*Ṭāghūt* in Arabic) and the equally strange word *Jibt* mentioned just previously, in 4:51, and which, al-Ṭabarī indicated, might refer to "two idols whom polytheists were worshipping to the exclusion of God."[67] At 55:14, Robert likewise transliterated the rare word *ṣalṣāl*: "He indeed . . . created man from *celcal*."[68] An interlinear note just above reads "that is, from mud" (*id est de limo*).[69] This is the definition of the term that Muslim commentators advance as well, al-Qurṭubī, for example, explaining that what was meant here was "dry clay" (*al-ṭīn al-yābis*).[70] In a famous passage (61:6), Jesus promises to send another prophet "whose name was Aḥmad." Just as the Muslim commentators do, so the Latin annotator here explains that this future prophet is understood to be "Muhammad" (*Mahumetus*).[71]

The most striking examples of the dependence of these annotations on the Muslim exegetical tradition are, however, the cases where they tell us about what Muslims call the "occasion of revelation"—the specific incidents in the Prophet's life, or in the lives of others, that prompted God to reveal particular passages. We see a brief example of this at the beginning of surah 54, whose enigmatic first verse reads, "The hour approached and the moon was divided." In both Robert's unusually close translation (*Appropinquauit hora, lunaque bipertito diuisa est*) and in the Arabic original, this sentence is strikingly opaque, not only because dividing the moon lies beyond our ken, but also because the following verses shed little light on this one. The Qur'ānic exegetical tradition, however, concluded that it referred to a miracle worked one night near Mecca by Muhammad, who pointed at the moon, which then split in half and fell to earth in two pieces.[72] In conformity with this view, the Latin note on Robert's version of this verse derisively observes that "some sign had occurred in the moon which he says to have been worked through himself."[73]

Sometimes, the information supplied concerning the occasion of revelation serves fairly obvious polemical goals, as at verse 3:54. This verse comes in the middle of a longer narrative about Jesus, and, without clear connection with what is before or after, remarks that "they plotted, and God plotted, and God is the best of plotters." After indicating that the first plotters described here are "the Jews" (*iudei scilicet*), a marginal note goes on to say that "Here [Muhammad] means to say that certain Jews wanted to kill Christ but, shrewdly removing himself, he escaped, leaving some unidentified person in his place, whom they crucified, thinking that he was Christ. But the Creator raised Christ to himself."[74] Such an account would seem shocking to any Christian reader, so decisively does it depart from the Gospel accounts of the crucifixion, and it doubtless served the interests of showing readers where to be horrified by the Qur'ān that it did so. But it also happens to be rather like what Muslim commentators said when they explained this difficult verse and its occasion of revelation.[75]

At times, the language of such notes reflects the very analytical structure of the exegetical source, whether human or written, that the annotators have turned to. At verse 2:243, the Qur'ān invokes the memory of those who abandoned their dwellings in fear of death, only to have God bring death upon them anyway, after which he restored them back to life. A note that flows from the margin just next to this verse over into the space above the following column of text reads as follows:

> Here they tell a certain fable, namely that certain people fleeing on account of earthquakes and lightning to caves under mountains and rocks, dwelt there thinking themselves removed from the power of God, and on account of this fearing him not at all; these God made die and rise again so that there he might show himself to

be equally powerful everywhere. According to some this happened to certain people fleeing lest they go into battle, and he seems more likely to mean this.[76]

That "they tell a certain fable" here nicely describes the process, so ubiquitous in Qur'ānic exegesis, of quoting a hadith that is thought to give the background details necessary to understand a difficult verse. That we are given alternative explanations is also powerfully reminiscent of Muslim exegetical practice, for alternate, and often completely different, hadiths are often provided for the reader, and indeed the Arabic commentaries on this verse cite a number of different hadiths similar to those mentioned here.[77]

It was a complex form of reading, then, that lay behind these notes. On the one hand, we will take up no other single source that is so relentlessly hostile to Islam. None of the several Latin Qur'ān commentaries or sets of marginal glosses that we will examine in the following three chapters, for example, will so viciously decry Islam's "stupidity" and the Prophet's "ridiculous" teachings. On the other hand, very few other sources demonstrate such detailed familiarity with Islam and Muslim Qur'ān exegesis, or as much interest in reading the Qur'ānic text within that tradition of Muslim exegesis. In fact, polemic and philology mix together in nearly equal measures in these annotations, and the ensuing interaction between those two kinds of reading is not the end of the complexity of these notes. For one thing, it is worth pointing out that sometimes the polemical value of the philological notes—their usefulness, in other words, in understanding and refuting the key teachings of Islam—is not entirely obvious. How exactly does it help the cause of Christian apology to be presented with a detailed summary of the Islamic names of God? To what polemical purpose can one put the knowledge that the transliterated term *celcal* (*ṣalṣāl*), the substance out of which humans were made, in 55:14 means "mud"? Can the further information about those people abandoning their homes in fear of death in 2:243—that is, that they were fleeing an earthquake or afraid of going to battle—be seen to serve an obvious purpose in Christian-Muslim disputation?[78] Almost any piece of information about Islam could presumably be put to some sort of polemical use, but suffice it to say that none of these things is typically at issue when medieval Christians dispute Muslims. In fact, in these cases one cannot help sensing a sort of philological slippage, a half-conscious drifting away from the obvious anti-Islamic purposes of most of the philological analysis in these notes and into something else. We may, in fact, be witnessing a kind of scholarly vanity here, the virtuoso textual analysis of philologists who are enjoying their mastery of their tools, and who can't resist parading their knowledge before later readers. Or we may be seeing something even more intriguing, the gradual and unaware transformation of purpose that extensive engagement with a text sometimes brings, an insensible shifting of pragmatic, polemical interest in the text into a "drive for completeness" and systematic coverage.[79] We have no way of knowing for sure which impulse is at work, but such slippages will show up in later Qurʾān readers too.

The question of who, after all, composed these remarkable notes is a complex one. There are abundant annotations, in the same hand, in the other works in the Arsenal manuscript, many of them serving the same complex purposes as those on Robert's Latin Qurʾān.[80] D'Alverny and others have taken up the question of their authorship before, and her argument, that they must have been written by a team, probably consisting of members of Peter the Venerable's group of translators, is almost surely correct. That the notes show such remarkable knowledge of Islamic thought and Qurʾānic interpretation means that their authors had to have been scholars of matters Arabic and Islamic; that they are so unendingly hostile to Islam indicates that they had to be non-Muslims; that they periodically make fairly serious mistakes while elsewhere handling complex issues well suggests that all the members of the annotating team were not equally learned; and that they are virtually contemporary with the translations themselves suggests that members of the original translation team itself were responsible. For d'Alverny this all meant that some member of Peter the Venerable's team less familiar with Islam and the Qurʾān—probably Peter of Poitiers, Peter the Venerable's secretary—must have actually written them based on information supplied by others who knew Islam far better, such as the Mozarab Peter of Toledo, translator of the *Apology of al-Kindī*, which follows the Qurʾān in the Arsenal manuscript, and Robert of Ketton. This would explain both the notes' extensive learning and their periodic slipups.[81] Such a view must be substantially correct, and to it I would make only one adjustment. Given the fact that—and this is something that d'Alverny was not aware of—Robert clearly knew a great deal about Islamic Qurʾānic exegesis, his translation being repeatedly shaped by it, the argument that he played a role in compiling these notes must be seen as very strong indeed. If I am right in assuming that he, like Dominicus Germanus of Silesia in the early sixteenth century,[82] must have compiled a large number of notes based on his reading of Qurʾānic commentaries or on his conversations with learned Muslims, such notes would be the natural sources upon which much of the marginalia was based as well. At any rate, it is impossible not to notice the obvious continuities between how Robert translates certain passages and how the annotations then comment upon them.[83]

The Rest of the Toledan Collection: A Further Polemical Frame

But Robert's restrained Latin Qur'ān was not just inserted within the complex frame provided by the abundant annotations; it was also lodged in the Arsenal manuscript between a series of further works that, pressing in on it from all sides, attempted in a much less ambivalent way to insure that Christians read it with a properly apologetic and polemical eye. Of course Robert's own short preface to his translation, with its abusive comments on Islam,[84] functioned in this way, but much more important were a series of other texts that consisted, first of all, of a trio of short compilations of Islamic tradition. The first of these, called the *Fables of the Saracens*, and bearing a subtitle similar in tone to the hostile rubrics in Robert's Latin Qur'ān, *A Lying and Ridiculous Chronicle of the Saracens*, is a grab bag of Islamic traditions also translated by Robert himself.[85] We learn, for example, of the four things that God was believed to have created directly (the Pen, Adam, the Throne, and Paradise); of the process of human gestation; of the chronology of the patriarchs and prophets; of the events of the Hijrah; of the lives of the first caliphs.[86] Many of these traditions are widely known in the Islamic world, but James Kritzeck was not able to find a single Arabic work that embodies them all and of which this is a direct translation. It may be a compilation of extracts from various works.[87] Under the title of *The Book of the Generation of Muhammad and His Upbringing*, the second of these works recounts many legends about creation, the lives of Old Testament figures, and the life of Muhammad, all in order to illustrate how the miraculous prophetic light can be traced from the beginning of the world and through the Jewish prophets to Muhammad himself.[88] Earlier prophecies of the coming of Muhammad play a role here, as do marvels associated with Muhammad's birth. In this case the Arabic original has been clearly identified as *The Book of the Lineage of the Messenger of God*.[89] The third work bears the title *The Teaching of Muhammad*.[90] A translation of an Arabic work called *The Questions of ʿAbd Allāh ibn Salām*, this dialogue presents Muhammad answering queries about all manner of things put to him by an early convert to Islam. Ranging from questions such as "Are you a prophet?" and "Has God sent you a book?" to amusing riddles, these questions, and Muhammad's astute answers to them, lead the questioner to recognize Muhammad as the messenger of God.[91]

This extensive sampling of Islamic tradition affixed to the front of Robert's Qur'ān translation in the Arsenal manuscript is balanced by a far more important work attached to the end. The last thirty-eight folios consist of a translation of the most widely read Arab-Christian treatise against Islam, *The Apology of al-Kindī*.[92] Written in Arabic in the ninth or tenth century, this work consists of a short letter attributed to a Muslim, called al-Hāshimī, inviting a Christian friend, named al-Kindī, to embrace the Prophet's religion. This is followed by a vast epistle by the Christian al-Kindī, who both attacks Islam and defends Christianity so ferociously that most scholars have argued that the stereotypical name of the Christian—ʿAbd al-Masīḥ ibn Iṣḥāq al-Kindī (i.e., "Servant of the Messiah, Son of Isaac, al-Kindī")—is a pseudonym, and that the equally stereotypical name of his Muslim correspondent, ʿAbd Allāh ibn Ismāʾīl al-Hāshimī (i.e., "Servant of God, Son of Ishmael, al-Hāshimī"), must likewise be a literary fiction, the letter attributed here to a Muslim almost certainly having been written by the same anonymous Christian who wrote the lengthy refutation. But while this work attacks Islam zealously, it is nevertheless informed by extensive learning in Islamic thought, and as a guide to both the nature of Islam and how to rebut it, it would have centuries of influence in Christian Europe.[93]

But the collections of Islamic tradition and the *Apology of al-Kindī* were not the only works that framed Robert's Latin Qur'ān in the Arsenal manuscript. Standing at the very beginning of it were two further short texts, both by Peter the Venerable. First we find a *Summary of All the Heresy and Diabolic Sect of the Saracens or Ishmaelites*.[94] Here Peter described, and energetically refuted, Islamic beliefs about God, Muhammad, the Qur'ān, the Last Judgment, and a whole host of other issues.[95] Just after that we find a letter from Peter to the leading Christian thinker of the age, Bernard of Clairvaux,[96] explaining that he had caused all these works to be translated so that Christian thinkers might effectively demonstrate the wrongness of Islam's teachings, just as Augustine had taken on all the heresies of his age, and inviting Bernard to embrace this task. Bernard did not take up the inivation.

Now there is no doubt that, taken as a whole, this series of works that hemmed in Robert's Latin Qur'ān embodied some of the same polemical philology that informed the extensive marginal notes that we have already looked at. The overtly polemical works—Peter's *Summary* and the *Apology of al-Kindī*—showed very clearly where Christian readers should find the Qur'ān and Islam scandalous and erroneous. The three collections of Islamic tradition—each of them an authentically Islamic work, after all—provided something of what the philological notes did, extra-Qur'ānic sources useful in understanding Islam and its holy book. Like the annotations, then, these further works are testament to a basic insight: that the Qur'ān by itself, especially in Robert's nonpolemical translation, was not a sufficient introduction to Islam. It required two kinds of supplement: warning about what in it was not true, and clarification of what it said so that it could be more effectively refuted.

Manuscript Layout and Scholastic Reading Practices

But the frame that surrounded Robert's Latin Qur'ān consisted not only of philological-polemical annotations and a series of overtly anti-Islamic works that hedged it in front and back. It also consisted of a series of manuscript-design features, rooted in a specific set of ideas about how books should be read. In examining now these design features of Arsenal MS 1162, we will have a chance to reflect on some of the larger goals of the makers of this manuscript and to think through how those goals—and ways of reading—fit in with the dominant intellectual movement of their day. For it is as a tool for the new scholastic readers, who were beginning to flourish at just the period when this manuscript was produced, and who had equal interests in polemic and philology, that we can best understand this remarkable codex.

To understand and use a written text effectively, a reader not only must know how to read the necessary language, but must also be guided into the text by a series of manuscript techniques that orient him to the material—making him at home, as Jacques Monfrin has pointed out, with the written words that are to meet him. Such "simple or infinitely complex signals"[97] guide his reading by anticipating the questions he will want answered and the ways he will want to use the book in front of him. Just as they would have done with any other text, the creators of the Arsenal manuscript had choices to make about how they wanted to guide readers into this anthology of Islamic texts. What they chose was to place these works within the revolutionary new manuscript layout associated with the twelfth-century Renaissance. In so doing they made clear two things: that they themselves read the Qur'ān according to the new reading procedures that flourished in and shaped that period, and that they believed that the readers of the manuscript they were producing would want to read it that way too.

The scholastic book began to emerge during the early twelfth century. It was the product of the huge shift from the early medieval monastic culture of reading, where one ruminated over a few texts but in great depth, to the scholastic reading culture fashioned to suit the needs of scholars who no longer ruminated over texts but discursively analyzed them, and who now were awash in a thousand new texts by Greek and Arab scientists and philosophers and by new theologians trained in recently founded cathedral or collegiate-church schools.[98] Twelfth-century book makers did not invent devices to make written texts easier to search, digest, and analyze in the scholastic way, but, in the first half of that century especially, they brought together a whole series of such techniques, creating the basic template of the scholastic book—a template which in many ways is still with us, modern books being its direct descendants.[99] What drove this change was "the insufficiency of memory as a finding device," as Richard and Mary Rouse have put it, in the world of the multiple texts and innovative analytical methods of the new schools.[100] Under this pressure, manuscript makers combined more than a dozen mechanisms that transformed many far older texts into books that scholastic thinkers found congenial. These included running headlines, chapter titles in brightly colored ink, alternating red and blue initials, variation in the size of initials, paragraph markers, tables of contents, cross-references, citations of quoted authors, and elaborate marginal annotations.[101] The Arsenal manuscript by no means employs all of these devices—though we will see in the next chapter that later copies of it contain most of them—but it certainly makes use of some of the key techniques.

Though there is no table of contents in the strict sense, instructing readers on which works could be found in this codex, a short prologue on folio 1ra, though present in no later manuscripts, does describe the contents of the manuscript with varying degrees of clarity—while the collections of Islamic tradition and even the Qur'ān are only alluded to here vaguely, the *Apology of al-Kindī* is described rather precisely.[102] Furthermore, the reader is assisted notably in finding what interests him by the colorful titles that appear at the beginning of each text. The eye of the reader is drawn to the titles, for example, of *Liber generationis Mahumet* and *Doctrina Mahumet*, for these appear in bright lettering stretching across both columns of the page.[103] While we lack the first folio of Robert's translation in the manuscript, it must certainly have had a similar title. Since the Qur'ān consists of more than one hundred separate surahs, we should not be surprised to discover that their titles are in the same vivid red as well, and often any blank space left in lines with such titles is filled in with a looping pattern also in red.

It is easy to find the beginnings of individual works within this manuscript, then, and easy to find the beginnings of new surahs of the Qur'ān in particular. But the early surahs of the Qur'ān, other than the short *Fātiḥah*, are quite lengthy. The second occupies fully eight folios (26r–34r), which is a great deal of text to find one's way through. Interested in serving the needs of the new twelfth-century reader, therefore, Robert of Ketton did something that was common in his age, but of which readers for the last five hundred years have been derisively critical:[104] he subdivided these early surahs, creating a Latin Qur'ān of 123 surahs rather than the standard 114.[105] There was nothing unusual about this in the intellectual world in which Robert dwelt. Aristotle's works received new chapter divisions in that century, after all, and Stephen Langton created the chapter divisions still used in biblical books at the beginning of the following century.[106] Readers faced with many books to digest needed them to be cut up into manageable, and citable, portions. Here, then, a Latin-Christian reader was applying to the Qur'ān one of the layout devices applied contemporaneously to many other Latin texts. Yet in doing so, Robert actually drew on the Islamic frame of the Qur'ān for guidance. While it has been suggested that these redivisions in Robert's Latin Qur'ān were simply arbitrary,[107] Bobzin, following the intriguing suggestion of d'Alverny,[108] has elegantly shown that Robert placed new surah divisions at points in the text where there were already other divisions in the Arabic Qur'ān as Muslims read it. These were the beginnings of new *ḥizb*s, or sixtieths. The division of the text in this way—together with the ever-present surah divisions—was common in Arabic manuscripts, and it is quite clear that when Robert wanted to subdivide a surah, he always adopted the beginning of a new *ḥizb* as the beginning of his newly created surah, and it is not surprising to find that when he did so, he was using a system of *ḥizb* divisions that circulated in Tunis and North Africa, rather than one typical of Cairo and farther east.[109]

But in twelfth-century manuscripts even the chapters were presented to the reader as consisting of smaller, easily identifiable subunits. Thus in Gratian's *Decretum*, new subsections were often signaled by the insertion of a paragraph sign into the text.[110] Typically, this was a curved bracket, something like a large C, often with a horizontal line running from the top of the bracket to the right, and covering part of the following word, and often written in brightly colored ink. In the Arsenal manuscript, a very different marker was devised to signal each successive subdivision, a symbol that looks very like a minuscule q and a minuscule p written back to back, sharing the same descending line, and preceded and followed by a dot on the line: .qp. (figure 2).[111] The formal origin of this sign is not clear, but, given its unusual shape, it readily arrests the eye of the reader, focusing his attention on the beginning of a new section. Yet again, in producing a searchable text for the twelfth-century European reader, Robert was drawing on a model provided by Arabic Qurʾān manuscripts. For it turns out that the divisions these unique symbols mark off almost always correspond to still another set of Qurʾānic divisions marked in many Arabic Qurʾān manuscripts: the division into groups of ten verses (called an *ʿushr*, or "decade"). Throughout almost all of the second surah, for example, the subdivisions of Robert's Latin Qurʾān correspond very closely with the decade divisions of medieval Arabic Qurʾān manuscripts such as Paris, BnF, ar. 384, a thirteenth-century codex. There are two places—at the second and third decades—where no paragraph mark can be found, and there are two places where Robert's new surah divisions take precedence over a decade division, and for which there are consequently no paragraph marks, but with one exception, all the remaining twenty-six paragraph divisions of this surah fall where decade divisions do in the Arabic manuscript. Later in Robert's Latin Qurʾān, these divisions often become less frequent, but where they do occur, they likewise tend to fall where decade divisions would be in the Arabic text.[112] The subdivisions of this first Latin Qurʾān turn out, therefore, to be derived from Arabic Qurʾān-reading practices, something that the annotators of the manuscript were quite conscious of, for, as we have seen, they oriented readers of this codex by pointing out that this new sign was simply "the Arabic paragraph sign."[113]

Closely connected functionally with the Arsenal manuscript's "Arabic paragraph sign" is the use of brightly colored initials. The letter following immediately after each paragraph sign is a large initial copied in the bright red ink of the surah titles, this making the beginning of new sections even more clearly discernible, even at a glance. Contemporary Latin intellectuals such as Hugh of St. Victor recommended that manuscripts employ vividly colored initials to divide up the text, partly because this would assist readers to remember what they read—the particular pattern of initials on each folio sticking in the reader's mind and aiding recall at a later date.[114] The combi-

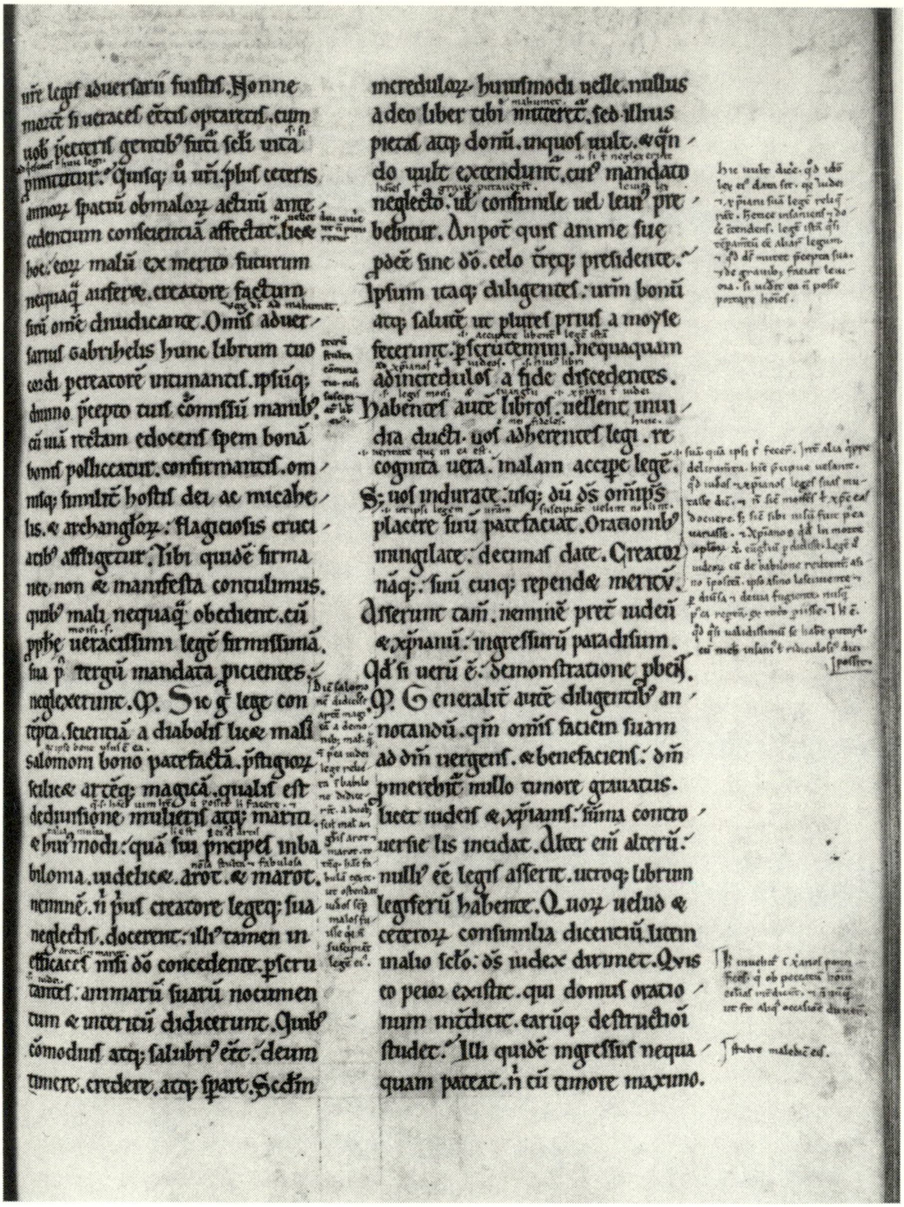

Figure 2. Paris, BnF, MS Arsenal 1162, fol. 28r. Notice the unique paragraph sign in line 22 of the right column and line 22 of the left, marking the decade divisions that typically appear in Arabic Qur'ān manuscripts. The presence of both marginal and interlinear glosses intriguingly mimics contemporary Latin biblical manuscripts. By permission of the Bibliothèque nationale de France.

nation of paragraph signs and red initials in the Arsenal MS seems perfectly suited to this purpose.

In addition to tables of contents, readily recognizable book titles, and chapter divisions, all helping the reader find his way through a text that had also been divided up into manageable subdivisions, another key element of the new scholastic book was, of course, an authoritative set of glosses.[115] The Arsenal anthology of Islamic texts is, as we have already seen, no exception. These extensive annotations, moreover, embody many of the same features as do other scholastic glosses that were compiled in the same century. If the first step in achieving the systematic knowledge to which the scholastic movement aspired was the creation of a detailed commentary on a key text that both digests it and "clarifies [its] ambiguities,"[116] then these annotations surely qualify as scholastic. Like Andrew of St. Victor's contemporary glosses on the books of the Old Testament, for example, these Latin annotations apply grammatical, philological analysis to the text. Where Andrew turned to Jewish rabbis, consulting them on the meaning of the *Hebraica veritas* of their scripture and frequently incorporating their views directly into his glosses, so the authors of these notes turned directly to Arab-Muslim sources of Qur'ān exegesis, using information gained in this way to explicate transliterated words and puzzling passages. Where Andrew undertook, when necessary, to correct corrupt passages of the Vulgate, so these notes, as we have seen, include many glosses that do nothing but emend the text of Robert's Latin Qur'ān.[117] Like Andrew's works, therefore, these annotations are the fruit of "an exciting exercise in close reading."[118] But the Latin notes on Robert's Qur'ān translation were not just grammatical and historical. They were also overtly polemical, and as such they contributed directly to one of the main projects of the scholastic movement: defending orthodox Christianity against heretics and unbelievers.[119]

In this light, the striking combination of philological and polemical reading that the annotations embody begins to seem ever less surprising. Not only did the sort of apologetic and polemical mindset that most medieval Christian readers brought to the Qur'ān require a certain amount of philological analysis of that text—it must be understood properly to be attacked effectively—but the specific intellectual movement within which the Qur'ān was first introduced into Latin Christendom particularly emphasized both the close textual analysis and the ideological combat of which these notes consist. The philology and polemic of these Latin annotations were as much a fruit of scholastic ways of reading as the newly subdivided surahs and the innovative paragraph sign.

But in thus transforming the Qur'ān into a scholastic textbook, the designers of Arsenal MS 1162 had also paradoxically granted to Islam's holy book a surprising visual authority. The Qur'ān, domesticated and controlled by a scholastic layout and explanatory commentary, looks, in this manuscript, very much like the many other authoritative scholastic books so central to Latin-Christian culture, for in medieval culture glosses often connoted authority. Built on a series of irreplaceable authoritative texts—the Bible, the writings of Augustine and the other Fathers, as well as the works of Plato and, increasingly, of Aristotle—medieval Latin education was studiously oriented toward canonical texts. For this reason, "the most widely practiced literary form . . . was the commentary, the genre," as Martin Irvine put it, "that seeks to disclose the meaning of an institutionally validated text."[120] As a result, commentaries themselves are a sign of a text's high status.[121] This is especially so for sets of glosses that became so widely used that they amounted to an authoritative part of the very text they sought to explain and for which manuscript makers had therefore to configure the page layout to allow for abundant marginalia and interlinear notes. Manuscripts of this kind often included faint ruling lines, drawn in lead or with a sharp, pointed object, not only for the columns of text itself, but also for the canonical glosses that illuminated the canonical text.

There was a range of works, from Virgil's *Aeneid* to Gratian's *Decretum*, that achieved this status, but for our purposes the most relevant is the Vulgate Bible, which, in the course of the twelfth century, came to be surrounded by the dense apparatus of the *Ordinary Gloss*, a compilation of earlier medieval glosses on both the Old and New Testaments that acquired both a relatively stable form and unchallenged authority during that century, and in the course of doing so drove remarkable changes in biblical manuscripts. Where earlier biblical exegesis had tended to take the form of running commentary on specific lemmata of the Bible, and was published in separate volumes from the Bibles that people actually read, the *Ordinary Gloss* came to be written both in the margins and between the lines of specially designed manuscripts.[122] That it consisted of both marginal and interlinear notes meant that the biblical text itself had to be laid out with abundant wide spaces, both between the lines, to accommodate up to two lines of interlinear glossing, and in the margins. So abundant was all this commentary, in fact, that eventually a standard layout developed, with a single column of Vulgate text surrounded and indwelt by marginal and interlinear glosses. It must have been laborious work to design such manuscripts—working out the proper ratio of text to glosses, something that varied, potentially, with each page, and ruling the manuscript for both biblical text and marginal and interlinear commentary. While some glossed Bibles were expensive books with glorious illuminations, a great many were practical products meant more for serious study than impressive display.[123] They were the books of teachers and scholars, prestigious, authoritative books to be studied by the new masters of the twelfth century.[124]

While the Latin Qur'ānic gloss in its margins and between its lines would be copied into a large number of later manuscripts,[125] and so might well deserve the name *Glossa ordinaria in Alcoranum*, Arsenal MS 1162 is by no means identical in layout to these glossed Bibles. The Qur'ānic notes are not extensive enough to force the Latin Qur'ān to be written in a single column surrounded by commentary, so that glossed Qur'āns are usually written in two columns. But there are very interesting parallels. While there is no ruling in the margins for the annotations, as there is, of course, for the Qur'ānic text itself, the notes are nevertheless written in a disciplined and readable hand similar to that of the text.[126] They are undoubtedly there, like the biblical gloss, for the benefit of later readers; they are not just the random jottings (of the sort we will examine later) of particular readers for the benefit only of themselves. For their intended later readers, these notes have the function, once again like the biblical gloss, of both disclosing the meaning of the text, something their philological portions do admirably, and imposing an institutionally authorized interpretation on it, the task of their hostile anti-Islamic contents.[127] Like the biblical *Ordinary Gloss*, once again, they are laid out in both marginal and interlinear glosses.

In fact, if we set the Arsenal manuscript side by side with contemporary glossed Bibles, such as MS Auct. D. 1. 13 of the Bodleian Library in Oxford, we cannot help but be struck by how similar they appear.[128] This mid-twelfth-century copy of the Pauline Epistles together with the *Glossa ordinaria* is ruled for both text and glosses, and its hand is nearly identical to that used in the Arsenal manuscript. It uses colored ink in the same relatively modest ways. There is one beautiful illuminated initial in blue, red, green, black, gold, and brown on folio 1r, but no others. After this, there are red titles at the beginning of each epistle, often followed by large initials in red with green and red flourishes. The incipits and explicits of each book are also in red. There are no red initials at the beginning of important subsections, however, as there are in the Arsenal manuscript.

An even more interesting comparison can be made with MS Laud. lat. 29 of the same library (figure 3, cf. figure 2), a manuscript of the glossed Epistles also dating to the mid-twelfth century.[129] Where the previous

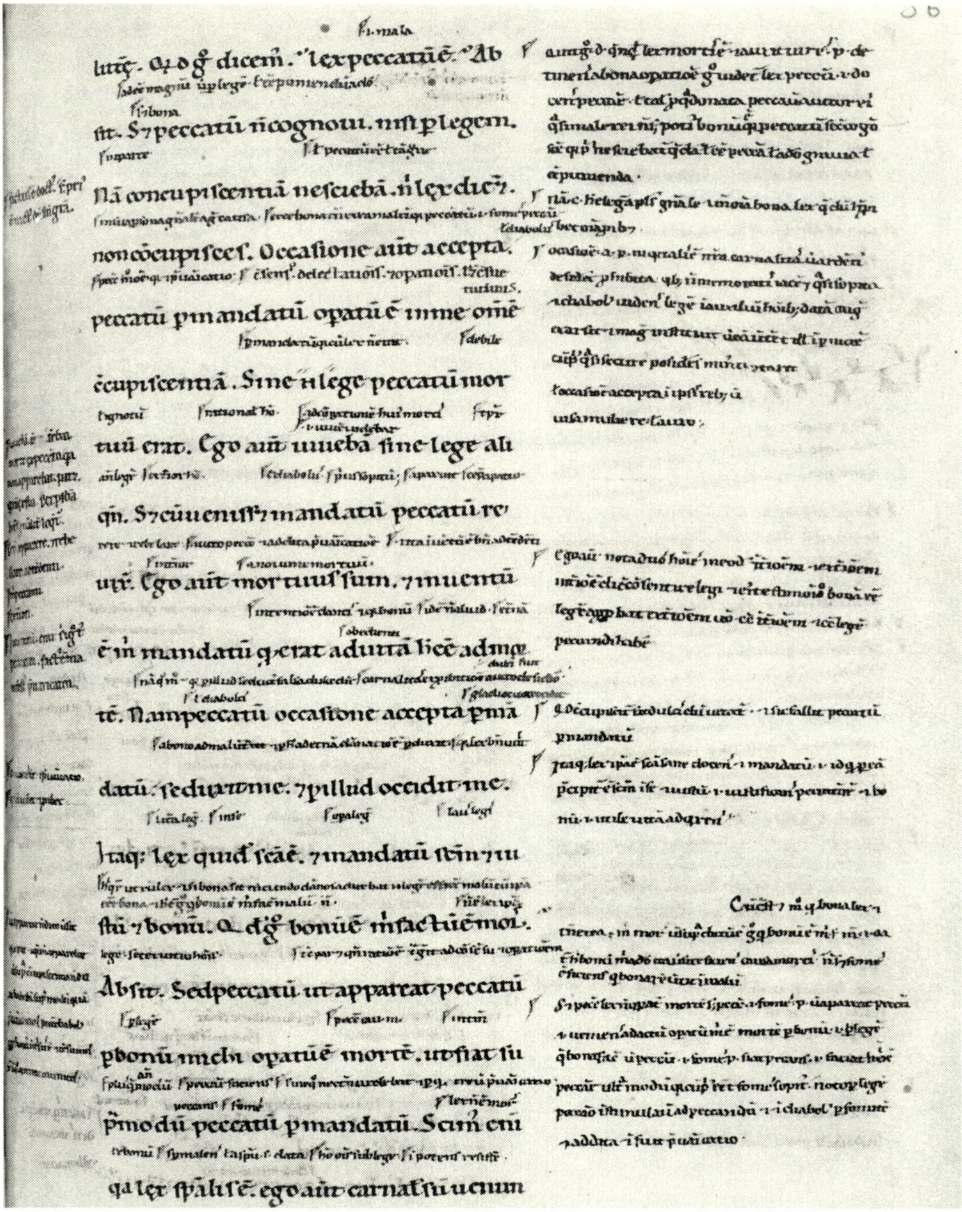

Figure 3. Oxford, Bodleian Library, MS Laud. lat. 29, fol. 36r. A mid-twelfth-century manuscript of the Epistles with the *Glossa ordinaria* written both interlinearly and in the margins. By permission of the Bodleian Library, University of Oxford.

manuscript benefited from rather careful preparation, this one was not so exactingly made. While its single central column is consistently ruled for the biblical text, and the margins are usually ruled for the glosses, this is by no means always the case, for there are passages of commentary that have the same somewhat sloppy appearance (for example, folios 36r, 103r) as they often do in the Arsenal manuscript. Furthermore, the use of color is on par with the Qurʾānic manuscript. There are some initials fully seven lines high, in yellow and red with interlace patterns (for example, folio 50r), and others three lines high, in red or blue with decoration in the opposite color (for example, folio 22v), though these are fairly rare. There is red touching of initials here and there, and a few larger black initials with yellow decorations (for example, folio 69v). Red titles show up occasionally too (for example, folio 75r). But in general this is a rather plain manuscript in comparison with Arsenal MS 1162; in fact, it is a little shabby in some ways, especially in the notably inconsistent use of decoration. By comparison, the Qurʾānic manuscript gives the impression of being a more finished piece of work.

To read the Qurʾān as it appeared in the precious Arsenal manuscript was, then, to read a dangerous, heretical pseudoscripture—or so its many marginal notes instructed. But it was also to read a book that had been the object of careful and extensive linguistic analysis; a book that had been reconfigured to satisfy the reading methods of its new scholastic readers; a book that, translated into elegant, elevated Latin, had been laid out on the page in such a way that it mimicked the appearance of the canonical texts that these scholastic readers dedicated themselves to understanding. That the Qurʾān had thus been, in its initial Latin form, so thoroughly inserted into the manuscript conventions, textual analysis, and ideological discourse of the twelfth century—that it was read and was expected to be read in so fully a scholastic mode—is doubtless the natural result of the tremendous ambition and optimism of the scholastic movement. As we will see in the following chapter, Robert's Latin Qurʾān would frequently be inscribed in later manuscripts and printed books within frames that both replicated and extended the logic of this originating scholastic frame. But that frame would also be reworked, subverted, and intriguingly transformed.

Chapter 4

New Readers, New Frames: The Later Manuscript and Printed Versions of Robert of Ketton's Latin Qur'ān

Robert's translation had entered circulation in its original, twelfth-century, form, as we have just seen, framed by a complex system of both polemical and philological glosses, hostile surah titles, and largely anti-Islamic accompanying works meant both to illuminate this difficult text and to control how Christians understood it. It became something of a best seller. The surviving twenty-four manuscripts and two sixteenth-century printed editions attest a wide readership—much wider, at any rate, than the circulation of the other Latin translations combined.[1] If we try now to understand how Robert's Latin Qur'ān was read, by examining how the frames in which it was presented to readers changed over the course of the following four centuries, we find that later Latin Christians often did as they were told—reading Islam's holy book in a properly Christian, anti-Islamic way—but sometimes not. And even when they did fall into line, they by no means always did so passively.

A sizable minority of the later manuscripts essentially reproduced that twelfth-century frame. But the majority of the manuscripts, as well as both printed editions, reworked the twelfth-century frame in important ways. Often the removal of a crucial element—the annotations, for example—simply made room for other works that facilitated the same polemical Christian reading. As indexes and tables of contents were added to many other scholastic books in the high Middle Ages, for example, so they were also affixed to Robert's translation. Such study aids could make for more efficient polemical reading, allowing the Christian apologist to locate the useful bits of the Qur'ān more quickly. But sometimes the organizing principles of such search tools had little to do with assisting religious disputation, aiming rather at something like a comprehensive exposition of the Qur'ānic text. Abridged and excerpted editions of Robert's Latin Qur'ān were produced as well. All these ways of reframing his text allow us to see how readers both were shaped by the earlier frames in which they found the Qurʾān, and yet could also actively, and sometimes subversively, reshape them.

It is true that, unlike the other Latin Qurʾān translations, we never find Robert's *Lex Mahumet* traveling without at least some polemical framing works. It is likewise true that we do not have evidence of later readers applying the tools of philology in the intensive way that Robert himself did as he translated, or indeed in the way that we will see them applied to other Latin versions of the Qurʾān. Polemical reading nearly always predominates, then, and its concerns are always present even if they are muted at times. Yet throughout, we will see that philology continues to play an important role, as polemical readers find themselves checking one manuscript against another for textual accuracy, or correcting Robert's eccentric surah titles, or examining his version against the Arabic original.

The large number of surviving copies of Robert's version allows us, finally, to see more historical change than in the case of the other European versions of the Qurʾān. If authoritatively glossed manuscripts—replicating the scholastic layout of the original twelfth-century manuscript—predominate in the thirteenth and fourteenth centuries, the fifteenth and sixteenth centuries present us with diversity: study aids that seem only minimally concerned with polemic; reading approaches clearly connected with a humanist interest in Oriental languages and exotic, postbiblical Jewish texts; Protestant-Catholic disputes played out over the text of Islam's sacred book—all this developing even as old-fashioned Christian polemical reading remained ever attractive.

The Qurʾān as Christian Textbook: Glossed Manuscripts of the Thirteenth and Fourteenth Centuries

The manuscripts that most fully reproduce the framing elements of the Arsenal manuscript are those that include not only the majority of the other works in Peter the Venerable's anthology but also the hostile surah rubrics and, most important, the abundant marginal annotions. Nearly two fifths—nine—of the later manuscripts do so. While the great majority of these are thirteenth- and fourteenth-century manuscripts,[2] one was produced in the sixteenth century.[3] Typically, these manuscripts include most of the marginal, though only a few of the interlinear, notes that the Arsenal manuscript contained,[4] preserving in addition most of the other characteristic physical features of the Arsenal manuscript, often in fact giving greater emphasis to them. They generally include a prologue describing the manuscript's contents at the beginning[5] and use red ink for the titles of individual works and the Qur'ān's surahs. They all maintain the new surah divisions introduced by Robert, as well as the paragraph divisions based on the *ʿushr* divisions of the Qur'ān, and the unique paraph mark that he also devised to indicate them. The Arsenal manuscript had bright red initials following each paragraph sign. Many of these manuscripts adopt an alternating red and blue pattern for those initials[6] and several do the same for the much larger initials that begin each surah.[7]

As we saw in the last chapter, this sort of layout functioned in effect as "a finding device," allowing each page to be scanned quickly for relevant material and, as Hugh of St. Victor had recommended, assisting readers to remember what they had read by giving each page its unique cast.[8] In these thirteenth- and fourteenth-century manuscripts, this authoritative, scholastic-textbook character is even more striking. In the majority there is careful ruling not only for the text of the Qur'ān itself, but also for the marginal notes, so that they too would appear in perfectly spaced, perfectly horizontal lines, inscribed within marginal columns kept elegantly separate from the text columns.[9] If ruling for marginal glosses is a sign of a prestigious text in the book culture of Latin Christendom, then these manuscripts are brimming with prestige. In the Corpus Christi manuscript in Oxford, the annotations on a number of pages occupy both left and right outer margins, as well as top and bottom margins in a very carefully planned layout.[10]

That Robert's Latin Qur'ān was read in these manuscripts in the way that other authoritative, glossed Latin textbooks were read can be seen in the marginalia found in the folios of one of this group of manuscripts, Oxford, Bodleian Library, MS Selden Supra 31. Here two later medieval or early modern students of Robert's Latin Qur'ān have drawn brackets in pencil around material that interested them, and in doing so, they were clearly guided by the twelfth-century notes that occupy the manuscript's margins.[11] This is most strikingly apparent in the places where the second reader has bracketed not only portions of the Qur'ānic text but also parts of the annotations that concern the same passages. Verses 2:183–87, for example, explain the fast of Ramadan, and the adjoining marginal note asserts that during this month, though Muslims fast in the day, "during the whole night they eat, drink, and have intercourse without ceasing."[12] The second reader has bracketed just this section of the note, and then gone on to bracket all of the relevant verse in the Latin text itself.[13] Not every bracket by these two readers was instigated by a marginal note,[14] but many clearly were, these readers relying on the twelfth-century marginalia to do their job of clarifying and controlling the text in front of them, treating both text and marginal notes as one interconnected system. As more than one scholar has pointed out, this is very much how the authoritative books produced by medieval intellectuals were read.[15]

A Mendicant's Polemically Searchable Pocket Qur'ān

A still larger group of the manuscripts of Robert's Latin Qur'ān reworks the original twelfth-century framing in notable ways. Of these, the most interesting are those that leave out the twelfth-century annotations. The willingness to construct manuscripts without these authoritative notes is striking evidence of Latin readers "turning the tables" on the framing devices in which Robert's Latin Qur'ān came packaged, in order to create new frames of their own.[16] An excellent example of this process is a tiny manuscript now in the National Library of France that demonstrates how removing the marginal notes could be but a prelude to adding other, more current, study aids. Produced in the thirteenth century, Paris, BnF, MS lat. 3668[17] lacks the annotations on Robert's Latin Qur'ān, as well as the *Apology of al-Kindī*, but contains the rest of the works assembled and translated by Peter the Venerable's team, and in many ways resembles the other red-and-blue, textbook-like manuscripts of the collection.[18] An ex libris from the fourteenth century identifying it as the property of the "monastery of Saint Adalbert in Wratislava [i.e., Breslau] of the Order of the Brothers Preachers,"[19] and an illumination, in gold, blue, grey, pink, and red, of a friar preaching to a dark-faced listener on folio 4v (see figure 4), confirm that it traveled among the Dominicans.[20]

One cannot help but notice, however, how this manuscript imitates the exactly contemporary Paris "pocket Bibles" and other small, academic books that circulated widely in this period, especially among the mendicant orders. Measuring 182 x 130 mm, it falls well within the upper limits of medieval pocket books[21] and, like them, is written on extremely thin parchment. Pocket Bibles tended to have sober decoration, but it was "always present and of great elegance"[22]—an apt description of this tiny Latin Qur'ān as well. Achieving their standard form by about 1230, and made in

Figure 4. Paris, BnF, MS lat. 3668, fol. 4v. A (presumably Dominican) friar in the historiated initial preaches to a dark-faced (presumably Muslim) man in this copy of the Latin Qur'ān that clearly circulated among the Dominicans. By permission of the Bibliothèque nationale de France.

large numbers throughout the thirteenth and fourteenth centuries, these pocket books grew out of the greater emphasis on teaching and preaching the scholastic age brought, especially among the new mendicant orders who brought the form to perfection.[23] A small codex, containing the whole of the scriptures, had obvious appeal to the often itinerant friars.[24] Moreover, the Latin text of Robert's translation has been carefully checked, with corrections, normally surrounded by a box drawn in red ink, studiously entered in the margin.[25] Just as the Dominicans were interested in correcting the biblical text, therefore, so some member of the Order of Preachers expended considerable energy in getting the Qur'ānic text right as well.[26]

Such pocket Bibles—the scholarly books of scholastic readers—

typically came packaged with research tools such as "indexes (by topic and word), cross-references, canon tables, chapter lists and, most often, Jerome's *Interpretation of Hebrew Names*,"[27] reference works that could quickly direct preachers or university professors to the parts of the texts they needed to cite.[28] In its original format this mendicant pocket Qurʾān notably lacked such study aids, and since it was such a small book, it also lacked the twelfth-century annotations, which were very much a research tool in themselves.[29] But sometime in the fourteenth century, perhaps at the Dominican house in Breslau, a pair of Latin-Christian readers corrected this problem. Just after the end of Robert's Latin Qurʾān one of them added a short table of the "Errors of the Qurʾān,"[30] consisting of statements such as "That sins are from God, and that God blinds humans" and "That in paradise there will be wine, milk, and honey."[31] That some entries take the form of vague subject headings—"Likewise, on the food of paradise. Likewise, on the drink of paradise"[32]—suggests that this table was intended to be not just a list of errors but an index that would point readers to where such errors could be found in the Qurʾān. This suspicion is confirmed by the fact that after some of the entries folio numbers have been written in, in the same hand as the rest of the list. Thus, after "Likewise, that God has no son" (*Item quod deus non habet filium*), we have six folio numbers: ".4.d. item .44.b. item 61.d. item 69.b. item 66.b. item .94a. item 96. c."[33] If we turn back now to the Qurʾānic text, we find that whoever drew up this list of errors also added foliation to the manuscript, with numbers appearing on the verso side, the accompanying initials (a, b, c, d) referring to the top and bottom halves of the numbered verso (a and b) and the top and bottom halves of the facing recto (c and d). On "4.d" therefore—the bottom half of the recto opposite the verso numbered "4" (folio 31r in the modern foliation)—we find that the Christian doctrine of the Incarnation is indeed attacked: "Certain people, with whom the truth by no means agrees, assert," Robert's translation reads, "that the creator of all things . . . has taken on a son (2:116)."[34]

This research tool, however, is incomplete. Of the total of twenty-five entries, only eight have references to passages in this manuscript where pertinent material can be found. It could be that this list was originally not conceived as a reference tool, but rather simply as a list of putatively untrue Qurʾānic teachings, something like a list that appears in still another Parisian manuscript of Robert's translation,[35] and adding reference numbers was only an afterthought. Or it could be that it was indeed designed as a reference work, like a very similar Latin list of Qurʾānic errors appended to the beginning of a thirteenth-century Arabic manuscript of the Qur'ān,[36] but was simply never finished.

What is certain is that this unfinished tool was soon rendered obsolete by a second searching device, longer and more useful. Written on a new gathering of folios added in the fourteenth century is an alphabetical index for Robert's Latin Qur'ān (fols. 152r–156v).[37] It was only in the late twelfth century that alphabetical indexes of the sort that appear in modern books began to be written, culminating in such massive alphabetical research tools as the biblical concordances that the Dominicans and Franciscans developed in that century.[38] Lacking a title, and written in three columns, the index that appears in this Parisian manuscript of the Latin Qur'ān is a modest[39] but sophisticated example of this new genre of reference tool (see figure 5). It is written in a hand very similar to that which drew up the immediately preceding list of Qur'ānic errors, and is built on the same reference scheme. The first entry, for example, reads, "Abraham founded Mecca" (*Abraham mecham fundauit*), followed by a series of references—"4.d. item 5.c. item 13.a. item 54.b. item 71.d."—each of which refers to a passage that describes or alludes to the building of the Kaʿbah in Mecca by Abraham and Ishmael.[40] Some entries are just phrases, others short sentences: "Adam: how he is created," "Jesus worked miracles," "the story of Jonah."[41] Occasionally there are single-word entries.[42] Each entry is followed by one to half a dozen references to relevant passages in the Latin Qur'ān, and some topics can be searched for in more than one way. Not only can we find verses that describe Abraham's work in Mecca by searching under *Abraham mecham fundauit*, as we have just seen, but also by looking up *Mecham Abraham fundauit*, where we find the same references.[43] It is a work, moreover, that continued to be elaborated on, for more than one entry very clearly was added later, usually written in smaller script to fit into blank spaces.[44]

Here, therefore, was a version of the Qur'ān with the framing of contemporary Latin pocket books, especially pocket Bibles. It had sober but elegant decoration; its text had been carefully checked; it had been made searchable for scholastic readers in a hurry to find the right passages. Building, therefore, on the logic of the Latin Qur'āns in the authoritative red-and-blue textbook format, this was a version of the Qur'ān suited specifically to the reading practices of the thirteenth and fourteenth centuries. Readers educated in the schools and universities could apply the study procedures that were familiar to them directly to the Qur'ān, for here was a

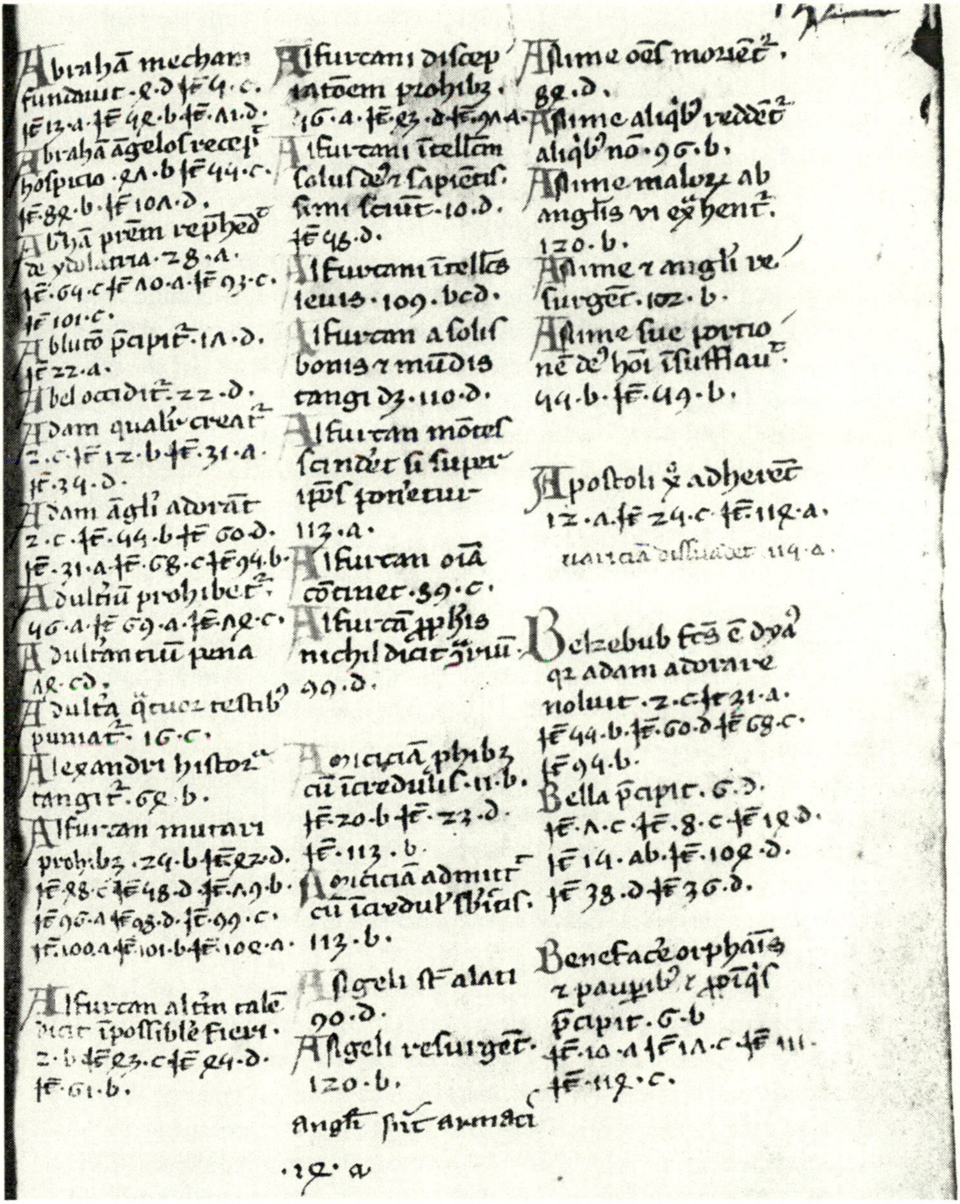

Figure 5. Paris, BnF, MS lat. 3668, fol. 152r. The beginning of the polemical index made for this pocket edition of Robert of Ketton's Latin Qur'ān. By permission of the Bibliothèque nationale de France.

manuscript which, like the pocket Bibles, was "designed both for reading . . . and for reference."[45]

What such readers were thought to be interested in as they scanned this manuscript's index is not difficult to figure out—for this was a research tool clearly intended to help the polemically and apologetically minded quickly find the most useful Qur'ānic passages. Entries such as "God makes men to err,"[46] "Jesus did not suffer [on the cross],"[47] "Muhammad does not know the future,"[48] and "How many wives it is licit to have,"[49] are all topics around which Christians repeatedly constructed anti-Islamic arguments.[50] On the other hand, entries such as "the Gospel and [Old] Testament teach straight ways,"[51] "Jesus worked miracles,"[52] "Jesus [is] the spirit and word of God,"[53] "Christ [is] the greatest of all prophets,"[54] and "Christ taught the upright way,"[55] refer to Qur'ānic statements of the kind that Christian apologists liked to single out when they wanted to make the case that the Qur'ān, if properly understood, actually confirms the basic Christian teachings.[56] But the sort of reader envisioned here was one who nevertheless desired a rather extensive knowledge of Islam, even if his main goal was demonstrating its untruth. A whole series of entries concerning *Alfurcan*—the Furqān or Qur'ān, that is—indicate that readers were thought to be interested in Islamic beliefs about the Qur'ān: that it must not be changed, that it is impossible to duplicate, that it contains all things, that it says nothing contrary to the prophets.[57] Other entries give us references to the Qur'ānic passages that prohibit certain foods, encourage charitable giving, prohibit fornication, require parents to be honored, and outline the annual pilgrimage.[58] If one read through all the passages singled out by this index, one would have a fairly extensive knowledge of Islam, though one notably slanted toward a Christian polemical and apologetic interpretation of it.[59]

This concern for a broad and fairly accurate knowledge of Islam is complemented by another adjustment to this Latin Qur'ān's frame, undertaken by the same hand that created the list of errors on folio 151v. Throughout much of the Qur'ānic text, we find marginal notes at the beginning of each surah giving us the correct surah number, according to the Islamic division of the text, thereby correcting Robert's redivision of the Qur'ān.[60] Moreover, in many cases the correct Arabic surah name in Roman transliteration has been added as well: "elbactara" for "al-Baqarah" at surah two, for example, and "xxii. sura elhats" for Sūrat al-Ḥajj (22).[61] The Dominican Order of the thirteenth century included some of the most learned Christian missionaries to Islam, and it would not have escaped the notice of members of the order that the works of Ramon Martí and Riccoldo da Monte di Croce, friars capable of reading the Qurʾān in Arabic, did not refer to its surahs using the eccentric division imposed on it by Robert of Ketton, but by clear references to the Islamic names of the surahs.[62] We should probably not be surprised, therefore, to find such philological corrections as these in a Dominican copy of Robert's Latin Qurʾān.

It should also not surprise us to find that a study aid has been devised here specifically for Christian polemical and apologetic purposes, since, as Laura Light has pointed out, the development of the pocket Bibles themselves, with their accompanying research tools, was closely connected to the church's struggle against heresy.[63] Many of the pocket Bibles, in fact, contained, among other study aids, a "short collection of Biblical passages, arranged by topic" and "designed to combat heresy," especially the dualist Cathar heresy. These antidualist study aids are very similar to the Qurʾānic index, in both length and content, for while some of what they contain has little direct relationship with heresy, there is a great deal of material that is "clearly directed against the teachings of the Cathars."[64] Furthermore, pocket books with similar research tools were devised to assist Christian preaching against Judaism. A tiny (170 x 115 mm) contemporary codex now in Paris, for example, contains an enormous compilation of *Extracts from the Talmud*.[65] Produced soon after the burning of the Talmud in Paris in the early 1240s, by a team that included two Christians who knew Hebrew extremely well, these extracts were intended to make clear the "errors, obscurities, and blasphemies of the Talmud."[66] To make these errors all the clearer, this codex has been made eminently searchable. Not only are there marginal notes throughout that provide cross-references to related biblical passages,[67] but there are useful study aids annexed to the end of the manuscript. One (fols. 231v–232v) is a list of the names of the principal rabbis cited in the Talmud, while the most relevant here is a title-less index of biblical references in the Talmud extracts (fols. 234v–238v). Scholastically trained Christian scholars had at their fingertips, therefore, an extraordinarily useful and quickly searchable collection of Talmudic extracts. The Paris pocket Qurʾān clearly reflects much the same set of concerns as led to the creation of both the lists of dualist errors found in many contemporary pocket Bibles and the Latin extracts of the Talmud preserved today in the same library.

This Paris pocket Qurʾān, moreover, is not unique. A late fifteenth- or early sixteenth-century copy made (almost certainly) directly from it and preserving both its small size and its polemical index is extant today in the

National Library of Russia in Saint Petersburg,[68] while a similarly small-format Latin Qur'ān sits right next to it on the shelf in the National Library of France. Bearing the shelf mark "lat. 3669," this latter codex is a fifteenth-century manuscript likewise lacking the original twelfth-century annotations, and even the polemical surah rubrics have been stripped from the text. Yet it contains a substantial list of Qur'ānic errors at the end—though it lacks a reference system guiding readers to the places in the Qur'ānic text where this material can be found—and has an anti-Islamic poem affixed at the beginning.[69] Removing the twelfth-century annotations to Robert's Latin Qur'ān, therefore, did not at all necessarily spell the end of polemical Qur'ān reading, which could, in fact, thrive perfectly well without them, as new polemical study aids more attuned to later ages' reading habits were devised and adjoined to Robert's widely diffused translation.

Yet it is worth bearing in mind the Rouses' observation that "the use of alphabetical order was a tacit recognition of the fact that each user of a work will bring to it his own preconceived rational order which differs from those of other users."[70] The polemical index in the Paris pocket Qur'ān is extensive enough in its range of topics that, although it was clearly contrived with the polemical reader in mind, it is conceivable that later readers could have used it for very different—and rather nonpolemical—purposes. There are numerous references to such topics as the Islamic law on charitable giving and money lending, the Qur'ānic account of Alexander the Great, the desirability of chastity, and the illegality of perjury.[71] All these topics may have been included in this index to allow missionizing Dominicans to gather a broad knowledge of Islam in order to undermine its teachings. But in themselves, such Qur'ānic passages have very little to offer the enthusiastic Christian apologist, and they could also conceivably be used for very different purposes.

A Nonpolemical Table of Contents for the Qur'ān

That Robert's Latin Qur'ān was, in fact, read in ways rather different from the polemical approach incarnated in the Paris pocket Qur'ān can be seen in the framing it receives in other manuscripts, especially in later centuries. Some of these also lack most of the twelfth-century polemical annotations, but in these cases no new polemical reading tools were devised to replace them. Perhaps the most intriguing is a sixteenth-century codex now in Dresden (Sächsiche Landesbibliothek, MS 120b).[72] Written on paper, this copy of Robert's Latin Qur'ān includes most of the standard accompanying works, though it has Riccoldo da Monte di Croce's *Contra legem Sarracenorum* in place of the *Apology of al-Kindi*, which certain other manuscripts contain instead.[73] While a few of the twelfth-century annotations have survived here and there, most have been left out.[74] Instead, a table of contents to Robert's translation has been added at the beginning. Present in none of the other known manuscripts of his version,[75] this table of contents, composed sometime before 1537,[76] is remarkable in the first place for its length: it is fully thirty-six folios long, making it roughly one quarter the length of the text of Robert's translation that it analyzes (which is 132 folios in this manuscript).[77] It was an enormous task to compile it, then, though not necessarily an unusual one. The changes in reading practices in the twelfth and thirteenth centuries that led to the creation of the new scholastic text, with its running headlines, its searchable page layout, and its indexes, also led scholars to begin constructing tables of contents. In many ways the simplest research aid—it is far easier to compile than a complex index—an analytical table such as this functioned much like the tables of contents that modern readers know.[78]

While many tables of contents in earlier periods had been compiled in a separate gathering of folios which was then tacked on at the beginning (or sometimes the end) of a work,[79] the *tabula* in this manuscript was copied in the same hand as the first part of the Qur'ān translation and so was clearly part of the original conception of this manuscript, not some later addition. It was itself, however, clearly copied from some other, currently unknown, manuscript, rather than having been compiled specifically for this codex. Two things make this clear. First, if the text of this table of contents is compared with a sixteenth-century printed version of it—a somewhat bizarre work that we will examine a few pages hence—it becomes clear that both this manuscript version of the *tabula* and the printed version derive from some other earlier version.[80] Second, this table of contents was clearly devised for a version of Robert's translation that had been subdivided differently from the version that actually appears in the same manuscript. The 115 divisions to which the Dresden *tabula* refer are called chapters (*capitula*), not surahs, and they are each of roughly equal length. The text of Robert's Latin Qur'ān that follows it, however, is subdivided into his eccentric 123 surahs of varying length.

Clearly intended, therefore, for a copy of Robert's translation that had been divided into different units, and obviously copied from a different manuscript, this *tabula* certainly was not devised to be used with the copy of the Latin Qur'ān that immediately follows it. In fact, anyone trying to search the Qur'ānic text by means of it would have found that after the first thirty-six verses of surah 2, it was quite useless. But in its original context—at the head of a Latin Qur'ān properly subdivided—it would have helped readers effectively find passages of the Qur'ān that were of interest to them thanks to its detailed summary of the contents of the Qur'ān. When such a reader found a topic that interested him as he scanned the table, he could then have turned quickly to the relevant chapter of Robert's translation to find the proper Qur'ānic text. The layout of the entries in the manuscript facilitates such research by presenting them in relatively short lines or, when necessary, by indenting later lines to make locating the beginning of the next entry easier. The analysis of the third chapter, for example, appears in part like this (I have added the verse number[s] to which each entry refers in brackets):

.The Third Chapter.
Jesus son of Mary for whom the spirit divinely served as help and testimony [2:87b].
Solomon the good learned magic from evil angels, which magic the Jews learned afterward in Babylon from angels, namely Arot and Marot [2:102].
The spirit inspires whom he wants and by what means and whenever he wants [2:105].
No one is able to accomplish anything for his soul without God [2:107].
God who looks into the secrets of hearts will return to each his reward [2:110].
Christians and Jews both had good law-givers, but both have deviated from them [2:113].
Since to God belong the East and the West, the one pouring out prayers in any direction finds God [2:115a].
The compassion of God is restricted to no place [2:115b].
The wisdom of God embraces all things [2:115c].[81]

This table does not, then, provide a connected summary but rather a disconnected list of what the compiler considered the most important points of each chapter. The statements themselves, moreover, are not all of the same sort.[82] Some describe the contents of long sections of the Qur'ān. The first entry, for example, is "The Prayer of the Arabs" (*Oratio arabum*) (fol. 37r), this being the rather apt description of the first short surah of the Qur'ān in the standard Arabic division of the text, a passage that is indeed a key element in the daily prayers of Muslims. Other entries take the form of instruction about Islamic beliefs and practices, as in the case of the entry that seems to cover all of verses 2:11–16: "The sect of Muhammad promises the highest good, that is God, saying that our riches will be God himself."[83]

Others are complete quotations or near quotations of Robert's translation, intended, perhaps, to get across some of the feel of the Qurʾānic narrative. Still others—the great majority—take the form of short, almost maxim-like statements based fairly closely on Robert's own wording.

If we ponder the sorts of topics that the table's compiler thought that Christian Qurʾān readers would be interested in, we can only be impressed by how little of his effort went into signaling the polemically and apologetically useful portions. For first of all, where we do find references to such material, its formulation is strikingly muted. The first such entry concerns 2:25, the first verse of the Qurʾān to describe the pleasures of the Islamic paradise. Christians saw it and similar passages as evidence of the carnal nature of Islam, and hostile arguments against this conception of paradise were common in Christian polemical writings.[84] Yet the entry here is curt and relatively sober: "The sensual delights of paradise" (*Paradisi uoluptates*)[85] is all it says, drawing no attention to the specific sensual pleasures mentioned in the verse—food and sex—that shocked Christian readers. The compiler used similar restraint in formulating other entries that might have been of use to polemicists. "The religion of Islam is the confirmation of the ancient laws, that is of Moses, Christ, and the rest of the prophets," reads the entry for verses 2:135–36.[86] Even when referring to Qurʾānic verses that deny the Incarnation or the Trinity, the compiler is studiously mild-mannered: "Those who say that God has a son lack knowledge,"[87] reads the description of verse 2:116, while the famously anti-Trinitarian description of God in surah 112—that he "does not beget, is not begotten, and there is no one comparable to him"—is largely quoted by the compiler in Robert's faithful translation.[88] Like Robert's translation itself, then, this table of contents neither plays up the Qurʾānic passages potentially damaging to Islam nor glosses over those prejudicial to Christianity.

Of course, the polemicist on the hunt for good material could tell even from these restrained entries that here were Qurʾānic teachings that needed refuting, but what is also surprising about them is that there are relatively few such entries. Of the sixty-two total entries for surah 2, verses 1–173, for example, only fifteen (about 25 percent) obviously touch on the traditional polemical and apologetic topics of Trinity, Incarnation, Muhammad's life, and Islam's supposed carnal and warlike nature. All the rest cover Qurʾānic material that virtually never plays a role in Christian-Muslim disputation: "There are many good people walking on the right road, but there are more evil people"[89] (2:26b); "The wicked person is his own punishment"[90] (2:27b); "Just as works of virtue to depraved people are irksome and heavy, so to good people they are easy and fun"[91] (2:44); "God perfects all things by his word and command"[92] (2:117). Not much here of polemical use.

Moreover, the compiler actually leaves out entirely references to many verses that Christian polemicists consistently used in their attacks on the Qur'ān and Islam. We find, for example, that the famous incident (alluded to in 33:37) involving Zayd and Zaynab—the locus classicus of the argument that Muhammad was a lustful pseudoprophet who invented revelations to justify his immorality—is passed over in silence.[93] This is particularly striking when we bear in mind that the annotations on Robert's Latin Qur'ān actually contain a rather stridently polemical note on this passage. Muhammad, the note asserts, had concocted this verse "on his own behalf, introducing God speaking to [Muhammad] so that the wife of a certain man whom he loved very much . . . he might afterward take as wife, as if by the command of God who gave permission to him."[94]

In fact, if we read this vast table of contents alongside those influential twelfth-century annotations, we cannot help but notice the striking differences in emphasis and interest. Next to 2:30–38, for example, a passage that recounts the temptation of Adam and Eve in paradise, a twelfth-century note reads, "an extremely stupid fable—I do not know where he found it—follows about God and Adam and the angels and the devil."[95] The Dresden table of contents, on the other hand, mildly describes these verses as "The creation of Adam and the command to him."[96] Just afterward, in its analysis of the specific content of verse 2:30, where God says to the angels, "I know what you know not," the Dresden table observes that "God knows many things which the angels do not know."[97] In contrast, the twelfth-century note on this verse fulminates about this "ridiculous thing, that God has boasted that he knows what the angels do not know."[98] Likewise, when the compiler of this *tabula* came to verse 2:62, the famous passage that describes how Jews, Christians, and Sabaeans will have their reward on the day of judgment, he essentially quotes Robert's version of it with no comment.[99] But the authors of the twelfth-century annotations felt compelled to point out that "here he [i.e., Muhammad] is entirely in contradiction with himself, for afterward he asserts almost everywhere that no one can be saved without his [Islamic] religion."[100] We have seen above the compiler's unprovocative description of 2:116—"Whoever says that God has a son lacks knowledge."[101] The tone of the twelfth-century annotation on this verse is very different: "And this is the chief point of all of his heresy, which this devil often repeats, that God is never believed to have had a son."[102]

The way that this compiler read the Qur'ān, then, was strikingly different from how the twelfth-century annotators did: where they saw a text in need of equal parts polemical attack and philological explanation, he viewed it as requiring neither. As the author of a table of contents, he was concerned with comprehensiveness, with getting across a relatively complete description of the whole contents of the Qurʾān, both the clear minority that were polemically useful and the great majority that were not.

The Dresden *Tabula*, the *Compendium Alchorani*, and Johann Albrecht von Widmanstetter's *Epitome Alcorani*

There is surprising evidence both that there were other readers who shared the interests of the compiler of the Dresden *tabula*, and that polemical Qurʾān reading nevertheless remained as popular as ever in the mid-sixteenth century, in the strange afterlife of the Dresden table of contents. For it was soon reworked into an abridged version of the Qurʾān, which survives in at least five manuscripts. This abridged Qurʾān then found its way into the hands of a humanist and Orientalist named Johann Albrecht von Widmanstetter, who published it in 1543 but added to it what amounts to a new polemical commentary. Just as Robert's largely nonpolemical Latin Qurʾān was given a starkly polemical framing of accompanying works and annotations, so also, therefore, could this largely nonpolemical table of contents/abridged Qurʾān be reinserted into an explicitly anti-Islamic framework.

This abridged Qurʾān deriving from the Dresden table of contents circulated from at least 1537 on under the name *Compendium Alchorani* (*The Abridgment of the Qurʾān*).[103] Its anonymous creator produced it by the simple but bizarre expedient of extracting the chapter titles and stringing together the discrete entries of the *tabula* so that they became what looks like a connected narrative. The Dresden *tabula* begins as follows (once again I have placed the surah and verse to which each entry refers in brackets):

> Table [of Contents]
> The First Chapter
> The prayer of the Arabs [Surah 1].
> They attribute to God wrath and mercy [1:3, 7].
> What in itself is true appears as it is to the pure alone [2:1–5].
> Those whom God hardens, no one will soften or instruct [2:6–7].

Those who praise virtue with the mouth and not in deed deceive themselves, gaining for themselves nothing other than harm for their souls [2:8–9].[104]

The same passage of the *Abridgment of the Qur'ān* reads as follows:

Compendium alcorani, that is, the laws of the Muslims
The prayer of the Arabs. They attribute to God wrath and mercy. What in itself is true appears as it is to the pure alone. Those whom God hardens, no one will soften or instruct. Those who praise virtue with the mouth and not in deed deceive themselves, gaining for themselves nothing other than harm for their souls.[105]

This looks like a connected narrative, but of course it isn't. That each sentence originally described a discrete Qur'ānic passage cannot be papered over simply by placing them one after the other. The resulting disjointedness is particularly striking in the passages that, in the *tabula*, had consisted of sentence fragments. On the following page, for example, we have a line that reads, "Commands of God to men. The world of the dead. The pleasures of paradise."[106] In the table of contents, these phrases described verses 2:21–25, and in the analytical structure of that study aid they made sense. In this new form, they must often have seemed baffling.

The fact that this abridgment of the Qur'ān consists of disjointed sentences and sentence fragments is evidence by itself that the table of contents had to have come first: the text as a whole makes far better sense as an analytical table of contents than as an abridged Qur'ān. But there is other relevant evidence as well. Partway through *The Abridgment of the Qur'ān* there is a large interpolation, nearly a folio in length, in at least two manuscripts.[107] Derived from certain of the other works which circulated with Robert's Latin Qur'ān—in particular Peter the Venerable's *Summa breuis*, the *Chronica mendosa*, *De generatione Mahumet*, and the *Doctrina Mahumeti*[108]—this interpolation has much the same character as the abridgment into which it has been inserted: it consists of disjointed sentences and phrases as well. It is possible that it also, therefore, is derived from a (presumably lost) table of contents designed for these other works of the Collectio Toletana, and that at some point folios of it came to be intermixed with folios of the table of contents for the Qur'ān.[109] Whatever the origin of this interpolation, it does not exist in the Dresden *tabula*, and surely did not exist in the original form of that study aid.[110] As we have no clear evidence of where or when the *tabula* was written, other than that it exists in a sixteenth-century manuscript, so also we have no evidence of the origins of this abridged Qurʾān that derives from it, other than that it too circulates in several sixteenth-century manuscripts.

What does this new framing for the Qur'ān—its reconfiguration as an abridgment—tell us about Qurʾān reading? In part it appears to be a continuation of the same set of concerns that motivated the compilation of the Dresden *tabula* to start with: a desire to have a quick way to gain some idea of the whole contents of the Qurʾān, not just the polemically or apologetically useful parts. Abridgments of important texts had become common during the scholastic period—just as indexes and tables of contents had, and for the same reasons. Though humanist readers were wedded to the idea of returning to the original sources themselves, they still turned to compilations of extracts and abridgments in large numbers.[111] If such abridgments are understood as study aids, as research tools to help readers find the material that they most need, then, like the *tabula* from which it derives, this abridged Qurʾān seems intended for readers who are at least partly interested in gaining something like a comprehensive understanding of the Qurʾān. Nevertheless, the notably odd character of the *Abridgment of the Qurʾān*—its nearly unreadable disconnectedness—makes one wonder whether it did not also serve a different interest as well. Latin readers were predisposed by a long tradition of polemic to view the Qurʾān as a bizarre and incomprehensible compilation of the intelligible and the unintelligible, this very quality being seen as a fundamental argument against its truthfulness.[112] It seems likely that upon opening the *Compendium Alchorani*, Latin readers would have had this prejudice powerfully confirmed. This abridgment, therefore, might just as well be seen as a primarily polemical framing for the Qurʾānic text.[113]

What is certain is that at least one later reader of this abridgment approached it very much along polemical lines and went on to design still another frame for it that reinforced such a reading. This later reader was the sixteenth-century Catholic German humanist and Orientalist Johann Albrecht von Widmanstetter (1506–57).[114] Having studied law and Hebrew in Tübingen and perhaps Heidelberg and Basel as a young man, Widmanstetter went on, as Hartmut Bobzin put it, to live an "eventful" and "restless" life,[115] traveling widely, working in ecclesiastical and lay courts, and studying in Italy and Germany, encountering along the way a series of like-minded scholars. Like Pico and Egidio da Viterbo, Widmanstetter's humanist interest in Greek and Latin combined with a fascination for Semitic languages and related esoterica, especially Kabbalah.[116] By 1530, moreover, he was learning Arabic in Bologna, and not long after, he was in Rome continuing his Arabic studies with Egidio da Viterbo. An indefatigable book collector, he had a library that included a large number of Hebrew and Arabic volumes,[117] and his most important scholarly contribution was probably his edition of the Syriac New Testament (Vienna, 1555).[118] Reading the Qurʾān was a natural part of this program of studies. Widmanstetter may well have produced a full translation of it by 1541, though such a work never was published and perhaps was made from an Aragonese version rather than the Arabic,[119] and he made repeated references to the Qurʾān in his commentaries on Hebraic and Kabbalistic works.[120] In 1543 he produced a printed edition of the *Abridgment of the Qurʾān* under the title *Epitome of the Qurʾān*, which appeared in Nuremburg in a small booklet that also included a revised version of the *Doctrina Mahumet* which had been translated by Herman of Carinthia as part of Peter the Venerable's anthology of Islamic works.[121]

To his studies of the Qurʾān, then, he brought this noticeably philological orientation, but also, as Bobzin has made clear, notable polemical and apologetic concerns of a very traditional sort.[122] All this is plain to see in his work on the *Epitome of the Qurʾān*. In the booklet containing it[123] the reader is greeted first by a letter to Duke Ludwig X of Bavaria-Landshut, which explains the purpose of the collection,[124] and then by a second letter to a bookseller from Nuremberg named Johannes Otto discussing the texts to follow.[125] The *Doctrina Mahumet*, its twelfth-century text having been modernized, occupies the next twelve folios under the title *The Theology of Muhammad son of ʿAbd Allāh Arranged in a Dialogue*,[126] the *Epitome of the Qurʾān* occupying the following thirty.[127] The next five folios consist of Widmanstetter's annotations on the *Theology of Muhammad*, and at the end of these, he inserted a short *Life of Muhammad* (*Mahometis vita*) that repeats the standard anti-Islamic commonplaces.[128] The final seven folios of the booklet are dedicated to Widmanstetter's annotations on the *Epitome of the Qurʾān* itself.[129]

As is always the case, then, Robert's Latin Qurʾān, even in abridged form, is offered to readers within a frame of anti-Islamic accompanying works, and, not surprisingly, these polemical preoccupations are particularly clear in Widmanstetter's annotations on the Qurʾān itself.[130] He entitles them *Annotations of Various Things and Impious Opinions Which Occur in the Epitome of the Qurʾān*.[131] As this title suggests, a fairly large number of these notes—there are seventy-three of them in total—are Christian polemical commonplaces. Yet there is something new in these intriguingly complex notes. Many draw parallels between the Qurʾān and a range of classical, Byzantine, and especially Kabbalistic and other postbiblical Jewish texts. Sometimes these latter notes seem little concerned with attacking the Qurʾān, Widmanstetter wanting simply to point out the connections among the variety of classical and Semitic texts that so interested him. At other times, however, exposing the similarities between the Qurʾān and Jewish texts is part of his strategy to expose the "impious opinions" of Islam's holy book, for these Widmanstetter often sees as derived from the Jews. Finally, some of the Catholic Widmanstetter's notes are intended to undermine the position of Protestant reformers as well as of Muslims. His sixteenth-century humanism and Orientalism, together with his Counter-Reformation Catholicism, therefore, have exercised an intriguing influence on his rather traditional Christian anti-Islamic thought.

Something like a third to a half of the annotations could have been written by nearly any premodern Christian thinker. Note 2, for example, referring to the passage "Those who say that God has a son are lacking in knowledge" (2:116), points out that "Here he denies that Christ is the son of God, although elsewhere he calls him both 'the word of God' and 'the spirit [of God].' "[132] That Muhammad contradicted himself repeatedly in the Qurʾān was a favorite argument of medieval polemicists.[133] Similarly traditional in their polemical approach are Widmanstetter's argument that Muhammad made God say specifically in the Qurʾān that he, Muhammad, lacked the ability to work miracles as cover for Muhammad's embarrassing lack of miraculous powers;[134] his pointing out of what he sees as fictitious prophets (*prophetae . . . commenticii*) dreamed up by Muhammad;[135] and his derisive observation that this "libidinous goat" (*libidinosus hircus*) had no business calling on people to avoid fornication.[136] Like many earlier anti-Islamic polemicists, he often asserts that the Qurʾān's errors derive from the "insolent Jews, in the footsteps of whom Muhammad follows."[137]

But Widmanstetter's notes go beyond standard Christian anti-Islamic polemic, such as when he reflects on the abridged Qurʾān's assertion that "water is the principle of all things." Here Widmanstetter draws connections among the Qurʾānic text, the Kabbalah, and pre-Socratic philosophy:

> Scripture teaches that the world was created by the mercy of God, but the Kabbalists attest that by the mercy [of God] the severity of the waters is tempered under the name of wine. Whence to the ancient philosophers of the Greeks, among which number was Thales of Miletus, was attributed the celebrated opinion that water was the prime matter of all things, which [philosophers] Aristotle appears to want to reprehend with more zeal than to understand."[138]

Here we seem, more than anything else, to have a learned humanist and Orientalist taking pleasure in showing off his knowledge of esoteric Jewish lore and classical texts.[139] We find references, in fact, to a host of thinkers whom we have not seen before in conjunction with Qurʾān reading: Aristotle, Averroes, Greek Patristic authors, the Talmudists,[140] and most especially the Kabbalists.

Like the note on water as the principle of all things, not a few notes of this sort lack any overtly polemical purpose. On the *Epitome of the Qurʾān*'s statement that the "Religion of God is faith," Widmanstetter simply observes, for example, that the fifteenth-century Aragonese Jewish thinker Joseph Albo "writes that faith comprises all the principles of the Jewish religion."[141] Many of the half-dozen notes that mention the Kabbalah[142] similarly lack obvious polemical content. One comments that the Kabbalists made mention of the same "Three orders of stars" of which the *Epitome* spoke.[143] Indeed in note 22, which refers to one of the many sentence fragments in the *Epitome* ("the beauty of Christ"), Widmanstetter, far from attacking the Qurʾān by associating it with Kabbalist teachings, sees both as bearing witness to Christian belief:

> the truth is manifested [here], ignorantly and unwillingly by Muhammad, for the Kabbalists have set up the seat of the Messiah on the *sefira* of beauty, which itself is divinity according to them, on which account he will clearly reach for the [idea that] the Messiah is the son of God in this place.[144]

But some of these notes referring to post-biblical Jewish texts clearly are meant to undermine the validity of the Qurʾān by associating its teachings with erroneous Jewish and Kabbalistic ideas. Commenting on the abridged Qurʾān's assertion that "All kinds of animals . . . will return to God," Widmanstetter describes a Kabbalistic teaching that he views as similar. In consequence of this view, he observes that

> by certain [Kabbalists] it is understood that the hope of salvation is offered to each kind of living thing. I have mentioned these things in order to point out that the endless monstrosities of opinions from this Kabbalah of the Jews, as if drawn forth from the Trojan horse, have attacked the Church of Christ."[145]

Here Widmanstetter indicates the wrongheadedness of both the Qurʾān and the Kabbalistic ideas that run in parallel to it, but also seems to strike out at contemporary Christian Kabbalists—such as his friend Egidio da Viterbo—who have, dangerously, introduced the Kabbalah into the church.

All this suggests that although Widmanstetter took a great interest in post-biblical Jewish texts, he was by no means convinced, as Pico, Egidio, and Reuchlin were, that Kabbalist literature substantially confirmed Christian beliefs.[146] This critical attitude of Widmanstetter toward the Kabbalah, which Secret pointed out many years ago,[147] shows up in other notes as well, though Widmanstetter sometimes suggests that Muhammad went astray not so much by adopting Kabbalist ideas as by misunderstanding them, or by following the "more obtuse" rather than "the more acute" Kabbalist thinkers.[148]

Widmanstetter's early sixteenth-century humanist Orientalism, therefore, has reshaped what is otherwise a typically polemical way of reading the Qur'ān. But he was also a pious Catholic worried about the spread of Protestant ideas, and sometimes his notes reflect this as well. In 7:40–49, the Qur'ān described the interaction between the dwellers in paradise, those in hell, and certain people in between who stand on a barrier between paradise and hell. The *Epitome* succinctly summed this up in the phrase *Paradisi, inferi, intermedii.*[149] Widmanstetter, (rather mistakenly) seizing on the parallels that this suggests with the Catholic doctrine of purgatory, commented at length on the origins of this doctrine, suggesting that news of this teaching must have reached Muhammad from Jews and Christians. The idea developed first among the Hebrews, he argues, but was taken up by Pythagoreans[150] and later by the Christians. After discussing the Christian theology of baptism and purgatory, he argues that these views have been confirmed by a whole host of Church Fathers. Then he comes to the point:

> Since the mores of the Christians are more and more corrupted by vices every day, so that as, step by step, remedies for the extinguishing of the fire of purgation are sought by all, rather than aids against the tyranny of the vices, the understanding of the fire of purgatory, both useful and necessary to the Church, has perished, even among those by whom it ought most especially to have been preserved."[151]

There can be little doubt that Widmanstetter has in mind Protestant reformers who rejected the Catholic doctrine of purgatory.[152] The interest he shows in predestination in a later note likewise suggests Protestant preoccupations.[153]

The twelfth-century annotations on Robert's Latin Qur'ān both attacked the Qur'ān polemically and explained it philologically. Johann Albrecht von Widmanstetter's notes embody a reading approach that differs strikingly with respect both to its aims and to the set of books, as it were, alongside which he read the Qur'ān. At the end of his notes on the *Epitome of the Qur'ān*, Widmanstetter succinctly describes his approach when he asks any who might be offended by the "frequent mentioning of Kabbalist teaching in these annotations" to bear in mind that it was only "necessity that impelled me to pluck such things from their [i.e., the Kabbalists'] recondite books, as would point out the frauds of the Jews, the fickleness of the Christians who have fallen away from the bosom of the Church, and the inconstancy of Muhammad and the hideousness of [his] crimes."[154] As this comment suggests, Widmanstetter's notes were never intended to explicate the Qur'ān philologically; rather they were meant to engage only those passages that he could refute on traditional anti-Islamic grounds, relate to some classical or extrabiblical Jewish teaching, or connect to the Protestant ideas that he opposed. While Widmanstetter obviously shares the abiding Christian concern with pointing out the Qur'ān's errors, this preoccupation with classical, Jewish, and especially Kabbalist texts is a particularly vivid departure from the twelfth-century approach. Where those original annotations were informed by equal measures of Islamic Qur'ān exegesis and Arab-Christian polemic and apologetic, Widmanstetter, who knew a good deal of Arabic,[155] did not use any Arabic sources to speak of in his editorial work on the *Epitome Alcorani* and its accompanying notes,[156] turning instead to Hebrew works.[157] Reading the Qur'ān polemically and apologetically, then—with an eye to those parts which could be used either against Islam or for Christianity—was perennially attractive to Latin Christians throughout the whole period from 1140 to 1560, but that did not make it perennially the same.[158]

Bibliander's *Machumetis . . . Alcoran*: A Protestant Qur'ān Edition and Its Catholic Reader

In the same year (1543) that Widmanstetter published his quirky Qur'ānic epitome, Robert's Latin Qur'ān found its way into print in its entirety as well, through the energetic work of a Swiss reformer, Hebraist, and Arabist named Theodore Bibliander (1504–64).[159] Widmanstetter does not seem to have been aware that this edition was coming out,[160] and asserts that what Robert had translated was precisely the abridged Qur'ān that he had published, using as a source text an abridgment of the Arabic Qur'ān made by some anonymous Muslim. Widmanstetter appears, in fact, never to have examined Robert's full translation at all. If he had, it would have been clear that the epitome he published was an abridgment of that, not a translation of some Arabic original. At any rate, while Widmanstetter's *Epitome Alcorani* would remain a scarce, nearly unread work,[161] Bibliander's edition would be consulted widely in the following centuries, many copies of it and of the slightly revised edition of 1550 surviving in libraries to this day.[162] This edition perpetuated much of the typical Latin framing; yet in intriguing ways, the frame in which Bibliander inserted the Qurʾān here is different from any that we have encountered. It is the work of a humanist, but a humanist with rather different interests than those of the Catholic Widmanstetter, whose Oriental studies connected him to the circles of both biblical humanists and Christian Kabbalists. Rather, Bibliander was a passionate protestant reformer whose way of reading the Qurʾān was connected with his desire to renovate both Christian society and the Christian church.

The complex story of how Bibliander's edition made it into print has been thoroughly told elsewhere.[163] It suffices to say here that Bibliander chose to insert Robert's Latin Qurʾān into a framework that was in many ways typical. To start with, it is surrounded by most of the original anthology that Peter the Venerable had commissioned four hundred years previously. Bibliander even included the twelfth-century annotations—at least in his 1543 edition—though he stripped them from the margins of Robert's text itself and placed them elsewhere in the volume. But Bibliander did not stop there. Rather, building on the basic logic of Peter the Venerable's anthology, he supplemented all these works with a series of further (and in some cases excerpted) polemical, apologetic, and historical treatises that had been written in the centuries since, the result being large enough that it required three books in one large volume to accommodate it. The reader is greeted first by a short preface by Melanchthon, and then by Bibliander's own notice to his readers and apologia for his edition, all of which attack Islam in unstinting language.[164] Some copies of the 1543 edition also contain an "In Alcoranum Praefatio" by Martin Luther himself—he had played a key role in getting a license for the printing of Bibliander's edition—and it too ferociously attacks Islam.[165] The later two books of the anthology contain anti-Islamic works by Juan Luis Vives, Savonarola, Nicholas of Cusa, Riccoldo da Monte di Croce, and a series of works, including papal letters, illuminating the contemporary state of the Turks.[166] Here was a comprehensive anthology of anti-Islamic works in addition to the Latin Qurʾān itself, this long list of accompanying works ensuring that, as Bibliander militantly put it, "the teaching of Muhammad . . . is not promulgated in public on its own, but rather with an overwhelming army of [other] writers who both refute and disprove, and slaughter and kill it."[167]

The reading that Bibliander had in mind was, without a doubt, a polemical and apologetic one, therefore, and the few woodcuts that decorate his edition's pages viscerally urge such an approach by portraying Islam as aggressively warlike: the background of the large capital "M" (for "misericordi") that begins surah 1 in the 1543 edition is illustrated with a fighter brutally kicking a man flat on his back, for example, while the capital "Q" (for "quum") with which Bibliander's *Apologia* begins in the 1550 edition sits on a background image of a naked man bound to a pole and carried off to captivity by two soldiers. Yet if we look for evidence both of how he read the Qur'ān as he prepared this edition, and of what he thought later readers might need to know about it as they read, we find once again that a polemical reading of the Qur'ān can be much more complicated than we might think.

Bibliander does not tell us much explicitly about his reading approach in his lengthy apologia for his edition, which, as its title suggests, is largely preoccupied with defending his decision to issue the Qur'ān in print for the first time in Europe.[168] As part of his defense, however, he argues that a comparison of the Qur'ān with the Bible both demonstrates the excellence of Christian doctrine and reproaches the corruption of human society,[169] and here he gives us some intriguing clues as to how he engaged the Qur'ānic text. Examining the Qur'ān, he points out, makes clear that negligent Christian rulers and the lax Christian society they govern contrast badly, in fact, with Turkish society, in which religious leaders "have the power of retracting the rulings" of their rulers "if they are repugnant to Muslim law";[170] it likewise exposes how imprudently Christian rulers act—he clearly has in mind Catholic princes—who forbid the preaching of the Gospel, and who oppose renewal of church and society;[171] it even illuminates the dangers of any Christian society ignorant of its own doctrines, such as, he asserts, the Arab-Christian society at the time of Muhammad, which was able to be lured away from true teaching by a pseudoprophet, and here Bibliander adds that "our age has a recent and vivid example" of the same thing "in the reign of the Anabaptists in Münster."[172] This reading was not to be just a refutation of Islam's holy book, therefore, but also an attack on the Zwinglian Bibliander's own Christian enemies—both Catholic and radical Protestant—as well as a call for the renewal of a Christian society whose degeneration was obvious, inasmuch as even the society of the false religion of Islam was more godly.[173] "[C]omparing the Qur'ān with the divine scriptures" (*collatio Alcorani ad scripturas diuinas*)—Bibliander's term for the procedure that demonstrates all these things—is a good description of what he does as a reader of Islam's scripture.[174]

But it is not a complete description, for before undertaking such a comparison, Bibliander found himself, like so many previous Latin-Christian readers, having to contend with philological matters. Like the Dominicans who prepared the Paris pocket Qur'ān,[175] Bibliander showed a real interest in getting the text of Robert's translation right. He compared the principal manuscript he used—which he knew to be a rather poor one[176]—with two other Latin manuscripts and with an Arabic manuscript, using them to help establish a more reliable text.[177] There are signs of this editorial work at a number of points in his edition,[178] but its most intriguing fruit is a set of *Annotations on the Variant Readings of the Four Different Exemplars*,[179] which consists of some nine hundred textual comments keyed to page and line number. Most of these signal disagreements between the manuscripts, such as a note that tells us that for *annuunt* in verse 2:11, another manuscript or manuscripts read *amminutis*.[180] Usually, these notes concern single-word variants, but sometimes Bibliander records larger textual differences as well, such as the absence in some witnesses of whole phrases.[181] Moreover, another large group of notes, rather than recording manuscript variants, amounts to a linguistic and stylistic commentary on Robert's translation. A note on 2:24, which in Robert's version begins *Sin autem*, observes that the translator mistakenly "writes *sin autem* in place of *sin minus*."[182] Though he made no real adjustments to the Latin Qur'ān on the basis of the Arabic manuscript that he consulted—as Bobzin and others have shown, his knowledge of Arabic was relatively modest[183]—Bibliander also included here a series of notes that gave the Arabic original, printed in Hebrew characters, of many terms that Robert had transliterated, such as at verse 19:98, where Robert had transliterated the word *qarn*, meaning "generation" or "era," as *alchirna*.[184] Some of these latter notes, clearly the fruit of an extensive comparison of Robert's Latin Qur'ān with the Arabic original, include learned exposition. Robert translated the word *Rūm* in 30:2, which means Romans or Byzantines, rather inadequately as "Christians" (*Christiani*). Bibliander explained that "in Arabic *Rūm* [this written in Hebrew characters] is the Roman people. For thus the Emperor of Constantinople was then called."[185] His study of the Arabic Qur'ān also reveals itself occasionally in his marginal notes on the Qur'ān. At the beginning of surah 3 he points out that "in Arabic it begins, 'In the name of God the

Righteous, the Merciful.'"[186] In a note on surah 107, he observes that "not everything which is in the Arabic has been included here."[187]

Hartmut Bobzin has rightly pointed out that Bibliander's printed version of the Latin Qur'ān was in no sense a complete critical edition, his editorial adjustments confining themselves to only a few essential passages.[188] Nevertheless, as with a number of other earlier readers, it is striking to see Bibliander's encounter with the Qur'ān become in part an energetic encounter with its textual problems, whether Latin or Arabic. This same interest in textual accuracy inspired him to insert a third translation of the short first surah, this one by Guillaume Postel, after Robert's and the Mozarab translation that usually accompanied it.[189] In all this he shows an interest in the whole of the Qur'ānic text that in some ways seems at odds with the obvious polemical preoccupations of his edition. Yet as we have had ample occasion to see before, a polemical reading of the Qur'ān often existed side by side with rather different tendencies—an interest in Qur'ānic philology or, as here, a concern to understand the whole text or at least possess a correct version of it.

But Bibliander's editorial activity went beyond collating manuscripts and comparing the Latin and Arabic texts of the Qur'ān; he also added an enormous number of marginal notes of his own to Robert's Latin Qur'ān. These marginal notes demonstrate some of the same complexity of reading. In the first place, it is worth bearing in mind that these notes are an intentional replacement of the twelfth-century notes that so often accompanied Robert's version. While at least one of the manuscripts that Bibliander consulted contained those notes, he chose to place them out of sight, some thirty-four pages after the end of the Qur'ān.[190] One could turn there and find both the polemical notes that decry how "most full of stupidities and fables and impieties" the Qur'ān is[191] and the learned philological notes that explain, for example, that Hebrew and Arabic are both written in the same way, from right to left,[192] but one had to go well out of one's way to do so. Here, then, we have another example of a reader "turning the tables" on the earlier framing of the text he takes up, deciding to replace it with his own frame.

What Bibliander replaced that part of the twelfth-century frame with is a set of annotations that combine his polemical purposes with the interest in the whole text of the Qur'ān attested by his collation of Arabic and Latin manuscripts. Where the twelfth-century annotations were polemic and philology, both based on wide reading in Arab-Islamic and Arab-Christian sources, Bibliander's annotations are polemic, based heavily on a comparative reading of the Qur'ān and the Bible (the *collatio Alcorani ad scripturas diuinas* that he described in his apologia) together with a systematic description of the Qur'ān's contents. The majority of Bibliander's marginal notes amount, in fact, to a running analysis of the text, consisting variously of single words, sentence fragments, and whole sentences—all meant, as Bobzin has pointed out, to make the Qur'ān accessible to the Christian reader.[193] If we were to string them together, the result, in fact, would be something very like the Dresden table of contents. The first several notes on surah 2 read as follows: "What the Book of the Qur'ān conveys; what sort of disciples it requires" (on 2:1–10);[194] "A simile for those who abandon the sect which they had made an appearance of following" (on 2:19–20);[195] "Paradise" (on 2:25);[196] "The resurrection of the dead by God. The seven heavens created." (on 2:28–29).[197] Notes such as these, appearing on every page of Bibliander's edition, describe the Qur'ān's contents in a way that the twelfth-century notes, preoccupied with pointing out its apparent absurdities and explaining its obscurities, do not—not least because Bibliander's notes cover all of Robert's translation, whereas the twelfth-century notes become quite thin after the first score of folios. While Bibliander does not describe every verse, the coverage is extensive enough to give readers an impressive guide to the whole text of the Qur'ān. As a searching device, these notes would surely be rather useful: easily legible, concise, they provide a relatively quick way of finding interesting passages in the Qur'ānic text.

As should be clear from these examples, Bibliander has drawn the attention of readers to a wide range of passages, many of them without obvious polemical or apologetic use, and this is true throughout, but it should also be clear that the interests of religious disputation are being served here as well. Like so many Qur'ān readers, Bibliander did not fail to point out the first Qur'ānic description of the Islamic paradise in 2:25, and his single word description—"Paradise"—was surely all that was necessary by the mid-sixteenth century to alert readers to a passage likely to contain a description of that carnal paradise for which Christians so regularly censured Islam. And indeed a large minority of these notes seem intended for readers with such concerns. "He asks of others a demonstration which he himself does not produce,"[198] Bibliander writes next to 2:111, which tells how Jews and Christians claim that only they will enter Paradise, and calls on them to produce a proof (*burhān/demonstratio*). This is ammunition for Christians attempting to undermine Muhammad's claims to prophecy, Muhammad's lack of miracles—at least in orthodox Sunnī Islam—being widely cited as evidence that he was not a real prophet.[199] Not surprisingly, Bibliander points out passages that deny Jesus' divinity, observing with some exasperation on the last page that "he does not cease to deny the son of God."[200] He alerts readers to "fables" which Muhammad uses in his depiction of the resurrection in 2:259.[201] As Bobzin has pointed out, he even occasionally draws the reader's attention to Qur'ānic teachings that reproduce "Jewish fables."[202] He likens the last few verses of surah 2 to the teachings of Pelagius,[203] implying, like so many Christian polemicists before him, that the Qur'ān contained many teachings of Christian heresiarchs.[204]

Although polemical notes such as these[205] make up only a minority of Bibliander's annotations, there is no shortage of them, nor is there a shortage of another sort of note that we have not really seen before—systematic references to parallel biblical passages—which also make up a substantial minority of the notes. The intensive comparison of Qur'ānic and biblical texts that these latter notes embody is, of course, the natural result of the Reformers' view that "All doctrines . . . had to be tested in light of Scripture, and rejected if they were inconsistent with it."[206] As Bobzin has pointed, out many of these notes simply cite without comment the biblical passage(s) that tell(s) much the same story as a given Qur'ānic passage.[207] While a few only allude to such biblical parallels without mentioning them specifically,[208] Bibliander normally identifies the relevant biblical passages by book and chapter.[209] Often such notes summarize the Qur'ānic passage—in this way contributing to Bibliander's running marginal description of the Qur'ān's contents—and also cite the related biblical passages. Verse 2:221, for example, warns Muslims not to marry polytheist women until they convert, which Bibliander summarized in the margins as "Marriage may be among coreligionists. Deuteronomy 7."[210]

Frequently, when Bibliander points out biblical parallels, he also "censures" what he sees as Muhammad's reworking of them.[211] Next to an account of the wanderings of the Children of Israel in the desert, including Moses' miraculously making water flow from a rock, Bibliander observes that "He mixes two stories, Exodus 15 and 17, the story of Exodus 16 having been corrupted."[212] Later, when the Qur'ān describes the incident of the yellow calf in 2:67–69, Bibliander points out the parallel passage in Numbers 29, but then complains that Muhammad "intermixes fabulous things, no doubt from the traditions of the Jews."[213]

Now it is quite likely that Bibliander based a few of these notes on the twelfth-century annotations,[214] but they are overwhelmingly his own work, and represent still another reading of Robert's by this time venerable translation, bringing together concerns and techniques, many of which we have seen separately elsewhere, into a unique, new whole. Like the twelfth-century annotator, Bibliander is anxious both to explain and to attack the Qurʾānic text, but he approaches both tasks rather differently than did his medieval forebears. He only rarely engages in the sort of philological commentary that Peter the Venerable's team so often concerned itself with, and, like Widmanstetter's, his reading of the Qurʾān does not involve any extended consultation of the Qurʾānic exegetical tradition. But like the maker of the Dresden *tabula*, he grapples with the whole of the Qurʾānic text—preparing a running description of all of it—and like the Dominican makers of the Paris pocket Qurʾān, he goes to a great deal of trouble over the Latin text, collating his version with other versions and carefully recording hundreds of variant readings. And while braiding all these strands together, he adds something new, at least in the intensity with which he does it: a systematic comparison of the Qurʾān with the Bible, this often being the source of his criticism of the Qurʾān's teachings. This attack on the Qurʾān founded on a close reading of the text of the Bible itself is a procedure that should not surprise us in a Protestant humanist.

As luck would have it, it is possible to gain intriguing insight into how Bibliander's edition was itself read by contemporaries from a still further reframing of Robert's translation that was made, based on Bibliander's 1550 edition, probably sometime before 1560. Extant in a manuscript in a small Austrian convent, this reworking consists of a set of extracts from the Qurʾān, made near the highpoint of the Ottoman threat to Europe, and reveals a reader who—like so many we have seen already—is shaped by the particular packaging in which he found the Qurʾān, but also reads against it, ignoring what does not interest him. Once again, there is no doubt that this reader approaches the Qurʾān guided by polemical and apologetic concerns; yet he still reveals an interest in more of the Qurʾān than just the disputational commonplaces.

Like earlier repackagings of Robert's Latin Qurʾān, this one reflects the reading practices of its age, for while humanist scholars famously professed to be interested in the original sources alone, without commentary or abridgment, the making of extracts of the kind found here was really quite common in this period, and had, indeed, been recommended by humanist intellectuals such as Guarino and Erasmus.[215] The extracts in question—described in the manuscript as *Selected Extracts from the Qurʾān, the Faith of the Turks*—only exist today, so far as I know, in a little known codex of the Franciscan convent at Güssing in Austria.[216] Rightly described by a modern cataloguer as a "Theological Miscellany," this manuscript contains a range of works, all written in the same hand—a treatise on the eucharist, a sermon delivered to a Hungarian audience (though written in Latin), a compilation of dominical sermons.[217] Some of the works, moreover, are specifically concerned with current religious disputes: a dialogue between a Lutheran and a Catholic attributed to the Dominican inquisitor and anti-Protestant polemicist Johannes Bunderius (d. 1557)[218] called *Confutations of Modern and Ancient Heresies*;[219] excerpts from Nicholas of Cusa's *Cribratio Alcorani*;[220] the Qur'ānic extracts themselves;[221] and excerpts from the *Doctrina Mahumet* from Peter the Venerable's anthology.[222] Even here, in the mid-sixteenth century, therefore, Robert's Qur'ān cannot be prised away entirely from those original accompanying works. This range of works makes complete sense in a theological anthology produced somewhere on the Austrian-Hungarian border where Catholic-Protestant and Christian-Muslim conflicts were ever present.[223] That the compiler was a Catholic, moreover, seems the obvious conclusion based on the contents of the manuscript. From internal evidence, it is clear that much of the compilation was copied by a single hand between 1557 and 1560.[224]

For reasons that will become clear just below, there is no doubt that these *Selected Excerpts from the Qur'ān* were made using Robert of Ketton's translation in the edition of Theodore Bibliander. Furthermore, there is notable evidence suggesting that they were made using the edition of 1550 specifically: whereas in the 1543 edition Bibliander took out the new Qur'ānic divisions that Robert had introduced within the second surah, only indicating where they had been by marginal notes, in the 1550 edition they are prominently restored, and the compiler of these extracts uses them with equal prominence.[225]

The compiler's procedures are not difficult to isolate. Written in short paragraphs the second and following lines of which are always indented, his extracts take several different forms. Occasionally, they are direct quotations of Robert's translation, with no other comment. One extract, for example, which is not directly connected to the extracts before or after, abruptly gives us a word-for-word quotation of the Latin version of 23:97: "beseech God in order that he protect you from all diabolical urgings, and that he cast them away from you."[226] But generally, each extract is preceded by a sort of headline or rubric, written in larger letters in purple/brown ink and describing the content of what follows, which is in a smaller hand in brown/grey ink.[227] When the compiler quotes 24:22 in Robert's version, which tells us that the wealthy should assist both their relatives and the poor, he prefixes it with the rubric, "Who is to receive good works."[228] In most cases, though not in this last instance, the rubrics themselves—and this is how we know the compiler was using Bibliander's edition—are drawn directly from Theodore Bibliander's marginal annotations. Before the compiler's quotation of 20:131, for example, which calls on believers not to be envious of the happiness of other married couples, he inserts this rubric in large letters: "Another's wife is not to be desired."[229] At the corresponding passage in Bibliander's edition, we find that the marginal note is identical: *Non concupiscenda uxor aliena.*[230]

Sometimes, in fact, the compiler of these extracts quotes only Bibliander's notes, ignoring the real Qurʾānic text entirely. His extract for surah 98 begins with a rubric—"Neither Jews nor Christians"—that abridges the first part of Bibliander's note on this surah. The summary that follows then simply quotes the same marginal note in full: "In this surah he writes that before Muhammad, neither the Jews nor the Christians understood anything. At his advent, however, dissension appeared."[231] At other times, his extracts are really combinations of Robert's Latin text and Bibliander's notes. At surah 104, his rubric reads, "Who is to be condemned," which is based on the first few words of Bibliander's note. The extract then mixes the rest of that note together with paraphrased material from the Qurʾānic text itself (these paraphrased sections are in italic here): "Especially *he says that* committers of fraud, shirkers, the avaricious, *are to be burned in most fervent flames.*"[232]

It is clear, then, that to a remarkable degree, Bibliander's notes guided the reading of this compiler of Qurʾānic extracts, and this is true as well of the themes that preoccupy him, for like Bibliander's annotations, these extracts show a wide interest in both the polemically useful and the polemically useless portions of the Qurʾān. One extract, for example, begins with the rubric, "God is everywhere," and consists of a quotation of 2:115 in Robert's translation: "Since to God belong East and West, toward whichever direction one pours out prayers one will find God. For his mercy is restricted to no place; his wisdom embraces all things."[233] This verse caught many Qurʾān readers' attention, despite the fact that it was of little value in attacking Islam, consisting as it does of entirely unobjectionable monotheistic piety that Christian readers could not help but admire.[234]

But alongside the many extracts of this sort, there are just as many whose role in attacking Islamic belief and defending Christianity cannot be doubted. Like countless previous readers, this compiler focuses on what seemed the fradulent nature of the fast of Ramadan: "In the temples let there be no sex with women," he writes, quoting 2:187b verbatim; "Fasting all day, break the fast at night, eating and drinking then as much as will be agreeable, until almost the beginning of the hour which precedes the rising of the sun. Let no one transgress these boundaries constituted by God."[235] Extracts of this sort are surely intended to make clear the false teachings of Islam.[236] Other passages—such as the quoted portion of 21:91 which describes how God breathed into the Virgin Mary, thereby presenting her and her son as a miracle to the nations[237]—are jotted down because they seem to confirm Christian doctrine.

The reading approach of this compiler of Qurʾānic extracts, then, is in many ways very like that of Bibliander, whose notes he followed so closely; but in one striking way, his interests diverge from Bibliander's. While the compiler relied heavily on Bibliander's notes to help him identify passages of interest in the Qurʾān, he entirely ignored all the references to biblical parallels that Bibliander went to so much trouble to include. Though the compiler quotes, as we have seen, all of 2:115, indicating that it teaches that "God is everywhere,"[238] he does not include any reference to the fourth chapter of the Gospel of John, as Bibliander did right beside this verse.[239] He draws no attention to the Qurʾānic passages that Bibliander sees as "mixtures" of different biblical narratives.[240] In fact, the compiler mentions absolutely none of the some twenty-five biblical references that Bibliander includes in his notes for surah 2, even though Bibliander's notes influence him so thoroughly otherwise, and this is true of the other surahs as well.[241]

This anonymous Catholic reader, therefore, followed the Protestant Bibliander in expressing interest in the whole text—he jotted down thirty folios of extracts, covering almost all the surahs of the Qurʾān—and shared his contemporary's interest in both the polemically useful and much that was not, but had no interest in seeing the Qurʾānic text through the lens of biblical parallels. In fact, in his ways of engaging the text of Robert's Latin Qurʾān, this mid-sixteenth-century reader is intriguingly representative of how that work was read over these four centuries. Polemic certainly predominates. For this Latin Christian, who may well have remembered vividly the Turkish siege of Vienna in 1529 and who was all too aware of the proximity of the enormous Ottoman empire, Islam was primarily something to be attacked and exposed. Attacking and exposing it was made far easier by having a version of Robert's Latin Qurʾān, supplemented by Bibliander's helpfully polemical notes, and this reader was happy to let them do their job. Yet attacking and exposing Islam did not require following Bibliander slavishly. Where Bibliander's biblicism seemed irrelevant, it could be passed over entirely. And attacking and exposing Islam also did not limit this reader to examining only the Qurʾānic passages that most suited that task—he did not approach the Qurʾān or Islam looking only for good ammunition, but read and made notes quite widely on Qurʾānic material very far removed from the polemical commonplaces.

Much the same thing could be said for most of the other readers whose approaches to Robert's *Lex Mahumet* are revealed in the manuscripts and printed books examined here. Among them, too, polemical reading predominated, and in their polemical reading they happily allowed themselves to follow the controlling guidance of the frames in which they found the Qurʾān. But like this Catholic reader of Bibliander's edition, they often ignored or effaced what seemed useless to them, inserting new framing devices instead, updating Robert's Latin Qurʾān to suit the reading practices of new centuries. The choices they made regarding what books to read alongside the Qurʾān—Kabbalistic treatises, for example, or the Bible itself—are striking indicators of the freedom with which they approached Robert's translation, even if they continued to read it in the familiar polemical mode. And just as with this Counter-Reformation excerptor, the overriding polemical preoccupations of other readers of Robert's *Lex Mahumet* did not keep them from reading the Qurʾān in ways that were not inherently polemical, even if they could also serve polemical purposes: checking the Latin text carefully for accuracy, or seeking out, in an Arabic Qurʾān manuscript, the Arabic original of terms that Robert had transliterated. Reading the Qurʾān polemically was neither simple nor unchanging.

That the compiler of the lengthy table of contents in the Dresden manuscript does not really fit this pattern—polemical preoccupations seem strikingly secondary in this reader who was so concerned to get across a comprehensive description of the Qurʾān's contents—indicates that Latin-Christians could, at least from time to time, approach Robert's Latin Qurʾān very much against the grain of the predominant polemical concerns that hedged it about in the books in which it traveled. As we turn in the following two chapters to the manuscripts in which the other Latin Qurʾāns circulated in Western Europe we will encounter plenty of evidence that polemical Qurʾān reading often predominated among them as well. But we will also find that the Dresden compiler was no fluke.

Chapter 5

The Qurʾān Translations of Mark of Toledo and Flavius Mithridates: Manuscript Framing and Reading Approaches

Compared with the twenty-four manuscripts of Robert of Ketton's *Lex Mahumet*, there are relatively few surviving manuscripts of any other Latin version of the Qurʾān—in fact, only fifteen manuscripts survive for the other three combined—and none of these versions found its way into print, either abridged or in its entirety.[1] Yet in these fifteen manuscripts, we have evidence, as we will see in this and the next chapter, of a broader range of reading practices and attitudes than we saw in the codices of Robert's Latin version. Some of what we see here will be familiar: Mark of Toledo's Qurʾān translation, for example, occasionally circulated surrounded by much the same set of polemical works that typically surrounded Robert of Ketton's version; and we will continue to encounter evidence—sometimes astonishing evidence—of philological Qurʾān reading. But rather than dwell on the familiar here, I will emphasize in Mark's and in Mithridates' Latin versions two different aspects of Qurʾān reading that we have not really seen before.

The most striking aspect of how readers approached Mark of Toledo's Latin Qurʾān grows directly out of the very decision he made about how to translate. We saw earlier that Mark carefully followed the Arabic syntax of the Qurʾān, usually word for word. This meant that Mark's version could easily be read side by side with the Arabic Qurʾān, and there is remarkable evidence from at least two later readers that this is exactly what they were doing—carefully comparing the two versions line by line. Robert's complex paraphrase, on the other hand, can only be read alongside the Arabic with great difficulty, and I know of no evidence of this occurring from the period under consideration. Mark's particular translation method made possible, therefore, a very particular reading practice.

The most distinctive thing that the manuscripts of Flavius Mithridates' translation have to tell us, on the other hand, has more to do with attitudes toward the Qurʾān than with ways of reading it. On the surface, his translation seems to be intended for thoroughly philological Qurʾān study. His Latin version is laid out in parallel columns alongside the Arabic original, all this supplemented by impressive-looking notes, and not a whiff of polemical sentiment can be found anywhere. Yet these erudite trappings turn out to be a sort of philological trompe l'oeil: the translation, as we have seen earlier, is often quite defective; the seemingly scholarly notes likewise often prove, upon inspection, to be misleading, at times apparently the result of pure invention. So dodgy is the scholarship here, in fact, that it is hard to imagine that philological Qurʾān reading was the real motivating force behind the creation of this edition. Yet the impressive appearance of humanist scholarship that we find here, I suggest, does have an intriguing connection with what actually did bring this work into being: the concern to create a beautifully ornate version of the Qurʾān, one that would be suitable for the library of a wealthy lay book collector, someone who liked fancy codices as much for how they looked as for what texts they contained. The original owner of Mithridates' Qurʾān edition—Federigo da Montefeltro, Duke of Urbino—was just such a man, the Qurʾān becoming here not so much the object of polemic or philology as an expensive, desirable consumer commodity.

Manuscripts of Mark of Toledo's *Liber Alchorani*

We have seen that Robert of Ketton retitled Islam's holy book, naming it the *Religion of Muhammad* (*Lex Mahumet*), and that he reworked the standard surah divisions of the Qurʾān, adding nasty rubrics intended to warn Christian readers about the "lying and stupid fables" that awaited them in that text.[2] Mark's translation never seems to have suffered such rough treatment. Rather, he seems to have maintained the Arabic Qurʾān's traditional divisions and to have perpetuated its standard surah titles as well, throughout the whole of the Qurʾān. While Mark's Latin Qurʾān certainly could be read in the Christian polemical mode, his version facilitated philological study in a way that Robert's did not, and, perhaps for this reason, found itself circulating in a form that Robert's never did: as an entirely standalone work, with no polemical notes, no hostile preface, no apologetic appendices or supplementary works. As we will see below, it is between the lines of one such stand-alone Qurʾān that, intriguingly enough, we find striking signs of the philological reading that Mark's translation method made possible.

While we have a clear idea, as we have seen, of the earliest physical form of Robert of Ketton's translation, we are not so fortunate in the case of Mark's Latin Qurʾān. Seven manuscripts survive (one only fragmentarily), but no one has worked out the relationships among them, so that we do not know which of them preserves his text most accurately or has maintained the original frame that he gave it in its most pristine form.[3] Nevertheless, there are striking similarities in how these manuscripts present the Qurʾānic text that probably go back to Mark's original version itself or that, at the very least, certainly give us a clear idea of how Mark's version normally circulated.

In six of the seven manuscripts, Mark's translation is called *The Book of the Qurʾān* (*Liber Alchorani*), while one gives it no title at all.[4] His Latin Qurʾān, therefore, generally circulated in Europe under something rather like its proper Arabic name. This is also true of the surah titles. While there are variations, in most manuscripts they appear under their original titles either in Latin translation or, in the case of surahs whose titles are really proper names such as Ḥūd, in transliteration. Though in one case, a manuscript now in Vienna dated to about 1500, the surahs are identified by number only,[5] the majority of the manuscripts follow the pattern of the two oldest, both apparently from the fourteenth century: in Milan, BA, MS L 1 sup., Sūrat (11) Ḥūd is entitled "Hud. One Hundred Twenty-one Verses";[6] and in Paris, BnF, MS lat. 14503 we have nearly the same thing, "The Prophecy of Hud, One Hundred Twenty-one Verses."[7] All this corresponds closely to what contemporary Arabic versions have in the way of surah titles,[8] and is typical of these two manuscripts throughout: they usually give both the surah names and the numbers of verses, though the Paris manuscript eccentrically refers to each surah as a "prophecy" while in the Milan manuscript no term for "surah" is used at all.[9] Neither manuscript, however, has titles for all the surahs.[10] The later manuscripts are rather similar.[11]

The exception is a remarkable manuscript dated 1400 and preserved in the Mazarine Library in Paris. Here the titles have almost certainly been reworked in careful consultation with an Arabic manuscript of the Qurʾān. Each surah is actually called a "surah" (*curat*), and the specific titles usually appear in both translation *and* transliteration: *Curat Ioseph Iucuf* ("The Surah of Joseph, Yūsuf"), for example, or *Curat alnahel id est de ape* ("The Surah *Alnahel*, that is, of the Bee").[12] Sometimes the title appears in translation; at others we have only transliteration.[13] What this manuscript does not have, however, is any indication of the number of verses in each surah, except in the case of the first surah.[14] Rather, it normally supplies the surah number: "the Surah of the Table, *Almeyda*, chapter five."[15] As we will see below, this Mazarine manuscript derives from the thirteenth-century Milan manuscript (BA MS L 1 sup.) or its exemplar. These features that appear in the Mazarine codex but in no other manuscript of Mark's version—features that depend, moreover, on familiarity with Arabic Qur'ān manuscripts—almost certainly do not go back to Mark's original manuscript, therefore. They are the fruit, rather, of some later reader comparing Mark's version with the Arabic original, and there is other evidence that we will encounter a few pages hence pointing to this same conclusion.

The seven surviving manuscripts of Mark's Qur'ān translation, therefore, perpetuated to a considerable extent the external form of the Qur'ān, just as his translation itself perpetuated much more of the Qur'ān's linguistic form in its verbatim translation than Robert of Ketton's did.[16] There are, moreover, other ways in which Mark's Latin Qur'ān circulated differently from Robert's. We saw that Robert's Latin Qur'ān often took the form of a handsome, glossed, scholastic textbook. None of the surviving manuscripts of Mark's version gives quite this impression. It is true that a set of closely related glosses does appear in two of the seven manuscripts, the fourteenth-century Milan manuscript and the intriguing Mazarine manuscript copied in 1400. Both these sets of glosses are integral parts of these two codices and intended to be study aids for later readers. This is clear not only from their content but also from the fact that they were set out on the page as an essential and original part of the framing of the Qur'ān—like the text itself, they frequently are ornamented with red touching in the Milan manuscript, and in the Mazarine manuscript are written carefully in the vivid vermilion ink used for the surah titles. In the Milan manuscript, the notes are very concise—rarely more than three words. Some are polemical, some not, and though they appear at irregular intervals in this manuscript, they have something of the character of the running subject headings that Theodore Bibliander devised for the margins of his sixteenth-century printed editions of Robert of Ketton's Latin Qur'ān. Verse 2:25, for example—the first reference in the Qur'ān to the Islamic paradise—is signaled by a curt "paradisus" written in the margin; the discussion of the eternal destiny of Jews and Christians in 2:62 inspired the commentator to write "Judei et Christiani"; and Mark's misleading translation of the "sacred place of worship" (*al-*

masjid al-ḥarām) in 2:144 as "the illegal/forbidden oratory" engendered a simple, marginal restatement: "oratorium illicitum."[17]

These infrequent, brief notes are the core out of which someone later devised the much more extensive annotations we find in the Mazarine manuscript. Almost every note in the Milan manuscript appears here also. Sometimes they are repeated virtually unchanged, such as the "oratorium illicitum" note on 2:144, or the unusually long note on 2:120 which explains what its author considered the thrust of that verse: "one should follow neither Jews nor Christians."[18] But in most cases the Milan notes have been substantially augmented. The one-word note "devil" next to verse 2:36 in the Milan manuscript has become "the devil deceived Adam" in the Mazarine codex.[19] The Milan manuscript's single-word note on 2:275, "usury" (*fenus*), reads "he prohibits usury or lending at interest" (*prohibet fenus uel usuram*) in the later manuscript.[20] Probably the majority of the notes in the Mazarine codex, however, are not found in the Milan codex at all, but are entirely new, and often lengthier, annotations, now appearing regularly throughout the manuscript—often several to a page. Notes such as "That God taught Adam all names and he [Adam] recounted them to the angels" at 2:31 have no obvious polemical overtones, while others, like that on 2:187 ("That on [each] night of the fast it is allowed to them to take their pleasure with women"), clearly do.[21] But their concern with identifying the main contents of successive Qur'ānic passages for later readers is obvious, and as such, these notes are further evidence that manuscript designers did envision Qur'ān readers with interests that went beyond the strictly polemical.

But there is something else that deserves our attention in the expanded version of these glosses preserved in the Mazarine manuscript. Here and there we find comments that suggest knowledge of the Arabic Qur'ān itself, and in at least one case, of the standard Muslim interpretation of a verse. Just as the expanded surah titles in this same manuscript depend on familiarity with specifically Arabic texts, so also, therefore, do some of these notes. This is clearest at verse 2:131. Mark's translation captured the basic meaning of the Arabic except at the key word: "When his creator said to him, 'offer up [to God],' he said, 'I have been offered up to [God] the creator of nations."[22] The verb that Mark has translated somewhat ineptly as "offer up" (*offerte, oblatus sum*) surely means "to surrender" (*aslim, aslamtu*) in this context in the Arabic. Without explaining why he has done so, this annotator actually writes out the two conjugations of this Arabic verb in Roman script in the margin immediately adjoining this verse: *azlam* and *azlamtu*. Other than a vocalization error—we should have *azlim* in the first case, not *azlam*—this is entirely correct.[23] It is hard to see how anyone who did not know the specific Arabic of this verse could have written these glosses, and we find the same thing again just two verses later, in 2:133. Mark, translating "We have submitted to Him," wrote "We have been offered up to him." Here a note reads "*Muzlimuna*, that is, Muslims,"[24] and this time the annotator's transliteration is perfect.

This precise knowledge of the Qur'ān's Arabic is matched by accurate knowledge of Muslim Qur'ān exegesis a few folios later. The beginning phrase of verse 2:230, "If he divorce her," as we have seen elsewhere, was normally understood by Muslim commentators to mean, "If he pronounce the divorce a third time."[25] While Robert of Ketton actually translated the verse in such a way as to reflect this traditional interpretation, Mark did not, his version reading simply "And if he repudiated her."[26] The adjoining note in the Mazarine manuscript clarifies this phrase much as the Qur'ānic commentators did: "that the woman repudiated *for the third time* is not allowed to return to the man until another contracts marriage with her" (my italics).[27] The author of these expanded glosses in the Mazarine manuscript, then, has some familiarity with both the Arabic Qur'ān and its exegesis. We will see evidence below, while looking at another manuscript, that a later reader of Mark's version had even more knowledge of both these things.[28]

So we do have what looks like a standard set of glosses developed for Mark's version, glosses that in the Mazarine codex are based in part on some amount of Arabic learning, and we do find some of the other features of scholastic textbooks in these manuscripts. The Mazarine codex (MS 708) is the most expensively produced manuscript of this translation. Here the surah titles and surah numbers are vivid red, as are the running headers on each page that indicate which surah is being read. Large initials are in blue with red flourishes or in red with blue flourishes.[29] Like Robert's Latin Qur'ān as it appears, for example, in the thirteenth-century Bodleian manuscript,[30] Mark's version must, then, have been read at times much like other searchable, scholarly scholastic textbooks. Yet although frame lines were provided dividing each page into two columns, no ruling was provided here for the copyist ahead of time so that the lines of the text tend to list away from the horizontal, giving the page a sloppy feel. The fourteenth-century codex now in Milan—BA, MS L 1 sup.—is of similar quality.[31] Both these manuscripts, moreover, have only some of the features of the thirteenth- and fourteenth-century manuscripts of Robert's translation that are so like contemporary textbooks. Neither they nor any other manuscript of

Mark's version have illuminations, or indexes, or tables of contents, for example. Moreover, in neither manuscript do the marginal glosses appear on the page in quite the way that the glosses on Robert's translation do: no ruling has been inscribed in the margins to insure that the glosses are copied along straight lines, so in neither case do we have a page layout that reminds us so obviously of contemporary glossed Bibles or other scholastic textbooks. And the other manuscripts of Mark's version are even less like scholastic textbooks—and even less handsome.[32]

But if the framing of Mark of Toledo's Latin Qur'ān was different from Robert's in being less often like the "red-and-blue" scholastic textbooks, it was also different in the range of accompanying works that surrounded it. We have seen that in no case did Robert's *Lex Mahumet* manage to free itself entirely from the other works of the *Collectio Toletana*, though other elements were added to them, and not all of them were always present. At times, Mark's version came bundled in much the same way. In Paris, BnF, MS lat. 14503, it is essentially annexed into the Toledan Collection, for this fourteenth-century codex is the only known manuscript that contains *both* Mark's and Robert's translations. All of the other works commissioned by Peter the Venerable were copied here as well, and to all this were added such further works as the *Liber Nycholay*, a legendary and polemical life of Muhammad in which he is portrayed as having originally been a heretical cardinal named Nicholas. Long part of the library of St. Victor in Paris,[33] this large manuscript was copied entirely in the same scriptorium, and possibly all by the same hand. It was clearly designed to appeal to readers with polemical and apologetic interests in mind—and not just against Islam.[34]

But in general, Mark's Latin Qur'ān lived a freer life, at times appearing in the manuscripts accompanied by quite different works, at times having no accompaniment at all. The Mazarine manuscript of the year 1400 gives us Mark's preface to, and all of his translation of, the Qur'ān, but then follows these by works that appear nowhere else in Latin Qur'ān manuscripts.[35] First, we have Mark of Toledo's other important Islamic translations: his versions of Ibn Tūmart's *Creed* (*ʿaqīdah*) and other short works[36] which summarize Ibn Tūmart's teachings, which formed the ideological core of the Almohad dynasty and religious movement that dominated North Africa and Islamic Spain from the mid-twelfth through the first two decades of the thirteenth century. Both highly rationalist in its tendencies and highly legalistic,[37] the Almohad movement was the main Islamic enemy against which Rodrigo Jiménez de Rada had to rally the northern Christian kings as he orchestrated the great crusading campaign, in the years from

1209 to 1212, that culminated in the decisive defeat of the Islamic rulers of al-Andalus at Las Navas de Tolosa in 1212. In translating these short treatises, Mark was clearly hoping to give Latin readers greater insight into the dominant variety of Islam that faced them in southern Spain. But these translations by Mark are followed in the manuscript by a copy of the *Historia Alexandri Magni*, a Latin version made in about 950 of a Greek life of Alexander by Pseudo-Callisthenes. Usually known as *Historia de praeliis*, this text was a major source of knowledge on Alexander in the Latin world, as was also the short and famous text that followed it, the fictional *Letter of Alexander of Macedon to Aristotle*.[38] It is clear, moreover, that while these last two works were added to this manuscript as something of an afterthought (the last folio and a half of the previous gathering are blank, the *Historia Alexandri Magni* beginning on a new gathering), they are nevertheless written in a hand very like that which copied the rest of the manuscript, and were doubtless produced in the same scriptorium.

It is not easy to know what conclusions to draw from all this. Christopher de Hamel has pointed out that versions of Alexander's life were commonly copied into expensive manuscripts intended for aristocratic owners in just this period, these exotic tales meant "to be enjoyed by the rich" alongside "stories of . . . Charlemagne, and King Arthur."[39] As d'Alverny and Vajda have suggested, moreover, this Mazarine manuscript may have been copied from an exemplar in the papal library in Avignon.[40] While this manuscript is not handsomely illuminated, as the expensive codices containing the stories of King Arthur and Alexander the Great often were, it is nevertheless possible that we have here a codex similarly meant for some member of the aristocracy, whether ecclesiastical or secular—the Qurʾān, the short works of Ibn Tūmart, and the Alexander material being presented to readers as a collection of oriental exotica. At any rate, we will see later in this chapter that within a century, sumptuous Latin Qurʾāns were certainly being produced, not for the polemicists and philologists whom we have seen so far, but for wealthy book collectors of just this sort.

If Mark of Toledo's version is unusual at times for the strange company it keeps in the manuscripts, it is unusual at others for the *lack* of company. In one manuscript, Milan, BA, MS L 1 sup., Mark's Latin Qurʾān is preceded only by his preface, and followed by nothing else. Now this manuscript is clearly incomplete, and other accompanying texts may have been intended.[41] The preface by itself, moreover, as we have seen, contains a vicious attack on Islam and the Qurʾān, so that by itself it places the Qurʾān in a fully polemical context. Yet in another manuscript from about 1500

(Vienna, Österreichische Nationalbibliothek, MS 4297),[42] Mark's Latin Qur'ān appears stripped entirely of framing works other than an odd "prophecy" of nine short lines, written by the same humanist hand that copied the rest of the manuscript, and appearing on the last folio of Mark's translation just after the explicit. Imitating Qur'ānic language, this "prophecy" amounts to a sort of parody of a Qur'ānic surah, seemingly depicting Islam as a polytheistic religion, and mentioning how Muhammad was found "in the error of the day of Venus," a clear reference to his supposed sexual immorality.[43] While this short text is shot through with typical polemic, we cannot help noticing that the polemical frame is becoming ever more attenuated in these two codices. It is clear, moreover, that this Vienna manuscript was specifically designed to present Mark's Latin Qur'ān without his polemical preface, for the text of his translation begins at the top of the first folio of what is certainly its first gathering—it is not as if the folios containing his preface had been torn out of the manuscript at some point.[44]

This trend reaches its logical conclusion in the fifteenth-century manuscript now in Turin (Biblioteca Nazionale Universitaria, MS F. V. 35). Here the Qur'ān appears for the first time in Latin with no accompanying texts whatsoever—no commentary or preface of any kind to tell readers "where to be outraged," no polemical lives of Muhammad or attacks on Islam to frame Islam's holy book in a properly Christian manner—and like the Vienna manuscript, this codex was clearly designed this way, Mark's Latin Qur'ān beginning once again at the top of the first folio of what is clearly the first gathering of the manuscript.[45]

Just as it is difficult to know exactly what it means for Mark's Latin Qur'ān to be bound into a manuscript with legendary works on Alexander, so it is hard to know what it means to find his translation almost or even entirely on its own. On the one hand, though Theodore Bibliander observed in 1543 that the Qur'ān should not be allowed to travel abroad without a phalanx of properly Christian polemical works surrounding it,[46] we might well wonder whether such a framing was really necessary for Christian readers after three hundred fifty years of that text's circulation in the Latin world. Surely any Christian scholar who might read it in 1500 would know where to be outraged by its contents. Perhaps, therefore, we have little or no polemical framing in these cases because the tropes of Christian apologetic and polemic against Islam had long since become woven into the intellectual fabric of the Latin world. But on the other hand, it is worth recalling that in this same period, we have encountered at least one reader of Robert's Latin Qur'ān—the compiler of the Dresden table of contents—

who seems remarkably uninterested in the polemical commonplaces. The lack of polemical apparatus is perhaps, then, an expression of a lack of interest in polemic.

In fact, we have evidence that firmly supports both positions. A set of marginal notes written in the Vienna manuscript by its copyist presents us with evidence of just the sort of polemical Qurʾān reading that should be familiar by now. While some are simply corrections to the text[47] or attempts to clarify or emend difficult passages,[48] others clearly dwell on the passages most of interest in anti-Islamic polemic. Like so many other Latin-Christian Qurʾān readers, this glossator could not help pointing out Qurʾānic references to the Islamic paradise, writing, for example, *de paradiso* at verses 2:111–13. Where the Qurʾān discusses the earlier revelations to Moses and Jesus at 2:87, we have a similar note, and where those who ask for miracles are upbraided at 2:118, a bracket and a *nota* call Christian readers' attention to what seemed to be the Qurʾān's admission that Muhammad worked no miracles.[49] Here, therefore, is a copy of Mark's Latin Qurʾān with almost no polemical frame, and yet this did not mean that it could not be read polemically.

But such a Qurʾān manuscript could also be read in a very different way. A set of annotations in the Turin manuscript—the only copy that presents Mark's Qurʾān entirely by itself—is remarkably unconcerned with the traditional polemical or apologetic topics. Rather, these annotations focus on philological tasks. Many of these notes, which were almost certainly written by the copyist of the manuscript, attempt to clarify Mark's Latin by providing alternative translations. At verse 2:16, for example ("These are those who have purchased guidance with error . . ."), an annotation above *comparauunt* ("they have purchased") reads *id est emebant*, "that is, 'were buying.'"[50] In such cases the anonymous reader is thinking through the text's meaning and clarifying it by adding paraphrasing glosses.[51] Sometimes these notes solve problems in Mark's text. At verse 2:26, for example, Mark had left a puzzlingly erroneous translation for his readers. Where the Qurʾān says here that by the parable of the mosquito, God "leads many astray," Mark had written *oberrabit in ea multos*. Now unlike the Arabic verb it translates (*yuḍillu*), *oberro* is not normally a transitive verb (it means "he wanders," not "he makes [someone else] wander"), even though in Mark's formulation it must be read as such to give the clause any meaning. The annotator duly corrects this awkward usage in an interlinear note: "that is, 'he will make wander.'"[52] This last note, however, and a number of notes like it, make us suspect that this reader actually knows Arabic and is reading Mark's text alongside an Arabic version of the Qur'ān, for in thus making the intransitive Latin verb transitive, this annotator has corrected the text perfectly. His correction, in fact, sounds almost like the grammatical explanation of an Arabic teacher.

A series of notes that includes material actually drawn from standard Arabic Qur'ān exegesis confirms this suspicion. Several passages of the second surah, for example, begin with the phrase *wa-idh*, "and when," each typically introducing a new, short narrative involving some earlier prophet (see, for example, 2:63, 2:84, 2:93, 2:124, 2:125). Often, Qur'ānic commentators have pointed out that to understand this repeated phrase properly, one must supply the imperative verb *udhkurū*, "remember," between the "and" and the "when," yielding "and *remember* when"—for the Qur'ān reader is being asked to recall the experiences of earlier prophets.[53] Strikingly enough, the annotator of this manuscript supplies the exact Latin translation of this verb at all of the passages I have just listed, writing above "and when" (*et quando*) in verse 2:93, for example, the word *mementote*—"remember" in the plural imperative just as in the Arabic commentaries.[54] He may also have been consulting Qur'ānic commentaries when he wrote "that is, 'dryness' (*siccuritas*)" over the word "death" (*mors*) at verse 2:164. Here the Qur'ān had told of how God "gives life to the earth after its death."[55] Qur'ānic commentators, seeking to explain what exactly this clause meant, had observed that it referred to the state of the earth "when rain did not fall upon it," on account of which "it did not bring forth vegetation . . . and so in this way it was like a dead thing."[56] The annotator may have derived his gloss from the context, but his concise "dryness" captures well the gist of the Muslim exegesis of this passage. That he so clearly knows the traditional Muslim interpretation of other portions of the text makes us wonder whether Arabic commentaries are the source of this note as well. What is unmistakable here, however, is that, at least as he made these annotations, this reader was not interested in the standard concerns of polemic or apologetic. Rather, he was reading the text in the philological way that Robert and Mark and the other translators did when they translated the Qur'ān—paying minute attention to the meaning of words, turning here and there to the Arabic original and to Qur'ānic commentaries to help him understand difficult passages.[57]

When we look, therefore, at how Mark of Toledo's *Liber Alchorani* was read in the manuscripts that present it as a stand-alone text, we find written out in the margins precisely the set of dual reading practices that has preoccupied us so extensively in this book. In the Vienna manuscript, a concern to correct the text serves the interests of what is primarily traditional polemical and apologetic reading. In the Turin manuscript, philology predominates entirely. A set of marginalia in the sixteenth-century fragmentary manuscript now in Milan (BA MS R 113 sup.)—which may well, like the Turin manuscript, have originally presented Mark's Latin Qur'ān without any supplementary texts—intriguingly combines both of these approaches.[58] In these and the handful of other manuscripts of Mark's version, we see once again how willingly later readers reworked the Latin Qur'ān's framing and how energetically they introduced their own concerns into the marginal annotations they wrote on the manuscripts that came into their hands. Archbishop Rodrigo Jiménez de Rada had commissioned this new Latin Qur'ān as part of his orchestration of a crusade against the Muslim Almohads of the south, and Mark of Toledo's own preface had urged a highly polemical reading of the Qur'ānic text.[59] While it is clear that his Latin Qur'ān continued to be packaged for just such a reading, and that, indeed, it continued to be read in just that way, we cannot help but notice that two of the seven extant manuscripts of this translation indicate that it eventually found an audience with very different concerns. The later annotator who carefully inserted transliterated surah titles and made marginal notes based on his knowledge of the Arabic text, and the reader of the Turin manuscript comparing Mark's Latin text with the Arabic original and Qur'ānic commentaries, were doing things—undertaking philological inquiries—that neither Mark nor his episcopal patron probably expected when they produced this Latin Qur'ān. And yet Mark himself had made it much easier for later readers of his translation to apply such philological methods to it because of the very choices he had made as a translator. A stand-alone version of his Latin Qur'ān, with its perpetuation of the Qur'ānic surah names and its prosaic, literal translation in which the Latin text follows the Arabic word order carefully, could, of course, be read in the polemical mode so familiar in Latin Christendom; but it was also the perfect object for a careful, philological comparison with the Arabic original, a much more suitable object, at any rate, than was Robert's elaborate paraphrase.

Flavius Mithridates' Latin-Arabic Qur'ān Edition

Flavius Mithridates' translation in 1480–81 of two Qur'ānic surahs was contrived—on the surface at least—for a reader like that annotator of the Turin manuscript of Mark's Latin Qur'ān that I just described; for, in its earliest manuscript, this new Latin version and the Arabic original were presented to readers in parallel columns that would have facilitated the sort of line-by-line comparison of the Latin and Arabic texts that the Turin reader undertook. In offering Christian readers the Latin Qur'ān and the Arabic side by side, Mithridates was, in fact, clearly part of a trend that, we will see in the concluding chapter, actually began a generation earlier in Juan de Segovia's now-lost trilingual Qur'ān (Arabic, Castilian, and Latin); a trend, moreover, that will continue in Egidio da Viterbo's translation and edition a generation later. This trend is a vivid sign of an interesting development in Christian Qur'ān reading in this period—that it had become connected to the humanist, and especially biblical humanist, movements which produced facing-page, polyglot editions of classical and scriptural texts in significant numbers, and did so specifically to facilitate the parallel reading of texts in their original and translated forms. But in the case of Mithridates' translation and edition we should not allow ourselves to be misled by this seemingly humanist framing, for, as we will see, it was really meant more for show than for scholarship, his real goal being to create an expensive and exotic book that a wealthy layman would find attractive. Indeed, we cannot help but be struck by the fact that, at least in its original manuscript form (Vatican City, BAV, MS urb. lat. 1384), Mithridates' edition can only be described as—in Angelo Michele Piemontese's words—"ornato" and "bellissimo."[60] No other European version of the Qur'ān from this four-hundred-year period is so beautiful. We have already seen that the Qur'ān, without ceasing to be considered an heretical scripture, could be conceived of and experienced as a scholastic textbook. Here we will see that it could be packaged and presented as an expensively ornate collector's book as well, once again without ceasing, necessarily, to be reckoned a dangerous fraud.

As I mentioned earlier, the two surahs of this edition that actually were published were only a fragment of what was intended, judging from Mithridates' introduction to them, to be a much larger project: a polyglot Qur'ān with complete Arabic, Hebrew, Syriac, and Latin versions, all appearing side by side.[61] It is not at all clear that this idea of a four-language Qur'ān really originated with Duke Federigo—Mithridates' assertion of this may well be part of his extravagant praise of him—and Mithridates says, moreover, that he was also encouraged to take on this task by one of his other patrons, the cardinal archbishop of Molfetta, who at this time, as Bobzin points out, was Giovanni Battista Cibò, who was later Pope Innocent VIII.[62] Wherever the idea came from, the parallels between it and the polyglot Bibles are obvious, not least in Mithridates' description of the project: "In short, each language will be placed in its [own] column, but the most noteworthy statements among them, which contain a great deal of ambiguity as they are set forth in Arabic, are put into each translation, and at the end of the work are clarified."[63] We were to have, then, parallel columns of text in multiple languages, accompanied by explanatory notes. Mithridates does not explain to us exactly why such an edition was desirable to him or his patrons. Such a collation of differing Qurʾān translations could hardly serve the same purpose that polyglot Bibles did: making the Bible available to biblical scholars in all the versions in which it was actually used in the Christian world. The Qurʾān apparently did not exist in this period in any of these languages besides Arabic and Latin, after all.[64]

Yet there is no doubting the general parallels of all this with the polyglot biblical editions that were the most striking achievements of the biblical humanist movement. Such editions, with the original languages and ancient and modern translations laid out in parallel columns alongside commentaries, were not, of course, entirely novel in the Renaissance.[65] Yet the biblical humanists produced these polyglot Bibles in unprecedented numbers in the sixteenth and seventeenth centuries.[66] The urge to create them was—it must be added—hardly disinterested, as Jerry Bentley has observed. Cardinal Cisneros, the driving force behind the Complutensian Polyglot, the first great multilingual Bible of the biblical humanist period, aimed at far more than academic philology. He hoped, for example, that his polyglot version of the Christian scriptures would encourage piety; and he was anxious as well for it to help "unify the disparate religious and cultural elements of early modern Spain."[67] But even though such multilingual projects were connected with particular theological or religious goals, we cannot help but notice that they were specifically created to facilitate philological investigation. That is the immediate point, after all, of putting a text in one language next to a version of the same text in another language—so that one can compare how the languages work; so that one can use a sound knowledge of one language to gain a fuller knowledge of another; so that one can dwell upon fine points of grammar, morphology, and usage. Facing-page editions bring philological questions to the surface, pushing aside—without necessarily suppressing—doctrinal or theological issues.

The original manuscript of Mithridates' Qurʾān translation must be seen as privileging philology in this same way, at least on the surface. The Latin and Arabic texts are written, respectively, in the inner and outer of the two columns on each page (see figure 6), the end of each Arabic verse

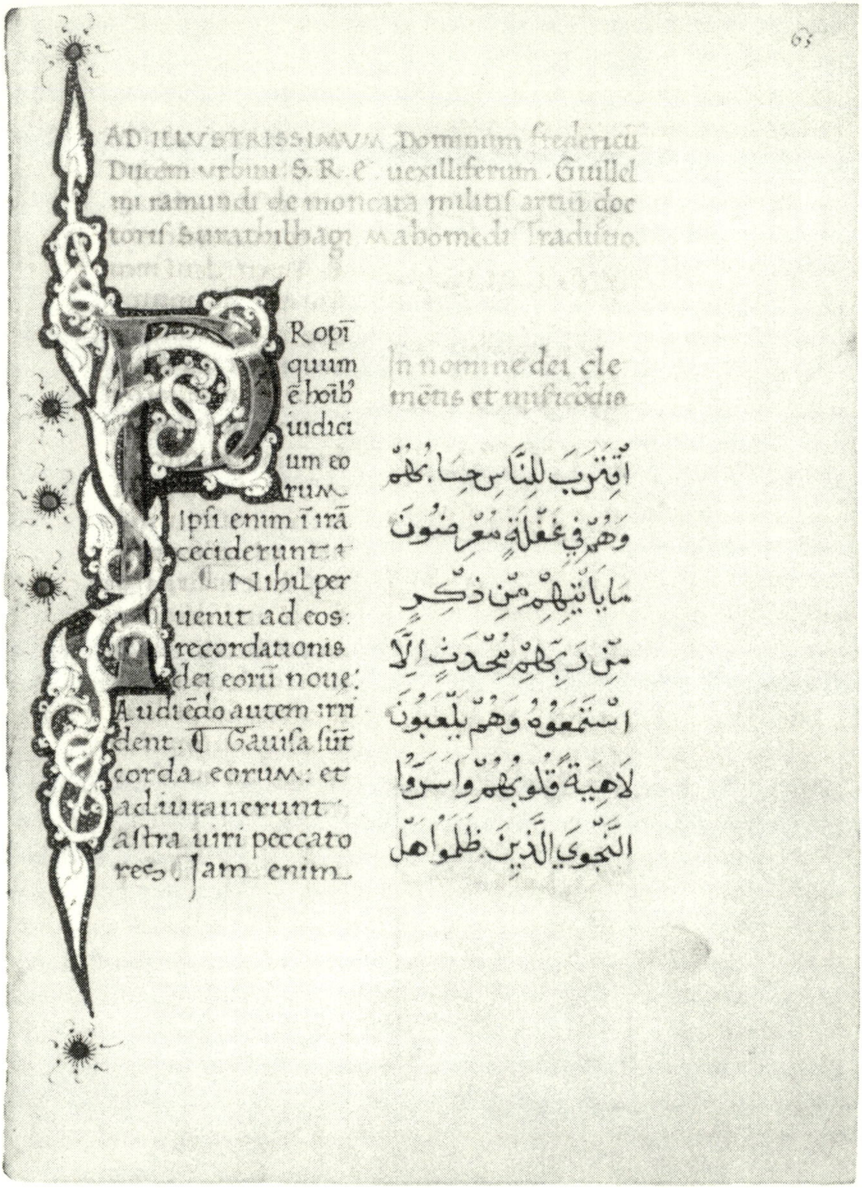

Figure 6. Vatican City, BAV, MS urb. lat. 1384, fol. 65r. The first page of Flavius Mithridates' edition and translation of surah 21 (mistakenly given the title here of surah 22: *Surathilhagi* = Surah of the Ḥajj). The illuminated P is decorated with gold leaf and is 76 mm high by 35 mm wide. © Biblioteca Apostolica Vaticana (Vatican).

signaled by a red mark that looks like a large inverted comma, the beginning of each Latin verse indicated by a prominent paragraph sign in alternating red and blue. The copyists have, moreover, made sure that the Arabic and Latin versions of each verse always appear side by side—the text of one language never falls behind that of the other, as happens in one manuscript of Egidio da Viterbo's bilingual Qur'ān.[68] The eyes of readers who know both languages, or of readers who know one well and want to learn the other better, are quickly and effectively drawn into comparing the two versions.

Other elements of the layout and framing of this edition embody the same concern with introducing readers to the original Arabic—and Islamic—form of the Qur'ānic text. Mithridates has preserved the Muslim divisions of the Qur'ān into *ḥizb*s (or sixtieths) and *ʿushr*s (groups of ten verses), these words appearing at the standard places in the text in Latin transliteration and in Arabic, the former inserted into the Latin column, the latter appearing in the outer margins. It is somewhat troubling, however, that while in general the Arabic text seems to have been carefully copied and vocalized, the respective words for these divisions are oddly transliterated into Latin, Mithridates giving us *hisbi*, and *haxra*, respectively, though neither final vowel is really correct (we should have either no final vowel, or *-un*). Furthermore, the Arabic orthography of the word *ḥizb* in the two places where it occurs is puzzling (fols. 70r and 81v), for the first consonant has a dot above it, giving us a *khā* rather than the required *ḥā*. This reminds us of the fact that this translation is very poor indeed,[69] something that the careful coordinating of the two versions on the page brings out all the more forcefully. Right on the second page of his edition, in fact, the reader is confronted with Mithridates' embarrassing misreading of *nūḥī*, "we communicated, revealed," as *Nūḥ*, meaning "Noah": "We sent before you Noah," where we should have "We sent before you none but men whom we inspired."[70]

The impressive philological layout of the Arabic and Latin texts in this manuscript, is not, therefore, matched by much exacting philological care in translation, transliteration, or, as we will see, commentary;[71] but the approach to the Qur'ān embodied here is also, nevertheless, strikingly nonpolemical. Rather than being surrounded by a hedge of other anti-Islamic texts, as Robert of Ketton's version usually was and Mark of Toledo's translation sometimes was, Mithridates' Latin Qur'ān is accompanied in this codex only by two astrological works. The first is his own Latin translation of a treatise called *On the Celestial Images* and attributed to one Ibn al-

Ḥātim, which appears here (fols. 1ra–27ra) with Arabic and Latin in facing columns, the Latin text graced by a number of beautiful miniatures. This is followed by a work on eclipse computations attributed to Mithridates himself (folios 30ra–61vb).[72] In this manuscript, therefore, the companions of the Latin Qurʾān are works of natural philosophy for which the Arabs were admired, not polemical treatises pointing out the defects of Islam. Nor is Mithridates' bilingual Qurʾān preceded by a hostile preface.[73] His brief introductory remarks, in fact, contain nothing that could be construed as an attack on Islam and its holy book or as a defense of Christianity from Islamic polemic.

The brief set of notes (folios 86va–87vb) on these two surahs that Mithridates added at the end has these same tendencies. While purporting to be the work of a learned philologist, the scholarship here is at best unimpressive, at worst shockingly misleading; yet at no point do the notes really indulge in polemic. They are supposed to explain the words that Mithridates simply transliterated rather than translating. Yet even in this original manuscript, this commentary is clearly not complete. It proceeds in alphabetical order, covering all the transliterated words in the two surahs up through the letter "m," but then suddenly leaves off, even though there are two transliterated words, *il rahmani* (*al-Raḥmān*, "the Merciful") and *il zabur* (*al-Zabūr*, "the Psalms"), both of which begin with letters after "m," which have not been commented on.[74] Instead, with no intervening rubric or title, a rather different reference work—a simple Arabic-Latin lexicon—begins on the immediately following folio (88ra), as if it were part of this commentary, though it clearly is not.[75] What seems to have happened is that two quite different works, Mithridates' alphabetically organized commentary on his Qurʾān translation and an Arabic-Latin glossary, have been merged together, part of the former, apparently, having been lost in the process.[76]

Despite its fragmentary nature, however, there is no mistaking this commentary's (at least superficial) philological orientation.[77] Its interest in linguistic issues is apparent from the very first note:

> *Al. Il. Ul.* are the articles just as in our [Italian] vernacular, *lo. la.* And sometimes, according to the variation of the preceding vowels, it is pronounced in uttered speech *il* and sometimes *ul*, since these Arabs only have three vowels, *a. i. u.* But the Hebrews have only two articles, manifestly *ha* and <missing word>, and the Chaldeans have one, manifestly *yath*.[78]

Mithridates insists on explaining the Arabic article here because it occurs in several of the transliterated terms in his Latin Qurʾān, and his note is the work of a scholar of Semitic languages examining this part of speech from the point of view of comparative linguistics. This comparative element recurs in later notes.

But most of the commentary is concerned with the meanings of nouns or proper names that appear in the two surahs, on the model of the second note: "*Baith*: that is house or temple, whence *baith al macdas*, that is the temple of the sanctuary."[79] Here Mithridates gives his reader the correct definition of the word *bayt*, and then offers an example of its use with this meaning, *bayt al-maqdis*, "the Holy House," the standard Arabic name for Jerusalem. In this case, as in the case of the Arabic article, he is explaining a single linguistic element that actually only occurs as part of longer transliterated phrases in his Latin text.[80]

What becomes clear, however, as one reads these notes is that while Mithridates knows a range of basic features of both the Arabic language and the Islamic religion, his knowledge of them does not seem to go at all deep; rather, he is often passing off as detailed and authentic knowledge of how Muslims understand the Qur'ān what is in some cases clearly pure (and rather inept) guesswork and in others information drawn from thoroughly non-Islamic sources—often Jewish ones—that have no real bearing on the Qur'ānic text at all.[81] As a result, while he has no trouble with simple matters,[82] his commentary is sometimes comically misinformed and misleading. His assertion that *Muslimīn* (plural of *Muslim*) means "the saved"[83] is troubling enough: *Muslim* means "one who submits," and this is something that any Qur'ān translator should have known. Even more disturbing is his note at verse 21:85, where the Qur'ān speaks of Isma'īl, Idrīs, and *dhū al-kifl*. Now this last term, literally meaning something like "the possessor of security/guarantee," presented real interpretive difficulties. Mithridates, unsure what to do with it, translated the first term, *dhū*, meaning "the possessor of," quite wrongly as *genus* ("the nation, people"). The second term he simply transliterated, *ilchifli*, and then observed in the accompanying note that this term "is the religious name in the sect of Muhammad for those who suffer for their devotion to him."[84] This looks like pure speculation based largely on the immediate context: the second half of the verse does imply that Isma'īl, Idrīs, and *dhū al-kifl* did indeed suffer for their devotion, but this does not at all tell us to whom Muslims believed the third term referred. Qur'ānic commentators did not speak with one voice about this, but they all agreed that this term referred to a specific person (both here and in 38:49) rather than a group of people, seeing it as a second name for Ezekiel, or Elijah, or another prophet, or identifying him with a magician named Bishr (or Bashīr) son of Ayyūb, or specifying that he was simply a righteous man among the Children of Israel, but not a prophet.[85]

Most egregious, perhaps, is Mithridates' insistence that the term *musrifīn* ("the excessive, prodigal ones") in verse 21:9 "is the name of a sect that they say was in the time of Noah." Here he was steered in the wrong direction by his own ineptness as a translator, for just previously in 21:7, as we have seen, he had mistaken the verb *nūḥī*, "we communicated, revealed," for *Nūḥ*, meaning "Noah," and so had wrongly assumed that this passage referred to the builder of the ark, when it most certainly did not. He then went on to explain in his note that this sect from the time of Noah did not believe in paradise or the immortality of the soul, this suggesting that he had some idea of the literal meaning of the term (SRF IV means "to exceed, go beyond what is right"), but these particular wrong beliefs seem closer to those of the biblical Sadducees than to the polytheists and unbelievers to whom Qurʾānic commentators assume the term refers.[86]

Mithridates' commentary, then, was often as execrable as his translation, but there is some real learning mixed in with these mistakes. Somehow he has gathered that at least some Muslim commentators believed that Gog and Magog were very short ("the Arabs say that they are men of small stature so that they do not exceed the measure of one arm"),[87] and he knows that they were believed by Muslims to be connected to Alexander the Great. Yet we nowhere find evidence of the sort of sophisticated, detailed knowledge of Islamic Qurʾān exegesis or tradition that we find quite frequently in the twelfth-century annotations on Robert of Ketton's Latin Qurʾān, or that we will see on such thorough display in the notes on Egidio da Viterbo's Qurʾān edition of a few generations later. While Mithridates seems to know something of the etymology of the Arabic word *jahannam* (21:98), meaning "hell" or "hellfire" and drawn, like the English "Gehenna," from the biblical Hebrew, he tells us nothing about the rich Islamic traditions, some of which personify it as a vast beast pulled along by seventy thousand angels, while others consider it merely the name for one part of a multilevel hell.[88] He seemingly knows nothing of the complex set of Muslim traditions that saw Idrīs (21:85, mentioned earlier), as a prophet who ascended into heaven while still alive, and was often identified with the biblical Enoch or Elijah, or with Hermes Trismegistus, and who was typically thought to have lived at some point between Adam and Noah. Instead, rather suspiciously, we are told that Idrīs "is the name of a prophet who Muhammad says existed at the time of Abraham, but Abū Bakr says he was the anointed Jesus," views for which I know no Islamic precedent.[89]

In fact, where Mithridates' notes seem particularly erudite, they tend to be based on irrelevant Jewish traditions rather than Arab or Muslim sources. His commentary on the name *ʿĀd* (*Iadus*) in 22:42 is an eloquent example. The standard Islamic view is that ʿĀd, like Thamūd, the proper name that appears just after it, refers to a numerous ancient people who lived after the time of Noah.[90] Mithridates gives his readers a very different interpretation:

> I have found in the books of the Kabbalah of the Jews that *Iadus* was a certain Simeon Justus son of Jehozadak, the high priest who lived for a long time after the great synod convened in the time of Ezra. In his days Alexander of Macedon came in order to lay waste to Jerusalem, and this Simeon came out to meet him. When Alexander saw him, he prostrated himself on the earth and venerated him and conceded to him whatever he asked. And the servants of that man marveled at why he did this, to whom [Alexander] said, 'do not be amazed. I saw his image always in battle, and I vanquished."[91]

Where the Qurʾān spoke of ʿĀd, a term Muslims believed referred to a whole people contemporary with Noah, Mithridates saw a reference to Jaddus (or Jaddua), a Jewish high priest who, Josephus tells us, managed to persuade Alexander to spare Jerusalem in a manner very like that described here (*Jewish Antiquities*, 11, 329–36). The same legend appears in the Talmud (Yoma 69a), and that version is even more similar to Mithridates' account—here Jaddus is referred to as Simeon the Just, for example, and Alexander explains that he bowed down before him because "His image it is which wins for me in all my battles."[92] This note demonstrates a certain amount of sophisticated knowledge, but not of Islamic thought. It is Jewish tradition that Mithridates knows, his version conflating aspects of Josephus' account with that of the Talmud.[93] He claims to have learned this "in the books of the Kabbalah," so he may well have been using some later account in which the two earlier versions had already been merged, and since Mithridates' knowledge of Kabbalah is undisputed, such a later source may well have been a Kabbalistic one in the narrow sense.

Mithridates' reading of the Qurʾān, therefore, and the kind of reading that his edition and translation were meant to foster, were unlike anything we have seen before. There is some evidence elsewhere that he had a real interest otherwise in anti-Islamic polemic. The two Qurʾānic quotations in his sermon before Pope Sixtus VI occur in a rather apologetic context.[94] Yet there is no obvious polemic in his Latin-Arabic Qurʾān edition, but rather an impressive appearance of philology. Nevertheless, when probed, all this philological apparatus proves rather defective. So while polemical concerns were not, then, the main motivation behind this work, it is hard to see how philological concerns were either, for there is good reason to think that Mithridates—when he set his mind to it—really was capable of sound Semitic and Arabic philology. He was truly learned in the Hebrew language,[95] and his translation of the astronomical work of Ibn al-Ḥātim in the same manuscript appears to be competent.[96] Even more striking, however, is the evidence residing in another Vatican codex contemporary with Mithridates' Qurʾān translation that contains, among other things, a few surahs of the Qurʾān in Arabic, but written in Hebrew characters. Abundant Latin notes in several hands, from the late fifteenth and early sixteenth centuries, litter every folio of the Qurʾānic surahs. The great majority of these notes are by a single author writing in vivid reddish-purple ink between the lines and in the margins. Intriguingly enough, at the end of his notes, this particular annotator wrote "Finis: Fl[avius] Guillelmus Raimundus Monacates."[97] This, of course, is one of the several slightly different names that Mithridates used,[98] indicating, as Piemontese has argued, that the author of these many Qurʾānic glosses is Mithridates himself.[99] If so, then we are faced with an intriguing puzzle, for if we look closely at these notes, we might easily conclude that they were written by an entirely different person from the inept scholar who produced the Qurʾān edition in Vatican MS urb. lat. 1384. For one thing, the author of these Qurʾānic glosses is relying extensively on Qurʾānic commentaries.[100] At 22:19, for example, where the Qurʾān tells of "The two adversaries" who "are opponents who contend concerning their Lord," we find an interlinear note above the word *khaṣmān* ("two adversaries"). Just who or what these two adversaries were is not at all clear in the Qurʾānic text, and medieval Arabic Qurʾān commentators often asserted that they are to be understood, as a hadith quoted by al-Ṭabarī put it, as "the unbelievers and the believers who dispute about their Lord."[101] The Latin gloss at this point in the Vatican manuscript simply reproduces this view, identifying the *khaṣmān* as "two, namely, the faithful and the unbelievers."[102] Yet we have seen that one of the things that makes Mithridates' translation of the Qurʾān so defective is his apparent failure to consult just such Qurʾānic commentaries as this "Flavius Guillelmus Raimundus Monacates" was clearly turning to here and at many other points in these notes.

Furthermore, the interlinear glosses in this Arabic Qurʾān manuscript amount, as Piemontese has noted, almost to an interlinear translation. Bizarrely enough, Flavius Monacates gets things perfectly correctly here that

Flavius Mithridates botched badly in his translation. So at 22:5, where Mithridates translated *rayb* ("doubt") entirely wrongly as *intellectus* ("understanding"), this glossator properly gives us *dubium* ("doubt"); where in the same verse Mithridates had wrongly read *ardhal* as *arḍ* ("earth") and so gave his reader *terram*, the glossator rightly recognizes it as an elative form qualifying the following word *al-ʿumur* ("span of life") and therefore translates the whole phrase, much more adequately, as "a viler life" (*viliorem vitam*).[103] If indeed the Flavius Guillelmus Raimundus Monacates who wrote these Qurʾānic glosses is the same man as Flavius Mithridates, then we must conclude that Mithridates surely knew good Qurʾānic philology when he saw it, and that, therefore, philological concerns can hardly have been the real motivation behind his edition, translation, and commentary on the two Qurʾānic surahs, for he must have known that his work there was not even close to adequate.[104]

The real driving force behind this project is vividly suggested, in fact, by something else: the sumptuous physical features of its original (and at least one later) manuscript. I have already cited Piemontese's description of it as "ornato" and "bellissimo."[105] This is no exaggeration. Upon opening this vellum manuscript, we find a glorious title medallion, of the kind frequently found in deluxe Florentine manuscripts of this period,[106] laying out the contents of the manuscript.[107] The first page of the text proper, the beginning of Ibn al-Ḥātim's treatise, has elegant gold, blue, green, and red floral ornamentation in the top, bottom, and side margins, in patterns common in Renaissance Italian manuscripts.[108] At the bottom of the folio we find the shield of the Dukes of Urbino, since the manuscript was dedicated to Federigo da Montefeltro. Ibn al-Ḥātim's astronomical treatise has a series of handsome illuminations featuring the images of the signs of the zodiac, all of them drawn in medallions 50 mm in diameter, often against dark blue backgrounds. When we come to Mithridates' preface to his Qurʾān edition (see figue 6 above), we are greeted by a beautiful illuminated initial P at the beginning of surah 21, fully 76 mm high and 35 mm wide, with flourishes extending from the top of the page to the bottom. The initial itself is in vivid gold; the vining interlace that ornaments it is in white, with blue, red, and green used to form the background. The initial at the beginning of the other surah is quite similar.[109] As Piemontese has pointed out, the Arabic text has been copied in good oriental calligraphy,[110] while the Latin text is in a humanist book hand.

Christopher de Hamel has described the very period in which Mithridates produced his Qurʾān edition as the age "of the great building of libraries for the princes of the Renaissance."[111] Here was a beautiful, expensive book designed to appeal to just such a princely collector, for that, famously, is just what Federigo da Montefeltro, the dedicatee of this manuscript, was. He probably had, as Cecil Clough has pointed out, more wealth to spend on patronage than any other contemporary prince in Italy, and "perhaps even in western Christendom," for he possessed an annual income of at least fifty thousand ducats.[112] It was said that Federigo spent thirty thousand ducats, a simply vast sum, on manuscript books alone, many of them with just the design features contained in the manuscript of Mithridates' Qur'ān edition.[113] Like other Renaissance princes, therefore, he was acquiring a huge, humanist library "for"—as Clough put it elsewhere—"the social status it bought."[114]

Moreover, that a copy of part of the Qur'ān should have figured among Federigo's many deluxe books is hardly surprising given the great fondness of wealthy fifteenth-century Italians for Islamic goods of all kinds. Islamic carpets, glass, and ceramics all "acquired widespread cachet" in lay Italian society, as Rosalind Mack has shown, "as leading elites throughout the peninsula collected them in increasing quantities."[115] Islamic works of art, then, like expensive manuscripts, were signs of high status, and their public display won admiration in the increasingly secular society of northern Italy.[116] Particularly suggestive in this connection is the widely shared fondness in this period for paintings that contained Arabic (or at least Arabic-looking) writing. In the Church of S. Giovanni in Monterrone at Matera, for example, St. James the Lesser is depicted wearing a mantle which has pseudo-Arabic decoration painted in white on red.[117] "Such exotic inscriptions," Mack intriguingly observed, "served principally as erudite accessories, meant to be recognized but not necessarily read."[118] Much the same thing could be said of Mithridates' Qur'ān edition. Not only is its translation deeply flawed, making it largely a waste of time to read, but, unlike most other Latin Qur'ān manuscripts, it contains almost no marginalia: it seems not, in fact, to have been read with any intensity. It was—apparently as were not a few of Federigo's other beautifully produced but textually flawed manuscripts—meant rather more to be collected and displayed than read.[119] In fact, I suggest, the side-by-side Arabic and Latin texts and the supposedly erudite notes are really meant primarily to add to this book's collectability. They helped make its "humanist bibliophile" owner feel that not only did he possess an exotic, Islamic book, but one that had been properly valorized by the trappings of humanist scholarship.[120] That Mithridates, who seems to have been a truly learned linguist, would take part in the creation of such a thoroughly unscholarly book should not, by the way, surprise us—"he was not always scrupulous," Alastair Hamilton has said of him, "certain that nobody could check his sources"; and he had a hand in other similarly questionable scholarly enterprises.[121]

Whether this Latin-Arabic Qurʾān edition was Mithridates' own hasty, uncorrected work or the defective work of someone else that he passed off as his own is impossible to say. What is certain is that it was the product neither of a primarily polemical engagement with the Qurʾān, nor of a truly philological reading of it, though it clearly exemplifies some of that spirit. Rather the Qurʾān here is primarily a kind of consumer commodity, packaged specifically for wealthy lay collectors who "enjoyed being surrounded by books."[122] Moreover, other roughly contemporary Latin Qurʾān manuscripts suggest the same thing. Sometime before 1537, for example, Mithridates' Latin translation of the two surahs, together with the notes that accompanied it in the Vatican manuscript—but without the two astronomical works—were copied into a second Italian manuscript, this one now in Paris (BnF MS lat. 3671).[123] The maker of this manuscript left out not only the astronomical works that accompanied Mithridates' edition in the Vatican manuscript, but also the Arabic text of the two surahs that Mithridates had translated, so that we now have only his rather defective Latin translation. Yet like Mithridates' original manuscript, this one is also both ornate and beautiful, intended to be possessed and admired by a book collector and his friends. The first page of the translation itself is typical of the manuscript's production values throughout. At the top is Mithridates' dedication of the work to Federigo da Montefeltro in elegant humanistic cursive letters, written in green ink. The *basmalah* ("In the name of God, the merciful and compassionate") is in similarly elegant red. The faceted P that begins the surah itself ("Propinquum . . .") is three lines high and written in gold against a deep blue background. The text of the surah is in the same fine humanistic cursive, the bottom margin featuring the coat of arms of the Giustiniani family (figure 7), such coats of arms being commonplace in fine Renaissance manuscripts.[124]

It is worth noticing that many of the physical features of this manuscript, and indeed of its Vatican ancestor, are characteristic of Renaissance books containing specifically classical—rather than scholastic—texts. While Bibles, biblical commentaries, canon-legal works, and scholastic philosophical and theological treatises continued to be copied in Gothic handwriting in this period, and were typically placed on the page in two columns, classical texts were typically copied in humanistic hands and in a single wide

Ad ſſ[m] D. Federicum Ducem Vrbini S.R.E. Vexilliferz
Guiglemi ramundi de Moncata Militis Arcium Doct. Surathil.
hagi Maumethi Traductio. /

In nomine Dei clementis & misericordis.

R opinquū eſt hominibus iudicium eoꝝ. Ipsi
enim in iram ceciderūt. Nihil puenit ad eos re
cordatiōis Dei eoꝝ none. Audiendo aūt irridēt
Gauisa sunt corda corū. et adiunauerūt astra viri peccatoris.
Iam enim ſ similes nobis hoibus carneis. qui uenitis ad nos
magicis: et prʒudetis. Dixit deus meus scio que dicitur. et
que in celo sunt & que i terra: e ipse est auditor scientiarū
oīm hns. Dixerunt nunqd somnias / aut a te ipso dicis aut
poetice loqueris? Cur nō uenit ad nos scriptis suis sicut misit
ad primos? Non crediderūt qui ante eos fuerūt ciuitatum de
struximus eos & effecti sunt credentes: et quod misimus ante
te Noe ad uiros interrogare populū: q recordatur fortasse vos
nescitis: et q fecimus eos corpora nō comedēba cibos neq bea
ti fuerūt. Illis aūt quod promisimus suauimus et liberauim°
eos qui placuerūt nobis. & IL mus zasim destruximus. Iam
ex alcc dedimus nobis scripturas i qbus est memoria vestra
& non cognoscitis. /

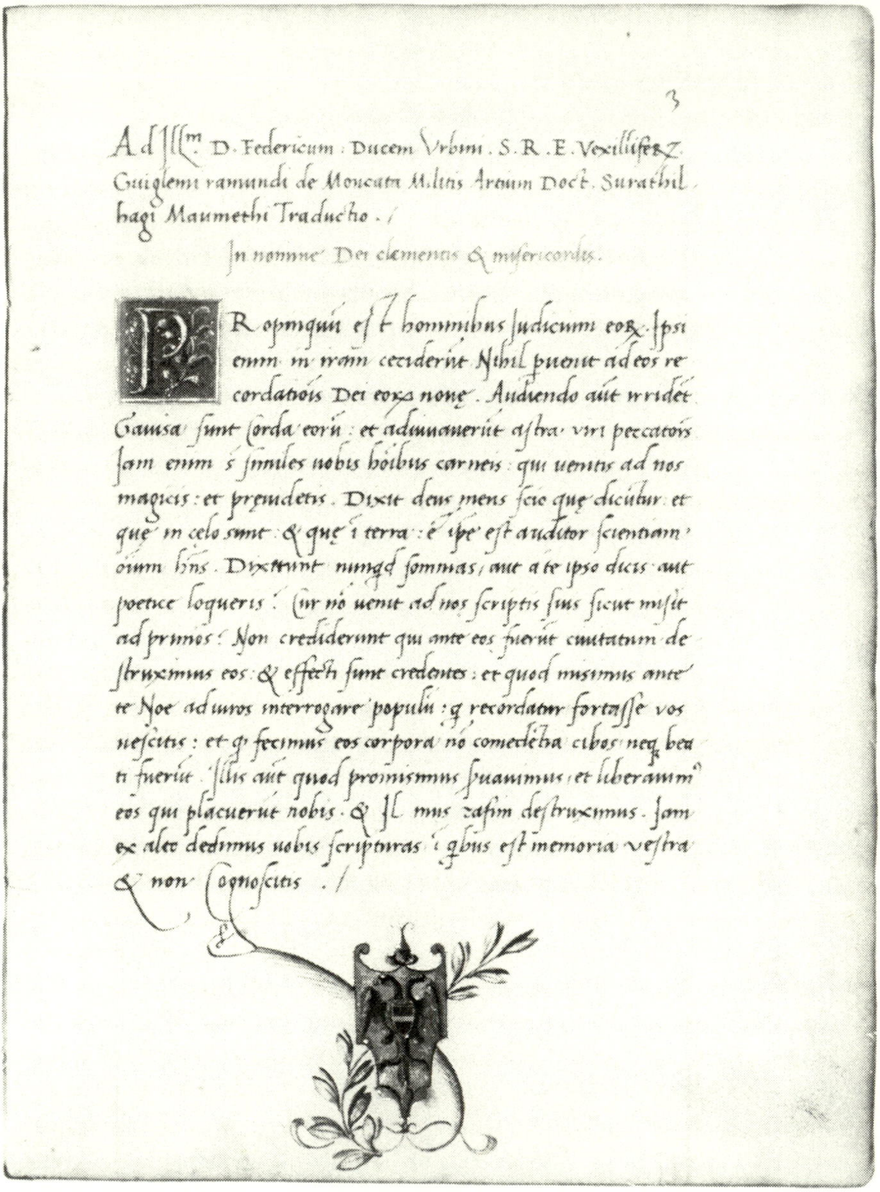

Figure 7. Paris, BnF, MS lat. 3671, fol. 3r. The first page of Mithridates' Latin
translation of surah 21 in an early sixteenth-century Italian manuscript given to a
member of the powerful Venetian Giustiniani family, whose coat of arms appears
at the bottom. By permission of the Bibliothèque nationale de France.

column of text.[125] Inserting the Qur'ān into a classicizing format, as we find it in the Paris manuscript, therefore, seems of a piece with the desire to produce a version of the Qur'ān suited to Renaissance book collectors, whose secular culture and concerns have been much emphasized by modern historians.[126] Islam's holy book, so universally seen in the Latin-Christian world as a pseudoscripture, is partially transformed, by this calligraphic and codicological classicization, into a humanist-approved book, authorized, we might say, by virtue of being dressed in the external form of the Ciceronian and Platonic texts that the same collectors acquired and which had in the same way been domesticated—despite their non-Christian provenance—for consumption by elite Christian society. This Parisian manuscript, then, once the property of another wealthy and powerful Renaissance layman, perpetuates thoroughly the same attitude toward the Qur'ān as did Mithridates' original manuscript, now in the Vatican. A letter of dedication by Friar Gabriele della Volta at the beginning of the Parisian codex, telling us that he could think of no gift either more exceptional (*rarius*) or more agreeable (*gratius*) to give to his patron, Antonio Giustiniani, than Muhammad's irreligious work,[127] eloquently captures this transformation of the Qur'ān into what is in large part a valued consumer commodity.[128] That this is so is also suggested—as it was in the case of the Vatican manuscript—by the fact that this Parisian codex seems not to have been much read. Not even a hint of marginalia can be found in its pages.[129]

In tracing through the evolution of the manuscript versions of Mark of Toledo's and Flavius Mithridates' Latin Qur'āns, I have stressed how each has its own trajectory, Mark's literal translation finding itself read, by virtue of its very literalness, alongside the Arabic Qur'ān in a way that Robert of Ketton's version was not, Mithridates' ornate edition appealing to wealthy late medieval book collectors whose interests lay less in the content than in the sumptuous form and humanist embellishment of their codices. The subtle transformations that Mithridates' version underwent as it was recopied indicate, however, that these trajectories were not invariable. In still another manuscript now in Milan (BA, MS R 113 sup.), closely related to the Parisian manuscript that I have just described, we find Mithridates' Qur'ān translation copied once again in humanist cursive and laid out in the single column of text preferred by humanists for classical works. Yet there is little here to suggest that this manuscript was meant primarily for consumption by lay book collectors. While handsome red ink was used for the titles and for the words discussed in Mithridates' commentary, we have no elegant facetted initials, no dedicatory letter to a wealthy prince, no coat of arms, no glorious title medallion. What began as an expensive book for collectors has now found itself inhabiting a rather workaday codex—one that seems to have been used largely by someone interested primarily, in fact, in apology and polemic.[130] Moreover, the cultural concerns or intellectual preoccupations that shaped one Latin Qur'ān's trajectory as it was recopied and repackaged for new audiences could from time to time shape the paths of other versions as well, and thus we can find Robert's *Lex Mahumet* transformed into an illuminated Italian collector's book as well.[131]

Finally, as we have been working our way through the manuscripts and printed editions of the various Latin Qur'ān translations that circulated in medieval Europe, we have seen the balance between polemical reading and philological reading gradually shifting—Robert's version never freeing itself from a polemical framing, Mark's translation often circulating in just the same way, but occasionally appearing shorn of all polemical packaging, Mithridates' translation originally presented to its readers without any polemical apparatus at all. In turning now to the final Latin version of the Qur'ān from this period, Egidio da Viterbo's remarkable achievement of 1518, we will see that, on the surface at least, philology has finally won out entirely. Yet we will also see that it is worth paying attention to potentially polemical preoccupations that lie just beneath the surface of what is an astonishing monument to philological learning.

Chapter 6

The Manuscripts of Egidio da Viterbo's Bilingual Qur'an: Philology (and Polemic?) in the Sixteenth Century

Where Mithridates' ambition to create a multilingual Qur'ān achieved only partial (and rather flawed) fruition, Egidio da Viterbo managed to have a bilingual Qur'ān produced in 1518 that substantially accomplished many of the goals that Mithridates at least claimed for his work. Here, in parallel columns, the reader found the Arabic Qur'ān, a new Latin translation, exegetical notes, and something we have not seen before: the Arabic text *transliterated* into Latin. While Egidio's motivations in commissioning this new Qur'ān edition are not clear, the final product was one that served the interests of philological Qur'ān readers in remarkable, indeed unprecedented, ways. And, as luck would have it, extensive evidence survives of how at least one, and perhaps two, readers made use of this philological edition before the mid-sixteenth century.

But what is so impressive both about Egidio's edition and about these later readers of it is not merely how concerned with philological issues they were but how unconcerned they appear to have been with traditional anti-Islamic polemic. We should bear in mind, after all, that in the first half of the sixteenth century, as we have already seen, polemical Christian reading of the Qur'ān still flourished: Robert of Ketton's Latin Qur'ān was still being copied together with the twelfth-century notes that so viciously attacked Islam; Johann Albrecht von Widmanstetter was publishing his peculiar abridged Qur'ān with polemical notes informed by his reading of Kabbalah and Greek philosophy; Theodore Bibliander was publishing his edition of Robert's translation with a new set of marginal glosses whose polemical concerns are obvious throughout. Such polemic seems surprisingly absent in Egidio's learned edition, at least on the surface, and in the reactions of the two readers.

Instead, philological reading is pressed forward with breathtaking consistency in ways that fully anticipate the sophisticated philological scholarship of Ludovico Marracci, whose 1698 edition of the Qur'ān is usually singled out as the initiator of modern Qur'ān study in the West. Indeed, in some ways we might see this approach to Qur'ān reading as even more "modern" than Marracci's engagement with the Qur'ān, for Marracci's bilingual edition is still meant specifically to serve the cause of attacking the Qur'ān, its learned translation and notes being joined to a vast refutation of the Qur'ān's teachings. It is true, however, as we will see at the end of this chapter, that there is reason to think that Egidio's edition is not nearly so innocent of polemical preoccupations as it appears on the surface, polemic continuing, perhaps, to play its age-old role even here, in what looks like a work of pure philology. What is certain is that to an astonishing degree, philology has come to predominate over polemic in both the framing of the Qur'ān and in later marginalia added to it.

Philology is predominant in another way as well, for while there are real parallels between Egidio's edition and that of Mithridates—both providing us with the Qur'ān in Arabic and Latin, both attaching notes of a humanist sort to the text—there is a key difference: nothing about Egidio's edition suggests that it, like Mithridates' work, might really have been intended for wealthy consumers who would have valued its ornate appearance and exotic contents over its scholarly merit. Rather, Egidio's edition was a strictly practical and truly learned tool for philologists. There are no expensive illuminations, no dedication medallions, no lovely initials, no dodgy Semitic scholarship in the notes. Both the Qur'ān as the target of Christian attack and the Qur'ān as an elegant consumer product for the superwealthy have been largely pushed aside in favor of the Qur'ān as the object of humanist philology.

Egidio's Edition

Though neither of the surviving manuscripts of Egidio's edition fully reproduces its original format, together they nevertheless provide sufficient information to allow us to reconstruct what the original would have looked like. One of the surviving copies is a manuscript (Milan, Biblioteca Ambrosiana, MS D 100 inf.; see figure 8) produced entirely by the hand of one David Colville,[1] a seventeenth-century Catholic Scot and Orientalist. To this manuscript he appended a long note describing the codex he himself copied—very likely the original manuscript—which was housed in Spain at the library of El Escorial.[2] What Colville found before him, he tells us, was a manuscript of the Qurʾān laid out in four parallel columns. The first column contained the Arabic version itself, while the second consisted of the same text transliterated into Roman characters. In the third column resided a new Latin translation, and in the final column were explanatory notes which were not, however, complete, for they gave out around the fourth or fifth surah, picking up again, as Colville made clear in a later note in his manuscript, at the beginning of surah 38 and continuing for only a few more surahs. The manuscript consisted of two volumes, and at the end of the first of these, Colville observed, a certain Iohannes Gabriel Terrolensis was identified as the copyist of the first three columns. Colville, however, judged that this same Iohannes Gabriel was also the translator, for, from the translation itself, he deduced that the translator was "by nation Spanish or Spanish-Italian" (*fuisse natione Hispanum, vel Hispano-Italum*) because of the Romance idioms that had made their way into his Latin version. At some point after Colville wrote this, he apparently came across information confirming his guess, for in the second part of the prefatory note, which appears to be a later postscript, he notes that Iohannes was in fact a Spaniard from Zaragoza who had copied and translated the text for Cardinal Egidio,[3] and as Natalie Zemon Davis has recently suggested, our Iohannes Gabriel was, in fact, very likely an Aragonese Muslim convert to Christianity.[4] It is particularly fortunate that Colville provided all this information in his preface, because the manuscript that he was copying in El Escorial has since been lost, and there is no other known source which tells us anything about the circumstances under which this bilingual Qurʾān came into being. It is fortunate as well because Colville himself decided to simplify his task by copying only the Arabic text itself and the new Latin translation of it in facing columns, leaving out entirely the Latin transliteration of the Arabic and—or so it appears at first—the notes from the fourth column.

Until recently, Colville's Milan copy was the only known witness to Egidio's original edition, but it turns out that a second copy survives in the Cambridge University Library (MS Mm. v. 26; see figure 9). This much earlier manuscript, probably from the 1530s, is incomplete, containing only parts of the first forty-nine surahs. Yet its layout is intriguing, for, in its conception at least, it clearly conforms to the manuscript design that Colville described for the Escorial manuscript. Like that lost codex, the Cambridge manuscript was originally set out in four parallel columns stretching across the verso and recto of the folios open to the reader. The first column contains the Qurʾān in Arabic (in North African script, just as in Colville's

Caput de Gentibus in Modo

in eo 77. vers.

— stat. in India
diabolos ha in
esse 7 et hat 7 ̃
in ipsa aquamobilg.
in plieg

Jn — oie de p̃j potuerp.

1 Oberong licet de ̃ opre et q quia
terre ay tpg et
licet de tora est ay - exa.

2 in Dio que de hig reliquas g
in tira de que
utica qd lectat et eyciet. — in
pigay pigatore - in et idobg torg
eoteg uidey ee non erut idii sed erut
pena dei terribilis.

3 et in eoilog sut q deputant de des abg
sientia et sequntur une diabolo
a lectul

4 ̃ scripl ̃fde ̃ q y qui Eabeth ander
ipln y faict erore ̃ et dirige ̃
D pra Zagep

5 o Eonęp f estg veg in Ilis de repemtine
g la ay venioncy ay en terre postea in
lga ole postea ernim postea en postea cry
erebli et inerebli
obp formatore et declaracey aby et
efteng a ratiacby qd ueberey tp d
lapp determinal postea efaciny ay
puray postea longlog lamp epet
et ir noby est q ureli.

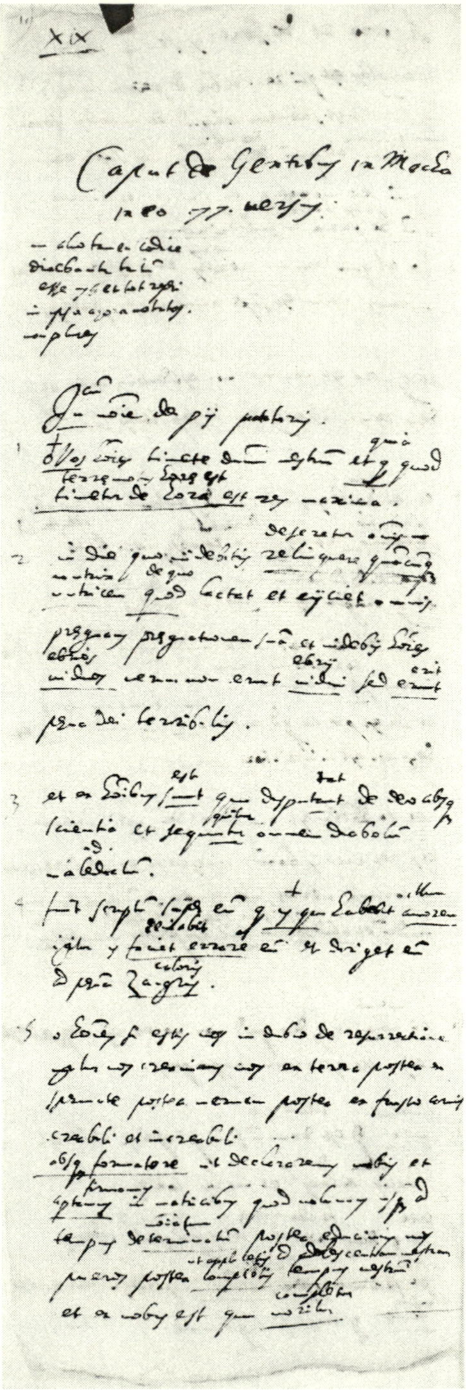

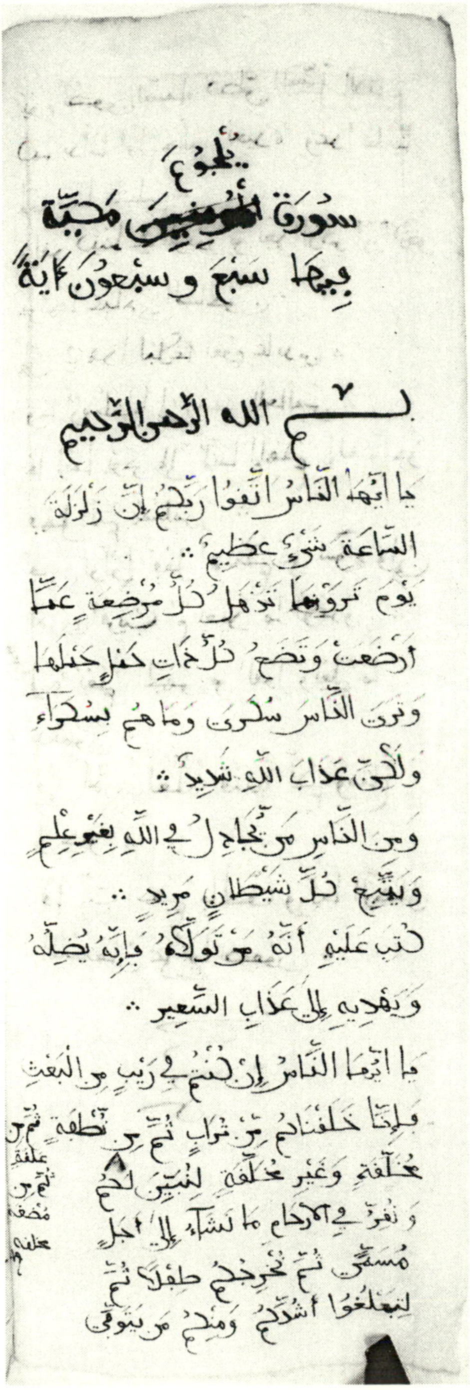

Figure 8. Milan, BA, MS D 100 inf., fols. 311v–312r. The beginning of surah 22 with the Arabic and Iohannes Gabriel Terrolensis's Latin Qur'ān translation on facing pages. Copyright Biblioteca Ambrosiana Auth. No F 120/06.

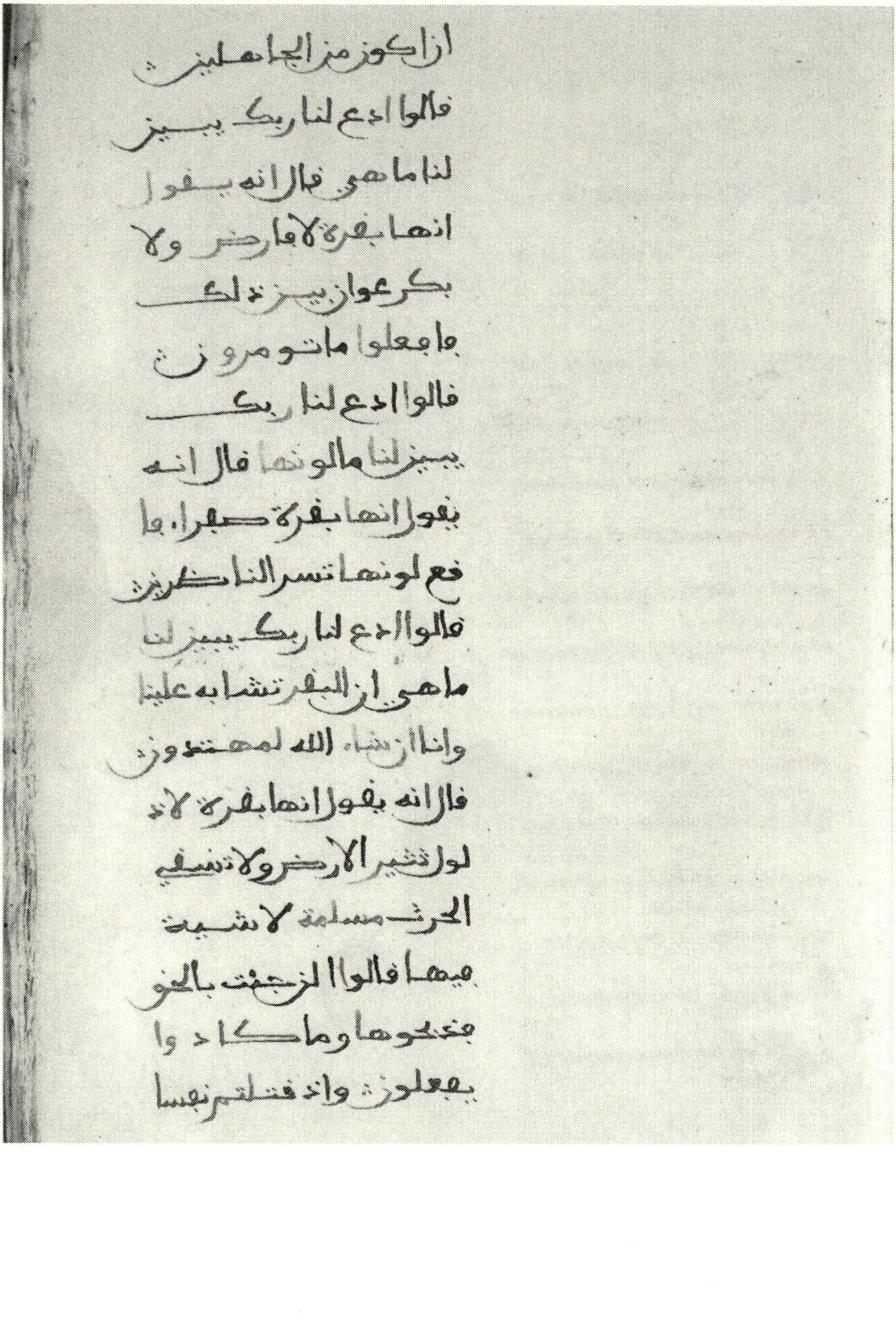
ان اكون من الجاهلين
قالوا ادع لنا ربك يبين
لنا ما هي قال انه يقول
انها بقرة لا فارض ولا
بكر عوان بين ذلك
فافعلوا ما تومرون
قالوا ادع لنا ربك
يبين لنا ما لونها قال انه
يقول انها بقرة صفراء فا
قع لونها تسر الناظرين
قالوا ادع لنا ربك يبين لنا
ما هي ان البقر تشابه علينا
وانا ان شاء الله لمهتدون
قال انه يقول انها بقرة لا ذ
لول تثير الارض ولا تسقي
الحرث مسلمة لا شية
فيها قالوا الان جئت بالحق
فذبحوها وما كادوا
يفعلون واذ قتلتم نفسا

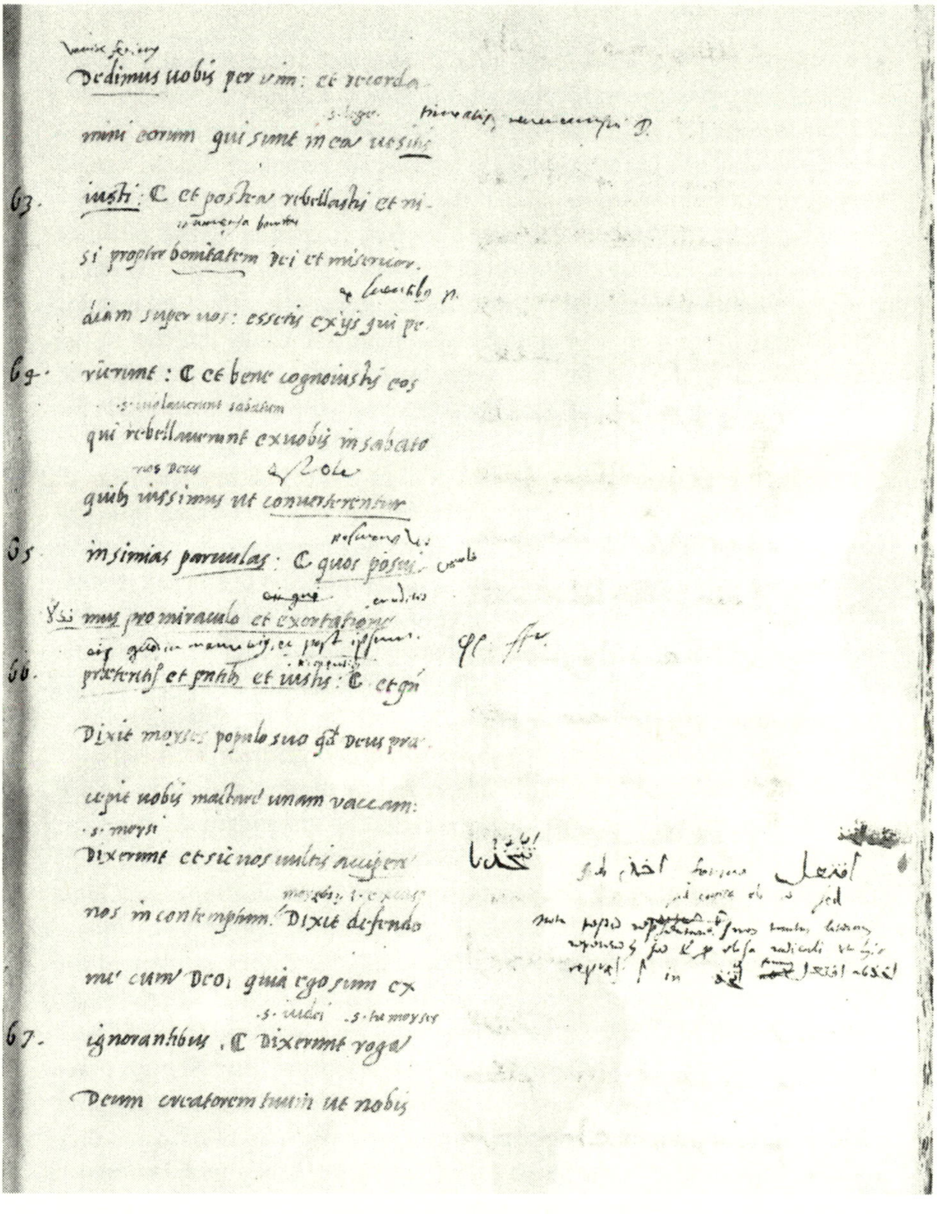

Figure 9. Cambridge, Cambridge University Library, MS Mm. v. 26, fols. 11v–12r, 2:63 ff. The Arabic Qur'ān and Iohannes Gabriel Terrolensis's translation are again side by side. The blank second and fourth columns were intended for the Latin transliteration of the Arabic and the explanatory notes from the now lost Escorial manuscript, but neither was ever copied into this manuscript. The note in the lower right column—including a few Arabic words—was written by a later reader who may well have been William Tyndale. By permission of the Syndics of Cambridge University Library.

copy), while the third has a Latin translation which is clearly just a slightly different version of the text from that found in the Milan manuscript. But, as happened frequently, a manuscript begun was left unfinished, the second and fourth columns in the Cambridge manuscript remaining blank, though they were clearly intended to contain the original manuscript's Latin transliteration of the Arabic and the notes. In fact, it apparently did not take long for the copyist(s) to give up on the idea of reproducing the original as they found it, for after folio 50, the Arabic ceases altogether, so that for many folios (from there to folio 226), the manuscript only has text in the third column. In the last fifty folios, finally, the Latin copyist decided that all this valuable paper ought not be wasted, and used all four columns for the Latin translation.[5]

It is obvious that Egidio's Qur'ān edition was set up in such a way as to overwhelmingly favor philological reading. This should be clear not only from what I have said so far, but also from further evidence provided by the two surviving manuscripts themselves, especially the Milan codex. While that manuscript contains nothing like a title, either at the beginning or in a colophon, the Cambridge manuscript refers to itself as "Book one of the Qur'ān," this suggesting that, like Mark of Toledo's translation, this sixteenth-century Latin Qur'ān originally bore its proper Islamic name.[6] What is even more certain is that this edition perpetuated the specifically Islamic surah names and surah divisions, in both Arabic and Latin. In the Milan manuscript the first surah is preceded by a standard Arabic title: "The Opening of the Book, and it is Meccan, in which are seven verses."[7] The Latin title on that we find on facing pages is much the same: *Clauis Alcoran facta in Mecha ubi continentur septem uersus.*[8] There is an embarrassing translation error here,[9] but otherwise the translator has followed the typical Islamic practice of giving the surah name, the place of its revelation, and the number of verses, and he followed this practice throughout.[10] These proper surah titles appear elsewhere too. In a departure from Muslim practice, running heads appear at the top of each page in Latin or Arabic,[11] and so that these running headlines can be particularly useful to scholars, they include, beginning with the Surah [4] of the Women, an internal reference system: *Azoara .3.a de mulieribus. liber .I.*, "The Third Surah, Book I, Of Women." Like certain other Western readers,[12] Egidio and his translator have followed the practice sometimes adopted in the Islamic world of dividing up the Qur'ān into four books, book 1 ending at the end of the Surah [4] of the Women, book 2 ending at the Surah [18] of the Cave, and book 3 ending at the Surah [37] of the Ranks. The running heads then gradually evolve so that they refer to each surah not only by overall surah number, but also by the surah number of a specific book. The Surah of Joseph, for example, is called "The Eleventh Surah, Joseph, or the Sixth of the Second Book," while the last surah is referred to as "The Hundred Sixteenth Surah, Of Humans, or the Seventy-second of the Fourth Book."[13]

While the running heads do not occur in the Cambridge manuscript, which, as we have seen, is incomplete, vestiges of the division of the Qur'ān into four books do remain, and both the Cambridge and the Milan manuscripts contain something else that is quite innovative for both Europe and the Islamic world: verse numbers, these appearing at the beginning of each verse, though this practice is not consistent in either manuscript.[14] In the original manuscript, however, the verse numbering system must have been fairly thorough, since the explanatory notes that were in the fourth column of the manuscript that Colville copied make extensive use of it and of the internal reference system of the running heads.

The Notes of the Fourth Column

This is a Qur'ān edition meant for serious study, then, by intellectuals who wanted to see the Arabic right next to the Latin translation, who wanted to have the text before them in the format that it has in Arabic manuscripts, who wanted to be able to cite it by surah and verse, and who wanted to be able to look up cited passages quickly. It is a textual scholar's research tool, and nowhere is this philological orientation of Egidio's edition clearer than in the explanatory notes to which I have already alluded. While David Colville indicates in his prefatory note that the fourth column of the manuscript that he copied contained these notes, he appears originally to have intended to leave them out entirely, reproducing only the Arabic text and the Latin translation of the Escorial manuscript. Yet eventually, Colville changed his mind and saw fit to copy a large sampling of these notes anyway, though not in either of the two columns of his own manuscript. Rather, he copied them—they are clearly in his handwriting—on loose sheets of paper, and these sheets, fortunately for us, eventually were placed between the pages of the manuscript, the greater part of them eventually coming to be bound into it.[15] There are twenty-three of them, generally located in the manuscript near the Qur'ānic passages to which they pertain.[16] Most concern surahs 2 and 3, with the largest single concentration relating to the end of the latter.[17] There can be no doubt, moreover, that these notes are drawn from the fourth column of Egidio da Viterbo's original edition, rather than being, say, the work of Colville himself, for he actually describes them as such quite explicitly at the top of the first leaf: *glossae desumpsae ex columna 4a*, "the glosses extracted from the fourth column" (figure 10).[18]

These twenty-three leaves, therefore, preserve at least some of the explanatory notes of Egidio's original edition, though it is impossible to know either how many of the notes survive in this way or to what extent Colville may have abridged them.[19] Formally, however, they clearly follow a pattern. They begin with a reference to the relevant passage using the edition's verse numeration,[20] after which we are given a gloss placed in the mouth of Muslims. While sometimes these glosses are attributed, apparently, to Muslims in general,[21] perhaps more notes are ascribed either to unnamed exegetes,[22] or to specific Qur'ānic commentators, as in a note on the forbidden tree of paradise that reads, "*al-Zamakhsharī* says that that tree which was prohibited to them was a fig" (my italics).[23] At the end of many notes, the reader is supplied with cross-references using the edition's division of the Qur'ān into books, surah numbers, and verses. A note on 2:29, for example, comments that al-Zamakhsharī says, "regarding the Qur'ān, book 4, chapter 4, verse 10," that God made earth before he made heaven.[24]

As these few examples suggest, these notes are overwhelmingly concerned with explaining the Qur'ān using Islamic sources. If we look now at a large and representative sample—the notes on the first two surahs—this becomes even clearer. In fact, of all the earlier sets of Latin Qur'ān annotations, the ones that these notes most resemble are the philological annotations that circulated in Robert of Ketton's translation alongside the hostile polemical notes. Like those twelfth-century annotations, many of these notes explain general Islamic beliefs or common Qur'ānic themes alluded to in the text, as well as certain conventions of Qur'ānic narrative and structure. The first note, for example, concerns the short first surah as a whole, describing accurately its role in the five daily Islamic prayers.[25] Similarly, a note on 2:67 informs us that here "begins the story of the cow on account of which this surah is called *baqarah*."[26]

A much larger portion of the notes imparts what is more properly textual explanation or interpretation. In verse 1:7, Iohannes Gabriel Terrolensis had translated the Qur'ān's *al-maghḍūb ʿalayhim* ("those with whom [God] is angry") rather misleadingly as "evil speakers" (*maledictores*), and *al-ḍāllūn* ("those led astray") more adequately as "those who have gone astray" (*errantes*). A brief note points out, much as interlinear and marginal notes on Robert of Ketton's translation did, that "glossators explain" that

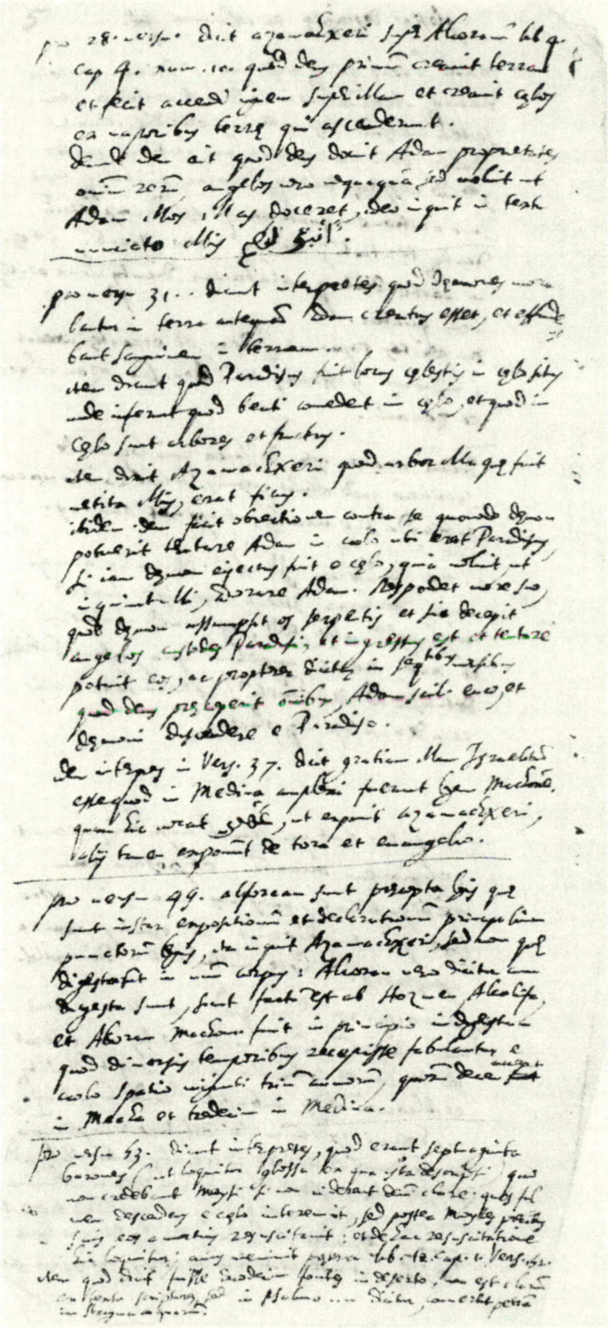

Figure 10. Milan, BA, MS D 100 inf., fol. 5v (though foliated on the side visible here, the reverse of this loose leaf is properly the recto). This is the first of the twenty-three leaves of paper on which David Colville copied substantial portions of the explanatory notes in the lost Escorial manuscript's fourth column. The first note here ("pro 28. versu") quotes the Muslim commentator al-Zamakhsharī ("azamachxeri") on verse 2:29. Copyright Biblioteca Ambrosiana Auth. No F 120/06.

these groups "are Jews" and "Christians."[27] As we saw in the case of those earlier notes, this is indeed precisely what Muslim "glossators," including al-Zamakhsharī, whom the note here specifically mentions, say is meant by these two terms.[28] A note on the mysterious letters at the beginning of surah 2 explains them—once more like notes on Robert's Latin Qur'ān—by drawing on well-known Muslim views of their meaning.[29] The note on 2:138 explaining that *ṣibghah*, "color" or "dye," refers here to "the baptism of the Christians" conforms completely with many interpreters' views on this verse—including the view of al-Zamakhsharī, who is mentioned here specifically once again.[30] Among the explanations that Muslim commentators advanced for the name of Mount *ʿArafāt* in 2:198 was that "Adam and Eve met there and they became reacquainted with each other (*taʿārafā*)."[31] The Latin note here provides the same exegesis,[32] while a long comment on Hārūt and Mārūt, the two angels who taught Solomon magic, follows an Islamic tradition often recounted by Muslim commentators on this verse.[33] Many other examples could be cited.[34]

The author of the notes occasionally assumes advanced learning on the part of his readers. Sometimes they discuss specifically Arabic terms that do not appear in the Latin version in transliteration, such notes being useful, therefore, only to readers who can decipher—at least minimally—the Arabic text itself.[35] Other notes seem intended for readers interested in Hebrew as well as Arabic, as in the case of a long note on 2:104. Here the Qur'ān calls on believers to say to Muhammad, not *rāʿinā*, a relatively rare word meaning "Take care of us!" or "Listen to us!" but rather *unẓurnā*, a common expression meaning "Look after us!" Muslim interpreters explained that this unexpected command was necessary because while the former expression was perfectly suitable, Jews were using it disingenuously, either by pronouncing it like a similar Hebrew word, which meant "insult," or by changing it into another Arabic word, *ruʿūnah*, meaning "frivolity, levity," this also demeaning the Prophet.[36] "The author of these annotations," begins the Latin note on this passage, "said that *rāʿinā* [written here in Arabic characters], which he writes in Latin letters in this way, *rahine*, is both an Arabic and Hebrew word and in the Arabic language it means 'Look after us!' and in Hebrew an insult." The note then goes on to explain that "when the Muslims said to Muhammad *rahine* they meant 'Be well!' but when the Hebrews said this, they meant 'May God destroy you!'" For this reason Muhammad "ordered that the Jews not use the word any further."[37]

But these notes do not just explain difficult terms or usages; they also frequently inform us about the broader context in which Muslims thought certain verses had been revealed. Verses 2:55–56 discuss those who said to Moses that they would not believe him until they saw God plainly, God then striking them with a bolt of lightning, after which he "raised [them] up after death" so that they might be grateful. In explanation of all this, Qurʾānic commentators typically cited Islamic traditions that told how, after the Children of Israel had repented of their worship of the Calf, God had ordered Moses to come to him with a group of the Israelites who would apologize to him. So he chose seventy men. But after making their way to the place where they would apologize to God, they spoke the words of the verse—"We will not believe you until we have seen God plainly"—after which, as the Qurʾānic verse had said, they were struck by a thunderbolt, died, but were then brought back to life after Moses began to weep and beseech God.[38] The Latin note sets out a concise version of the same story: "the interpreters say that there were seventy men (*barones*) . . . who would not believe Moses if they did not see God clearly. A bolt of lightning descending from heaven killed them, but afterward Moses by his prayers resuscitated them from the dead, and it is about this resuscitation that he speaks here."[39] The use of the Romance *barones*, which the copyist Colville seemed to deride,[40] is doubtless explained by the attempt of an Iberian translator to come up with a way to translate the Arabic *shuyūkh* ("sheiks"), this being the term that some of the hadiths recounting these events use for the seventy men chosen by Moses,[41] but the thoroughly Islamic function of this note—explaining the occasion of these verses' revelation—is very clear, and other similar notes could be cited.[42]

These Latin annotations are also notable because they identify explicitly many of the Islamic sources upon which they are based.[43] Not all the commentators mentioned can be identified,[44] but references to al-Zamakhsharī are frequent,[45] and in at least two cases he is cited alongside one *Abanatia* or *Bnatia*.[46] This very probably transliterates *Ibn ʿAṭīyah* (d. 1147), an Andalusī scholar who was the author of a rather lengthy Qurʾān commentary called *The Succinct Composition in Interpretation of the Noble Book*.[47] And indeed, some of the Latin notes may well be based on his commentary.[48] A much later note mentions al-Bukharī, the great scholar of Islamic tradition, whose massive hadith collection also includes a section on Qurʾānic commentary.

The most important source is al-Zamakhsharī himself, whom the notes mention far more than any other commentator, this Muʿtazilite interpreter being apparently as popular with the Christian author of these notes as he was in the Islamic world in general.[49] In many cases it is possible to show that views attributed to al-Zamakhsharī in these Latin notes can indeed be found in his commentary on the relevant verses, as examples that we have already examined make clear.[50] The author of the notes at one point even imparts to his readers some of the flavor of al-Zamakhsharī's particular analytical methods: "in the same place [al-Zamakhsharī] proposes an objection against himself"—an objection, that is, to the view that he had just offered on the location of Adam's Paradise mentioned in 2:35. If, the note observes, it was in heaven, as al-Zamakhsharī had argued, "how will the demon [i.e., Satan] have been able to test Adam in heaven where Paradise was, if the demon had already been ejected from heaven," for that testing had occurred when Satan had urged Adam and Eve to eat of the tree. Al-Zamakhsharī "responds in his usual way," the Latin note explains, "that the demon assumed the mouth of the serpent and thus deceived the angels, the guardians of Paradise," and so was able to enter Paradise, despite being banned from it, and was thus able to tempt Adam and Eve.[51] Such dialectical exposition—much more typical in Islamic theological texts than in Islamic exegetical literature—is indeed rather common in al-Zamakhsharī's notably rationalist commentary,[52] and his explication of this verse is no exception: "How did [Satan] manage to make [Adam and Eve] sin and to whisper temptation [to them]," al-Zamakhsharī asks in his commentary, "after what had been said to him [in another surah]: 'Get out from [Paradise], for you are cursed' (15:34)?" He offers his readers several explanations, including just that offered in the Latin notes as well: "it is related that he wanted to enter, but the guardians forbade him, so he entered into the mouth of the snake so that it entered with him and [the guardians] were not aware."[53]

There is no doubt, then, that the author of the Latin notes made frequent, direct use of al-Zamakhsharī's commentary. But there may well be more than one source behind interpretations that he ascribes to al-Zamakhsharī alone. Indeed, the composition of these Latin notes appears to have been a remarkably complex process involving not only the consultation of several Muslim commentaries but perhaps even the laborious searching of the Qur'ān itself for parallel or related passages. At verse 2:106, for example, one of the key passages concerning Qur'ānic abrogation, the notes relate that "al-Zamakhsharī says that there are certain verses of the Qur'ān which have been changed or thoroughly deleted from the Qur'ān," this summarizing (somewhat inaccurately) al-Zamakhsharī's relatively brief comments about the process of abrogation. But then the notes go on to give us a series of examples, using the edition's internal reference system: "such as that which was in chapter 6, book 3 at the beginning of it, in which verse the stoning of adulterers was proscribed."[54] A series of further examples follows, but none of them is mentioned by al-Zamakhsharī. Rather, the list of abrogated verses here seems to be the result of the author of the Latin notes having examined other commentaries and other parts of the Qurʾān itself in order to find examples of abrogated verses.

Other than the extensive twelfth-century notes that so often filled the margins of manuscripts of Robert of Ketton's Latin Qurʾān, then, no other set of Latin glosses on the Qurʾān demonstrates as much Islamic learning as these Latin notes that once graced the fourth column of Egidio da Viterbo's sixteenth-century bilingual Qurʾān. It is striking that David Colville himself, the learned seventeenth-century Orientalist who produced the Milan manuscript, confessed that he was delighted when these notes picked up again toward the end of the Qurʾān, after many surahs' absence, for they explained "the things which I was not understanding."[55] There is, of course, one vivid difference between the two Latin commentaries: In Egidio's notes we find none of the vicious denunciation of the Qurʾān that exists alongside all the philology that we find in the twelfth-century notes—no cursing of Muhammad as a *mendax*, no snide dismissals of the Qurʾān's ridiculous fables. Indeed, if we consider Egidio's edition as a whole, we cannot escape the conclusion that, like the contemporary *Octoplex Psalterium* of Giustiniani, completed just before (1516), or the Complutensian Polyglot edition of the Bible, appearing soon after (1523), this was a scholarly tool meant for serious philological study. Like Egidio's bilingual Qurʾān, these earliest of the sixteenth-century biblical polyglot editions, modeled on Origen's massive *Hexapla* with its six parallel columns of Hebrew and Greek text, presented the Bible to readers in original languages as well as new translations, together with explanatory notes.[56]

In fact, if we set what we know of Egidio's edition side by side with the work that has customarily been hailed as the initiator of modern philological Qurʾān study in the West—Marracci's *Alcorani textus universus* of 1698—the similarities are striking. As in Egidio's edition completed a hundred and eighty years earlier, Marracci has put the Arabic version of the Qurʾān and a Latin translation next to each other, though not in parallel columns: Marracci preferred to break the Qurʾān up into relatively equal portions a page or two long which he presents first in elegantly printed and vocalized Arabic and then in his learned new Latin version. Immediately after the translation, Marracci provides his reader with a set of notes tied to specific verses whose lexical, grammatical, or interpretive difficulties he attempts to clear up. These notes, like those in Egidio's edition, are based almost exclusively on mainstream Islamic authorities, who are also identified by name. Often the concerns of both sets of notes are nearly identical. We have already seen that in Egidio's edition, verse 2:104,[57] with its puzzling proscription of the phrase *rāʿinā*, "Watch over us!" when applied to Muhammad, inspired a note that repeated the Qurʾānic commentators' view that this was because Jews were abusing the term by mispronouncing it so that it turned into an insult. Marracci inserts a very similar note in his translation, pointing out that in Arabic both *rāʿinā* and *unẓurnā*, the term Muhammad's followers were to use instead, "mean almost the same thing, that is: 'watch over us' [*respice nos*, cf. Egidio's definition: *aspice nos*,[58] "look over us"] or 'have regard for us.'" He then cites the views of the commentator al-Suyūṭī, quoting him in Arabic and then in Latin translation, these views being quite similar to the explanation set out in Egidio's edition: The Jews were greeting Muhammad derisively with this word since in Hebrew it meant "heckling, flippancy" (*ruʿūnah, conuicium*), and therefore it was prohibited to Muhammad's followers.[59]

The many striking similarities in concern and content between the surviving annotations from the fourth column of Egidio's edition and the notes of Marracci's *Alcorani textus*[60] are rendered all the more remarkable if we bear something else in mind: Marracci's life's work (he published it after forty years' labor, just two years before he died) is not just an edition, translation, and explanation of the Qurʾānic text; it is also a refutation of it. Not only does he preface his edition and translation with an enormous introduction that attempts to refute Islam in rather traditional ways,[61] but after the notes that clarify each section of the Qurʾān, Marracci provides further commentary under the heading "Refutata" or "Refutationes." Here he systematically attacks Islamic belief and the Qurʾānic text from a Christian point of view. Marracci's refutations of the first twenty-nine verses of surah 2, for example, begin with the pointed observation that "These three individual letters"—the mysterious letters, that is, *alif-lām-mīm*—"are placed for no good reason at the beginning of this surah if the understanding of them is reserved only for God, and they cannot be understood by men."[62] He then goes on at considerable length to attack, among other things, the Islamic beliefs that Jews and Christians corrupted their scriptures (nearly eight columns of text on this topic alone), that "men sin not freely, but necessarily" (*hominem non libere, sed necessariò peccare*), that Paradise contains carnal pleasures, and that God created the earth before the heavens, rather than the other way around.[63] All the information about Egidio's edition suggests, on the other hand, that it had no such set of "refutationes." David Colville mentions no such thing; neither of the known surviving manuscripts contains evidence of any such obviously apologetic and polemical annotations.

Leo Africanus's Notes

Egidio's bilingual Qur'ān edition, then, deserves far greater recognition in the history of European scholarship on the Qur'ān and Islam. It accomplishes much of what Marracci accomplished two centuries later, and does so without the explicit polemical concerns that are so obviously central to Marracci's vast project. But just as all the other Qur'ān translations that we have been looking at had further stories to tell about Latin-Christian Qur'ān reading when we looked at later manuscripts of them, so too does Egidio's bilingual Qur'ān. Our sample of later manuscripts in this case is especially small—only two, as we have seen, and one of those is a seventeenth-century manuscript copied well after the terminal date for this study. Nevertheless, these two manuscripts preserve between them extensive further notes by (at least) two later readers who used the edition within a few generations of its completion and who shared the philological approach to Qur'ān reading that Egidio's edition was meant to encourage.

One of these sets of notes amounted to extensive corrections to the whole of Iohannes Gabriel Terrolensis's translation and was copied into both later manuscripts, becoming, in effect, still another study aid for readers of this philological edition of the Qur'ān. As it happens, David Colville, the erudite Scotsman who produced the Milan manuscript, provides us with valuable information concerning the origin of this first set of additional notes. The Latin translation, located in the third column of the El Escorial manuscript, he tells us, had been "corrected and interpolated in many places" (*in multis locis correcta et interpolata erat*),[64] and he indicates that the author of these notes was another Iohannes—Iohannes Leo Granatinus.[65] An educated Granadan, born a Muslim and named al-Ḥasan al-Wazzān, he had been kidnapped in 1518 by a Sicilian pirate and presented as a gift to the pope in 1520. After converting to Christianity, he took the name of Iohannes Leo in Latin (but also used the corresponding Arabic name, Yūḥannā al-Asad) and was often known as Leo Africanus. Eventually, he found his way to North Africa and apparently reverted to Islam, but during his years as a Christian, he not only wrote the well-known *Description of Africa* but also became one of Egidio da Viterbo's Arabic teachers.[66] In the second postscript section of his introductory note, Colville confirms this identification as well, this time by actually quoting what appears to be a letter of dedication from Leo Africanus to Cardinal Egidio: "The Qur'ān, which before was contrary and contradictory in certain places, and in some totally obscure," had now been made accessible. For "I [Leo Africanus] have put all my power into correcting it," translating literally what he could, and by means of some other suitable phraseology what he could not.[67] Leo added these corrections in Viterbo in 1525 to what was probably the original manuscript of the edition, David Colville tells us, after it had been brought to Italy from Spain.[68] Industrious as ever, Colville then attempted to copy "the Latin translation . . . together with the corrections [of Leo] in the same way" that he had found them,[69] so that the Milan manuscript of Egidio's edition actually contains two translations: Iohannes Gabriel Terrolensis' original version and Leo Africanus' extensive revision of it. Copying Egidio's edition "together with the corrections" left by Leo seemed a wise plan to the copyist of the Cambridge manuscript as well, for, like the Milan manuscript, it contains throughout a vast number of correcting notes. As we will see presently, many of these notes are largely the same as Leo's notes, and clearly derive from them. But by no means are the two sets of notes identical. At some point, in fact, it seems likely that at least one other reader with extensive knowledge of Arabic and Islam reworked Leo's notes so that the version preserved in either the Cambridge or Milan manuscripts is really an elaboration or revision of Leo's original corrections.[70]

The character of these notes is quite consistent throughout. The note on 2:33 in the two manuscripts is typical. This verse reads, "He said, O Adam, inform them of their names, but when he informed them of their names, he said, did I not tell you that I know what is hidden (*ghayb*) in the heavens and on earth, and I know what you reveal and what you have hidden?" All is not entirely clear here—who, for example, is the subject of the several third-person verbs?—and Leo's notes attempt to clarify. Over the first verb in Iohannes's translation, *dixit*, "he said," the Milan manuscript has "namely, God" (*scilicet deus*) while the Cambridge manuscript has "God" (*deus*), and when the verb recurs later in the verse, the same notes appear again. Above "inform them of their names"[71] the Milan note reads, "namely, announce to the angels the names of them, that is, of things," while the Cambridge manuscript has an abbreviated version of the same note: "to the angels, that is, [the names] of all things."[72] Where Iohannes Gabriel's translation reads, "I know everything that you conceal and reveal" (*scio omnia quę uos absconditis et manifestatis* in both manuscripts), the Milan note observes "that which you, that is, the angels reveal and conceal," while the Cambridge note gives us the one-word gloss "angels."[73]

The Milan notes tend to be longer, therefore, but both sets are primarily concerned with explicating the literal meaning of the text and clearing up potential confusion. In doing so, the author or authors of these notes draw—as so many other Christian readers had done in the past—on the Islamic tradition of Qur'ānic commentary itself, as can be seen just a few verses hence, where God, in 2:38, tells Adam and Eve, who have been tempted into error by Satan, to "go down from [paradise] all together." Above Iohannes's translation, both sets of notes instruct us that "all" (*omnes*) here refers not just to Adam and Eve but to "Adam, Eve, and the Demon."[74] Though there was disagreement about whom, exactly, this command addressed, it was often said by Muslim commentators that God was speaking here to Adam, Eve, the snake, and Iblīs (Satan), as al-Ṭabarī[75] suggested, or "Adam, Eve, Satan, and their offspring," according to an opinion cited by Ibn ʿAṭīyah.[76] Leo's explanatory notes here clearly draw on this Muslim interpretation, and there are many other examples.[77]

In the above examples, the two manuscripts contained the same or largely the same annotations, and the many notes of this kind seem most likely to have been the glosses composed by Leo Africanus himself. At many points, however, there are notes that are unique to one or the other manuscript, and some of these, therefore, may not be the work of Leo Africanus but of some other reader. Yet whoever wrote them, their character is very much in line with Leo's notes. Since the Cambridge manuscript contains only something like half of the Qur'ānic text, there are many parts of the Qur'ān in Iohannes's version that survive only in the Milan manuscript, but there is no shortage of interlinear annotation for these portions. At 2:1, for example, the Milan manuscript has a note rather similar to those left by other Christian readers, interpreting the mysterious letters that appear here (*alif-lām-mīm*) as standing for Allāh, the angel Gabriel, and Muhammad, a view that was widely advanced in Qur'ānic commentaries.[78] The same sort of notes have been added to the final surahs of the Qur'ān, which are also lacking in the Cambridge manuscript. In the first verse of surah 108, for example, Iohannes had simply transliterated a difficult word—one of the so-called "strange" or "foreign" words of the Qur'ān: *alcautar* (for the Arabic *al-kawthar*). Meaning literally something like "abundance,"[79] this word was interpreted in a number of different ways by Muslim commentators, but among the most common views was that it referred to "a river in paradise," Leo's notes suggesting the same thing.[80] On the other hand, there are many notes in the Cambridge manuscript that are lacking in the Milan manuscript, and some of these are based on the Muslim exegetical tradition too. At 46:10, for example, the Qur'ān speaks of "a witness from among the Children of Israel" who testified to the validity of the Qur'ān. Above the Latin translation of this verse, a note in the Cambridge manuscript informs us that this Jewish witness "was called Abdaghir who became a Muslim."[81] *Abdaghir* is almost certainly a corruption (and such corruptions of Arabic names in Latin texts are notoriously common) of ʿAbd Allāh ibn Salām, who was a famous early Jewish convert to Islam and was often identified in the commentaries as the witness to whom this Qur'ānic verse refers.[82]

In both manuscripts, these notes attributed to Leo Africanus have been copied carefully between the lines of Iohannes Gabriel Terrolensis's version, essentially as a set of standard glosses for the benefit of later readers. Just as the twelfth-century annotations of Robert's Latin Qur'ān quickly became a sort of authoritative commentary on his version, so these notes have been built into the very layout of Egidio's edition. Where the twelfth-century notes, however, had the dual function of explaining the text philologically and attacking it polemically, these annotations exclusively serve the cause of philology. Informed by an impressive knowledge of Arabic and of Islamic Qur'ān exegesis, they effectively replace the original notes of the fourth column which, as we have seen, were left out of both later manuscripts, though added to the Milan manuscript as an apparent afterthought. They represent, therefore, and are the fruit of precisely the sort of philological reading that Egidio's edition in its original form was meant to inculcate. Once copied into the later manuscripts as authoritative glosses, they were meant in turn to assist the same sort of reading in still other readers.

The Cambridge Reader

Remarkably enough, we have evidence of still another reader of Egidio's edition, one who very likely took up the Cambridge manuscript within a few decades after it was completed[83] and who, while he left far fewer notes than Leo Africanus (they cover only a part of surah 2), read the text in a similarly philological way. Beginning at verse 46 and continuing through verse 231, these notes occur both interlinearly and in the empty right column, from folio 7r to folio 39r. There are now two large lacunae in the text in this section of the Qur'ān, each amounting to more than thirty-five verses and arising from leaves having been lost at some point before the last rebinding of the manuscript. There must at one time, therefore, have been something like another ten folios of the text that contained notes, since the annotator passes over both gaps without any comment, even though in the first case the gap begins in the middle not just of a verse but of a word.[84] And while the author of these notes is as philological in his concerns as Leo, his reading approach is intriguingly different. Leo was concerned both with correcting the Latin translation and explaining its meaning as Muslims understood it; this second reader is interested in the literal meaning of the Arabic text alone, not the Muslim exegesis of it.

Whoever this reader was, he had a very impressive knowledge of Arabic, his competence showing up clearly at points where his notes, like so many of Leo's before him, are essentially corrections of Iohannes Gabriel Terrolensis's version. At verse 2:49, for example, Iohannes had translated the Arabic's *balā'un* ("trial, affliction") quite wrongly as *beneficium* ("benefit, favor"). This humanist annotator corrects this interlinearly to *tentationes* ("trials, temptations"), which, other than being in the plural, is a vast improvement.[85] At other points, he corrects the text by adding lines or phrases that have been left out.[86] But in general, this reader's notes represent not so much a correction of the Latin text as the insistent working through of the literal meaning of the Arabic, for a much larger percentage of his notes take the form of verbatim Latin versions of the Arabic at points where Iohannes had provided quite competent but nonliteral translations. There is no more vivid example of this than his reworking of verse 2:177. Here God provides a list of the kinds of people to whom the pious should give charitably—their kinsfolk, orphans, the poor, and, in Iohannes's version, strangers or foreigners (*hospites*). Over this last word, the annotator carefully writes *filiis viarum*, "to the sons of the highways," this being the literal translation of the Arabic idiom used here: *ibn al-sabīl*, "the son of the road," meaning "wayfarer, vagabond."[87] Iohannes's translation here is not really wrong at all; it just does not follow the Arabic literally, so the reader added this clarifying note. This he does over and over. At 2:53, Iohannes had correctly translated the Arabic verb *ātaynā* ("we have brought, given") as *dedimus* ("we have given"). This reader's interlinear notes, however, instruct us that this verb means *venire fecimus* ("we have made come"), for this is the literal meaning of this verb (ATY) when used in the fourth form.[88] This humanist annotator continued to explicate the literal meaning of the Arabic to the end of his notes where, at verse 2:230, he points out that the Qur'ān's *qawm yaʿlamūna* should, technically speaking, be translated as "people who know" (*populus qui sapit*) rather than "knowledgeable people" (*homines scientes*) as Iohannes had it.[89]

As all these notes imply, this reader was actively moving back and forth between the Arabic and Latin columns of text,[90] and as his eyes moved back and forth, he often found himself writing above or beside the Latin words the specific Arabic words that they translated. On the first page that bears any of his notes, therefore, he wrote the Arabic word *āl* ("family, clan") above the Latin *gens* ("family, tribe") in verse 2:49, which describes how God delivered the Children of Israel from the "family of Pharoah"; there are a number of other examples.[91]

But it is not just his handwriting and his energetic interest in linguistic issues that suggest that this reader is a humanist: his frequent use of Greek words suggests this as well. At many points where his notes retranslate the Arabic in a more literal way—such as in verse 2:93, where he points out that Iohannes's "they introduced the cows into their hearts" ought more precisely to be translated "they drank the cow into their hearts"—he indicates that his version conforms to the Arabic text by writing "φϱ. Ar." next to his note. This appears to be an abbreviation for the mixed Greek/Latin "φϱάσις (*phrasis*) Arabica," meaning something like "the Arabic expression."[92] On several occasions, he offers two slightly different Latin formulations that he believes capture the Arabic more closely than Iohannes's translation, and in these cases he signals which one he believes is the better by inserting the Greek ἀντί (*anti*), meaning something like "rather than," between them, such as at verse 2:113. Here Iohannes had written "and the Jews said that the Christians do not have truth" (*et dixerunt iudei non habent christiani ueritatem*), the last part of which this reader recognizes as a paraphrase for the very idiomatic Arabic expression *laysat al-Naṣārá ʿalá shayʾin*, "the Christians are not on anything" (i.e., "they are supported by no substantial truth"). Over Iohannes's *ueritatem* ("truth"), therefore, he writes *supra rem*. φϱάσις *Arabica* ("on top of a thing—the Arabic expression"), capturing the literal Arabic fairly well. But he wants to make clear that literally the Arabic reads precisely as he has just retranslated it, *supra rem*, "on top of a *thing*," by writing ἀντί *quicquam*, that is, "rather than [on top of] *anything*."[93] At a few other points he uses Greek words to translate an Arabic term that he seems to think cannot adequately be captured in Latin. At 2:102, for example, where the angels Hārūt and Mārūt say *innamā naḥnu fitnah*, he is uncertain how exactly to understand the last word.

He first translates all this in the empty right column as "we are thoroughly seditious" (*tanto sumus nos seditiosi*), but then above *seditiosi* he writes ἀπόστασις ("defection, revolt"), before going on to capture the Arabic more literally by writing "or misfortune" (*vel infortunium*) next to this, the last suggestion yielding the phrase "we are thoroughly a misfortune," which comes closest of all to the Arabic ("we are merely a sedition, a discord"). This is impressive linguistic analysis: all of the reader's suggestions are better than Iohannes' translation—*sumus probantes* ("we are testers, provers").[94]

This humanist reader's translations are far from being perfect in every case,[95] but in general, he shows remarkable understanding of the Arabic in front of him. This shows up particularly vividly in a few longer notes that discuss Arabic morphology and lexicography. At verse 2:67, where the Children of Israel ask Moses, "do you take us in derision?" the humanist annotator observes that the verb in question here, *tattakhidhunā* ("do you take us"), which he writes in Arabic in the margin, is derived from the root *akhadha* ("to take"). Moreover, just as Arab grammarians would explain this specific form of the verb—what modern Western grammarians call the eighth form—by using the paradigmatic root Fʿ L ("to make, do"), he goes on to point out that it is "in the form *iftaʿala*" (see figure 9).[96]

We might expect that a man with such an advanced knowledge of Arabic might be reading Qurʾānic commentaries as well—we have seen many other Latin readers using Arabic *tafsīr*s in this period—and there is some rather slim evidence that he might be doing so. When he writes "that is the Qurʾān" over "that which which had been offered afterward" (*quod fuit delatum postea*/ *mā warāʾahu*) in 2:91, he is repeating just what Qurʾānic commentators say about this part of the verse.[97] But this is something that he could have worked out for himself from the context. And there is much more evidence that suggests that he either was not reading commentaries at all as he made his way through the Qurʾān or that, if he was, he intentionally ignored what they said. Indeed, his adjustments of Iohannes's Latin text often involve removing from it the very commentary influences that are there because Iohannes had, as we have seen, frequently turned to Qurʾānic commentaries as he translated. Iohannes had translated the Arabic "what their hands have sent before" (*mā qaddamat aydīhim*) in 2:95 as "their sins which they have committed" (*sua peccata quae fecerunt*) because Muslim commentators explained that what their hands have sent before are "their sins and their crimes."[98] The humanist annotator stripped out this commentator's interpretation, giving us the very literal "that which their hand made come before" (*id quod praevenit manus eorum*).[99] Likewise, Iohannes had made verse 2:173 speak of "those things which were offered to idols" even though the Arabic text said "that which was offered to something other than God" because the commentators said that, as Ibn ʿAṭīyah put it, "other than God (*ghayr [Allāh]*)" here means "what is sacrificed to graven images and idols."[100] Returning the text to its literal sense, the humanist annotator instructs us that what is at issue here is what was offered "to things other than God."[101]

As luck would have it, there is evidence concerning the identity of this annotator on the Qurʾān's literal meaning. On a blank folio near the beginning of the manuscript we find—remarkably enough—the name "William Tyndale" written in Arabic characters (*Wilyām Tindalun*). The somewhat inept and almost certainly European hand that wrote this name—very likely, by the way, as what paleographers call a "pen-trial" to test the quill before setting to work—is much the same as that which wrote the Arabic words that appear in the humanist notes we have just looked at. Moreover, Tyndale's hand as it appears in at least one autograph document resembles the hand that wrote the Latin of these notes as well.[102] Tyndale (d. 1536), the first of the great Protestant translators of the Bible into English, knew Hebrew very well, and there is other evidence that he knew some Arabic.[103]

While more research is necessary both to identify and to date this reader securely, the intriguing connection of these annotations with Tyndale suggests, I think, the context in which we can best understand these erudite and nonpolemical notes. If the scholar who wrote them was indeed Tyndale, or at least from a circle of scholars with similar interests, then we need not look far for explanations for the reading approach that informed them. There is no polemic here not because this humanist was an Islamophile or an anachronistic liberal relativist in religious matters but because he, like many other biblical humanists in this period, viewed the study of the Arabic language as of real use in understanding the Hebrew Bible. This is something that contemporary Christian Hebraists, such as Tyndale's fellow Englishman, Robert Wakefield, frequently recommended,[104] and given the general lack of Arabic works available to European scholars, the Qurʾān—especially one constructed so as to facilitate philological study—was the most likely text on the basis of which one could undertake such Arabic study. It is almost certain that, if pressed to comment on the nature of the Qurʾān as a scripture, the author of these notes (especially if he was the passionate reformer William Tyndale) would have advanced the Christian polemical view that had been around for centuries. But that was simply not his concern here. His goal was learning Arabic to help himself learn better the Hebrew and Aramaic of the Bible.

Assuming that these notes were written by Tyndale or by someone of like mind, then, we should read them not as the product of thoroughly disinterested scholarship (if such a thing can be said to exist) but rather as arising from deeply held—and deeply interested—Christian humanist beliefs about the value of understanding the Bible in its original languages in order to reform both church and society. Something very similar can certainly be said about Egidio's edition itself. We have already seen that Egidio shared many of the central concerns of the biblical humanists, and was deeply concerned to reform the church, playing an extensive role in the reforming of his own order. To these Christian humanist concerns he added extensive learning in Hebrew and other Semitic languages (including Arabic). He traveled, therefore, in the circles of the scholars who produced the biblical polyglots and shared their outlook, and the edition of the Qurʾān that he commissioned shared the philological character of their ambitious biblical editions. Moreover, Egidio was fascinated, as not all other biblical humanists were, by postbiblical Hebrew literature, seeing the Kabbalist tradition as testifying to the essential truth of Christian belief.[105] For him, therefore, the study of Hebrew was doubly important and the necessity of learning Arabic doubly pressing. While largely nonpolemical, at least in its outward form, then, Egidio's Qurʾān edition was nevertheless still the product of deeply held Christian beliefs. For while such beliefs had consistently, as we have seen, inspired Latin scholars to engage the Qurʾān as a text that needed to be refuted, those same Christian beliefs could also, in the right Christian humanist circles, inspire them to embrace it as a way of learning a difficult but necessary language.

Polemical Undercurrents?

It is hard to resist the pressure to conclude that in Egidio's edition and in the reactions of these two early readers to it, we are, for the first time, in the presence of Latin-Christian Qurʾān reading that is pure philology unadulterated by polemical concerns; that, even if real religious motivations inspired Egidio and at least one reader of his edition, attacking Islam was not part of those motivations. The date of 1518, moreover, inclines us to see in this remarkable accomplishment just the sort of careful historical and philological textual criticism that humanists frequently held up as the only legitimate form of interpretation and which culminated in such works as Lorenzo Valla's irrefutable demonstration of the fraudulent nature of the *Donation of Constantine.*[106] Yet modern commentators are increasingly loath to see the scholarship of any movement or period as entirely objective. About the Renaissance in particular, Anthony Grafton has pointed out that "few of the humanists actually reveal on close inspection that commitment to a strictly historical approach [to textual criticism] which most secondary sources lead one to expect."[107]

In fact, it is possible to see the traditional polemical and apologetic themes of Christian Qur'ān reading residing just behind the impressively philological exterior of those deeply learned notes in the fourth column of Egidio's edition. While we have no ugly accusations of Muhammad's untruthfulness, it is hard not to notice the Christian preoccupations both in what the notes say and in what they do not say. The second note points out, as we have seen, that those with whom God is angry and those who have gone astray in verse 1:7 are Jews and Christians respectively, this of course being exactly what Muslim commentators said.[108] Other than the immediately previous note, which describes at length the five prayers required of Muslims and specifies the number of times this surah is said during each, this is the only note on this first surah, the *Fātiḥah.* Yet Muslim exegetes found in it many more problems that required attention. The very first verse, "Praise be to the lord of the worlds," occasioned discussion on at least two issues. First, as al-Ṭabarī asked, why does "praise" (*ḥamd*) have an article (*al-*) attached to it? Why do we have "*the* praise to God" rather than "praise be to God"? His answer, which later commentators such as the Andalusī Muslim Ibn ʿAṭīyah essentially repeated, was that the article here implies that "all praise" or "all kinds of praise" belong to God."[109] Even more discussed was the final phrase of the verse: *rabb al-ʿālamīn.* There was no doubt about its literal meaning; it clearly meant "lord of the worlds." But what was being referred to here? Typically commentators explained that these "worlds" were to be understood as all groups and communities in the cosmos, whether "men, or Jinn, or anything else," as Ibn ʿAṭīyah put it. Al-Ṭabarī suggested that it referred not only to all these groups or communities, but also to each generation of them.[110] Verse 5 of the same short surah also attracted comment on the phrase "the straight path." Here the commentators reported a range of views as well. According to some, the straight path should be understood as Islam itself, while others said it referred to the Qur'ān, or to Muhammad together with Abū Bakr and ʿUmar.[111]

But the Latin notes in Egidio's edition tell us nothing about any of these philological issues, preferring instead to focus on the only interpretive problem in the first surah that pertained to Christians and Jews: the identities of those in verse 7 who have called down God's wrath and those who have gone astray. This silence on linguistic and interpretive problems that have no Christian connection is particularly striking if we notice that Iohannes Gabriel Terrolensis, who translated the Qurʾān for Egidio da Viterbo, clearly understood some of these further textual problems and adjusted his translation accordingly. As we have seen, he, like Robert of Ketton and Mark of Toledo before him, turned to Muslim exegesis to help him resolve difficulties,[112] and in doing so, he clearly came across the idea that "lord of the worlds" in 1:1 meant, as al-Ṭabarī suggested, "lord of the generations," for that is what he gives his readers: *dominus generationum*.[113] Not only, therefore, was the likely author of these notes well aware of the Muslim discussions about the meaning of this phrase, but he also then gave his readers a puzzling translation—"generations" where we would expect "worlds"—without explanation. The bilingual readers for whom this edition was clearly intended had natural cause to be perplexed by this, but the author of the notes felt no pressing need to explain, though he had gone out of his way to make clear that the most important Islamic prayer considered Jews and Christians to be well outside God's favor.

If we look beyond the first short surah, we find a similar pattern in these notes: their impressive historical and philological analysis is directed overwhelmingly at passages that turn out to be relevant to Christian-Muslim disputation. Muslim exegetes found a whole range of problems to discuss in the first thirty-five verses of surah 2. To what does *ghayb* refer in 2:3 ("those who believe in the *ghayb*")? Literally meaning "the invisible, the concealed," this word was variously said to refer to God himself, or to his fate and divine decree, or to the Qurʾān, or to the straight path, the resurrection, or the garden.[114] What sort of sickness afflicted the hearts of the unbelievers in 2:10—doubt, as some said, hypocrisy, "a corruption which is in their doctrines," grief? All these were suggested as possible meanings.[115] In 2:19, the word *raʿd*, normally meaning "thunder," inspired disagreement. Some commentators said it referred to an angel moving clouds, some a wind making a great noise; others said it was the name of this great noise itself. The nearby word *barq* ("lightning") provoked a similar discussion.[116] Verse 2:26 says that God is willing to coin an analogy with even a gnat "and what is beyond it" to clarify the state of unbelievers. Did this mean what is beyond the gnat in largeness or smallness? The commentators had much to say about this,[117] but while Iohannes Gabriel Terrolensis chose the former (*similitudo unius culicis et illo maioris*), no explanation appears in the notes.[118] At 2:28, as we have seen in another connection, Muslim exegetes were very puzzled, and had much to say, about how God could be said to have brought humans in the beginning out of death and into life.[119]

All these problems—and many others besides—typically inspired commentary by Muslim Qurʾān scholars but are passed over in silence in the Latin notes in Egidio da Viterbo's edition. Rather, we find notes on the meaning of the mysterious letters at the beginning of surah 2 and, at verse 2:24, on how Muhammad made war on a rival prophet. Notes at verses 2:31–33 dwell on how Muslims believe that Adam taught the angels not just the words for things, but an understanding of "the properties of all things" (*proprietates omnium rerum*), while at 2:35 we learn that Muslims believe that Adam and Eve's paradise was in heaven, and are given an outline of al-Zamakhsharī's views on how Satan was able to slip into paradise in the mouth of the serpent to tempt humanity's parents.[120] As we have seen earlier in this chapter, many of these notes are based on thoroughly sound Islamic exegesis.[121] But taken collectively, they emphasize the Qurʾān's alien qualities in their preoccupation with the mysterious letters, Muhammad's warlike character, and the differences between Qurʾānic and biblical accounts of the same events—all these the common concerns of polemical and apologetic Qurʾān reading.[122]

Likewise, notes later in the second surah on how the direction of prayer was changed,[123] on how the Bible originally contained prophecies concerning Muhammad,[124] on the nature of Jihād,[125] on the supposed "idols" that Muhammad allowed to remain in the Kaʿbah,[126] on the unfamiliar angels, Hārūt and Mārūt, and their sexual misadventures,[127] and on the principle of Qurʾānic abrogation,[128] all played into the traditional Christian interpretation of the Qurʾān and Islam: it was a violent religion founded by a pseudoprophet who claimed to have been foretold in nonexistent biblical prophecies and who made up revelations to suit his immediate needs, all the while introducing unheard-of prophets and angels and tolerating pagan religious practices at the heart of his monotheistic religion.[129]

Not all the Latin notes of the fourth column of Egidio's Qurʾān edition fit into this polemical way of reading, but it should be clear that we cannot see in these learned annotations simply a Latin translation of a Muslim Qurʾān commentary. Rather—in the form, at least, in which they survive today—they make up a Latin commentary based on authoritative Islamic sources that, in its procedures follows the philological and historical methods of interpretation celebrated by humanists but, in its selective use of those sources, turns out to advance the same polemical ends that Christian Qurʾān reading had so often served in the past. Assuming, therefore, that David Colville has provided us with a representative sample of the notes in the fourth column in Egidio's original edition, then even in this impressively philological research tool, the Christian desire to undermine the Qurʾān's validity, to point out how it conflicts with the Bible, and to stress what seemed to Christians its weakest points, lives on, even if in a muted way. Short of finding a complete manuscript of Egidio's extraordinary edition, we cannot, of course, know this for certain, since it is entirely possible that Colville himself excerpted those notes in such a way as to emphasize polemical themes (though there is nothing else about his copy—including his comments in the preface—that suggests such concerns). Yet the fact that throughout the period from 1140 to 1560 we have seen polemical and philological ways of reading the Qurʾān interact with each other so commonly suggests that this undercurrent of Christian polemic in the surviving notes to Egidio's edition may well be original to it, and not an artifact introduced by a later copyist. Just as the overwhelmingly polemical framing of Robert of Ketton's Latin Qurʾān concealed substantial philology, so the overwhelmingly philological framing of Egidio's bilingual Qurʾān may well have concealed substantial polemic.

Conclusion

Juan de Segovia and Qur'ān Reading in Latin Christendom, 1140–1560

There were times—after the fall of Acre in 1291, for example, or in the years after Constantinople's conquest by the Turks in 1453—when Islam became an especially pressing problem for Latin intellectuals.[1] It is with the reaction of one Latin scholar to the latter calamity that I want to bring this book to a close. For in the aftermath of the loss of that great Christian city, what Juan de Segovia, a leading Latin churchman, did was to read the Qur'ān—though "read" is really too mild a verb: he studied it, he grappled with it, tirelessly, intensively, nearly passionately.[2] What is more, he wrote about all this, producing the only narrative account of Christian Qur'ān reading in these centuries of which I am aware. To read this precious, gregarious document, I want to suggest here, is to see written out all the complexities of Qur'ān reading that I have been trying to demonstrate using the other, rather different sources that have been the focus of this study.

Juan de Segovia was born about 1393[3] and studied and taught at Salamanca, residing there almost continuously from 1407 to 1431 and eventually holding a prestigious chair in theology.[4] The fall of 1431, however, found him at the Council of Basel. Not only was Juan one of the most active members of this council, but he soon became the leading conciliar theorist[5] and played a key role in the council's deposition of Pope Eugene IV and election of Felix V. The new pope made Juan a cardinal and he was sent on important diplomatic missions. But Juan's prosperity did not last, for at length the opposing papalist position triumphed at the council and Felix was forced to resign. As a result, Juan lost his cardinalate, though he was given two bishoprics by the newly elected Pope Nicholas V in exchange, as well as the titular archbishopric of Caesarea. Having been granted a pension to reside at a priory in the Savoy, he retired there in 1451, where he wrote his history of the Council of Basel and, more important for our purposes, took up Qur'ān study in a nearly obsessive way. He died in 1458.

Juan had certainly thought about Islam before. As early as 1426 and 1427, he was giving university addresses that dealt with Muslims and their religion,[6] and in 1431, he participated in a religious debate with a learned Muslim ambassador of the Kingdom of Granada.[7] He had been trying, in fact, since the 1430s to obtain a trustworthy translation of the Qurʾān, and may have examined copies of it in Arabic (though he seems to have known almost no Arabic at this point).[8] Nevertheless, it was only after Constantinople's fall that he devoted his full attention to the issue of Islam.[9] Concerned, as many European Christians were, with the continued expansion of Islam, Juan turned his restless intelligence toward finding a way to end conflict between Christians and Muslims. A remarkable correspondence between Juan and two other titans of the age—the theologian and philosopher Nicholas of Cusa and the future pope Pius II, Aeneas Silvius Piccolomini—attests both to Juan's preoccupation with Islam and to the fact that this preoccupation was not unique to him.[10]

Where earlier historians underlined the novelty of Juan's approach to Islam, especially his emphasis on what he called the "way of peace" through informed and irenic interreligious discussion, in the last few years scholars have stressed—quite rightly—the many ways in which his thought on Islam was thoroughly traditional. Islam for Juan was a vile, militant, and sexually promiscuous heresy: no Islamophile he.[11] Yet his conviction that Muslims could only be converted through peaceful means was deeply held, and his hostility to all forms of anti-Islamic crusade was authentic and frequently expressed.[12] Islam was a heresy, yes, but military conflict with Islam had only made the world more dangerous and Christianity's long-term success even less likely. What was needed, he argued, was an engagement with Islam consisting of three interconnected elements: peace must be maintained as thoroughly as possible; relations—especially cultural relations—between Latin Christianity and Islam must be intensified in order to generate an atmosphere of mutual comprehension; and there must be peaceful discussion of the basic beliefs that separate the two.[13] Juan had enormous confidence that reasoned debate carried on by learned scholars would naturally lead to agreement among groups whose positions seemed profoundly irreconcilable, a view that characterized both his approach to Islam and his earlier career in Basel as a leading conciliarist.[14] Of necessity, this peaceful interaction with Islam required deep study of the Qurʾān and an adequate Latin translation.

That this preoccupation with Islam would then lead to intensive study of the Qurʾān was also not unique to Juan. Nicholas of Cusa, one of Juan's learned correspondents, himself read the Qur'ān with remarkable thoroughness, leaving behind for posterity both a massive Christian apologetic work based on this reading—his *Sifting the Qur'ān*[15]—and also his personal copy of Robert of Ketton's Latin Qur'ān, which contains on every folio his own marginal notes recording his reactions to the text as he read it.[16] What Juan did that was unusual was to write in such detail about that experience of reading the Qur'ān. For this we can thank his garrulousness. Juan's very gift for verbosity allowed him to write at length about a topic concerning which others only left stray hints.[17]

And Juan's account of his Qur'ān reading is a bracingly complex one. He depicts it for us in a lengthy preface to a new trilingual edition of the Qur'ān in Arabic, Castilian, and Latin, of which he was both patron and cocreator. His edition itself has, sadly, vanished,[18] but somehow Juan's preface survived, and in the course of telling us why the earlier, and by then standard, Latin version of the Qur'ān by Robert of Ketton was not adequate for properly understanding Islam, and how his version would conform "wholly to the substance and style of the Arabic language,"[19] he describes in some detail his own extended encounter with Islam's holy book.

It was an engagement informed in equal parts by polemic and philology. On the one hand, Juan is profoundly hostile to Islam: it is the most complete heresy, he asserts, the very beast described in the Apocalypse of St. John.[20] But on the other hand, like the humanist-trained biblical philologists who would begin to flourish soon after his lifetime and who "lavished their attention on the text [of the Bible] itself,"[21] Juan became committed to gaining a thorough understanding of the Qur'ān. Hostility to Islam leads him to the study of the Qur'ān; picking up the Qur'ān leads to reflections on whether the version in his hands is adequate for his polemical tasks; the meaning of the Arabic original must, therefore, be determined; authorities must be consulted, either in person or in writing; the thoroughly non-Latin structures and abounding vocabulary of the Arabic language must be mastered; the conventions of Qur'ānic narration must be considered, the practices of Arabic, and specifically Qur'ānic, orthography thought through. And then one must come up with a Latin translation, that process entailing a similarly long list of philological problems. What began for Juan in polemic rapidly ballooned into heavy-going philology, without ever explicitly abandoning its polemical goals.

The preface that tells us all this moves back and forth between all these stages in Juan's confrontation with the Qur'ān. Though by his lifetime the Qur'ān had been translated at least twice into Latin, Juan appears to have known only of Robert of Ketton's version; intriguingly, given the large number of manuscripts of it that survive, he found it difficult to get hold of—it had, in his view, "hardly entered into the common awareness of Christians" at all.[22] More importantly, he insisted, it "deviates in many things from the contents of the Arabic text."[23] And this latter conviction grew the more Juan studied Robert's translation and the more he became acquainted with the Arabic original. Though, at this point in his Qur'ānic studies, he does not seem to have known any Arabic, he asserted that he became more convinced of the flaws in Robert's version after "having seen . . . certain parchments of the Qur'ān."[24] Even before he could actually read them, Juan was looking at what were presumably Arabic Qur'ān manuscripts.

What Juan saw as the defects of Robert's Latin Qur'ān, together with his inability to find another, more reliable translation, inspired him to plan a new Latin version. For this purpose, he turned to his homeland. Juan describes how he arranged for a prominent, learned Muslim scholar known variously in the sources as Içe de Gebir or Iça Gidelli (the later perhaps from "al-Shādhilī," i.e., a member of the Shādhilīyah Sufi order) who, like Juan, was from Segovia, to come to his priory in Aiton.[25] With a salary agreed upon, this Muslim faqih traveled from Spain to the Savoy, arriving at Juan's priory in December of 1455 with a Muslim friend[26] and with "books of their doctors which expound the Qur'ān."[27]

Juan's plan was to have Iça translate the Qur'ān from Arabic into Castilian, after which he himself would translate it into Latin.[28] Juan had very specific ideas about how he wanted Iça to work: he was to "make a translation of the Qur'ān from the Arabic language and conforming to the text, without glosses, limitations, expositions, or insertions in the text," which, Juan implies, Iça did exactly as asked, though he also added "certain very brief and rare [notes] in the margins for the annotation of certain words."[29] Juan then intended to transform this verbatim Castilian Qur'ān into Latin, so that Latin Christendom would have available to it the proper tool with which to refute Islam. But this seemingly simple project soon became—as all translation must—a much more complicated task than it had appeared at first. Very quickly, philological issues began to preoccupy Juan as he watched Iça work.

Iça's task required four months, Juan tells us. During the first, he copied out the whole of the Qur'ān, making, presumably, the fair copy for Juan's edition. In the second month, he added the vowel marks that all copies of the Qur'ān have. During the third month, "he translated [the Qur'ān] into the Hispanic vernacular, writing the translation with his own hand."[30] In the final month, Juan and Iça read the Castilian and Arabic versions side by side in order to correct the translation. [31]

Juan found all this immensely interesting, and soon Iça was actually teaching him the rudiments of Arabic.[32] As Juan's teacher of Arabic, Iça seems to have had some success. It was not long before he "was beginning to read as by pronouncing the syllables," having learned the letters but not all the other markings that clarify the meaning of the text.[33] The Arabic alphabet—he is anxious to let us know—has twenty-nine letters, but does not include vowels, which they designate with small markings above the consonants. [34] He likewise comments on the Arabic case system and on the complex system of verbal conjugations[35] and observes that Arabic often uses the "nominative or ablative absolute" construction.[36] Not all of this is very clear—and some seems rather misleading, there being, for example, no such thing as an ablative absolute in Arabic which, indeed, lacks an ablative case altogether.[37] But despite his imperfect knowledge of its grammar, Juan's intensive encounter with the Arabic language comes across vividly.

So also does his engagement with Arabic manuscripts of the Qurʾān. We have seen that this interest goes back to Juan's earliest Qurʾān investigations, but it becomes a particular preoccupation during these months with Iça and in the following years. As he learns about the Arabic alphabet, he comes to realize that vowel markings do not normally appear in other Arabic books and explains, quite rightly, that in manuscripts of the Qurʾān, these sigla are often written not in black, but in a range of vivid colors—blue, red, green and yellow.[38] In comparing copies of the Qurʾān, he notices, moreover, that not all are exactly alike: at least one Qurʾān manuscript that he possessed contained far more vowel marks for case endings than did the copy Iça had made for him.[39] He is particularly attentive to the divisions of the Qurʾānic text as it appears in codices. It is divided, he observes, into four large books, and further into surahs (what he calls once again "Psalms"), and into verses.[40] The surahs themselves, he indicates, are organized in descending order of length, "with the exception of the first which is quite short and is reputed to be the substantial statement of all the others."[41] Because the early surahs are so long, they are also divided into paragraphs, Juan noticed, though the paragraph divisions are not the same in all Qurʾān manuscripts.[42] This examination of Qurʾān manuscripts allowed Juan to observe that the number of verses in each surah is set out, often in red characters, at the beginning of the surah, as is also the site of its revelation, "And there are two places [so] named, Yathrib [i.e., the original name of Medina] . . . and Mecca, the house which is reputed the holy of holies by them."[43] The subject matter "considered most important by them" also appears here, Juan referring to the names of the Qur'ānic surahs, which are drawn from notable events or references in each one.[44] All this is perfectly true: there is no mistaking that Juan had spent a lot of time with Arabic copies of the Qur'ān.

But it was not just the study of Arabic and the pondering of Qur'ān manuscripts that Juan's Latin Qur'ān project inspired in him: from the very beginning, he found himself reckoning with how Muslims interpreted their book and with the details of Islamic belief generally. In fact, it is clear from a comment made elsewhere by Içа that Juan had stipulated ahead of time that Iça's charge was not only to translate the Qur'ān but also to help Juan understand "the meanings and statements of its texts."[45] Even as Iça was teaching him Arabic, therefore, he was passing on to Juan "a summary of the understanding of any of the Psalms [i.e., the surahs] of the Qur'ān" that he had begun before he came to Aiton, and writing down a list of the thirteen articles of the Islamic faith "together with written reasons, according to their understanding, for the proving of them." He furthermore drew up for Juan a genealogy and short life of the Prophet and, what Juan considered most remarkable, Iça designated in his Castilian translation the Qur'ān's "227 revoked articles," or abrogated verses, and apparently explained why these verses were said, in orthodox Islamic belief, to be canceled by later Qur'ānic revelations.[46]

Iça's volumes of Qur'ānic commentary particularly caught Juan's eye. He not only made a point of mentioning that Iça had brought them with him from Spain[47] but also noticed that when Iça was perplexed by a given passage, he examined them. It struck Juan as surprising that, unlike the Qur'ān, these books largely lacked vowel markings.[48] As part of his ongoing evaluation of Robert of Ketton's twelfth-century Latin Qur'ān—a topic which Juan takes up more than once in the preface—he apparently asked Iça about places in Robert's text where it departed from the literal meaning of the Arabic. These conversations led Juan to the surprising and, as we have seen, entirely correct conclusion that "in many passages, just as one commenting, [Robert] explicates the Muslim meaning, though it scarcely is available in the Arabic letters, which meaning that master [i.e.] Iça acknowledged."[49] Juan not only noticed Iça's Qur'ān commentaries, therefore; he also found himself discussing Muslim Qur'ān interpretation.

When Iça had finished his Castilian version of the Qur'ān and he and Juan had read through it, Iça had to leave the Savoy, before Juan had learned Arabic thoroughly—before, indeed, a fair copy of the Castilian text had been produced.[50] Juan was forced to hire another copyist to help complete the latter task, but never succeeded in finding another Arabic teacher.[51] With no other option left to him, he decided that he must forge ahead anyway, making a Latin translation of the Qur'ān based on Içа's literal Castilian version and his own—admittedly imperfect—knowledge of the Arabic original.[52] Given his desire to present the Qur'ān to Christian readers without addition or gloss, and given his previous insistence that Iça translate it into Castilian word for word, it is not surprising to discover that Juan attempted to produce a verbatim Latin version, taking this approach, as a matter of fact, to remarkable extremes.[53]

This meant, on the one hand, faithfully transforming Iça's literal Castilian translation into Latin, a process that Juan strikingly described as "composing in the Latin language that translation made by [Iça] in Spanish" (*interpretationem per illum factam Hyspano, Latino condens sermone*).[54] But, on the other hand, it meant doing so with an eye ever more closely fixed on the Arabic original, shaping his Latin version in such a way that it began to preserve "the Arabic more than the Spanish way of speaking."[55] To accomplish this, Juan did not hesitate, in fact, to reshape the Latin language itself. His description of how he did this is not entirely intelligible, but there is no doubt that he innovated in unprecedented ways. He changed deponent Latin verbs (the fairly common verbs which are passive in form but active in meaning) into active verbs when the Arabic verbs they translated were active, Arabic having no verbal form like the deponent. In places where Latin would require a dative—presumably he was thinking here of instances where the dative is used as an object of a verb—he used the accusative in Latin, since Arabic lacks a dative case.[56] Latin possessive adjectives in the third person ("his," "her," "their") presented, he tells us, a particular problem. They vary in number not according to the possessor but according to the thing possessed. *Liber suus* in Latin, therefore, can mean either "his/her book" or "their book," depending on whether the antecedent is singular or plural, while *libri sui* means either "his/her books" or "their books." In Arabic, the possessive adjectives lack this ambiguity: "his book" is *kitābuhu*, "their book" *kitābuhum*; "his books" is *kutubuhu*, "their books" *kutubuhum*. This problem Juan addressed in two different ways. Early on in his translation, he adopted the practice, which was actually fairly common in medieval Latin, of indicating possession by means of a pronoun in the genitive rather than a possessive adjective, writing, say, *liber ipsorum*, "the book of those same ones," to clarify a plural possessor. But he was also not afraid to invent entirely new forms, and he did so here, creating a new plural variation of the possessive adjective, *sussuus*, which he used to refer to plural subjects, "so that where [the 's'] is duplicated it indicates that it is a plural in the Arabic language."[57]

Furthermore, Juan noticed many Qurʾānic words which were also in "the language of the Spanish in the vernacular" because of the Arabs' long occupation of the Iberian Peninsula. He therefore coined Latin words on the models of these Arabic-derived Castilian words, even when other Latin words were available.[58] He likewise noticed that Arabic frequently employed a construction called the nominal absolute. Here a noun phrase in the nominative case, referring to the subject of a following main verb, is stated at the beginning of a sentence "and left hanging," the sentence itself "carrying on . . . as though the [original statement of the subject] did not exist."[59] Thus in verses 2:4–5 of the Qurʾān we literally have "And those who believe in what we revealed to you and what was revealed to you previously, and who are certain of the next world, these are in dependence on the guidance of their Lord . . ." Though Iça, for the sake of intelligibility, had added finite "to be" verbs to such absolutes, "because the Spanish language . . . does not use absolutes," Juan, as he gradually came to follow the Arabic original more than Iça's Castilian translation, began to "set forth nominal absolutes without the verb."[60]

Many of Juan's methods of making the Latin text conform to "the Arabic way of speaking" were, therefore, remarkably innovative, he himself confessing that he had not hesitated "to rough up Priscian," the famous late antique grammarian, by making "frequent use of incongruous Latin."[61] It is likely, in fact, that his translation at many points would have been, as L. P. Harvey put it, "down-right incomprehensible" to readers unfamiliar with Arabic.[62] What appear to be a few fragments of Juan's Latin translation surviving as quotations in his own works suggest this may have been so.[63] At any rate, Juan clearly had in mind readers such as himself who knew at least some Arabic and who would use his Latin version as a sort of key to the Arabic text itself.

That this is so is strongly suggested by the format of the edition that Juan was preparing, something that he also describes in some detail. The Arabic text copied out and vocalized by Iça appeared in one column and Iça's Castilian version appeared next to it, in large and well-formed characters.[64] After finishing his Latin version, Juan had it written—in vivid red letters—between the lines of the Castilian translation, the result being a trilingual Qurʾān in a single great volume written, he tells us with noticeable precision, on thirty-three six-leaved gatherings.[65] To read Juan's Latin version usefully, therefore, it would have been necessary at many points to look over at the Arabic or, perhaps, down at the Castilian in order to be certain what Juan's hybrid Latin meant. Juan as much as admits this when he indicates that the work was intended for "the experts in the three languages" (*trium periti linguarum*).[66] What began as a tool for converting the worst of heretics became in the end, therefore, a book of supremely philological character, a volume that privileged lexical and grammatical inquiry and brought the reader's attention ever back to the Arabic text of the Qur'ān in all its particularity. That Juan actually attached the "Summary of the Understanding of the Psalms," the work apparently explaining the Muslim interpretation of the Qur'ānic surahs that Iça had copied for him in Aiton, to the end of the tri-lingual edition as a sort of Qur'ānic study aid only added to the philological uses of this volume.[67]

Yet immediately after describing the layout of his new Qur'ān edition, Juan makes clear that his considerable philological efforts had all been for polemical and apologetic ends: he had done all this, he says, "in order that it would make known . . . what the sect of Muhammad contains, its aim being to demonstrate how easily learned Christians are able to persuade Muslims out of their sect, and how one should be compassionate with those who are passing away in ignorance, lack of learning, and blindness."[68] It is on this evangelizing note that Juan concludes his preface. From polemic to philology and back to polemic once more.

It is clear, I hope, that just such an oscillation between polemic and philology characterized Latin-Christian Qur'ān reading in general. In fact, just as recognizing the coexistence of what Gilbert Dahan calls "confessional exegesis" and "scientific exegesis" is a key to understanding Latin-Christian biblical study in the same period, so attending to the intricate interaction between polemical and philological Qur'ān reading is central to understanding how Islam's holy book was read in Latin Christendom.[69] Not that all readers so enthusiastically embraced both approaches, but if we consider as a body the sources that have preoccupied us here, we find equally abundant signs of both ways of interacting with the Qur'ānic text.

Indeed, Latin-Christian scholars often found that philological Qur'ān reading was both necessary and many-sided. Not a few found themselves—at the most basic level—drawn into the marvelous complexity of the Arabic language. This was particularly true of those who translated the Qur'ān into Latin in this period, but it was also true of others such as the annotators of Robert's Latin Qur'ān, who were forced to explain the meaning of Arabic words that appeared in transliteration, or of the Protestant humanist Theodore Bibliander, who included a set of notes likewise explaining Arabic terms in his edition of that translation four hundred years later.[70] Juan de Segovia's Qur'ān edition actually facilitated such close grappling with the Arabic language, since it presented the Arabic Qur'ān side by side with Castilian and Latin translations. His was not the last to do so, for, as we have seen in the two previous chapters, in the following two generations both Flavius Mithridates and Egidio da Viterbo likewise provided Latin readers with the Qur'ān in Arabic in parallel columns with a Latin version.

As it did for Juan, Qur'ān reading for many Latin readers meant contending with that text's literary and structural conventions. The earliest manuscript of Robert's translation has paragraph marks that follow the traditional Islamic division of the Qur'ān into decades of verses, and the accompanying marginal glosses explain that certain abrupt changes in the narrative voice represent "asides of God to Muhammad." One later Christian reader laboriously wrote the proper Arabic surah names—often in both Arabic script and Latin transliteration—in the margins of a thirteenth-century copy of the same translation.[71] Later translators were far more studious about maintaining in their Latin versions the proper divisions of the Qur'ānic text and the proper names of the surahs, the sixteenth-century version produced for Egidio da Viterbo preserving these features of the Qur'ānic text quite minutely.[72] In doing all this, these readers were, like Juan de Segovia again, obviously spending a lot of time with Arabic manuscripts of the Qur'ān.

Juan, as we have seen, noticed that Iça had brought with him the "books of their doctors which expounded the Qur'ān," and made clear that he and Iça even spent time discussing Muslim exegesis of the Qur'ān. Of this engagement with the vast tradition of Qur'ānic commentary and with Muslim scholars themselves, there is also abundant evidence among other Latin Qur'ān readers. The translators—or at least those who did their job at all adequately—regularly found themselves turning either directly to Qur'ānic commentaries or to Muslim informants as they attempted to come up with Latin translations of particularly difficult passages of the Arabic original. But even readers who were not translators can be watched as they consult Qur'ānic commentaries or knowledgeable Muslims. The marginal notes on Robert's Latin Qur'ān are frequently based directly on Muslim Qur'ānic exegesis, as are the notes that centuries later came to occupy the fourth column of Egidio da Viterbo's Arabic-Latin Qur'ān edition.

Some Christian readers clearly read the Qurʾān with Arabic Qurʾān commentaries open next to them. The faint interlinear notes in a late medieval copy of Mark of Toledo's thirteenth-century Latin Qurʾān are certainly the work of such a reader, Mark's very literal translation method making it easy to follow his Latin version side by side with an Arabic commentary.[73]

To make his now-lost Qurʾān edition more useful for later readers, Juan de Segovia attached to it the "Summary of the Understanding of the Psalms [of the Qurʾān]" that Iça had copied down for him in Aiton. This also is something that we have found Christian Qurʾān readers doing—attaching study aids to the text to make it easier to consult and understand. A thirteenth-century copy of Robert's translation now in Paris (BnF MS, lat. 3668) was fitted out with a substantial alphabetical index allowing readers to find quickly specific Qurʾānic passages of interest to them, and the same index appears in a late medieval copy now preserved in the National Library of Russia. To a fifteenth- or sixteenth-century manuscript of the same translation now in Dresden, a similarly anonymous reader attached a comprehensive analytical table of contents that describes each section of the Qurʾān in exhaustive detail.[74]

But though such study aids in many cases assisted readers in "lavishing attention on the details" of the Qurʾānic text in the manner of a philologist, some—like that thirteenth-century alphabetical index—were primarily finding devices designed specifically for polemically minded readers. This is philology often in service of polemic, then, just as Juan's philology so clearly was, and the addition of polemical indexes to the Qurʾānic text was really part of a larger strategy of placing Islam's holy book within an all-encompassing frame that was supposed to insure that later readers read it in a properly Christian way. Though among the Latin Qurʾān manuscripts that circulated in western Europe there are a few that lack such a polemical frame,[75] the great majority of them—especially the manuscripts of the most widely read version, Robert of Ketton's Latin Qurʾān—enclose it within a series of anti-Islamic texts. The ugly rubrics that replaced the surah names in Robert's version warn Christian readers of the inanities they will find, their hostile tone continuing throughout the oft-copied marginal notes which, despite the careful philological reading that often informs them, are obviously intended to demonstrate to Christian readers the Qurʾān's fraudulence. Attached to the Qurʾān before and behind in most of the later manuscripts and printed editions are further works that urge a polemical reading: Peter the Venerable's own *Summary of All the Heresy*, for example, and the famous *Apology of al-Kindī*, the most widely read Arab-Christian attack on Islam, translated into Latin, like the Qur'ān itself, under Peter the Venerable's auspices.

The jottings of later readers indicate that they often shared this desire to attack the Qur'ān and to defend the beliefs of Catholic Christendom and were often assisted in doing so by the very polemical framing in which they found the Qur'ān. What appear to be two late medieval or early modern readers of a copy of Robert of Ketton's version now in the Bodleian Library in Oxford (MS Selden Supra 31) were fond of bracketing interesting passages in pencil. More than once, they marked off sections of the polemical marginal notes and then went on to bracket or underline precisely the parts of the Qur'ānic text to which the bracketed sections of the notes refer. We can almost see their eyes moving from the explanatory notes to the text, their way of reading guided by the marginal notes and their polemical concerns. Likewise, a reader of Theodore Bibliander's edition of Robert's translation copied down a lengthy series of excerpts now extant in the tiny city of Güssing, Austria. Written in a hasty hand sometime just before 1560, these excerpts, strikingly enough, incorporate almost as much material from Bibliander's marginal notes as from the Qur'ānic text itself, often moving from one to another in mid-sentence. For this reader, Qur'ān reading meant engaging Islam's holy book through the thoroughgoing polemical filter that Bibliander had conveniently placed in the margins of his edition.[76]

Yet we would be very mistaken in assuming that all Qur'ān readers were so easily controlled by the polemical frames which typically surrounded it. Readers late in the period, for example, brought a new set of concerns and sources to their polemical analysis of the Qur'ān.[77] The Catholic Orientalist Johann Albrecht von Widmanstetter (d. 1557), for example, first editor of the Syriac New Testament, brought novel interests in the Kabbalah to his study of the Qur'ānic text and, in demonstrating the Qur'ān's falsity, pointed to disturbing parallels not only with Kabbalistic texts but with Protestant thought as well.[78] Qur'ān readers, therefore, like the readers of all other texts, were often confoundingly free, perfectly capable, in fact, of reworking the apparatus of framing devices that was meant to control how they read texts.[79] The creative reworkings of the polemical tradition of Qur'ān reading that we see in Widmanstetter are signs of this freedom, as are instances in which we can actually follow later readers as they vividly reject at least parts of the polemical frames in which they encountered the Qur'ān. The excerpts in the Güssing manuscript follow Bibliander's approach closely, as I have just suggested; yet in one striking way, they are the result of a fit of independent readership. Where a substantial portion of

Bibliander's notes consists of references to the verses of the Bible that parallel Qurʾānic passages, the Güssing reader's excerpts ignore these cross-references entirely: he is interested in polemic, but his polemic is shorn of any fascination with the laborious comparison of biblical and Qurʾānic narratives so important to the Protestant Bibliander.

But readers do not just freely reject earlier polemical frames by ignoring what they have no interest in; just as often, they energetically reconfigure those polemical frames for the Qurʾān as they create new manuscript or printed editions of it. The Paris copy of Robert's Latin Qurʾān with the annexed polemical index designed to speed up the search for material useful in disputation noticeably lacks the original twelfth-century Latin glosses. Here a typically twelfth-century study aid (a marginal commentary) has been pushed aside in favor of a typically thirteenth-century research tool (an alphabetical index), and the whole has been designed to fit within the confines of another typically thirteenth-century piece of technology, the small pocket book written in tiny letters, the result being a Dominican friar's pocket Qurʾān, ready to take on the road in the cause of preaching against the holy book of Islam.[80]

But if later readers were capable of creating innovative polemical frames for the Qurʾān, they had the capacity for even greater freedoms as well. I have already mentioned the analytical table of contents prefixed to Robert's Latin Qurʾān in the Dresden manuscript. What impresses here is not only the vastness of this study aid (it is fully one quarter the length of the Qurʾānic text that it analyzes) but the largely nonpolemical nature of its contents. Unlike the polemical index in BnF MS lat. 3668, this research tool focused only minimally on the Qurʾānic passages of value for disputation, and the reader who painstakingly prepared it assumed that there were other readers whose Qurʾānic interests similarly fell outside the limitations imposed on the Qurʾān by the typical polemical framing devices that usually accompanied it. A striking but telling irony in this case is that a later reader, the Orientalist and Kabbalist Widmanstetter, then printed an abridged version of the Qurʾān, which, as we have seen, was merely a reconfiguration of this tabula, attaching to it his own innovative set of polemical framing devices:[81] from polemical to nonpolemical and back again. Both polemical and nonpolemical study aids and framing devices could be read, it seems, in more than one way.[82]

While it is true, then, that Juan de Segovia's Qurʾānic philology was always the handmaiden of his overwhelmingly polemical and apologetic goals, these examples of readerly freedom—especially those that, like the

Dresden table of contents, demonstrate little concern with anti-Islamic polemic in its usual forms—urge us to recognize that philology might at times become a powerful motivation on its own. Indeed, there are hints in Juan's garrulous prologue that even for him Qurʾānic philology could engender peculiar pleasures of its own, quite independently of its value in attacking Islam. His rambling, if flawed, descriptions of the Arabic method for marking vowels, of the tendencies of that language to use nominal absolutes, or of the practices of Qurʾānic copyists go well beyond what is strictly necessary for his immediate concerns.[83] He had spent a lot of time acquiring the beginnings of expertise in Qurʾānic philology and seems to want to display this learning for his readers. In his celebrated study of the development of a philological tradition among Confucian scholars in seventeenth- and eighteenth-century China—a tradition very similar to the humanist tradition that developed in Latin Christendom—Benjamin Elman has observed that when philological methods are applied to the language of classical or sacred texts, they "momentarily desacralize" it, so that studying that language can become, even if only briefly, the immediate goal of inquiry and not just the forerunner to larger theological or ideological concerns.[84] It is not going too far, I think, to recognize, in Juan's enthusiastic studies of Arabic and in other readers' nonpolemical Qurʾān reading, instances in which philological Qurʾān reading has momentarily "de-demonized" Islam's holy book, these readers slipping out, if only briefly, from under the constraining framework of polemical engagement.

Polemical ends did indeed dominate the widely practiced Qurʾānic philology of this period, the attempt to refute Islam serving as the central motive for sophisticated learning about Islam and its book,[85] but these moments in which Qurʾānic philology briefly "de-demonized" that text urge us to recognize that readers could express other attitudes toward the Qurʾān besides hostility. Thomas F. Glick has compellingly described how academic inquiries that had nothing to do with religious belief could be pursued collectively in the Middle Ages by members of more than one religious group—who might work together as a translation team or who might occupy roles of student and master—irrespective of which religious group was politically dominant. A Christian scholar's desire to learn medical knowledge from, say, a Jew living in Christian Spain might even lead him to refer to his teacher as "my master." This deferential title makes sense because the specific, narrowly defined arena of medical education, an arena in which non-Christians often were the authorities, could become what Glick and other scholars call "a neutral space." In such neutral spaces, which Glick argues are created by the "expectation of gain by [all] parties"—education on the part of the student, pay on the part of the master, for example—Jewish, Christian, and Muslim intellectuals could "bracket ideology," could step outside of polemically prescribed roles that they might well occupy in other circumstances, and interact, if only for a limited time, as fellow scholars pursuing the same scholarly ends. It is only the assumption, all too widespread in current scholarship, that medieval intellectuals were "always in the polemical mode" when dealing with members of other religious groups that makes us think otherwise.[86] The momentary "de-demonization" of the text that we see from time to time when Latin Christians apply philology to the Qurʾān suggests that similar "neutral spaces" can open up inside the individual personalities of Christian Qurʾān readers—that, despite the powerful polemical vocabulary that so often dominated their intellectual interaction with the Qurʾān, room could be made for other ways of thinking about and handling Islam's holy book.

At the same time that I have been making clear how polemic and philology interacted in such complex ways in Christian Qurʾān reading in this era, therefore, I have also been pointing out the ways in which the Qurʾān could, in such neutral interior spaces, be perceived and experienced as something besides a fraudulent scripture in need of (often highly philological) refutation. While there are times when readers explicitly reveal these other capacities, such as when one wrote "Bene" ("Well said!," "Yes, indeed!") next to verse 2:115 in a Parisian copy of Robert of Ketton's translation, expressing his unqualified agreement with that verse's moving description of God's omnipresence,[87] more often than not these attitudes and ways of experiencing were expressed more subtly. Robert of Ketton had nothing good to say about Islam in the preface to his translation, but he nevertheless went to enormous trouble to reshape this text into an elegant Latin document whose prose conformed to the canons of good style reigning in his day, and his was the version of the Qurʾān that was by far the most widely read in Latin Christendom. Neither he nor, as far as we can tell, any of his readers explicitly denied that it was a fraudulent text inspiring an evil religion; yet he still felt bound to give it a prestigious Latin form, and it was in that form that most Latin readers encountered it. The Latin Qurʾān could, as we have seen, be given the physical form of a polemical research tool for disputatious mendicants; yet in that process, it also became what was essentially a scholastic textbook of the sort that circulated in the great Latin universities of the later Middle Ages where, like other non-Christian textbooks by the likes of Aristotle and Maimonides, it could be used in the writing of what was essentially Christian theology. In the late Middle Ages the Qurʾān in various Latin versions would be reframed as something else again: an expensively produced book meant not for scholars but for book collectors, attracted to it not only by its costly illuminations and calligraphy but also by its exotic Oriental character. In the world of late medieval northern Italy, a vast range of products from the Islamic world—carpets, bronzes, cut glass—had found ready markets among the wealthy. The Qurʾān fit right in. While never ceasing to be seen as an anti-scripture, therefore, Islam's holy book was understood to be and experienced as other things besides simply that.

Qurʾānic philology existed far earlier in Latin Europe, therefore, than scholars have thought; that philology was typically welded onto the purposes of anti-Islamic polemic; and alongside this dialectic of philology for polemic, other, sometimes ambivalent, attitudes toward the Qurʾān could exist as well. Such has been the principal argument that I have advanced in this book, and this argument, it should be obvious, is in many ways an argument for continuity: a continuity of complex reading practices and ways of experiencing the Qurʾān that stretches from the mid-twelfth through the mid-sixteenth century, right over the apparently imposing barriers that have typically been thought to separate the twelfth-century Renaissance from the Scholastic period, and the Scholastic period from the age of Renaissance and Reformation. Yet it should also be clear that this is a continuity that exists alongside of or, better, contains within itself a series of equally interesting changes. Across the whole period from 1140 to 1560, Latin readers applied philological tools to and constructed polemical arguments on the basis of the Qurʾān, but in doing so, they produced texts of the Qurʾān that varied with the scholarly conventions of the day and which often unconsciously mimicked contemporary biblical editions. Robert of Ketton's Latin translation is a sort of amplified Qurʾān, the original text having been noticeably expanded by the inclusion of exegetical material drawn from Arabic Qurʾān commentaries. In this it resembles nothing so closely as the almost exactly contemporary *Scholastic History* of Peter Comestor, which similarly presents its readers with a version of the Latin Bible notably amplified by the interpolation of traditional biblical exegesis.[88] At the other end of the period, Egidio da Viterbo's bilingual Qurʾān with its parallel columns of Arabic text, Latin transliteration, Latin translation, and explanatory notes is inescapably reminiscent of the polyglot Bibles with their parallel columns of Hebrew, Aramaic, Greek, and Latin biblical texts and interpretive notes, the first of which was produced virtually contemporaneously and in the same region—eastern Spain.[89] Just as Juan de Segovia's Qur'ān reading exemplifies the powerful continuities of reading practice and attitude that I have just described, so it also contains vivid signs of this particular evolution. Had his trilingual Qur'ān survived, it would have been the first of three Qur'ān editions to set forth the original Arabic alongside a Western language in this period.

The polyglot Bibles were the work of the remarkable biblical humanists who flourished at the end of the fifteenth and beginning of the sixteenth centuries and there are, as we have seen, a number of close connections between that movement and Qur'ān reading in the same period. This alerts us to another factor in generating the complex patterns of Qur'ān reading, especially in the later Middle Ages and sixteenth century: Latin-Christian intellectuals were beginning to find other reasons to read the Qur'ān besides the desire to refute it or defend the Bible. It was a commonplace in the early sixteenth century that if one wanted to learn Hebrew—as a growing number of humanists were doing—then one ought also to learn Arabic and Aramaic, since knowledge of these two cognate languages would ease learning the language of the Old Testament.[90] But to learn Arabic, it turned out, sometimes meant learning it through the medium of reading the Qur'ān, copies of which had been circulating in Latin Europe since at least the early fourteenth century.[91] Thus it is that we find at least one sixteenth-century humanist intellectual—perhaps even that great biblical translator William Tyndale himself—making his way slowly through an Arabic copy of the Qur'ān, carefully revising and correcting the new Latin translation made for Egidio da Viterbo. Such a figure might well, in other circumstances, have attacked the Qur'ān according to the age-old model of Christian polemicists. But his interest as he worked through the Arabic Qur'ān was almost certainly the more mundane task of learning a difficult language related to Hebrew. When we look at his marginal annotations, we find minute philological investigation intermixed with no obvious polemical preoccupations.[92]

The circle of biblical humanists, however, often overlapped with that of another important group of late medieval intellectuals, the Christian Kabbalists. Following Pico della Mirandola's lead, these scholars used their knowledge of Hebrew and Aramaic to read the great works of Jewish mysticism and to merge many aspects of it with Christian belief, creating in the process a tradition of Christian Kabbalah that "caused an intellectual earthquake," the "seismic tremors" of which "shook everything from the structures of theological education to the practice of natural philosophy" in the early modern period,[93] including, as we have seen, Christian Qurʾān reading. Flavius Mithridates turned to Kabbalistic texts as he composed his rather dubious notes on the Qurʾān. Johann Albrecht von Widmanstetter attacked the Qurʾān by associating its doctrines with the Christian Kabbalist notions that he also disliked. Though I have come across no explicit connection between Egidio da Viterbo's Qurʾān edition and his intense—and very learned—interest in Kabbalah, there is certainly a relationship between these two initiatives at some level, both growing out of his broader and abiding interest in Semitic languages.[94]

While there are indeed, therefore, substantial continuities in Qurʾān reading from the mid-twelfth to the mid-sixteeth century, there are also, as all this suggests, some important changes, the most striking of them connected with the development of the new scholarly practices and interests that humanist scholars of biblical languages and postbiblical literature introduced into the scholarly culture of Latin Europe. But in clarifying the ways in which Latin-Christian Qurʾān reading changed as it came under the influence of different kinds of reading practices and such broader intellectual movements as biblical humanism and Christian Kabbalism, I have necessarily been saying much about the origins of scholarship specifically on the Qurʾān in the modern West as well. Some scholars have seen little in common between the investigations of post-Enlightenment linguists, historians, and scholars of Islam and the Qurʾān study of their medieval predecessors, positing a sort of dramatic modern break with medieval Qurʾān reading practices with the application of humanist scholarly methods to the Qurʾān in the sixteenth century, or asserting that it was only in 1698, with the publication of Ludovico Marracci's magnificent *Alcorani textus universus*, that modern Qurʾānic scholarship can be said to have begun in the West.[95] With much more nuance, Norman Daniel, while he rightly pointed out that while Marracci's edition and translation of and notes on the Qurʾān represent exemplary scholarship that any "modern" philologist cannot help but admire, nevertheless also stressed how fully Marracci's "refutations" of the Qurʾān—refutations which, in point of fact, comprise a major portion of the work—continue long-standing polemical approaches to Qurʾān reading.[96] As we have seen, the philological aspects of Marracci's enormously learned work were almost entirely anticipated by Egidio da Viterbo's bilingual Qurʾān of 1518, and the kind of Qurʾān reading that informed Egidio's own edition was not so radically different from that of Robert of Ketton, the first Latin translator of the Qurʾān in the middle of the twelfth century, who, like Egidio, turned repeatedly to sources of Islamic Qur'ān exegesis as he translated. All this requires us not only to do away with notions of a radical change in Western Qur'ān scholarship in the Renaissance or the Enlightenment, but to see in the development of the modern, Western study of the Qur'ān, and indeed Islam generally, a still more gradual evolution than even Daniel suggested. Modern Qur'ān scholarship must be seen as unfolding slowly out of the premodern practices of European Qur'ān reading, Qur'ānic philology for the purposes of polemic gradually, though rarely entirely, giving way to an ever more independent philology, the biblical humanist movement playing a key role in this transition.[97]

Of this gradual development of modern Qur'ān scholarship out of medieval Latin ways of reading the Qur'ān, Juan de Segovia's Qur'ān reading is also, for one last time, notably representative. His most intense period of Qur'ān reading occurred in the 1450s, a few generations before the biblical humanist movement got underway. His Qur'ān edition, as I hope will be clear from the foregoing, actually itself anticipated Egidio's work of sixty years later and thus also Marracci's accomplishment two hundred and fifty years in the future. Like both these later Qur'ān readers, he presented the Qur'ānic text to the reader in both Arabic and Latin, to which he added a Castilian version, and what amounted to a commentary (compiled by his Muslim collaborator Iça) that explained the meaning of each of the Qur'ān's "psalms." There are obvious ways in which his edition was more primitive than either Egidio's or Marracci's, but in providing the Qur'ān to Christian readers in both Western translations and the Arabic original, all this accompanied by exegetical notes, it was clearly the product of much the same approach to that text and therefore signals the key changes in Qur'ān reading that took place from the later fifteenth century onward. But that he was as preoccupied with polemic as he was with philology—in this like both Robert of Ketton and Ludovico Marracci as well—reminds us of the deep continuities in how Latin intellectuals engaged the Qur'ān throughout the whole period from 1140 to 1560.

Nancy Bisaha has recently shown that the response of humanists such as Benedetto Accolti (1415–64) to the Turkish conquest of Constantinople tended to draw equally on both classical and medieval models: he, like many contemporaries, adopted "classical elements . . . such as the addition, or invention, of speeches from key players," while nevertheless calling for a renewed crusade against Islam using much the same language as twelfth- and thirteenth-century crusade propagandists.[98] Juan de Segovia's passionately thorough Qur'ān reading, provoked by the same military defeat, similarly embodies both important later medieval innovations and centuries-old continuities in how Latin Christendom responded to Islam and its holy book. His precocious polyglot Qur'ān points toward the sixteenth-century emergence, in facing-page editions with their grammatical and textual notes based on Arabic Qur'ān commentaries, of a fully visible Qur'ānic philology more independent than the version that had till then been practiced largely in the service of anti-Islamic polemic, and had been hidden within the language of Latin Qur'ān translations and among the hostile framing notes that surrounded them. Yet even though his now lost edition privileged philological reading, much as would Egidio's edition in the next century, it was still explicitly linked in Juan's mind to the cause of attacking Islam and reinterpreting its book along Christian lines. Qur'ānic philology certainly grew in prominence during this period, as we have seen, and polemical Qur'ān reading clearly went through its own interesting transformations, but their tendency to work with each other in a complex tandem—as they did in Juan's encounter with the Qur'ān—remained constant throughout these four hundred years. And if, in the transparent pleasure that Juan took in his Qur'ān reading, we detect a capacity to think about and experience that book in ways that went beyond the compelling polemical and philological purposes that were uppermost in his mind, then here too we are in the presence of continuity. For, like him, other Latin readers had found in the Qur'ān not only a false scripture to be attacked polemically and a difficult text to be understood philologically, but a book whose elegant Latin form communicated prestige or whose exotic contents engendered desirability. Among its many readers in Latin Christendom, the Qur'ān was, like the powerful, feared, dynamic, and attractive civilization that it inspired, far too complex a thing to be approached or experienced in only one way.

Appendix
Four Translations of 22:1–5

Robert of Ketton's version of 22:1–5 (Paris, BnF, MS Arsenal 1162, fols. 89ra–b)

(1) Genus humanum deum time. quoniam hore maxime terremotus est timendus die resurrectionis. (2) quando nutrix suum alumpnum renuet. pregans aborsum faciet. omnisque licet falso. uidebitur ebrius. quoniam deus malum inferet grauissimum. (3) qui scripto notabit omnem insipientem rationantem in deum et sequacem diaboli mali. (4) singulos namque tales aberrabit et ad ignis penam mittet. (5) Quare de resurrectione dubitat quisquam? Nonne uos e terra primo plasmauimus secundo a spermate preiacente. sanquineque sequente tercio coagulata massa quarto forma similitudinis non nunquam dissimilitudinis produximus? Vobis quidem ad plenam noticiam explano singula: qui matris aluum conceptui mansionem ad terminum scitum efficio. post quem pueros educo. et ad uirilitatem integram adduco. et erit quidam mortis iuri cito suppositus. quidam autem ad uitam periorem deductus. ubi primo discretus: inscius efficitur. Terra quidem stabilis aqua super ipsam cadente: mouetur atque fructificat. et ex omni nascentium genere duo parilia decentia per eam orta sunt.

[(1) Race of the humans, fear God, for the earthquake of the greatest hour is to be feared on the day of resurrection; (2) when the nurse will reject her nursling, the pregnant woman will have a miscarriage, and each, though falsely, will appear drunk, for God will bring about a most weighty calamity (3–4) who, having written [it] out [already], will take note of each foolish arguer against God and [each] follower of the evil devil, for surely he will lead astray each one of such [followers] and cast [them] into the punishment of fire. (5) Why does anyone doubt about the resurrection? Did we not mold you first from earth, and second from preexisting sperm and ensuing blood, and third from a coagulated lump, and fourth did we not produce [you] from a form of similarity and sometimes of dissimilarity? To you indeed I explain each thing to the point of full information: [I] who make the womb of the mother the dwelling place of the conception until a known term, after which I bring forth boys, and I bring [them] to full manhood. And there will be a certain one placed quickly under the law of death, but another will be led to a worse life: at first wise, he becomes foolish. The steadfast earth, indeed, with water falling over it, is moved and bears fruit, and from all types of things being born two handsome equals rise through it.]

Mark of Toledo's version of 22:1–5 (Turin, Biblioteca Nazionale Universitaria, MS F. V. 35, fol. 44rb)

(1) O vos homines creatorem timete quia terre motus hore est magnum quid. (2) die qua uidebitis lactatricem stupefacere et obliuiscere quem lactauit et parturientem abortire et homines inebriatos nec erunt inebriati. verum supplicium Dei erit magnum. (3) et quidam hominum disputabunt in deo sine scientia et sequuntur omnem Sathanam proteruum (4) et scriptum est super ipsum quod qui imitatus fuerit eum faciet eum oberrare et diriget eum ad penam Averni. (5) O uos homines si dubitatis de die requisitionis nos quidem uos creauimus de terra deinde de spermate deinde de sanguinis suga. Deinde de carne consolidata et non consolidata ut declarem uobis et conquiescere faciam in matricibus quod uellem usque ad diem prescitum. Deinde uos educerem infantes usque dum peruenirettis ad robur uestrum. Et quidam uestrum decedunt et quidam ad deteriorem reducuntur etatem. ut postquam aliquid nouerunt desipiant et uidebitis terram aridam et cum dedimus desuper pluuiam contremissit et ebullit et producit de omni pares flores.

[(1) O you men, fear the creator, for the earthquake of the hour is a great thing; (2) on that day you will see the nursing mother be stunned and forget the one she nurses, and the one giving birth miscarry, and men drunk and they will be not drunk; but the punishment of God will be great. (3) And certain of men will dispute about God without knowledge and they will follow every brazen Satan. (4) And it was written above him that the one who has imitated him, he will make him stray and will guide him to the punishment of Avernus. (5) O you men, if you doubt about the day of examination, we indeed created you from earth, then from sperm, then from a sip of blood, then from consolidated and unconsolidated flesh, as I might declare to you, and I will make what I want to rest in wombs until a foreknown day; then I was bringing you up as infants until you might come into your strength. And certain of you pass away, and certain are reduced to a worse age so that after they know something, they become foolish. And you will see the arid earth, and when we have given rain from above, it shudders, and bubbles, and produces equal flowers from everything.]

Flavius Mithridates' version of 22:1–5 (Vatican City, BAV, MS urb. lat. 1384, fols. 75vb–76vb)

(1) O genus hominum timete deum uestrum qui tremere faciet illa hora quid mirabile. (2) Die qua uiderint illud expauescent omnes lactantes quę lactant: et clamabunt omnes pregnantes pro fetu earum et uidebuntur homines ebrii. et cur ebrii sunt. quia tormenta dei strictissima sunt. (3) Et hominum sunt qui murmurant contra deum absque scientia et efficientur omnes demoniorum ordinum. (4) Scriptum est enim super eo a quando natus est. quod pessime natus est: et offeretur tormentis tribulantibus. (5) O genus hominum cum fuerit in uos intellectus emissionis de sepulchris: et quod nos creauimus uos de terra quosdam uero de spermate etiam de menstruis: et de mistura eorum natos et abortiuos ex his: ut declaremus uobis: et formamus in matrice quod uolumus. ad tempus nominatum. postea uero facimus uos exire paruulos deinde perficimini in uires uestras. Et uestrum quidam moritur quidam ad terram reuertitur in breui uel in longo tempore absque eo quod quis sciat quod nos scimus. et uidetis terram aridam: et cum descendere fecerimus super eam aquam: madefit: et germinat: et floret parium specierum.

[(1) O race of men, fear your God who will make what [is] marvelous to tremble in that hour, (2) the day on which they will see that, all those nursing who nurse will panic. And all pregnant women will call out on behalf of their unborn child. And men will seem drunk: and why are they drunk? Because the torments of God are most severe. (3) And from among men are those who murmur against God without knowledge: and all will be made [to be] of the orders of demons. (4) It was written above him from when he was born, that he was most wickedly born, and will be taken to the oppressing torments. (5) O race of men, since in you has been understanding of the sending forth from the graves, and that we created you from earth, but certain ones from sperm, and even from menstrual [remains] and from a mixture of them, [we created you] born and miscarried from these, as we might declare to you; and we form in the womb what we want until a specified time. But afterward we make you to issue as small boys; from thence you are completed in your powers. And from among you a certain one dies, a certain one is brought back to earth in a short or long time without that which anyone knows which we know (?). And you see the arid earth, and when we have made water descend upon it, it moistens and germinates and makes flowers of equal species.]

Egidio da Viterbo's version of 22:1–5 (Milan, BA, MS D 100 inf., fols. 312r–v [Cambridge, Cambridge University Library, MS Mm. v. 26 lacks this surah])

(1) O vos homines timete deum uestrum et quia quod timetur de hora est res maxima. (2) in die quo uidebitis relinquere quamcumque nutricem quod lactet et eijciet omnis pregnans pregnationem suam et uidebis [*sic*] homines uiduos uerum non erunt uidui sed erit (erunt MS) pena dei terribilis. (3) et ex hominibus sunt qui disputant de deo absque scientia et sequuntur omnem diabolum maledictum. (4) fuit scriptum super eum quod is qui habebit amorem igitur is faciet errare eum et diriget eum ad penam Zangris.[1] (5) O homines si estis uos in dubio de resurrectione igitur nos creauimus uos ex terra postea ex spermate postea uermem postea ex frusto creabili et increabili absque formatore ut declararemus uobis et aptamus in matricibus quod uolumus usque ad tempus determinatum postea educimus uos pueros postea complemus tempus uestrum et ex uobis est qui moritur et ex uobis est qui reuertitur ad peiorem uitę quia (?)[2] [non] sciant post scientiam aliquod et uidebis terram securam et quando descendemus nos super eam aquam et mouebit et crescet et educet ex omni re paria et pulchritudinem.

[(1) O you men, fear your God because what is feared regarding the hour is the greatest thing. (2) On the day in which you will see each nurse abandon what she suckles, and each pregnant woman expel her pregnancy, and you will see people as widowed but they will not be widowed, but the punishment of God will be terrible. (3) And from among men are those who dispute about God without knowledge and follow every accursed devil. (4) It was written above him that he is the one who will have love; therefore, he will make him wander, and will guide him to the punishment of *saʿīr*.

(5) O men, if you are in doubt about the resurrection, [notice] therefore that we created you from earth, afterward from sperm, afterward as a worm, afterward from a piece creatable and uncreatable without a fashioner, as we might declare to you. And we furnish whatever we want in wombs until a determined time, and afterward we rear you as children, afterward we make complete your time; and from among you is he who dies, and from among you is he who is returned to a worse [state] of life so that they may not know something after [having] knowledge [of it]; and you will see the earth quiet, and when we will [make] water descend over it, it will move and grow and draw forth from each thing pairs and beauty.]

Abbreviations and Short Titles

Annotator	Anonymous twelfth-century annotations on Robert of Ketton's *Lex Mahumet.* Unless otherwise indicated, references are to Paris, BnF, MS Arsenal 1162.
BA	Biblioteca Ambrosiana (Milan).
BAV	Biblioteca Apostolica Vaticana (Vatican City).
al-Bayḍāwī	ʿAbd Allāh Ibn ʿUmar al-Bayḍāwī. *Anwār al-tanzīl wa-asrār al-taʾwīl. Beidhawii Commentarius in Coranum.* Ed. H. Fleischer. 2 vols. Osnabrück, 1968 (reprint of Leipzig edition of 1846–48).
Bibliander, *Alcoran* 1543	Theodore Bibliander. *Machumetis Saracenorum principis, eiusque successorum vitae, doctrina ac ipse Alcoran . . .* Basel, 1543.
Bibliander, *Alcoran* 1550	Theodore Bibliander. *Machumetis Saracenorum principis, eiusque successorum vitae, doctrina ac ipse Alcoran . . .* Basel, 1550.
BnF	Bibliothèque nationale de France (Paris).
EI2	*Encyclopaedia of Islam.* 2nd ed. 10 vols. Leiden, 1960–.
EQ	*Encyclopaedia of the Qurʾān.* Ed. Jane McAuliffe. 5 vols. Leiden, 2001–6.
Ibn ʿAṭīyah	Abū Muḥammad ʿAbd al-Ḥaqq Ibn ʿAṭīyah al-Andalusī. *Al-Muḥarrar al-wajīz fī tafsīr al-kitāb al-ʿazīz.* Ed. al-Raḥḥālī al-Fārūq et al. 15 vols. Doha, 1977–91.

Ibn Kathīr	Abū al-Fidā᾿ Ismā᾿īl Ibn Kathīr. *Tafsīr al-Qur᾿ān al-ʿAẓīm*. 4 vols. Beirut, 1990.
Iohannes Gabriel, *Alcoranus*	Iohannes Gabriel Terrolensis' translation of the Qur᾿ān completed under Egidio da Viterbo's auspices (c. 1518).
Mark of Toledo, *Liber Alchorani*	Mark of Toledo's Latin translation of the Qur᾿ān (c. 1210–11). Unless otherwise indicated, references are to Turin, Biblioteca Nazionale Universitaria, MS F. V. 35.
Marracci, *Alcorani textus*	Ludovico Marracci. *Alcorani textus universus . . . his omnibus praemissus est Prodromus*. Padua, 1698.
Mithridates, *Latin-Arabic Qur᾿ān*	Flavius Mithridates' edition and translation of surahs 21 and 22 (c. 1480–81). References are to Vatican City, BAV MS urb. lat. 1384.
al-Qurṭubī	Abū ʿAbd Allāh Muḥammad Ibn Aḥmad al-Qurṭubī. *Al-Jāmiʿ li-aḥkām al-Qur᾿ān*. 21 vols. in 11. Beirut, 1993.
PL	*Patrologia cursus completus. Series latina.*
Robert of Ketton, *Lex Mahumet*	Robert of Ketton's Latin translation of the Qur᾿ān (c. 1142–43). Unless otherwise indicated, references are to Paris, BnF, MS Arsenal 1162 and the sixteenth-century edition in Bibliander, *Alcoran* 1550.
al-Suyūṭī, *al-Itqān*	Jalāl al-Dīn ʿAbd al-Raḥmān ibn Abū Bakr al-Suyūṭī. *Al-Itqān fī ʿulūm al-Qur᾿ān*. Beirut, n.d.
al-Suyūṭī, *Tafsīr*	al-Suyūṭī's *Tafsīr al-Qur᾿ān al-Karīm* [his continuation of Jalāl al-Dīn Muḥammad ibn Aḥmad al-Muḥallī's *Tafsīr al-Qur᾿ān al-Karīm*]. Cairo, 1966.
al-Ṭabarī	Abū Jaʿfar Muḥammad ibn Jarīr al-Ṭabarī. *Jāmiʿ al-bayān fī ta᾿wīl āy al-Qur᾿ān*. 12 vols. Beirut, 1997.
al-Ṭabarsī	Abū ʿAlī al-Faḍl ibn al-Ḥasan al-Ṭabarsī.

Majma' al-bayān fī tafsīr al-Qur'ān. 5 vols. Qum, 1983.

al-Zamakhsharī — Abū al-Qāsim Jār Allāh Maḥmūd ibn 'Umar al-Zamakhsharī. *Al-Kashshāf 'an ḥaqā'iq ghawāmiḍ al-tanzī wa-'uyūn al-aqāwil fī wujūh al-ta'wīl*. Ed. Muḥammad 'Abd al-Salām Shāhīn. 4 vols. Beirut, 1995.

Notes

Introduction

1. See Bernard Guenée's discussion of the modern survival of medieval manuscripts as a gauge of the breadth of their readership in the Middle Ages in his *Histoire et culture historique dans l'occident médiéval* (Paris, 1980), 249–58, where he argues that a work surviving in thirty manuscripts was a great success. See also Ora Limor and Israel Jacob Yuval, "Skepticism and Conversion: Jews, Christians, and Doubters in *Sefer ha-Nizzahon*," in *Hebraica Veritas? Christian Hebraists and the Study of Judaism in Early Modern Europe*, ed. Allison P. Coudert and Jeffrey S. Shoulson (Philadelphia, 2004), 165. On the manuscripts of the Qur'ān in Arabic or Latin that circulated in medieval and early modern Europe, see the following: Marie-Thérèse d'Alverny, "Deux traductions latines du Coran au Moyen Âge," *Archives d'histoire doctrinale et littéraire du Moyen Âge* 22–23 (1947–48):69–131 at 108–13, 120–31; ead., "Marc de Tolède," in *Estudios sobre Alfonso VI y la reconquista de Toledo. Actas del II Congreso Internacional de Estudios Mozárabes (Toledo, 20–26 Mayo 1985)*, vol. 3 (Toledo, 1992), 25–59 at 49–59; ead., "Quelques manuscrits de la «Collectio Toletana»," in *Petrus Venerabilis, 1156–1956: Studies and Texts Commemorating the Eighth Centenary of His Death*, ed. Giles Constable and James Kritzeck (Rome, 1956), 202–18; Hartmut Bobzin, *Der Koran im Zeitalter der Reformation: Studien zur Frühgeschichte der Arabistik und Islamkunde in Europa* (Beirut and Stuttgart, 1995), 239–50, 344–46; on a manuscript of Robert of Ketton's Latin Qur'ān in a private collection, see ibid., 224; Angelo Michele Piemontese, "Il Corano latino di Ficino e i Corani arabi di Pico e Monchates," *Rinascimento: Rivista dell'Instituto Nazionale di Studi sul Rinascimento*, 2nd series, 36 (1996):227–73; *World Bibliography of Translations of the Holy Qur'ān in Manuscript Form* (Istanbul, 2000), I, 93–115; Fernando González Muñoz, *Exposición y refutación del Islam: La versión latina de las epístolas de al-Hāšimī y al-Kindī* (A Coruña, Spain, 2005), xcv–cxxiv. Professor José Martínez Gázquez is currently directing a team of scholars who are editing most of the Qur'ān translations that this study focuses on, and the results of their work are sure to add enormously to our understanding of Qur'ān reading in Western Europe. A website dedicated to that project and called "Islamolatina" can be viewed at http://seneca.uab.es/islamolatina/. It possesses a wealth of information relevant to the reading of Islam's holy book in Latin Christendom.

2. The bibliography here is enormous but see especially Beryl Smalley, *The Study of the Bible in the Middle Ages*, 3rd ed. (Notre Dame, Ind., 1978), and Gilbert Dahan, *L'exégèse chrétienne de la Bible en Occident médiéval, XIIe–XIVe siècles* (Paris, 1999).

3. On these, see most recently Gilbert Dahan, "L'enseignement de l'hébreu en Occident médiéval (XIIe–XIVe siècles)," *Histoire de l'éducation* 57 (1993):3–22, esp. 8–9, who supplies abundant bibliography. As we will see in Chapter 4, at least one and perhaps two copies of Robert of Ketton's Latin translation clearly circulated within the Dominican order.

4. In this, Qur'ān reading was like the study of Hebrew in this period. See Dahan, "L'enseignement de l'hébreu," passim.

5. But see Kurt Villads Jensen's impressionistic "Christian Reading of the Quran Before and After 1300," in *Rapports entre Juifs, Chrétiens et Musulmans: Eine Sammlung von Forschungsbeiträgen*, ed. Johannes Irmscher (Amsterdam, 1995), 173–78, and, much more importantly, Hartmut Bobzin's deeply learned *Der Koran im Zeitalter der Reformation*, and id., "Pre-1800 Preoccupations of Qur'ānic Studies," EQ 4:235–53.

6. Norman Daniel, *Islam and the West: The Making of an Image*, rev. ed. (Oxford, 1993) 70, and for further examples, 71–77. The author he is writing about here is Ramon Martí, though Daniel does not identify him.

7. Ibid., 78.

8. Ibid., 190–200 at 193–94. Daniel believed that the *Tractatus de statu saracenorum*, which he is citing here, was wholly the work of William of Tripoli. It has recently been shown to be the work of an anonymous author who used William's *Notitia de Machometo* as a major source. See John V. Tolan, *Saracens: Islam in the Medieval European Imagination* (New York, 2002), 204, 334n45 who cites Peter Engel's introduction to his edition of the text: Wilhelm von Tripolis, *Notitia de Machometo: De statu Sarracenorum*, ed. Peter Engels, Corpus Islamo-Christianum, Series Latina 4 (Würzburg, 1992), 52–74.

9. See Daniel, *Islam and the West*, 80, where he quotes Riccoldo carefully citing the first few verses of surah 109, which, since he was also an Arabist, he may have done using the Arabic text directly.

10. Ibid., 97, 198.

11. See especially Marie-Thérèse d'Alverny, "La connaissance de l'Islam en Occident du IXe au milieu de XIIe siècle," in *L'occidente e l'Islam nell'alto medioevo*, vol. 2, Settimane di studio del Centro italiano di studi sull'alto medioevo 12 (Spoleto, 1965), 577–602; Ugo Monneret de Villard, *Lo studio dell'Islam in Europa nel XII e nel XIII secolo* (Vatican City, 1944); and especially Tolan, *Saracens*.

12. Thomas F. Glick, "My Master, the Jew: Observations on Interfaith Scholarly Interaction in the Middle Ages," in *Jews, Muslims, and Christians in and around the Medieval Crown of Aragon: Studies in Honor of Elena Lourie*, ed. Harvey Hames (Leiden, 2004), 158.

13. See Camilla Adang, *Muslim Writers on Judaism and the Hebrew Bible: From Ibn Rabban to Ibn Hazm* (Leiden, 1996), 109.

14. Jeremy Cohen, "The Muslim Connection or On the Changing Role of the Jew in High Medieval Theology," in *From Witness to Witchcraft: Jews and Judaism in Medieval Christian Thought*, ed. Jeremy Cohen (Wiesbaden, 1996), 141–62 at 147.

15. Adang, *Muslim Writers on Judaism*, 254–55.

16. Daniel, *Islam and the West*, 35, 66, 98, 99, 201.

17. Glick, "My Master, the Jew," 157–58.

18. For another example of how choosing a different set of sources allows us to see interreligious relations in a very different light, see David Nirenberg's celebrated *Communities of Violence: Persecution of Minorities in the Middle Ages* (Princeton, N.J., 1996), 93ff.

19. James Hankins, *Plato in the Italian Renaissance*, 2 vols. (Leiden, 1990), vol. 1, 136–39 and 190–92, describes Decembrio's and George of Trebizond's tendentious distortions of Plato's works as they translated them.

20. See especially Roger Chartier, *The Order of Books: Readers, Authors, and Libraries in Europe between the Fourteenth and Eighteenth Centuries*, trans. Lydia G. Cochrane (Stanford, Calif., 1994), viii–ix and passim, and Guglielmo Cavallo and Roger Chartier, eds., *A History of Reading in the West*, trans. Lydia G. Cochrane (Amherst, Mass., 1999), especially the introduction (1–36) and the articles by Parkes, Hamesse, Saenger, Bonfil, and Grafton.

21. Studying other academic inquiries of the Middle Ages through their manuscripts has yielded similarly striking revisions in how they are understood. See Natalia Lozovsky, "*The Earth Is Our Book*": *Geographical Knowledge in the Latin West, ca. 400–1000* (Ann Arbor, Mich., 2000), 5n12.

22. Lozovsky, "*The Earth Is Our Book,*" 2–3, intriguingly discusses the necessity of and methods for studying such vaguely defined disciplines.

23. Anthony Grafton, *New Worlds, Ancient Texts: The Power of Tradition and the Shock of Discovery* (Cambridge, Mass., 1992), 7–8.

24. Ibid., 8.

25. I follow here the definition of philology typically used in conjunction with late medieval/Renaissance humanism: "A critical philologist pays close attention to words and the problems entailed in their transmission, translation, and explanation" (Jerry Bentley, *Humanists and Holy Writ: New Testament Scholarship in the Renaissance* [Princeton, N.J., 1983], 17–18; but see also Michael D. Reeve, "Classical Scholarship," in *The Cambridge Companion to Renaissance Humanism*, ed. Jill Kraye [Cambridge, England, 1996], 20–46). I am not suggesting that these Christian Qur'ān readers have embraced what James Hankins calls the "culture of criticism" that modern philologists, who aim only "to establish the original meaning of the author," practice (or at least claim to). Just as Hankins and others have shown that humanist philology was always closely connected to ideological, moral, or rhetorical concerns (see his *Plato in the Italian Renaissance*, 1, 364–66), so the Qur'ānic philology that I will be describing is rarely an end in itself.

26. Ora Limor and Israel Yuval have argued for a similar interaction between polemical and philological impulses among sixteenth-century Christian Hebraists in their "Skepticism and Conversion," 159–60 and passim.

27. See Chapter 1 below, pp. 32–35.

28. For abundant bibliography, see Cavallo and Chartier, eds., *A History of Reading in the West.*

29. Carol Everhart Quillen, *Rereading the Renaissance: Petrarch, Augustine, and the Language of Humanism* (Ann Arbor, Mich., 1998), 70.

30. See Ann Moss, *Ovid in Renaissance France: A Survey of the Latin Editions of Ovid and Commentaries Printed in France Before 1600* (London, 1982), 30–31, 44–

53, 60–61. For a similar interpretation of Petrarch, see Quillen, *Rereading the Renaissance*, 90–96, 104–5.

31. Anthony Grafton, "The Humanist as Reader," in Cavallo and Chartier, eds., *A History of Reading in the West*, 179–212 at 183.

32. Nicetas Philosophus in the ninth century, for example, appears to have been reading a Greek version of the Qur'ān. See "Translations of the Qur'ān," EQ 5:340–58 at 344 [art. Hartmut Bobzin], and Kees Versteegh, "Greek Translations of the Qur'ān in Christian Polemics (9th Century A.D.)," *Zeitschrift der Deutschen morgenländischen Gesellschaft* 141 (1991):52–68.

33. The bibliography here is enormous, but see most recently on Peter, Martí, and Riccoldo, Tolan, *Saracens*, 155–65, 233–54; Anthony Bonner, *Doctor Illuminatus: A Ramon Lull Reader* (Princeton, N.J., 1993), 1–56 contains an excellent introduction to Llull's thought and his study of Islam, but see also Tolan, *Saracens*, 256–74; on Cusa, see Ludwig Hagemann, *Der Ḳur'ān in Verständnis und Kritik bei Nikolaus von Kues: Ein Beitrag zur Erhellung islāmisch-christlicher Geschichte* (Frankfurt, 1976); on Alonso de Espina, see Ana Echevarria, *The Fortress of Faith: The Attitude towards Muslims in Fifteenth-Century Spain* (Leiden, 1999), 47–55 and passim.

34. Medieval copies of the Qur'ān in Arabic with Latin or Romance marginalia include Munich, Bayerische Staatsbibliothek, MS ar. 7 (on which see Bobzin, *Der Koran*, 309, 344); Paris, BnF MS ar. 384 (on which see François Déroche, *Catalogue des manuscrits arabes.* Deuxième partie: *Manuscrits musulmans*, vol. 1: *Les manuscrits du Coran. 2. Du Maghreb à l'Insulinde* [Paris, 1985], 53); and Vatican City, BAV, ebr. 357 (on which see Piemontese, "Il Corano latino," 264–67, 269–72). Perhaps the majority of manuscripts of the Qur'ān in Latin have some amount of marginalia. For bibliography see below, passim.

35. See Carlo de Frede, *La prima traduzione italiana del Corano sullo sfondo dei rapporti tra Cristianità e Islam nel Cinquecento* (Naples, 1967).

Chapter 1

1. See also 13:37, 16:103, 20:113, 26:195, etc. Unless otherwise indicated, all translations from Arabic, Latin, and other languages are my own.

2. On the Greek-to-Arabic translation movement, see Dimitri Gutas, *Greek Thought, Arabic Culture: The Graeco-Arabic Translation Movement in Baghdad and Early ʿAbbāsid Society (2nd–4th/8th–10th Centuries)* (London and New York, 1998). The literature on the later Arabic-to-Latin translation movement is enormous, but see Charles F. S. Burnett, "The Translating Activity in Medieval Spain," in *The Legacy of Muslim Spain*, ed. Salma Khadra Jayyusi (Leiden, 1992), 1036–58, for an excellent overview.

3. On humanist Arabic study, see Karl H. Dannenfeldt, "The Renaissance Humanists and the Study of Arabic," *Studies in the Renaissance* 2 (1955):96–117; and also Debora Kuller Shuger, *The Renaissance Bible: Scholarship, Sacrifice, and Subjectivity* (Berkeley, Calif., 1994), 13–16, 33–34; Hartmut Bobzin, "Geschichte der ara-

bischen Philologie in Europa bis zum Ausgang des achtzehnten Jahrhunderts," in *Grundriss der Arabischen Philologie*, ed. Wolfdietrich Fischer, Band 3: *Supplement* (Wiesbaden, 1992), 155–87; and Johann Fück, *Die arabischen Studien in Europa bis in den Anfang des 20. Jahrhunderts* (Leipzig, 1955), 25–53.

4. For a good introduction to Christian Kabbalah with abundant bibliography, see Joseph Dan, ed., *The Christian Kabbalah: Jewish Mystical Books and the Christian Interpreters* (Cambridge, Mass., 1997).

5. On Peter's translation project generally, see most recently José Martínez Gázquez, "Finalidad de la primera traducción latina del Corán," in *Musulmanes y cristianos en Hispania durante las conquistas de los siglos XII y XIII*, ed. Miquel Barceló and José Martínez Gázquez (Barcelona, 2005), 71–77, esp. 71–74; id. and Óscar de la Cruz Palma, "Las traducciones árabe-latinas impulsadas por Pedro el Venerable," in *Las órdenes militares: Realidad e imaginario*, ed. M. D. Burdeus, E. Real, and J. M. Verdegal (Castellón de la Plana, 2000), 285–95; José Martínez Gázquez, Óscar de la Cruz Palma, Cándida Ferrero, and Nádia Petrus [i Pons], "Die lateinischen Koran-Übersetzungen in Spanien," in *Juden, Christen und Muslime—Religionsdialog im Mittelalter*, ed. M. Lutz-Bachmann and A. Fidora (Darmstadt, 2004), 27–39 at 27–35; Marie-Thérèse d'Alverny, "Deux traductions," 69–113; ead., "Quelques manuscrits," passim; James Kritzeck, *Peter the Venerable and Islam* (Princeton, N. J., 1964), passim; and U. Monneret de Villard, *Lo studio dell'Islām*, 8–21.

6. For the sketchy details of Robert's life, see Charles S. F. Burnett, "Ketton, Robert of (fl. 1141–57)," *Oxford Dictionary of National Biography* 31:465–67. But see also id., "A Group of Arabic-Latin Translators Working in Northern Spain in the Mid-12th Century," *Journal of the Royal Asiatic Society* (1977): 62–70, esp. 63; id., "Some Comments on the Translating of Works From Arabic into Latin in the Mid-Twelfth Century," in *Orientalische Kultur und Europäisches Mittelalter*, ed. A. Zimmermann and I. Craemer-Ruegenberg, Miscellanea Mediaevalia 17 (Berlin and New York, 1985), 161–71; id., "The Translating Activity in Medieval Spain," 1043–45; id., Herman of Carinthia, *De essentiis: A Critical Edition with Translation and Commentary*, ed. and trans. Charles S. F. Burnett (Leiden, 1982), 4–5; Marie-Thérèse d'Alverny, "Translations and Translators," in *Renaissance and Renewal in the Twelfth Century*, ed. Robert Benson and Giles Constable (Cambridge, Mass., 1982), 449; and Kritzeck, *Peter the Venerable and Islam*, 62–65.

7. See here David Howlett's exhaustive analysis of Robert's use of elaborate numerological structures and the cursus in his introductory comments on his edition cited in the next note. On this preface see also José Martínez Gázquez, "Las traducciones latinas medievales del Corán: Pedro de Venerable-Robert de Ketton, Marcos de Toledo, y Juan de Segobia," *Euphrosyne* 31 (2003):491–503 at 492–95; and id., "El lenguaje de la violencia en el prólogo de la traducción latina del Corán impulsada por Pedro el Venerable," *Cahiers d'études hispaniques médiévales* 28 (2005):243–52, which includes an edition of the preface itself (244–45).

8. "tuus animus . . . studiosus sitiuit sterilem paludem Sarracene secte . . . fertilem efficere . . . propugnaculaque prorsus diruere" ("Praefatio Roberti tractatoris ad Dominum Petrum Cluniacensem Abbatem in Libro legis sarracenorum quem Alchoran vocant," ed. David Howlett in his *Insular Inscriptions* [Dublin, 2005], 168–75, ll. 1–3). Such language, as others have pointed out, suits quite nicely

the broader apologetic and christianizing goals of Peter the Venerable's project, which were often stated in very militant language. See Martínez and de la Cruz, "Las traducciones árabe-latinas impulsadas por Pedro el Venerable," 288, 293; Martínez, "Finalidad de la primera traducción latina del Corán," 74–76; id., "El lenguaje de la violencia," passim.

9. "Tibique . . . munus uoueo quod integritatem scientie in se conplectitur que secundum numerum et proportionem atque mensuram celestes circulos omnes et eorum quantitates . . . et earundem effectus atque naturas . . . diligentissime diligentibus aperit nunc probabilibus nonnunquam necessariis argumentis innitens" ("Praefatio Roberti tractatoris," ll. 55–62).

10. See Dorothee Metlitzki, *The Matter of Araby in Medieval England* (New Haven and London, 1977), 30–35 at 32.

11. For a brief account of what Robert says in his preface about his translation approach, see José Martínez Gázquez, "Observaciones a la traducción latina del Corán (Qur'ān) de Robert de Ketene," in *Les traducteurs au travail: Leurs manuscrits et leurs méthodes*, ed. Jacqueline Hamesse (Turnhout, 2001), 115–27 at 116–17.

12. "Lapides igitur et ligna ut tuum demum pulcherrimum et comodissimum edificium cementatum et indissolubile surgat nil excerpens nil sensibiliter nisi propter intelligentiam tantum alterans attuli" ("Praefatio Roberti tractatoris," ll. 28–30). See also d'Alverny, "Deux traductions," 86; and Martínez, "Las traducciones latinas medievales del Coran," 493.

13. For a sampling of scholarly reaction, see my "*Tafsīr* and Translation: Traditional Qur'ān Exegesis and the Latin Qur'āns of Robert of Ketton and Mark of Toledo," *Speculum* 73 (1998):703–32 at 705–7.

14. Gerard of Cremona, another (and more famous) twelfth-century Arabic-to-Latin scientific translator, for example, observed that he was attempting in his translations to transmit to Latin Christendom (*Latinitas*) "the most choice" writings of the Arabs. See Charles S. F. Burnett, "The Coherence of the Arabic-Latin Translation Program in Toledo," in *Science in Context* 14 (2000), 249–88 at 254–55, 275–76.

15. "Latinitas tamen omnis hucusque non dicam perniciosis incommodis ignorantie negligentieve pressa suorum hostium causam et ignorare et non depellere passa est" ("Praefatio Roberti tractatoris," l. 8–9). On this passage, see also Martínez, "Finalidad de la primera traducción latina del Corán," 76.

16. On Mark, see Marie-Thérèse d'Alverny and G. Vajda, "Marc de Tolède, traducteur d'Ibn Tūmart," *Al-Andalus* 16 (1951): 99–140, 259–307 and 17 (1952):1–56," and d'Alverny, "Marc de Tolède," 25–59. For an excellent introduction to his Qur'ān translation, see Nàdia Petrus i Pons, "Marcos de Toledo y la segunda traducción latina del Corán," in *Musulmanes y cristianos en Hispania*, ed. Barceló and Martínez, 87–94, but see also Martínez, "Las traducciones latinas medievales del Corán," 495–98; and id. et al., "Die lateinischen Koran-Übersetzungen in Spanien," 35–39.

17. See below, 232n4. As Petrus and others have pointed out, Mark makes no reference at all to Robert's translation and appears not to have been influenced by it. See her "Marcos de Toledo y la segunda traducción del Corán," 93; but also Martínez, "Las traducciones latinas medievales del Corán," 495.

18. Lucy K. Pick, *Conflict and Coexistence: Archbishop Rodrigo and the Muslims and Jews of Medieval Spain* (Ann Arbor, Mich., 2004), 14–20, 204–7, and passim. Nàdia Petrus i Pons rightly emphasizes the entirely Iberian nature of the motivations for this translation. See her "Marcos de Toledo y la segunda traducción latina del Corán," 87.

19. This preface is edited by d'Alverny and Vajda under the title "Préface à la traduction du Coran" in their "Marc de Tolède, traducteur," 260–68. For a detailed and insightful analysis of the biographical section see John [V.] Tolan, "Las traducciones y la ideología de reconquista: Marcos de Toledo," in *Musulmanes y cristianos en Hispania*, ed. Barceló and Martínez, 79–85.

20. "uenerabilis R[odericus] . . . sedem Archipresulatus Toletane metropoleos et insulam suscepisset, eamque ab inimicis crucis infestari cognouisset . . . quoniam quidem in locis ubi suffraganei pontiffices sacrificia sancta Ihesu Christo quondam offerabant, nunc pseudo-prophete nomine extollitur" (Mark of Toledo, "Préface à la traduction du Coran," 267. I read *pseudo-prophete* here as *pseudo-propheta*). On this and the following passages of the preface that express Rodrigo's motivations for the translation, see Tolan, "Las traducciones y la ideología de reconquista," 82–83; Petrus, "Marcos de Toledo y la segunda traducción latina del Corán," 88; Martínez, "Las traducciones latinas medievales del Corán," 496–97.

21. Mark of Toledo, "Préface à la traduction du Coran," 267.

22. "ut liber iste in latinum transferretur sermonem, quatinus ex institutis detestandis Mafometi a Christianis confusi, Sarraceni ad fidem nonnulli traherentur catholicam" (ibid.).

23. The same militant tone appears in connection with a related translation that Mark undertook later, this time of a short *ʿAqīdah* of Ibn Tūmart: "Transtuli [Mark says] . . . [librum] Habent[ometi] post librum Mofometi [*sic*], ut ex utriusque inspectione fideles in Saracenos inuehendi exercitamenta sumant ampliora" (Mark of Toledo, "Préface à la traduction d'Ibn Tūmart," ed. d'Alverny and Vajda in their "Marc de Tolède, traducteur," 268–69. On this passage, see also Martínez, "Las traducciones latinas medievales del Corán," 497.

24. D'Alverny and Vajda edit and comment on the Latin translations of these short works in their "Marc de Tolède, traducteur," 268–307.

25. On these manuscripts, see Petrus, "Marcos de Toledo y la segunda traducción latina del Corán," 90–91, who lists the six complete copies, and Chapter 5 below, where I discuss them all.

26. For the details of Mithridates' life that follow, I depend on Chaim Wirszubski, *Flavius Mithridates: Sermo de passione domini* (Jerusalem, 1963), 11–12, 48–59; Bobzin, *Der Koran*, 80–84; Angelo Michele Piemontese, "Il Corano latino," 252–63, and id., "Le iscrizioni arabe nella *Poliphili Hypnerotomachia*," in *Islam and the Italian Renaissance*, ed. Charles S. F. Burnett and Anna Contadini (London, 1999), 199–217 at 205, 213–15. For further bibliography on Mithridates, see Harvey Hames, "Elijah Delmedigo: An Archetype of Halakhic Man?" in *Cultural Intermediaries: Jewish Intellectuals in Early Modern Italy*, ed. David B. Ruderman and Giuseppe Veltri (Philadelphia, 2004), 39–54 at 52n11.

27. On the importance of this sermon for the history of Christian Kabbalah, see Wirszubski, *Flavius Mithridates: Sermo de passione domini*, 19–28.

28. Ibid., 50. See also David B. Ruderman, "The Italian Renaissance and Jewish Thought," in *Renaissance Humanism: Foundations, Form, and Legacy*, vol. 1: *Humanism in Italy*, ed. Albert J. Rabil (Philadelphia, 1988), 382–433 at 401–4.

29. "Quod petisti igitur de arabico in latinum sermonem uerti: deinde in hebraicum: et postea in chaldeum: et syrum" (Flavius Mithridates, preface to his Qur'ān translation. I quote here from Hartmut Bobzin's transcription [*Der Koran*, 81–82] of Vatican City, BAV, MS urb. lat. 1384, 63v–64v. Piemontese, who apparently did not know Bobzin's book, also transcribed it four years later in his "Il Corano latino," 260).

30. Vatican City, BAV, MS urb. lat. 1384. This MS will be discussed at length in Chapter 5.

31. Bobzin, *Der Koran*, 83–84.

32. For the manuscripts, see Bobzin, *Der Koran*, 81n266, and Piemontese, "Il Corano latino," 263–64.

33. On Egidio da Viterbo's life, see Bobzin, *Der Koran*, 84–88; François Secret, *Les Kabbalistes chrétiens de la Renaissance* (Paris, 1964), 106–21; and, most comprehensively, Francis X. Martin, O. S. A., *Friar, Reformer, and Renaissance Scholar: Life and Work of Giles of Viterbo, 1469–1532* (Villanova, Pa., 1992), whose "The Problem of Giles of Viterbo: A Historiographical Survey," *Augustiniana* 9 (1959):357–79 and 10 (1960):43–60 is still essential. On Egidio's failure to publish his works, see Martin, *Friar, Reformer, and Renaissance Scholar*, 174, and John W. O'Malley's foreword to that work, 7–10 at 8.

34. On Egidio as scripture scholar, see Martin, *Friar, Reformer, and Renaissance Scholar*, ch. 7 (153–79); see esp. 160–66 for his knowledge of Hebrew.

35. Secret, *Les Kabbalistes chrétiens*, 107, 110, 120. See also Martin, *Friar, Reformer and Renaissance Scholar*, 160–66.

36. For his fame as a preacher, see Martin, *Friar, Reformer, and Renaissance Scholar*, 181.

37. On his reforming ideas, see John W. O'Malley, *Giles of Viterbo on Church Reform: A Study in Renaissance Thought* (Leiden, 1968); and Martin, *Friar, Reformer, and Renaissance Scholar*, 93–117.

38. Bobzin, *Der Koran*, 86–87, and Martin, *Friar, Reformer, and Renaissance Scholar*, 173.

39. O'Malley, *Giles of Viterbo*, 19; see also 8, 21, 55.

40. For a complete transcription of Mark's translation of these verses, see appendix.

41. *Decipio*, "to ensnare, cheat," is, for example, completely incorrect for *lā yaʿlama . . . shayʾan*, "he knows nothing," in verse 5.

42. See esp. verse 2:5 ("Illi quidem sunt in directionem creatoris suis" < "ulā'ika ʿalá hudan min rabbihim") (Turin, Biblioteca Nazionale Universitaria, MS F. V. 35, fol. 1ra).

43. See al-Ṭabarī on 22:5, 9.110–11; and al-Ṭabarsī on 22:5, 4.71.

44. A transcription of Iohannes's translation of the whole passage can be found in the appendix.

45. Natalie Zemon Davis has recently discovered quite tantalizing evidence

for his having been a convert. See her *Trickster Travels: A Sixteenth-Century Muslim Between Worlds* (New York, 2006), 241.

46. A complete transcription of Mithridates' version appears in the appendix below.

47. This is Marmaduke Pickthall's translation, which makes good sense in this context. See his *The Meaning of the Glorious Koran*, with introduction by William Montgomery Watt, Everyman's Library 105 (New York, Toronto, 1909, 1992), 338.

48. Mithridates, *Latin-Arabic Qur'ān*, fol. 80r.

49. Ibid., fol. 65v. He makes the same error again at verse 25: "et missimus ante te ex missis noe . . ." (fol. 67r).

50. Ibid., fol. 68r–v.

51. As at 21:1 and 22:47 (ibid., fol. 65r, 82r).

52. Ibid., fol. 65v. *Ex alto dedimus* for *anzalnā* in 21:10 is likewise especially apt. See ibid., fol. 66r.

53. Giorgio Levi della Vida, *Ricerche sulla formazione del più antico fondo dei manoscritti orientali della Biblioteca Vaticana* (Vatican City, 1939), 96 and also 94.

54. See Bobzin's remarkable analysis of these passages and of an extant working draft of them (Paris, BnF MS lat. 3402, fols. 113r–116v) in his *Der Koran*, 447–97.

55. See Chapter 5 below.

56. Hankins, *Plato in the Italian Renaissance* 1, 66 and ff.

57. See, for example, Chapter 5 below.

58. "Nota quia talem paradẏsum ubique promittit. scilicet carnalium deliciarum. quę fuit olim alia heresis" (Annotator, fol. 26rb, rm).

59. On the Latin-Christian polemical view of the Islamic paradise, see Daniel, *Islam and the West*, 172–77.

60. Norman Daniel observed that, as far as Robert of Ketton and Mark of Toledo were concerned, this was true of their translations of *all* the Qur'ānic passages about the Islamic paradise. See Daniel, *Islam and the West*, 172.

61. "ubi dulcissimas aquas. pomaque multimoda. fructusque varios. et decentissimas ac mundissimas mulieres . . . possidebunt" (Robert of Ketton, *Lex Mahumet*, fol. 26rb; Bibliander, *Alcoran* 1550, 1:9).

62. "Et euangeliza illis qui crediderunt et operati sunt bona quod habebunt paradisos sub quibus flumina defluent. Quam cito collata sunt eis uictualia de fructibus dixerunt id est collatum nobis prius . . . et habebunt in eis uxores castas" (Mark of Toledo, *Liber Alchorani*, fol. 1rb).

63. "Nuncia autem iis qui crediderunt et fecerunt bona opera quia habebunt paradisos sub quibus fluunt fontes: et quandocumque fuerint nutriti nutrimento arborum eorum dicent hoc est quo antea fuimus nutriti . . . in quibus habebunt mulieres mundas in aeternum" (Iohannes Gabriel, *Alcoranus*, Cambridge, Cambridge University Library, MS Mm. v. 26, fol. 2r–3r; the text in the other extant manuscript of this translation, Milan, BA, MS D 100 inf., fol. 4v, is nearly identical. On these manuscripts and their relationship to each other, see Chapter 6 below).

64. For Trinitarian arguments based on the Qur'ān, see Daniel, *Islam and the West*, 205–9. On the "holy spirit," Jesus as the "word from God," and other related terms in the Qur'ān, see Geoffrey Parrinder, *Jesus in the Qur'an* (New York, 1977), 133–41, esp. 136, 139.

65. "Moÿsi ceterisque prophetis postea libro tradito. Christoque similiter filio Marie. cui spiritus diuinus auxilium atque testimonium extitit . . ." (Robert of Ketton, *Lex Mahumet*, fol. 27vb; Bibliander, *Alcoran* 1550, 1.11).

66. For Arab Christian Trinitarian thought in general, see Rachid Haddad, *La Trinité divine chez les théologiens arabes (750–1050)* (Paris, 1985), passim; for examples of *rūḥ al-qudus* referring to the third member of the Christian Trinity, see the extensive notes on 239. Muhammad Marmaduke Pickthall translates the phrase in 2:87 as "holy spirit"; see *The Meaning of the Glorious Koran*, 34.

67. "Et iam tradidimus moisi librum. et transmisimus post ipsum prophetas. Et dedimus ihesu filio marie testimonia et corroborauimus ipsum spiritu sancto" (Mark of Toledo, *Liber Alchorani*, fol. 2rb).

68. "Iam enim dedimus moysi scripturam postquem misimus nuncios et dedimus iesu filio marie declarationes quem adiuuauimus cum spiritu sancto" (Iohannes Gabriel, *Alcoranus*, Cambridge, Cambridge University Library, MS Mm. v. 26, fols. 17r–18r).

69. "Wa-huwa radd ʿalá al-Naṣārá." The quotation is from al-Qurṭubī (on 112:3, 20.168), who is citing Ibn ʿAbbās; al-Ṭabarsī (on 112:3, 5.567) also explicitly mentions Christians as among those whose teachings are being refuted here. It should be pointed out, however, that other commentators do not mention Christians at all, seeing the verse as revealed in response to the questions of "polytheists" (*mushrikūn*) or Jews. See, for example, al-Ṭabarī on 112:1–3, 12.740–41.

70. "Constanter dic illis deum unum esse. necessarium omnibus et incorporeum. qui nec genuit: nec est generatus. nec habet quemquam sibi similem" (Robert of Ketton, *Lex Mahumet*, fol. 138rb; Bibliander, *Alcoran* 1550, 1.188). In an important and too rarely read article, Ludwig Hagemann similarly observed that Robert accurately got across the Qur'ān's anti-Trinitarian passages and, more broadly, that his translation, despite its problems, communicated the essential belief content of the Qur'ān. See his "Die erste lateinische Koranübersetzung—Mittel zur Verständigung zwischen Christen und Muslimen im Mittelalter?" in *Orientalische Kultur und europäisches Mittelalter*, ed. Albert Zimmerman and Ingrid Craemer-Ruegenberg, Miscellanea Mediaevalia 17 (Berlin and New York, 1985), 55.

71. "[D]ic ipse est deus unus. deus eternus non genuit nec est genitus nec quicquid est ei simile" (Mark of Toledo, *Liber Alchorani*, fol. 84ra).

72. "Dic est deus unus, deus est potens. non fuit generatus neque generabit. et non ei equalis in eo" (Iohannes Gabriel, *Alcoranus*, BA MS D 100 inf., fol. 608r).

73. See Chapter 2, n. 145; see also Daniel, *Islam and the West*, 280.

74. Daniel, *Islam and the West*, 165. See also Martínez, "Observaciones a la traducción latina," 118, 121; id., "Las traducciones latinas medievales del Corán," 494–95; and Hagemann, "Die erste lateinische Koranübersetzung," 54.

75. "quo viso: omnes menstruate sunt" (Robert of Ketton, *Lex Mahumet*, fol. 69vb; Bibliander, *Alcoran* 1550, 1.77).

76. Daniel, *Islam and the West*, 165; Martínez, "Observaciones a la traducción latina," 121.

77. See al-Ṭabarī on 12:31,7.203; Ibn ʿAṭīyah on 12:31, 7.494–95; and cf. al-Qurṭubī on 12:31, 9.118–19.

78. Daniel, *Islam and the West*, 279–80. While José Martínez Gázquez has no-

tably pointed out the polemical distortions in Robert's translation elsewhere (see above, n. 74), his excellent recent article on how Robert translated the ubiquitous divine names in the Qur'ān makes clear that in general, Robert was quite unpolemical in his translation of these words, though his versions of them were by no means perfect. See José Martínez Gázquez, "Los primeros nombres de Allāh en la traducción latina del *Alchoran* de Robert de Ketton," *Euphrosyne* 33 (2005):303–13.

79. See Gilbert Dahan, "Les traductions latines de Thibaud de Sézanne," in *Le brûlement du Talmud à Paris, 1242–44*, ed. Gilbert Dahan (Paris, 1999), 95–120, esp. 98, 107–10, 115. Versteegh observed that the Greek version of the Qur'ān that circulated in Byzantium was also "not really a bad translation at all. . . . Within the limits of [its] literality the translator seriously attempts to translate the complete Arabic text." See Versteegh, "Greek Translations of the Qur'ān," 60–62.

80. Daniel, *Islam and the West*, 66.

81. For an insightful discussion of the errors of Robert's translation, see Hagemann, "Die erste lateinische Koranübersetzung," 52–54, whose criticisms strike me as fairer than those of d'Alverny, "Deux traductions," 85–86.

82. On these many critiques, see n. 85 below.

83. Robert of Ketton, *Lex Mahumet*, fol. 26rb; Bibliander, *Alcoran* 1550, 1.9.

84. See also Martínez, "Observaciones a la traducción latina," 118.

85. These criticisms have been widely discussed by modern scholars. See Darío Cabanelas Rodríguez, *Juan de Segovia y el problema islámico* (Madrid, 1952), 131–36; id., "Juan de Segovia y el primer Alcorán trilingüe," *al-Andalus* 14 (1949):157–61; Burman, "*Tafsīr* and Translation," 705–6; Martínez, "Las traducciones latinas medievales del Corán," 499–501.

86. "vix unam lineam reperies quadrare textui" (David Colville in his prefatory note to the manuscript copy he made of Egidio da Viterbo's sixteenth-century Latin-Arabic Qur'ān [Milan, BA MS D 100 inf.], a transcription of which appears in Oscar Löfgren and Renato Traini, *Catalogue of the Arabic Manuscripts in the Biblioteca Ambrosiana*, vol. 1 [Vicenza, 1975], 41–43 at 43). For more on this version of the Qur'ān, see Chapter 6 below.

87. See Burman, "*Tafsīr* and Translation," 706–7.

88. Bobzin, *Der Koran*, 481.

89. For his full translation of 22:1–5, see appendix.

90. See my discussion of Robert's version of surah 100 just below in this chapter.

91. Janet Martin, "Classicism and Style in Latin Literature," in *Renaissance and Renewal in the Twelfth Century*, ed. Robert Benson and Giles Constable (Cambridge, Mass., 1982), 537–68 at 538. See also E. Faral, *Les arts poétiques du XIIe et du XIIIe sìecle: Recherches et documents sur la technique littéraire du moyen age* (Paris, 1924), 48–49.

92. For the full text of 2:23–28, together with Robert's version and my translation of his Latin, see just above; for the text of the remaining verses before and after, which I analyze just below, see Robert of Ketton, *Lex Mahumet*, fol. 26rb; Bibliander, *Alcoran* 1550, 1:9.

93. See Martin, "Classicism and Style," 541–42, 544; see also *Rhetorica ad Herrenium*, 4.19–20, 26–28 (Marx, 134–37).

94. For the full text of this passage, see the appendix. On anaphora, see Martin, "Classicism and Style," 542.

95. Robert of Ketton, *Lex Mahumet*, fol. 137va; Bibliander, *Alcoran* 1550, 1.187.

96. On this technique, see *Rhetorica ad Herrenium*, 4.14 (Marx, 127).

97. See also my "Polemic, Philology, and Ambivalence: Reading the Qur'ān in Latin Christendom," *Journal of Islamic Studies* 15 (2004):181–209 at 199–201; and David Howlett, *Insular Inscriptions*, 174–75. D'Alverny, who was deeply suspicious of Robert's paraphrasing ways, nevertheless did point out that as a stylist he had "pretension to elegance." See her "Deux traductions," 79, 85. Metlitzki suggested that Robert's abilities as a prose stylist may have been "the reason why he was chosen to translate [the Qur'ān]." See her *The Matter of Araby*, 31. The elevated style also often made use of the *cursus*. Only further study can determine whether such rhythmical *clausulae* occur with signficant frequency in Robert's translation. On the *cursus*, see Tore Janson, *Prose Rhythm in Medieval Latin from the 9th to the 13th Century* (Stockholm, 1975), and Terence O. Tunberg, "Prose Styles and *Cursus*," *Medieval Latin: An Introduction and Bibliographical Guide*, ed. F. A. C. Mantello and A. G. Rigg (Washington, 1996), 111–16. On its importance in the elevated style, see Martin, "Classicism and Style," 543–44.

98. Martin, "Classicism and Style," 544–45, who follows Walter R. Johnson, *Luxuriance and Economy: Cicero and the Alien Style*, Classical Studies 6 (Berkeley, Calif., 1971), 23–30, 42–56.

99. On Meinhard, see Martin, "Classicism and Style," 546; on John of Salisbury, see Birger Munk-Olsen, "L'humanisme de Jean de Salisbury, un Cicéronien au 12e siècle," in *Entretiens sur la renaissance du 12e siècle*, ed. Maurice de Gandiallace and Édouard Jeauneau (Paris, 1968), 53–69 at 54.

100. See Martin, "Classicism and Style," 546–48.

101. See Louis Kelly, *The True Interpreter: A History of Translation Theory and Practice in the West* (Oxford, 1979), 44–45, 70, 99–100.

102. Speaking of his translation of al-Kindi's *Iudicia*, Charles S. F. Burnett, Keiji Yamamoto, and Michio Yano have pointed out that "In general, Robert abbreviates and recasts the text in his own words." See their "Al-Kindī on Finding Buried Treasure," *Arabic Sciences and Philosophy* 7 (1997):57–90 at 89. But it is clear from the passages that Burnett has edited of Robert's translation of al-Kindī's *The Forty Chapters* that his paraphrasing is a good deal less elaborate in this scientific text than in the Qur'ānic translation. For these, see Charles Burnett and Gerrit Bos, eds., *Scientific Weather Forecasting in the Middle Ages: The Writings of al-Kindī. Studies, Editions, and Translations of the Arabic, Hebrew and Latin Texts* (London, 2000), 397–405; and the former's "Al-Kindī on Judicial Astrology: 'The Forty Chapters,'" *Arabic Science and Philosophy* 3 (1993):77–117 at 111–17.

103. Kelly, *The True Interpreter*, 179–81.

104. See "al-ḳur'ān," EI2 5:400–32 at 420 [art. A. T. Welch and J. D. Pearson]; "Rhymed Prose," EQ 4:476–84 [art. Devin J. Stewart]; and Neal Robinson, *Discovering the Qur'ān: A Contemporary Approach to a Veiled Text* (London, 1996), 9–14.

105. See his translation of 22:4 in the appendix below.

106. It is worth pointing out that there is some possibility that the final form

of Robert's translation was in part the work of other hands, particularly those of Peter of Poitiers, Peter the Venerable's secretary, whom the latter clearly assigned to work with Peter of Toledo, the translator of the *Apology of al-Kindī*, one of the other works Peter the Venerable had translated (on which see Chapter 3 below). Though he probably did this because of Peter of Toledo's deficiencies in Latin, it is possible that Peter of Poitiers might have similarly improved the Latin of the other parts of this anthology of Islamic texts. (See d'Alverny, "Deux traductions," 795, and Martínez, "Observaciones a la traducción latina," 121–22.) That Robert was capable of writing good Latin prose is clear, however, from his other translations (as we have seen above), and there is no direct evidence that Peter of Poitiers or anyone else assisted him in translating the Qur'ān.

107. ". . . prohemio uero eius demonstrante splendidum fuisse rhetorem atque poetam. Visa arabici textus continentia suaque translatione, liquido apparet, descripta arabice in Alchurano in suum conuertisse eloquentie modum" (Juan de Segovia, "Prefatio . . . in translationem nouiter editam ex Arabico in Latinum uulgareque Hyspanum libri Alchorani," ed. José Martínez Gázquez, in "El prólogo de Juan de Segobia al Corán (*Qur'ān*) trilingüe (1456)," *Mittellateinisches Jahrbuch* 38 (2003):389–410 at 405, ll. 405–8). On this passage see also Martínez, "Las traducciones latinas medievales del Corán," 500–501.

108. Robert's version seems to have been the most widely read down to the publication of Marracci's *Alcorani textus* in 1698. See Daniel, *Islam and the West*, 279–80 and Hagemann, "Die erste lateinische Koranübersetzung," 55–56.

109. "At quod creauerit utpote alquid magne continentie nouiter fingendo, vel annichilauerit supprimendo, non fortasse reperitur, quin etsi alio alioque modo tota fere substantia Alchurani in ipsa reperitur translatione" (Juan de Segovia, "Prefatio . . . in translationem," 406, ll. 423–25). On this passage see also Martínez, "Las traducciones latinas medievales del Corán," 501.

110. See Daniel, *Islam and the West*, 279; and Hagemann, "Die erste lateinische Koranübersetzung," 55.

Chapter 2

1. Note, however, that not all Muslim scholars accepted the view—adhered to by modern Western scholars—that many of these "strange" words were foreign borrowings, developing complex arguments to demonstrate that they were truly Arabic terms. On these works in general, see Andrew Rippin, "Lexicographical Texts and the Qur'ān," in *Approaches to the History of the Interpretation of the Qur'ān*, ed. Andrew Rippin (Oxford, 1988), 158–74.

2. See Arthur Jeffery, *The Foreign Vocabulary of the Qur'ān* (Baroda, 1938), 99–100, 202–3.

3. See Ibn ʿAṭīyah on 4:51, 4.98–99.

4. See Edward Lane, *An Arabic-English Lexicon*, 2 vols. (London, 1863, rpt. 1984), 1.373.

5. Robert of Ketton, *Lex Mahumet*, fol. 41rb; Bibliander, *Alcoran* 1550, 1.32.

6. See Lesley Smith's introduction to her anthology of translated medieval Latin commentaries, *Medieval Exegesis in Translation: Commentaries on the Book of Ruth* (Kalamazoo, Mich., 1996), x.

7. See appendix below.

8. See al-Ṭabarī on 22:1, 9.104; but also al-Ṭabarsī on 22:1, 4.70, and Ibn Kathīr on 22:1, 3.197.

9. See appendix.

10. "ay yuqbaḍu rūḥuhu fa-yamūtu fī ḥāl ṣigharihi aw-shabābihi" (al-Ṭabarsī on 22:5, 4.71. See also al-Ṭabarī on 22:5, 9.112).

11. See, for example, Reuven Firestone, *Jihād: The Origin of Holy War in Islam* (Oxford, 1999), 55, 58–60, 84–85.

12. "Hostibus sicut et ceteris ad deum redeuntibus. ipse pius prebet ueniam" (Robert of Ketton, *Lex Mahumet*, fol., 30va; Bibliander, *Alcoran* 1550, 1.15).

13. "*Fa-in intahaw* ay imtanaʿū min kufrihim bi-al-tawbah minhu" (al-Ṭabarsī on 2:192, 1.286; see also Ibn Kathīr on 2:192, 1.216; and al-Bayḍāwī on 2:188 [*sic*], 1.106).

14. Robert of Ketton, *Lex Mahumet*, fol. 26vb; Bibliander, *Alcoran* 1550, 1.10. Though *discretum* has the form of a passive past participle, Robert appears to be using it in an active sense; the fact that Bibliander reads *descretiuum* here suggests the same interpretation.

15. "wa-yaʿnī . . . bi-al-furqān al-faṣl bayna al-ḥaqq wa-al-bāṭil" (al-Ṭabarī on 2:53, 1.323–24).

16. "al-furqān: wa-huwa mā yafruqu bayna al-ḥaqq wa-al-bāṭil wa-al-hudá wa-al-ḍalālah" (Ibn Kathīr on 2:53, 1.88).

17. See Jane Damen McAuliffe, *Qurʾānic Christians: An Analysis of Classical and Modern Exegesis* (Cambridge, England, 1991), 93–128.

18. See, for example, al-Ṭabarī on 2:62, 1.360–61.

19. "Al-Ṣābiʾūn jamʿ Ṣābiʾ, wa-huwa al-mustaḥdith siwá dīnihi dīnan . . . wa-kull khārij min dīn kāna ʿalayhi ilá ākhar ghayrihi tusammīhi al-ʿArab Ṣābiʾ" (al-Ṭabarī on 2:62, 1.360). Much the same definition of the term is found in several other commentaries. See al-Zamakhsharī on 2:62, 1.149; and al-Rāghib al-Iṣbahānī, *Al-Mufradāt fī gharīb al-Qurʾān*, 2 vols. (Cairo, n.d.), 1.405.

20. "Omnis recte uiuens. Iudeus seu Christianus. seu lege sua relicta in aliam tendens . . . indubitanter diuinum amorem assequetur" (Robert of Ketton, *Lex Mahumet*, fol. 27rb; Bibliander, *Alcoran* 1550, 1.10).

21. "wa-qīla kursīyuhi majāz ʿan ʿilmihi aw mulkihi" (al-Bayḍāwī on 2:254 [*sic*], 1.131).

22. Al-Ṭabarī on 2:255, 3.11, for example, explains that some interpreters say that the meaning of *kursī* here is *ʿilm Allāh*, "the knowledge of God," and he cites Ibn ʿAbbās's hadith. But see also al-Zamakhsharī on 2:255, 1.297, and al-Qurṭubī on 2:255, 3.180.

23. Robert of Ketton, *Lex Mahumet*, fol. 32vb; Bibliander, *Alcoran* 1550, 1.19.

24. ". . . ueniant ut sibi proficuum testificando uideant. diebusque determinatis deum nominando bestias sacrificent" (Robert of Ketton, *Lex Mahumet*, fol. 89va; Bibliander, *Alcoran* 1550, 1.108).

25. "Ḥadjdj," in EI2, 3.31–38 at 36 [art. A. J. Wensinck and J. Joumier].

26. "'*Alá mā razaqahum min bahīmat al-an'am*, ay 'alá dhabḥ wa-naḥr mā razaqahum min al-ibil wa-al-baqar wa-al-ghanam" (al-Ṭabarsī on 22:28, 4.81).

27. "'*Alá mā razaqahum min bahīmat al-an'am*, ya'nī bi-hi dhikr Allāh 'inda dhabḥihā" (Ibn Kathīr on 22:36, 3.211).

28. Verse 22:36, after referring to animals that God has provided for ceremonies ("sha'ā'ir"), orders Muslims to "recite the name of God over them." The commentators once again specify that the animals described here are those "that are allowable in sacrifice and immolations" ("wa-hiya al-ibil al-'iẓām wa-qīla al-nāqah wa-al-baqarah mimmā yajūzu fī al-hady wa-al-aḍāḥi"), and the recitation of God's name is to be done "in the case of the butchering of them" ("ay fī ḥāl naḥrihā"): al-Ṭabarsī on 22:36, 4.86; see also al-Ṭabarī on 22:36, 9.153–55. Robert here writes "bestias immolarent . . . in dei nomine" (Robert of Ketton, *Lex Mahumet*, fol. 89vb; Bibliander, *Alcoran* 1550, 1.108).

29. "Jeffery, *The Foreign Vocabulary of the Qur'an*, 43–44.

30. Al-Ṭabarsī on 105:3, 5.539, 542; see also al-Ṭabarī on 105:3, 12.691–93; al-Rāghib al-Iṣbahānī, *Al-Mufradāt* 1.7.

31. Robert of Ketton, *Lex Mahumet*, fol. 137vb; Bibliander, *Alcoran* 1550, 1.187.

32. "et misit super eos Babilonie aues" (Mark of Toledo, *Liber Alchorani*, fol. 83vb). For other examples of places where his translation is less informed by Islamic Qur'ān interpretation than Robert's, see my "*Tafsīr* and Translation," 709–24, and my "Exclusion or Concealment: Approaches to Traditional Arabic Exegesis in Medieval-Latin Translations of the Qur'ān," *Scripta mediterranea* 19–20 (1998–99):181–97 at 185–94.

33. "quantocius exire uoluerint ab angustia reducentur ad eam. dicentque eis. gustate supplicium incendii" (Mark of Toledo, *Liber Alchorani*, fol. 44va).

34. See al-Ṭabarī on 22:22, 9.127; and also al-Ṭabarsī on 22:22, 4.78.

35. Note, however, that the manuscript tradition is not in agreement here: I have followed here (as generally elsewhere) Turin MS F. V. 35, 44va which I consider one of the better manuscripts. But Vienna, Österreichische Nationalbibliothek, MS 4297 has "diceturque eis," the passive form we would expect (fol. 125v).

36. As in al-Ṭabarī on 108:2, 12.721: "waḍa'a yadahu al-yumná 'alá wasṭ sā'idihi al-yusrá, thumma waḍa'ahumā 'alá ṣadrihi."

37. Mark of Toledo, *Liber Alchorani*, fol. 84ra.

38. " . . . in terra habetis habitationem et bona pro tempore determinato uel usque ad mortem" (Iohannes Gabriel, *Alcoranus*, Cambridge MS Mm. v. 26, fol. 5r). In this case, though not in the cases to be cited just below, only the Cambridge MS contains this addition based on Islamic exegesis. The Milan MS has "terram habetis habitationem et bona pro tempore constituto," the "usque ad mortem" not appearing here (BA MS D 100 inf., 7r). As I have argued elsewhere, these two manuscripts contain slightly different recensions of the same translation, and this is but one more example of that fact. See my "Cambridge University Library MS Mm v. 26 and the History of the Study of the Qur'ān in Medieval and Early Modern Europe," in *Religion, Text, and Society in Medieval Spain and Northern Europe: Essays in Honor of J. N. Hillgarth*, ed. Thomas E. Burman, Mark D. Meyerson, and Leah Shopkow (Toronto, 2002), 335–63 at 342–43, 361–63.

39. Al-Ṭabarī mentions both views: "fa-qāla ba'ḍuhum: wa-la-kum fīhā ba-

lāgh ilá al-mawt. . . . wa-qāla ākharūn: yaʿnī . . . ilá qiyām al-sāʿah" (on 2:36, 1.279–80). See also al-Ṭabarsī on 2:36, 1.87.

40. Al-Ṭabarī on 2:58, 1.340. See also al-Ṭabarsī on 2:58, 1.119.

41. Iohannes Gabriel, *Alcoranus,* Cambridge MS Mm. v. 26, 9r; the Milan manuscript has *nostram culpam* but is otherwise identical (BA MS D 100 inf., fol. 9r).

42. See, for example, Ibn Kathīr on 17:1, 3.3: "*ilá al-masjid al-aqṣā*: wa-huwa bayt al-maqdis."

43. Iohannes Gabriel, *Alcoranus,* BA MS D 100 inf, fol. 260v (this surah is missing in the Cambridge MS).

44. "*Iqtarabat al-sāʿah:* danat al-sāʿah allatī taqūmu fī-hā al-qiyāmah . . . wa-hādhā min Allāh . . . indhār li-ʿibādihi bi-dunūw al-qiyāmah wa-qurb fanāʾ al-dunyā" (al-Ṭabarī on 54:1, 11.544; see also al-Ṭabarsī on 54:1, 5.186).

45. Iohannes Gabriel, *Alcoranus,* BA MS D 100 inf., fol. 536r. The Cambridge text is slightly different (and not entirely legible), but coincides on the point at issue: "Appropinquauit dies *judicii* et [illegible word] luna" (Cambridge MS Mm. v. 26, fol. 231vb).

46. "yaʿnī bi-hi al-malāʾikah" (al-Rāghib al-Iṣbahānī, *Al-Mufradāt,* 1:416).

47. "Per angelorum in celis seriem" (Robert of Ketton, *Lex Mahumet,* 109vb; Bibliander, *Alcoran* 1550, 1.139; many commentators specify, as Robert does, that the angels are in heaven: see, for example, Ibn ʿAṭīyah on 37:1, 12.332 where he quotes a hadith from Qatādah that states this explicitly); "[P]er ordines angelorum sanctos" (Mark of Toledo, *Liber Alchorani,* fol. 60ra); "Per angelos ordinatos" (Iohannes Gabriel, *Alcoranus,* BA MS D 100 inf., fol. 440r).

48. "*inna kitāb al-fujjār lafī sijjīn.* qāla: fī al-arḍ al-sābiʿah" (al-Ṭabarī on 83:7, 12.487; Ibn Kathīr on 83:7, 4.486; and Jeffery, *Foreign Vocabulary of the Qurʾān,* 165).

49. See "samāʾ," EI2 8:1014–18, and Q. 65:12.

50. Mark of Toledo, *Liber Alchorani,* fol. 81vb.

51. "Horum inquam liber. suis malis insignitus; in terrarum infima reconditur" (Robert of Ketton, *Lex Mahumet,* fol. 135va; Bibliander, *Alcoran* 1550, 1.183). Egidio's translator Iohannes Gabriel Terrolensis has *praesentatus* (then *praesentatio* where the word appears in the following verse) for reasons that I cannot fathom (Iohannes Gabriel, *Alcoranus,* BA MS D 100 inf, fol. 594r). Note that over both words David Colville, the copyist of this MS, has written ".d." In the prefatory note attached to the MS he explains what this means: "Litera 'd' supra voces indicat dubitationem, quod [*sic*] Leo [Africanus] non sciverat corrigere, sed dubitabat de expositione Gabrielis" (David Colville, preface, transcribed by Oscar Löfgren and Renato Traini in their *Catalogue of the Arabic Manuscripts in the Biblioteca Ambrosiana,* 3 vols. [Vicenza, 1975–1995], 1.41–43 at 43. On this preface and on Leo Africanus' relationship to this MS, see Chapter 6).

52. See Lane, *Arabic-English Lexicon* 1.1213–14; Reinhart Dozy, *Supplément aux dictionnaires arabes* (Beirut, 1881) 1.580; G. W. Freytag, *Lexicon arabico-latinum* (Beirut, 1975) 2.224.

53. See, for example, al-Qurṭubī on 96:18, 20.85 who explains that "huwa ma'khūdh min al-zabn wa-huwa al-dafʿ."

54. "*Al-zabn*: al-dafʿ, ka-annahum yadfaʿūna ahl al-nār fī-hā" (Ibn Qutaybah, *Tafsīr gharīb al-Qurʾān* [Cairo, 1958], 533). See Jeffery, *Foreign Vocabulary*, 148.

55. "Ipsum . . . retrahi iuberemus; ab aduocatis ipsum ad ignem ducturis" (Robert of Ketton, *Lex Mahumet*, fol. 137rb; Bibliander, *Alcoran* 1550, 1.186).

56. "wa-al-murād: malāʾikat al-ʿadhāb" (al-Zamakhsharī on 96:18, 4.770).

57. Al-Ṭabarsī on 96:18, 5.516: "yaʿnī al-malāʾikah al-muwakkalīn bi-al-nār"; see also Jeffery, *Foreign Vocabulary*, 148.

58. Mark of Toledo, *Liber alchorani*, fol. 83rb. The meaning of Iohannes Gabriel's translation of the term, *Tizionarios* (?), eludes me, but Leo Africanus, a slightly later reader (on whom see Chapter 6 below), supplied a much better, exegetically informed, interpretation in his interlinear note: "ministros scilicet suos inferorum" (Iohannes Gabriel, *Alcoranus*, BA MS D 100 inf., fol. 602v).

59. But see the conclusion to this book below.

60. See Chapter 1, notes 88–90.

61. "quoniam in quam multis passibus, uelud commentans, sensum explicat sarracenorum, uix ex arabicis literis aperientem, quem sensum magister ille fatebatur" (Juan de Segovia, "Prefatio . . . in translationem," 406, ll. 426–28). The "magister" mentioned here is Iça de Segovia, a Muslim faqih hired by Juan to assist him in this project. See the conclusion to this book below. See also Martínez, "Las traducciones latinas medievales del Corán," 501.

62. Gerard Wiegers, *Islamic Literature in Spanish and Aljamiado: Yça of Segovia (fl. 1450), His Antecedents and Successors* (Leiden, 1994), 108. On the vital intellectual traditions that still existed among the Mudejars under Christian rule, see Kathryn Miller, *Guardians of Islam: Muslim Minorities in Medieval Aragon* (forthcoming from Columbia University Press, New York), and the next note.

63. Mark D. Meyerson, *The Muslims of Valencia in the Age of Fernando and Isabel: Between Coexistence and Crusade* (Berkeley, Calif., 1991), 259–68.

64. Adang, *Muslim Writers on Judaism and the Hebrew Bible*, 110n2, 127, 253; and Lazarus-Yafeh, *Intertwined Worlds: Medieval Islam and Bible Criticism* (Princeton, N.J., 1992), 113–14.

65. See, for example, Nikolas Häring, "Commentary and Hermeneutics," in *Renaissance and Renewal in the Tweflth Century*, ed. Robert L. Benson and Giles Constable (Cambridge, Mass., 1982), 173–200; A. J. Minnis and A. B. Scott, with David Wallace, *Medieval Literary Theory and Criticism, c.1100–1375: The Commentary Tradition* (Oxford, 1988), passim. John B. Henderson shows that a profound emphasis on commented canonical texts is something common to virtually all premodern advanced civilizations; see his *Scripture, Canon, and Commentary: A Comparison of Confucian and Western Exegesis* (Princeton, N.J., 1991), passim, esp. 81: "For many medievals, glossing became second nature to the extent that they glossed whatever literature came within their reach."

66. Martin Irvine, *The Making of Textual Culture: 'Grammatica' and Literary Theory, 350–1100* (Cambridge, 1994), 17.

67. This has been convincingly shown by Rita Copeland in her *Rhetoric, Hermeneutics, and Translation in the Middle Ages: Academic Traditions and Vernacular Texts*, Cambridge Studies in Medieval Literature 11 (Cambridge, England, 1991) pas-

sim, but see also Christopher Baswell, *Virgil in Medieval England: Figuring the Aeneid from the Twelfth Century to Chaucer* (Cambridge, 1995), 6.

68. Copeland, *Rhetoric, Hermeneutics, and Translation*, 99–100, 127, 133–38.

69. Anthony Grafton, *Commerce with the Classics: Ancient Books and Renaissance Readers* (Ann Arbor, Mich., 1997), 17.

70. Copeland, *Rhetoric, Hermeneutics, and Translation*, 174–77.

71. On this shadowy figure and the references to him in the documents connected with Peter the Venerable's project, see Martínez and de la Cruz, "Las traducciones árabe-latinas impulsadas por Pedro el Venerable," 292 and n22; but also Kritzeck, *Peter the Venerable and Islam*, 32–33, 68–69; d'Alverny, "Deux traductions," 85; and on team translation generally, and the possible role of this Muhammad in particular, see ead., "Les traductions à deux interprètes, d'arabe en langue vernaculaire et de langue vernaculaire en latin," in *Traduction et traducteur au moyen âge: Actes du colloque international du CNRS organisé à Paris, Institut de recherche et d'histoire des textes, les 26–28 mai 1986*, ed. Geneviève Contamine (Paris, 1989), 193–206, esp. 194 (this article is reprinted in ead., *La transmission des textes philosophiques et scientifiques au moyen âge*, ed. Charles S. F. Burnett [Aldershot, England, and Brookfield, Vt., 1994]).

72. Kelly, *The True Interpreter*, 126.

73. See Dahan, *L'exégèse chrétienne*, 166.

74. See Smalley, *The Study of the Bible in the Middle Ages*, 154–56; Dahan, *Les intellectuels chrétiens et les juifs au moyen âge* (Paris, 1990), 283–84, 295–98; and, most recently, id., *L'exégèse chrétienne*, 376–87. It is worth mentioning that the translator of a Greek version of the Qur'ān available in ninth-century Byzantium may well have also turned to informants to assist him in his work. See Versteegh, "Greek Translations of the Qur'ān," 62.

75. See, for example, Johannes Mathesius's description of "translation committee" meetings in Wittenberg attended by Luther, Melanchthon, and others at which "The professors all brought their rabbis" in addition to their Hebrew and Greek editions of the biblical text (quoted in Stephen G. Burnett, "Reassessing the 'Basel-Wittenberg Conflict': Dimensions of the Reformation-Era Discussion of Hebrew Scholarship," in *Hebraica Veritas?*, ed. Coudert and Shoulson, 181–201 at 194).

76. Mark Meyerson's work suggests that there were still learned Muslims to be found in Christian Iberia at the end of the fifteenth century. See note 63 above.

77. Selden had translated, for example, Saʿīd ibn al-Baṭrīq's *Annals*. The autograph is in the Bodleian Library in Oxford (MS Arch. Selden A. 74*); on this manuscript, see Falconer Madan and H. H. E. Craster, *A Summary Catalogue of Western Manuscripts in the Bodleian Library at Oxford*, 7 vols. (Oxford, 1922–53), 2, part 1, 599. On Selden, generally see *Oxford Dictionary of National Biography*, 49:694–705.

78. This translates the Arabic—*wa-la-qad naṣarakum Allāh bi-Badr*—quite closely.

79. See al-Ṭabarsī on 3:123, 1.498; see also al-Ṭabarī on 3:123, 3.420.

80. See Oxford, Bodleian Library, V. 1. 16 Th. Seld. [Bibliander, *Alcoran*, 1543)], p. 26, l. 24 and left margin. The handwriting here, by the way, is identical to that in Selden's autograph copy of his translation of Ibn al-Baṭrīq's *Annals*, on which see n. 77 above.

81. Al-Qurṭubī on 3:123, 4.122.

82. Ludovico Marracci's edition of the Qur'ān was published in Padua in 1698. On him and his work see below in this chapter.

83. On Germanus of Silesia, see Marcel Devic, "Une traduction inédite du Coran," *Journal asiatique*, 8th series, 1 (1883):343–406, and F. Richard, "Le Franciscain Dominicus Germanus de Silesie, grammairien et auteur d'apologie en Persan," *Islamochristiana* 10 (1984):91–107. The unpublished manuscripts of his work are still at El Escorial, and include a fair copy of his Qur'ān translation, as well as his own autograph copy of Robert of Ketton's Latin Qur'ān made from the printed edition, this manuscript also including what look very much like his working notes for his Qur'ān studies. For more on him, see below in this chapter.

84. See n. 74 above.

85. McAuliffe, *Qur'ānic Christians*, 35.

86. See Chapter 6.

87. Mithridates, *Latin-Arabic Qur'ān*, fol. 76ra.

88. Ibid., fol. 82ra.

89. Al-Ṭabarī on 22:48, 9.172.

90. Mithridates, *Latin-Arabic Qur'ān*, fol. 76ra.

91. Al-Ṭabarī on 22:5, 9.110; al-Ṭabarsī on 22:5, 4.71.

92. "Et propterea ciuitates quae illis plenae sunt: sunt peccantes" (Mithridates, *Latin-Arabic Qur'ān*, fol. 82ra).

93. Consuelo López-Morillas, "Lost and Found? Yça of Segovia and the Qur'ān among the Mudejars and Moriscos," *Journal of Islamic Studies* 10 (1999):280.

94. Consuelo López-Morillas, *The Qur'ān in Sixteenth-Century Spain: Six Morisco Versions of Sūra 79* (London, 1982), 50–57; and ead., "Lost and Found?" 281.

95. On this manuscript in general, see F. Esteve Barba, *Biblioteca pública de Toledo. Catálogo de la colección de manuscritos Borbon-Lorenzana* (Madrid, 1942), 85.

96. Wiegers, *Islamic Literature*, 109–14.

97. López-Morillas, "Lost and Found?," passim.

98. *Alcorán: Traducción castellana de un morisco anónimo del año 1606*, ed. Lluís Roqué Figuls, introduction, Joan Vernet Ginés (Barcelona, 2001), 5. The words in italics are in red in the original MS (Toledo, Biblioteca Pública, MS 235). I thank Consuelo López-Morillas for allowing me to use her unpublished transcription of this manuscript as well. It is worth noting that this translation follows the Qur'ānic Arabic slavishly—to the point of incomprehensibility. The Castilian actually says "how do you disbelieve *with* God (*con Allah*)" which makes little sense in that language, but does follow the Arabic construction in which the verb KFR governs through the preposition *bi-*, which normally means "with," though not here. Likewise, he translates the first *wa-* here as "and," when it should be "when" or "while," thereby fumbling, as Latin translators occasionally do, a *waw* of accompanying circumstance. For a useful overview of the recent literature on Morisco Qur'ān translations, and for further discussion of the interpolation of Qur'ānic commentary into them, see Margarita Castells i Criballés, Review of *Alcorán: Traducción castellana de un morisco anónimo*, *Al-Qantara* 23 (2002):550–54.

99. See al-Ṭabarī on 2:28, 1.225, and al-Ṭabarsī on 2:28, 1.70.

100. "Lam takūnū shay'an; fa-khalaqakum" (al-Ṭabarī on 2:28, 1.222). This is

from a hadith related on the authority of Ibn Masʿūd. See also al-Ṭabarsī on 2:28, 1.71, who quotes the same tradition.

101. Al-Zamakhsharī on 2:28, 1.126; Ibn Kathīr on 2:28, 1.64.

102. "Hic namque uos ad uitam de non esse deducens: mortem inducet. et ad se uos resurgere faciet" (Robert of Ketton, *Lex Mahumet*, fol. 26rb; Bibliander, *Alcoran* 1550, 1.9).

103. See notes 17–20 above.

104. "Y aquellos que creen y aquellos que son judíos y los cristianos y los açҫabines *aquellos que adoran a los almalaques* . . ." (*Alcorán: Traducción castellana de un morisco*, 7).

105. See al-Ṭabarī on 2:62, 1.360–61, and also Ibn ʿAṭīyah on 2:61, 1.328.

106. Al-Ṭabarsī on 2:230, 1.330. See also Ibn Kathīr on 2:230, 1.262.

107. "Tertio uero sprete. nequaquam usquequo maritis aliis nupserint; et ab illis relicte fuerint" (Robert of Ketton, *Lex Mahumet*, fol. 31vb; Bibliander, *Alcoran* 1550, 1.17). For more on this passage of Robert's version in comparison with Mark of Toledo's version of the same verses, see my "Exclusion or Concealment," 190–93.

108. *Alcorán: Traducción castellana de un morisco*, 24.

109. See, for example, in the Morisco Qur'ān, the version of 22:22 (" . . . y serles a dicho: '¡Gustad el al@deb quemante!' " [ibid., 216. The translator here transliterates the key Arabic word, *al-ʿadhāb*, "punishment," the "@" in this edition standing for the Arabic letter "ayn."]; cf. Mark's version above, notes 33, 35); 2:36 ("Y a vosotros abrá en la tierra aturadero y espleyte hasta la ora de la *muerte*," ibid., 5, cf. Iohannes's version above, notes 38, 39); and 2:58 ("Abateçe *de nos nuestro pecado*," ibid., 7, cf. Iohannes's version above, note 41).

110. See al-Ṭabarī on 100:1, 12.665–67, al-Zamakhsharī on 100:1, 4.778, and al-Ṭabarsī on 100:1, 5.528.

111. "strepitum hanelo pectore emiserunt equi" (Robert of Ketton, *Lex Mahumet*, fol. 137va; Bibliander, *Alcoran* 1550, 1:187, l. 8).

112. Mark of Toledo, *Liber Alchorani*, fol. 83va.

113. Iohannes Gabriel, *Alcoranus*, BA MS D 100 inf., fol. 604v; this surah is lacking in the Cambridge MS Mm. v. 26.

114. *Alcorán: Traducción castellana de un morisco*, 403.

115. Ludovico Marracci, *Alcorani textus universus . . . his omnibus praemissus est Prodromus* (Padua, 1698). For the view that the seventeenth and eighteenth centuries were a watershed in Western Qur'ān scholarship, see Maxime Rodinson, *Europe and the Mystique of Islam*, trans. R. Veinus (Seattle, 1987), 37–44; Kenneth Setton, *Western Hostility to Islam and the Prophecies of Doom* (Philadelphia, 1992), 47–58; and Edward Said, who claimed that Europeans did not "let Muslim commentators of the [Qur'ān] speak for themselves" until the eighteenth century in his *Orientalism* (London and New York, 1978), 117.

116. Hartmut Bobzin, "Ein oberschlesischer Korangelehrter: Dominicus Germanus de Silesia, O.F.M. (1588–1670)," in *Die oberschlesische Literaturlandschaft im 17. Jahrhundert*, ed. Gerhard Kosellek (Bielefeld, 2001), 221–31.

117. Richard, "Le Franciscain Dominicus Germanus de Silesie," 96.

118. On this second manuscript, Montpellier, Bibliothèque de la Faculté de Médicine, MS H-72, see Devic, "Une traduction inédite du Coran," 343–45.

119. Devic, "Une traduction inédite du Coran," 360.

120. El Escorial, Real Biblioteca de San Lorenzo de El Escorial, MS ar. 1624, on which see H. Derenbourg, *Les manuscrits arabes de l'Escurial*, vol. 3: *Théologie—géographie—histoire* (Paris, 1928), 168–69.

121. "Mohhammaed ben Ahhmaed elmohhli esciphaei elkasciani. Expositor mysticus et tropologicus, insignis philosophus et metaphysicus" (Dominicus Germanus de Silesia, *Interpretatio literalis Alcorani*, El Escorial MS ar. 1624, fol. 3v).

122. "Nomina praecipuorum discipulorum, quos expositores ceu archigerontes et majores autoritatis prae caeteris citant" (ibid., fol. 3r).

123. "Non malè me otium ac studium meum impendisse arbitratus sum, si interpretationem Alcorani, non ex dictionariis lexicisque, sed ex ipsiusmet auctoris discipulorum, aliorumve ipsis coaevorum, uel aeuo proximorum, ac ipsiusmet Alcorani domesticorum expositorum sententia et declaratione venatus fuero" (Germanus, "Praefatio," ibid., fol. 1r; see also Darenbourg, *Les manuscrits arabes de l'Escurial*, 3.168–69).

124. "In nomine dei miseratoris misericordis. Nos utique dedimus te amnem paradiseum perpetuo currentem id est nunquam memoria tua in hoc et in altero mundo deficiet. Jugiter itaque ora dominum tuum et sacrifica primitias noualium tuarum. Is autem, qui odio te prosequitur, non relinquet ullam memoriam post se id est prolem aut aliquod opus bonum memoriae dignum" (Germanus, *Interpretatio literalis Alcorani*, El Escorial MS ar. 1624, fol. 526r).

125. The El Escorial manuscript lacks a title, but the colophon reads *Explicit Interpretatio literalis alcorani* (ibid., fol. 528v; see also Derenbourg, *Les manuscrits arabes*, 3.168–69). The Montpellier manuscript is titled "Interpretatio Alcorani litteralis cum scholiis ad mentem Autoris ex propriis domesticis ipsius expositoribus germane collectis." See Devic, "Une traduction inédite du Coran," 392–93.

126. "Ikhtalafū fī tafsīr al-kawthar fa-qīla huwa nahr fī al-jannah" (al-Tabarsī on 108.1, 5.549; see also al-Zamakhsharī, 4.801 and al-Rāghib al-Iṣbahānī, 2:642–43).

127. See, for example, al-Zamakhsharī on 108:3, who relates the "abundance" mentioned in this short surah to all of Muhammad's descendents among the believers, his memory (*dhikr*) which is mentioned in pulpits (*manābir*) and on the tongues of learned men until the end of the age (*ākhir al-dahr*) (4:802). For a substantial list of possible interpretations of the word, see al-Qurṭubī on 108:1; 20:147–48.

128. See al-Ṭabarsī on 108:3, 5.550; al-Zamakhsharī on 108:3, 4.802; and al-Qurṭubī on 108:3, 20.151.

129. "Dicunt quod iam natus fuisset Mohhammaedo filius masculus . . . appellavit eam nomine Abraham. . . . mortuus est infans. De cuius morte non tantum doluit propheta (aiunt) quantum de laetitia quam faciebant ipsius inimici . . . ac praecipuè Abu Giahel [*Abū Jahl*] et Eläassi bun Vaiel Elsahami [*al-ʿAṣ Wāʾil al-Sahmī*]. Qui mox illud mentiauerunt Makkensibus dicentes: Iam noster Mohhammaed, omni spe posteritatis frustratus desperat. quia post hunc nullum filium masculum amplius genuit. . . . Ecce (inquiunt) oraculum adfuit consolans eum, et dicens: Ipsius memoriam fore immortalem, non per semen masculinum, sed per multiplicationem fidelium suorum" (Germanus, *Interpretatio literalis Alcorani*, El Escorial MS ar. 1624, fol. 526v). The names of Muhammad's two enemies also ap-

pear in the margin in Arabic script, these names being specifically mentioned in this context in many commentaries. See al-Ṭabarsī on 108:3, 5:549; Ibn ʿAṭīyah on 108:3, 15.586; and the following note.

130. Al-Qurṭubī, for example, lists several possible personages to whom the last part of the surah might refer, including Abū Jahl, whom Germanus mentions by name (*Abu Giahel*, see previous note), and suggests that one or several of them were saying after the death of Muhammad's sons Qāsim and Ibrahīm that "Muhammad is cut off (*Muḥammad butira*) for he will have no one to rise up with his authority after him" (al-Qurṭubī on 108:3; 20:151).

131. "In domine dei pii et misericordis. (1) Tibi iam fontem in paradiso preparauimus. (2) Orationem igitur coram deo funde. ipsique suppliciter immola. (3) Tuus enim hostis. adiutoribus proleque carebit" (Robert of Ketton, *Lex Mahumet*, fol. 138ra; Bibliander, *Alcoran* 1550, 1.187–88).

132. Though Devic, who seems not to have looked at Robert's translation in any meaningful way, argued that the reason Robert's translation was—in his view—so inadequate was that he *did not* consult commentaries. See his "Une traduction inédite du Coran," 374, 400.

133. On Marracci and his great work, see Carlo Alfonso Nallino, "Le fonti arabe manoscritte dell'opera di Ludovico Marracci sul Corano," in *Raccolta di scritti editi e inediti*, vol. 2: *L'Islām: Dogmatica—Ṣūfismo—Confraternite*, ed. Maria Nallino (Rome, 1940), 90–134; Giorgio Levi della Vida, "Ludovico Marracci e la sua opera negli studi islamici," in *Aneddoti e svaghi arabi e non arabi* (Milan and Naples, 1959), 193–210; E. Denison Ross, "Ludovico Marracci," *Bulletin of the School of Oriental and African Studies* 2 (1921–23):117–23; and Hartmut Bobzin, "Latin Koran Translations: A Short Overview," *Der Islam* 70 (1993):198–99.

134. His discussion of Surah 74 ("The Cloaked One") is a good example. See Marracci, *Alcorani textus*, 2:762.

135. Marracci, *Alcorani textus*, 2:817. See above, notes 110–14.

136. "*Fa-al-mūriyāt qadḥan* hiya al-khayl tūrī al-nār bi-ḥawāfirihā idhā ṣārat fī al-ḥijārah wa-al-arḍ al-muḥaṣṣabah" (al-Ṭabarsī on 100:2, 5.529; see also al-Ṭabarī on 100:2, 12.667–68).

137. "Et ex suorum pedum ictibus ignis e lapidibus excussus" (Robert of Ketton, *Lex Mahumet*, fol. 137va; Bibliander, *Alcoran* 1550, 1.187).

138. For another example, see his version of 81:3: "Et, cùm montes ambulare facti fuerint (*idest sublati fuerint, et in pulverem redacti*)" (Marracci, *Alcorani textus*, 2:783). The bracketed portion is derived from commentaries, e.g., "wa-qīla: sayruhā taḥawwuluhā ʿan manzilat al-ḥijārah fa-takūnu kathīban mahīlan ay ramlan sā'ilan . . . wa-takūnu habā'an manthūran" (al-Qurṭubī on 81:3, 19.149). Cf. "montesque fient puluis" (Robert of Ketton, *Lex Mahumet*, fol. 135ra; Bibliander, *Alcoran* 1550, 1.182).

139. Marracci, *Alcorani textus*, 2:772.

140. "I. *Per missas.*] Nimirùm per intelligentias, seu Angelos. . . . Ita Zamachascerius, qui exponit, 'ṭawā'if min al-malā'ikah arsalahunna Allāh bi-awāmirihi' *ordines angelorum, quos mittit Deus cum mandatis suis*" (ibid.). Al-Zamakhsharī says exactly this on 77:1, 4.664.

141. "III. *Per Spargentes.*] Gelal: yaʿnī al-riyāḥ tanshuru al-maṭar *significantur*

venti, qui spargunt pluviam. Zamchascerius, ṭawā'if minhum nasharna ajnihatahunna fī al-jaww: *Ordines eorumdem* Angelorum, *qui expandunt alas suas in aere*" (Marracci, *Alcorani textus*, 2:773). "Gelal" or "Gelaleddinus" is how Marracci refers to the vastly prolific Jalāl al-Dīn ʿAbd al-Raḥmān ibn Abī Bakr al-Suyūṭī, whose famous *Tafsīr al-Qur'ān al-Karīm* (often known as the *Tafsīr Jalālayn*—the *Commentary of the Two Jalāls*—because it is al-Suyūṭī's continuation of a commentary begun by his teacher, Jalāl al-Dīn Muḥammad ibn Aḥmad al-Muhallī) he quotes directly and accurately here (see al-Suyūṭī, *Tafsīr al-Qur'ān al-Karīm* [Cairo, 1966], on 77:3; p. 542; see also Nallino, "Le fonti arabe manoscritte," 109, and "Exegesis of the Qur'ān: Classical and Medieval," EQ 2:99–124 at 113 [art. Claude Gilliot]). See al-Zamakhsharī on 77:3, 4.664 where the antecedent of *hum* is clearly *al-malā'ikah.*

142. "V. *Et immittentes monitionem.*] Conveniunt omnes cum Gelal, intelligi hic, al-malā'ikah tanzilu bi-al-waḥy ilá al-anbiyā' wa-al-rusul yulqūna al-waḥy ilá al-umam *angelos, qui descendunt cum revelatione ad prophetas, et legatos, ut annunciant eamdem revelationem gentibus*" (Marracci, *Alcorani textus*, 2:773). See al-Suyūṭī on 77:3, p. 542.

143. "Per angelos legationis efficaces. uentosque siccos et imbriferos. demonesque licitorum et illicitorum discreturos. ac prophetis diuina mandata correctoria uel instructoria conciso ferentes" (Robert of Ketton, *Lex Mahumet*, fol. 134ra; Bibliander, *Alcoran* 1550, 1.180).

144. Al-Qurṭubī on 77.2; 19:101. Here is an example, by the way, of Robert polemically distorting his translation. My "spirits" (vv. 4–5) translates *demones* which can mean "spirits" in classical Latin, but which usually means evil spirits—"demons"—in medieval Latin. Robert does use the word to translate *al-jinn*, as in 72:6: "Quidam tamen exercitus daemonum aliis tantum persuadent, ut in Deum nullatenus dicendo credant" (Bibliander, *Alcoran* 1550, 1.178). Earlier in the same surah he uses the term "diaboli" to translate *al-jinn*, in vv. 1 and 5 (ibid.). The *jinn* were intermediate spirits, some of them good and some bad; if there were traditions that said that *jinn*, instead of angels, were to distinguish between what is allowable and what is not in v. 4, then this might account for Robert's translation, but so far I have found no such traditions in the commentaries. That he is using *demones* in the classical sense is possible but not likely.

145. See above, note 123. Further examples: Marracci's version of 52:2's *wa-al-Ṭūr*: *per montem*, which he explains in his note *(nempè Synai)*, quoting the commentator al-Suyūṭī (d. 1505) and al-Zamakhsharī: "*Per montem.*] Exponit Gelal: ay al-jabal alladhī kallama Allāh ʿalayhi Mūsá . . . Eodem modo Zamchascerius" (Marracci, *Alcorani textus*, 2.679; cf. al-Suyūṭī on 52:1, p. 483; and al-Zamakhsharī on 52:1, 4.398); cf. Robert of Ketton's *Per montem sӯnai* (Robert of Ketton, *Lex Mahumet*, fol. 124ra; Bibliander, *Alcoran* 1550, 1.162). Compare Robert's and Mark's incorporation of the exegesis of *sijjīn* in 83:7 in their translations (see above, notes 50, 51) with Marracci's transliteration of it (*seggin*) elucidated similarly in his note (Marracci, *Alcorani textus*, 2:787). See also Marracci's version of 37:1 (*per Ordinantes ordinando*, which the attached note explains consist of angels; ibid., 2.586); Robert's and Mark's amplifying translations supply the same information (see above, note 47)

146. See, e.g., al-Ṭabarsī on 51:1–4, 5.152–53; and Ibn ʿAṭīyah on 51:1–4, 14.2–3.

147. N. J. Dawood, trans., *The Koran* (Harmondsworth, Middlesex, 1956), 116–17.

148. Pickthall's middle two verses read "And those that bear the burden (*of the rain*), and those that glide with ease (*upon the sea*) (*my italics*)" (Pickthall, trans., *The Meaning of the Glorious Koran*, 540; this translation was first published in 1930).

149. Mark of Toledo, *Liber Alchorani*, fol. 71rb. Robert's translation reads, "Per uentos sufflantes. attractasque nubes ponderosas. et naues equore currentes. angelosque nuntios" (Robert of Ketton, *Lex Mahumet*, fol. 123va; Bibliander, *Alcoran* 1550, 1.161). In Egidio's Latin Qur'ān, we have "Per ventos discurrentes, et per nubes oneratas, et per naves quae current, et per angelos iussos" (Iohannes Gabriel, *Alcoranus*, Cambridge MS Mm. v. 26, fol. 228va–b, with a nearly identical text in BA MS D 100 inf. fol. 526v).

Chapter 3

1. "Azoara .XXX.I. Insanis mendacibus et solitis neniarum replicationibus inuoluta" (Robert of Ketton, *Lex Mahumet*, fol. 89ra). This is actually the beginning of surah 22, numbered 31 here for reasons that I will explain presently.

2. See most recently Walter B. Cahn's comprehensive and erudite article, "The 'Portrait' of Muhammad in the Toledan Collection," in *Reading Medieval Images: The Art Historian and the Object*, ed. Elizabeth Sears and Thelma K. Thomas (Ann Arbor, Mich., 2002), 51–60, esp. 57–58; but also Martínez, "Finalidad de la primera traducción latina del Corán," 75. On this manuscript in general, see Henry Martin, *Catalogue des manuscrits de la Bibliothèque de l'Arsenal*, 9 vols. (Paris, 1885–92), 2.315–17; d'Alverny, "Deux traductions," 69–109, and Fernando González Muñoz, ed. and trans., *Exposición y refutación del Islam: La versión latina de las epistolas de al-Hāšimī y al-Kindī* (A Coruña, Spain, 2005), xcvi–xcviii, cxv–cxvii.

3. These works will be discussed further below.

4. See his introduction in González, *Exposición y refutación del Islam*, cxv–cxvii. González rightly argues on paleographical, codicological, and textual grounds that the several originally discrete sections of Arsenal MS 1162 must themselves have been copies of the archetypes of the various works in the collection and not the archetypes themselves. This view is an insightful refinement of d'Alverny's argument that each of the originally discrete portions of Arsenal MS 1162 was, in fact, the original exemplar of that work, the assembled manuscript, therefore, representing the original exemplar of the whole collection (see her "Deux traductions," 77–78, 96, 98). Both are in agreement, however, that a further copy of Arsenal MS 1162 was assembled at Cluny in the mid-twelfth century and that it is from this now lost archetype that all the manuscripts containing Robert's translation derive. For a description of that exemplar, see González, op. cit., cxvii–cxviii, and d'Alverny, "Quelques manuscrits," 204–6.

5. See, for example, the article by Roger Chartier cited in the following note.

6. This process has been well described by Roger Chartier in his "Reading Matter and 'Popular' Reading: From the Renaissance to the Seventeenth Century,"

in *A History of Reading in the West*, ed. Guglielmo Cavallo and Roger Chartier, trans. Lydia G. Cochrane (Amherst, Mass., 1999), 278.

7. John Tolan, "Peter the Venerable and the 'Diabolic Heresy of the Saracens'," in *The Devil, Heresy, and Witchcraft in the Middle Ages: Essays in Honor of Jeffrey B. Russell*, ed. Alberto Ferreiro (Leiden, 1998), 345–67 at 354–57.

8. On Hugh, see Paul Saenger, "Reading in the Later Middle Ages," in *A History of Reading in the West*, ed. Cavallo and Chartier, 120–48 at 121–22.

9. R. W. Southern, *Scholastic Humanism and the Unification of Europe*, vol. 1: *Foundations* (Oxford, 1995), 4.

10. I have shown this to be the case in my "Exclusion or Concealment," 194–95.

11. James H. Morey, "Peter Comestor, Biblical Paraphrase, and the Medieval Popular Bible," *Speculum* 68 (1993):6–35.

12. The earliest manuscript is Paris, BnF, MS lat. 16943, a manuscript that has striking resemblances to Arsenal 1162, the earliest manuscript of Robert's Latin Qur'an. On it, see most recently Agneta Sylwan's introduction to her edition of the book of Genesis in Comestor's *Scholastica historia. Liber Genesis*, CCCM 191, xl–xlv. Paris, BnF, MS lat. 372, a fourteenth-century copy of Comestor's great work, likewise makes no visible distinction between what is Biblical text and what is exegetical addition.

13. D'Alverny had almost nothing to say about these rubrics other than to note, quite correctly that they, like many of the marginal glosses that I will discuss below, "ont été inspirées par un esprit de dénigrement systématique." See her "Deux traductions," 101.

14. For an interesting discussion of the nature and origin of this practice, see al-Suyūṭī, *al-Itqān*, 1.122–23.

15. "Capitulum azoare matris libri .vii. uerba continens," and "Azoara de boue ducentorum octaginta quinque uerborum" (Robert of Ketton, *Lex Mahumet*, Oxford, Bodleian Library, MS Selden Supra 31, fol. 33r). While most often referred to as *al-Fāṭihah* ("The Beginning"), the first surah was also frequently called—as it is here—"the Mother of the Book" (*umm al-Kitāb*), this being one of the many different titles under which it was known, according to al-Suyūṭī (see his *al-Itqān*, 1.116–19).

16. For examples of titles that do not fit the space allotted for them, see Arsenal MS 1162, fols. 40rb, 42rb, 44ra.

17. On Robert's nonstandard method of dividing up the surahs, see below in this chapter.

18. "Hic non occidisse iudeos christum. sed nescio quem similem eius. nec deum habere filium. intra solitas insanias dicit. quod et sepe facit" (Robert of Ketton, *Lex Mahumet*, fol. 44ra).

19. Ibid., fol. 92rb.

20. Thus the rubric to Robert's *Azoara* 74 (*uanitate plenissima*), ibid., folio 129va. Daniel rightly stressed the repetitive nature of these rubrics. See his *Islam and the West*, 82.

21. The following surahs have polemical rubrics in the Arsenal manuscript: 7–10, 12–25, 28–34, 39–44, 46, 50–56, 58, 60–61, 63–65, 67–68, 71–74, 79–80, 82–85,

88. These numbers refer to Robert's division of the text, which, as I will make clear presently, is not the same as the standard Qur'ānic division.

22. Annotator, fol. 27ra, rm.

23. "Sequitur de deo et adam et angelis et diabolo fabula stultissima. quam nescio ubi repererit" (ibid., fol. 26rb, rm, at 2:29).

24. "Hic iactat quasi nullus hominum talem librum facere possit" (ibid., 26rb, interlinearly).

25. "Hoc furatur de euangelio" (ibid., 36ra, interlinearly on l. 10). See also 31ra, tm, where the Qur'ānic term Gehenna is similar identified as stolen from the Bible.

26. "Nota quam stulte et quotiens repetit istud sicut et alia multa. non habens quid loquatur" (ibid., 30ra, rm).

27. On verse 3:89, for example, a note asserts that "modo iterum concedit penitentiam. quam in aliis locis sepe solet negare" (ibid., 36rb, rm).

28. Ibid., 31vb, lm.

29. "Iterum quam stulta iuratio. qua facit deum iurare" (ibid., 133rb, rm).

30. See ibid., fol. 126ra, rm.

31. "Nota ubique stulticiam" (ibid., fol. 120va, lm).

32. Tolan, "Peter the Venerable," 357.

33. D'Alverny, "Deux traductions," 98.

34. Ibid., 99–102. Norman Daniel was likewise impressed by the learning of whoever wrote these notes, but said relatively little about their content or sources; see his *Islam and the West*, 22, 54, 58.

35. These textual correction notes and the rest of the annotations were all made at the same time: they are all in the same hand as, and the same lighter ink than, the text itself.

36. Annotator, fol. 134ra; cf. Bibliander, *Alcoran* 1550, 1.21.

37. Such as at 2:23: here the Arsenal manuscript had *huncque librum ueracem esse penitus credite, consimilem . . . perficite.* This makes grammatical sense but not the sense that the Qur'ānic original required. An interlinear note, therefore, supplies a *uel* before *consimilem*, yielding "Believe thoroughly in this book, *or* make . . . one resembling it." (See Annotator, fol. 26rb; cf. Bibliander, *Alcoran* 1550, 1.9.) The corrections in 2:23 and 3:1, and, as far as can be determined, all the many others are perpetuated in all the later manuscripts, this being a powerful demonstration that the Arsenal manuscript is the ultimate source of all twenty-four of the later manuscripts. See d'Alverny, "Deux traductions," 78.

38. "Sed ille quidem nec uobis nec parentibus uestris antea precepta; enodauit" (Robert of Ketton, *Lex Mahumet*, fol. 51va; Bibliander, *Alcoran* 1550, 1.48).

39. One such note is the paraphrase of Robert's rather confusing version of verses 2:142–43a, added in the margin nearby: "Hoc est ad quamcumque partem quis oret non curat inde deus. sed tamen tibi sicut amico meo et electo locum orationis ostendam. et genti tuę qui sunt mei proprii" (Annotator, 29ra, rm). A second translation of the first short surah inserted alongside Robert's translation—lacking in this manuscript because of the lost folio, but present in the other manuscripts—must have served a similar function since it is, as d'Alverny pointed out ("Deux traductions," 100–101), more literal than Robert's.

40. Ibid., 34vb, l. 20.

41. A similar example occurs at 2:272 where, next to Robert's translation (*Meum quidem est nequaquam tuum*, Robert of Ketton, *Lex Mahumet*, fol. 33va; Bibliander, *Alcoran* 1550, 1.20), an interlinear note reads *O Mahumet* (Annotator, fol. 33va). Al-Ṭabarī paraphrases this passage by inserting the same "O Muhammad" (*Yā Muḥammad*) for the same clarifying purpose (see his commentary on 2:272, 3.94).

42. "quod nos capitulum dicimus illi uocant azoaram" (Annotator, Oxford MS Selden Supra 31, fol. 33r, rm). This correct observation is, as d'Alverny pointed out, nested within a faulty etymology of the word which assumes that it is spelled in Arabic with an emphatic *ṣad* rather than a *sīn*: "Azoara arabice 'uultus' latine dicitur . . . Sicut enim uultus notat maxime quis uel qualis sit homo, sic capitulum quid sequens litteram dicere uelit" (ibid.), cf. d'Alverny, "Deux traductions," 102.

43. "alfurcam idem est quod alcoran" (Annotator, fol. 63ra).

44. "id est iudeis et christianis quos homines legum semper appellat" (ibid., fol. 43va, lm; see also 35vb, interlinearly ll. 18–19).

45. "Sciendum autem quod lingua arabica maximam cognacionem habet cum ebream, vnde et arabes isti . . . sicut iudei a dextera in sinistram, non a sinistra in dexteram sicut nos scribendo [litteras?] ducunt" (Annotator, Oxford MS Selden Supra 31, fol. 33r, rm). The manuscript has *dicunt* where I have read *ducunt*.

46. Ibid., fol. 33v; d'Alverny transcribes the whole of it from other manuscripts in her "Deux traductions," 99–100. Since it occurs near the beginning of Robert's translation, it does not appear in the acephalous Arsenal MS 1162.

47. "Vox quasi suorum professorum. et hoc sepe facit mutando personas in locutione. vt uideatur quasi propheta loqui" (Annotator, 29ra, rm).

48. A similar linkage of philology and polemic occurs at verse 2:22, where a marginal note explains that "hoc dicit propter christianos. quos . . . putat tres deos credere. . . . Et nota quod in isto heresis arriana reuixit" (ibid., fol. 26rb). Muslim commentators did sometimes assert that this verse was directed at Christians (see al-Ṭabarsī on 2:22, 1.61). The authors of this note had to explain the meaning of this verse as Muslims understood it—a philological task—before they could make their polemical point that Muhammad taught Arian doctrines.

49. "Primum capitulum istud breue matrem libri dicit ob hoc quoniam ex eo tota lex originem sortitur et fundamentum, et est initium et summa omnium orationum eorum" (Annotator, Oxford MS Selden Supra 31, fol. 33r).

50. "Wa-qīla umm al-shay' aṣluhu wa-hiya aṣl al-Qur'ān li-inṭiwā'ihā 'alá jamī' aghrāḍ al-Qur'ān wa-mā fīhā min al-'ulūm wa-al-ḥikam" (al-Suyūṭī, *al-Itqān*, 1.117).

51. I originally argued for the extensive influence of the Islamic exegetical tradition on these notes in my *Religious Polemic and the Intellectual History of the Mozarabs, c. 1050–1200* (Leiden, 1994), 137–43.

52. Annotator, Oxford, Corpus Christi College, MS 184, p. 50a. This is one of the earliest (thirteenth century) and most reliable manuscripts of Robert's Qur'ān after the Arsenal codex.

53. "Iudeos uocat hostes dei quia christum prophetam maximum absque pec-

cato semper uiuentem iustissimum et a uirgine natum absque reatu suspendere uoluerant" (ibid., p. 50b, top and right margins).

54. "Christianos dicit erroneos tum quia putant illos adore tres deos tum imagines" (ibid., p. 50b, rm).

55. See, for example, al-Zamakhsharī on 1:7, 1.26: "wa-qīla al-maghḍūb ʿalayhim hum al-Yahūd . . . wa-al-ḍāllūn hum al-Naṣārá." See also al-Ṭabarī on 1:7, 1.110–11, 113–15.

56. For a recent brief overview and ample bibliography on the "mysterious letters," see Irfan Shahīd, "*Fawātiḥ al-suwār*, The Mysterious Letters of the Qurʾān," *Literary Structures of Religious Meaning in the Qurʾān*, ed. Issa J. Boullata (Richmond, Surrey, 2000), 125–39.

57. Medieval copyists are notorious for failing to render accurately words or letters from other languages that show up in Latin texts, the variations in how these letters appear being but a further example of this.

58. "mim id est rex. lem id est sapiens. elif id est deus" (Annotator, Oxford MS Selden Supra 31, fol. 33r).

59. "Causa uero quod ab huiusmodi karactere incipit quoniam elif et in ordine litterarum et in nomine dei prima est aput eos; per lem uero maiestas dei, per mim imperium designatur" (ibid., 33r, bm). See also d'Alverny, "Deux traductions," 100.

60. Al-Ṭabarī on 2:1, 1.120.

61. See, for example, al-Ṭabarsī on 2:73, 1.137: "*fa-qulnā uḍribūhu bi-baʿḍihā* ay qulnā la-hum uḍribū al-qatīl bi-baʿḍ al-baqarah." See also al-Ṭabarī on 2:73, 1.402–3; and Ibn Kathīr on 2:73, 1.107.

62. "Fa-in qāla qāʾil: wa-mā kāna maʿná al-amr bi-ḍarb al-qatīl . . . ? Qīla: li-yuḥyā fa-yunabbiʾa . . . Mūsá . . . wa-alladhīna iddāraʾū fī-hā man qātiluhu" (al-Ṭabarī on 2:73, 1.404). See also al-Ṭabarsī, 1.137; and Ibn Kathīr, 1.107.

63. "Cum quis dei dogmate ipsoque fauente homicidam ignoratum patefacere studuerit. mortuum cum aliqua uacce particula; tangat. Sic enim suscitatus; rem ipsam edocebit" (Robert of Ketton, *Lex Mahumet*, fol. 27rb-va; Bibliander, *Alcoran* 1550, 1.11. For a fuller discussion of Robert's handling of this passage, see Burman, "*Tafsīr* and Translation," 714–16).

64. "Fa-qīla lisānahā wa-qīla fakhdhahā al-yumná wa-qīla ʿajbahā wa-qīla al-ʿaẓm alladhī yalī al-ghuḍrūf wa-huwa al-aṣl al-udhn . . ." (al-Zamakhsharī on 2:73, 1.155; see also Ibn Kathīr on 2:73, 1.107).

65. Annotator, fol. 27rb. For another example of a note matching the typical Muslim exegesis, see the marginal note on verse 2:25 which, above the phrase *mundissimas mulieres,* reads *scilicet a menstruis et egestione* (ibid., fol. 26rb), and see al-Qurṭubī who explains the phrase "pure wives" as follows: "wa-maʿná hādhā al-ṭahārah min al-ḥayḍ wa-al-buṣāq wa-sāʾir aqdhār al-ādamiyāt" (al-Qurṭubī on 2:14, 1.67).

66. "Theut idolum erat. antiquę ydolatrię arabum" (Annotator, fol. 41va, rm, commenting on the phrase "qualiter a Theut iudicium postulant").

67. "Fa-qāla baʿḍuhum humā ṣanamān kāna al-mushrikūn yaʿbudūnahumā min dūni Allāh" (al-Ṭabarī on 4:51, 4.133).

68. "Ille quidem hominem de celcal . . . condidit," (Robert of Ketton, *Lex Mahumet*, fol. 125vb; Bibliander, *Alcoran* 1550, 1.165).

69. Annotator, fol. 125vb.

70. Al-Qurṭubī on 55:14; 17.105; see also al-Ṭabarsī on 55:14, 5.200.

71. "cui nomen Ahaorethus," (Annotator, fol. 128[bis]rb; in Bibliander, *Alcoran* 1550, 1.171, *Machumetus* has replaced *Ahaorethus* in the text itself). Note that even in this earliest manuscript this name is badly garbled—as foreign names often are in Latin mss. Al-Qurṭubī on 61:6, 18.55: "wa-*Aḥmad* ism nabīnā." See also al-Ṭabarsī on 61:6, 5.279.

72. See, for example, al-Ṭabarī on 54:1, 11.544–47; and al-Zamakhsharī on 54:1, 4.420.

73. "aliquod signum contigerat in luna quod dicit propter se factum" (Annotator, fol. 125ra, rm). For another example, see the interlinear and marginal notes on 17:1, where, above "sacrosanct mosque" (*templum haran* [<Arabic *ḥarām*] in Robert's version), we have *scilicet meccę*; above *templum longinquum*, we have *scilicet ierusalem*, this and much else in the notes here conforming closely to traditional Islamic exegesis (ibid., fol. 78rb, and see Ibn ʿAṭīyah on 17:1, 9.7–10; al-Ṭabarsī on 17:1, 3.396).

74. "Hic uult dicere. quod iudei quidam Christum uoluerunt occidere. sed ipse callide se subtrahens euasit. dimittens nescio quem loco sui quem crucifixerunt putantes illum esse Christum. Creator autem leuauit Christum ad se" (Annotator, fol. 35va, lm).

75. See, for example, al-Ṭabarī on 3:54, 3.287, and Ibn ʿAṭīyah on 3:54, 3.140–41; see also my *Religious Polemic*, 139–41, where this particular marginal note and its Muslim sources are discussed at greater length.

76. "Hic narrant fabulam quandam. quod scilicet quidam propter terremotus et fulgura ad cauernas sub montibus et rupibus fugientes ibi habitabant. putantes se remotos a potestate dei. et ob hoc eum minime timentes; quos deus mori et reuiuescere fecit. ubi se ubique potentem equaliter demonstraret. Secundum quosdam istud contingit quibusdam fugientibus ne ad prelium irent. et hoc uidetur ipse magis uelle" (Annotator, 32ra–b rm–tm).

77. See al-Ṭabarī on 2:243, 2.600–605. He quotes hadiths very like the second, but cites none specifying that they fled because of earthquake or lightning, a narrative for which I can find no source. The majority of the traditions he cites specify, rather, that they fled "in fear of the plague." Other commentators give similar interpretations. See Ibn ʿAṭīyah on 2:243, 2.344–45; and al-Ṭabarsī on 2:243, 1.346.

78. On these passages, see above, notes 46, 68, 76.

79. I follow here L. E. Goodman's intriguing observations on an analogous transformation of motive and approach in the early movement to translate Greek and Syriac science into Arabic. See his "The Translation of Greek Materials into Arabic," in *Religion, Learning and Science in the ʿAbbasid Period*, ed. M. J. L. Young, J. D. Latham and R. B. Serjeant (Cambridge, England, 1990), 477–97 at 482–83.

80. See, for example, the explanations of the Kaʿbah and of Ramaḍan in notes to the *Fabulae saracenorum. Chronica mendosa et ridicula saracenorum*, Arsenal MS 1162, 6va, l. 10; 7rb, rm.

81. D'Alverny, "Deux traductions," 102–3; see also Burman, *Religious Polemic*, 87–89; Daniel, *Islam and the West*, 418; and Kritzeck, *Peter the Venerable*, 57–58, n. 31.

82. See Chapter 2 above.

83. See the discussion of the annotation on 2:73 above, notes 61–63.

84. On which see Chapter 1 above.

85. *Fabulae saracenorum. Chronica mendosa et ridicula saracenorum.* Arsenal MS 1162, fol. 5rb–10vb and margin of llrb.

86. Kritzeck describes the contents in some detail in his *Peter the Venerable,* 75–83.

87. See ibid., 75–76.

88. *Liber generationis Mahumet et nutritia eius.* Arsenal MS 1162, fol. 11ra-18rb.

89. See Kritzeck, *Peter the Venerable and Islam,* 84–88.

90. *Doctrina Mahumet,* Arsenal MS 1162, fols. 19ra–25bis.

91. See Kritzeck, *Peter the Venerable and Islam,* 89–96.

92. *Risālat ʿAbd Allāh ibn Ismāʾīl al-Hāshimī ilá ʿAbd al-Masīḥ ibn Iṣḥāq al-Kindī wa-Risālat al-Kindī ilá al-Hāshimī,* ed. A. Tien (London, 1888; Cairo, 1885, 1912).

93. *Epistola sarraceni ad christianum, Epistola Christiani ad sarracenum,* Arsenal MS 1162, fols. 140ra–178ra. See most recently Fernando González Muñoz, "La versión latina de la *Apología de al-Kindī* y su tradición textual," in *Musulmanes y cristianos en Hispania,* ed. Barceló and Martínez, 25–40; Professor González's excellent edition of the Latin text has just appeared as well; see n. 2 above.

94. *Summa totius heresis ac diabolicę sectę sarracenorum siue hismahelitarum.* Arsenal MS 1162, fol. 1ra–3va. Kritzeck edited this text in his *Peter the Venerable and Islam,* 204–11.

95. Kritzeck describes the contents of this treatise at great length in his *Peter the Venerable and Islam,* 115–52.

96. *Epistola domni Petri abbatis ad domnum Bernardum Claręuallis abbatem* . . . Arsenal MS 1162, fol. 3vb–4vb; Kritzeck edited this text in his *Peter the Venerable and Islam,* 212–14. On this letter, see also Martínez and de la Cruz, "Las traducciones árabe-latinas impulsadas por Pedro el Venerable," 287–89.

97. Jacques Monfrin, "Préface," to *Mise en page et mise en texte du livre manuscrit,* ed. H.-J. Martin and Jean Vezin (Paris, 1990), 9–10.

98. The bibliography on this topic is large, but for a recent overview, see the following articles, all published in *A History of Reading in the West,* ed. Cavallo and Chartier: M. B. Parkes, "Reading, Copying and Interpreting a Text in the Early Middle Ages" (90–102); Jacqueline Hamesse, "The Scholastic Model of Reading" (103–19); and Paul Saenger, "Reading in the Later Middle Ages" (120–48).

99. See Ivan Illich's intriguing essay, *In the Vineyard of the Text: A Commentary of Hugh's Didascalicon* (Chicago, 1993).

100. Richard H. and Mary A. Rouse, "*Statim invenire*: Schools, Preachers and New Attitudes to the Page," in *Renaissance and Renewal in the Twelfth Century,* ed. Robert L. Benson and Giles Constable (Cambridge, Mass., 1982), 201–25 at 205.

101. Richard H. and Mary A. Rouse, *Preachers, Florilegia and Sermons: Studies on the Manipulus florum of Thomas of Ireland* (Toronto, 1979), 27–32; id., "La naissance des index," in *Histoire de l'édition française,* ed. Henri-Jean Martin and Roger Chartier, vol. 1: *Le livre conquérant* (Paris, 1983), 95–108 at 98; M. B. Parkes, "The Influence of the Concepts of *ordinatio* and *compilatio* in the Development of the

Book," in *Medieval Learning and Literature: Essays Presented to Richard William Hunt*, ed. J. J. G. Alexander and M. T. Gibson (Oxford, 1976), 115–41 at 17–25.

102. D'Alverny transcribed this prologue in its entirety in "Deux traductions," 79.

103. See Arsenal MS 1162, fols. 11r, 19r.

104. See, for example, Juan de Segovia, "Prefatio . . . in translationem," 404, ll. 355–57, and d'Alverny, "Deux traductions," 86.

105. For a tabular overview of the relationship between the standard divisions and those found in Robert's version (as well as the slightly different—124-surah—division in Bibliander's sixteenth-century printed editions), see Bobzin, *Der Koran*, 229. It should be noted that Robert may well have intended 124 surahs himself, since what he entitles surah 17 is actually divided into two parts, the second of them simply lacking a rubric indicating that it is a new surah, the rubricator perhaps mistakenly passing over it. See Arsenal MS 1162, fols. 53va, 58va, 60ra.

106. On this tendency in general, see Parkes, "The Influence of the Concepts of *ordinatio* and *compilatio*," 125–26, but also Rouse and Rouse, "*Statim invenire*," 221; Saenger, "Reading in the Later Middle Ages," 133–34. On Langton specifically, see Amaury d'Esneval, "La division de la Vulgate latine en chapitres dans l'édition Parisienne du XIIIe siècle," *Revue des sciences philosophiques et théologiques* 62 (1978):559–68, and Dahan, *L'exégèse chrétienne*, 175–76.

107. See Ludwig Hagemann, *Der Ḳur'ān in Verständnis und Kritik bei Nikolaus von Kues: Ein Beitrag zur Erhellung islāmisch-christlicher Geschichte*, Frankfurter Theologische Studien 21 (Frankfurt, 1976), 26–27.

108. D'Alverny, "Deux traductions," 86.

109. See Bobzin, *Der Koran*, 226–30.

110. On the use of paragraphs in early copies of the *Decretum*, see Parkes, "The Influence of the Concepts of *ordinatio* and *compilatio*," 118–19.

111. D'Alverny described it as similar to an uncial "M", and suggested that it separated Qur'ānic verses. See d'Alverny, "Deux traductions," 100. While many Arabic Qur'ān manuscripts do use sigla to mark the end of each verse, this is certainly not the case here. Rather the novel siglum of the Arsenal manuscript is clearly indicating larger divisions.

112. As, for example, in surah 22, where we have only three divisions but each corresponds with one of the seven decades of that surah signaled in Arabic Qur'an manuscripts. See Arsenal MS 1162, 89va, 90ra, 90va.

113. "Ista littera non est aliud nisi paragrafum arabicum" (Annotator, fol. 26ra). See also d'Alverny, "Deux traductions," 100.

114. See Saenger, "Reading in the Later Middle Ages," 121.

115. See note 101 above.

116. Richard Southern, *Scholastic Humanism and the Unification of Europe*, vol. 2: *The Heroic Age* (Oxford, 2001), 26.

117. On Andrew, most recently, see Frans van Liere, "Andrew of St. Victor, Jerome, and the Jews: Biblical Scholarship in the Twelfth-Century Renaissance," in *Scripture and Pluralism: Reading the Bible in the Religiously Plural Worlds of the Middle Ages and Renaissance*, ed. Thomas J. Heffernan and Thomas E. Burman (Leiden, 2005), 59–75, esp. 62–63, 67–73. For more on the quite large bibliography on An-

drew, see ibid., and also Michael Signer, "Consolation and Confrontation: Jewish and Christian Interpretation of the Prophetic Books," in *Scripture and Pluralism*, 77–93.

118. The phrase is Frans van Liere's. See his "Andrew of St. Victor, Jerome, and the Jews," 67.

119. Southern, *Scholastic Humanism*, 1.4.

120. Irvine, *The Making of Textual Culture*, 392.

121. Ibid., 391.

122. On the meaning and function of this characteristic combination of marginal and interlinear glosses, see Christopher de Hamel, *Glossed Books of the Bible and the Origins of the Paris Booktrade* (Woodbridge, Suffolk, 1987), 14–27; Dahan, *L'exégèse chrétienne*, 125–26; and Smalley, *The Study of the Bible*, 56.

123. On the evolution of the gloss and, especially, of manuscripts to accommodate it, see Christopher de Hamel, *Glossed Books of the Bible*, 1–27; and Margaret Gibson, "The Twelfth-Century Glossed Bible," *Studia patristica* 33 (1989):232–44 at 233–37.

124. Dahan, *L'exégèse chrétienne*, 11–12.

125. See the beginning of the following chapter.

126. Daniel, *Islam and the West*, 186, mentioned the care with which they were inscribed in the manuscript.

127. Cf. Irvine, *The Making of Textual Culture*, 392–93.

128. See Margaret Gibson, *The Bible in the Latin West* (Notre Dame, Ind., 1993), 52–53, #14.

129. See de Hamel, *Glossed Books of the Bible*, 16n9, and F. Madan and H. Craster, *A Summary Catalogue of Western Manuscripts in the Bodleian Library at Oxford*, 2.1 (Oxford, 1922), 52, #1221.

Chapter 4

1. For a listing of the extant manuscripts, see d'Alverny, "Deux traductions," 108–12, and ead., "Quelques manuscrits," passim. The number twenty-four is attained by bearing in mind that three manuscripts she lists for the broader *Collectio Toletana* actually lack Robert's translation (these are Paris, BnF MS lat. 3649; Paris, BnF MS lat. 6225; and Cambridge, Corpus Christi College MS 335), and by adding to the remainder Karlsruhe, *Badische Landesbibliothek*, MS Reichenau 112, of which she was unaware (on which manuscript see Alfred Holder, *Die Reichenauer Handschriften*, Zweiter Band: *Die Papierhandschriften, Fragmenta, Nachträge*. Die Handschriften der Badischen Landesbibliothek in Karlsuhe, vol. 6 [Wiesbaden, 1971], 263–64). I thank Professor José Martínez Gázquez for sharing with me the results of his research on the manuscript tradition, which confirmed my own. For a recent overview of the later reception of Robert's translation, see Óscar de La Cruz Palma, "La trascendencia de la primera traducción latina del Corán (Robert de Ketton, 1142)," *Collatio* 7 (2002):21–28 [http://www.hottopos.com/collat7/oscar.htm].

2. Oxford, Bodleian Library, MS Selden Supra 31; Paris, BnF, MS lat. 3390;

and Paris, BnF, MS lat. 3391 are from the thirteenth century; Oxford, Corpus Christi College, MS 184 has been dated to either the thirteenth or fourteenth centuries; Paris, BnF, MSS lat. 6064 and 14503; Troyes, Bibliothèque Municipale, MS 1235; and Vatican City, BAV, MS lat. 4072 are from the fourteenth century.

3. Mantua, Biblioteca communale, MS A. III. I. On this manuscript, and those mentioned in the previous note, see d'Alverny, "Deux traductions," 109–11, and ead., "Quelques manuscrits," 212–13.

4. BnF MS lat. 3391 and Oxford, Corpus Christi MS 184 preserve the notes particularly fully, but even the latter lacks some of the interlinear notes: "id est quando benefit eis," on "commodo" in verse 2:14 of Robert's translation (Arsenal MS 1162, fol. 26ra) is lacking in that codex (see p. 50b).

5. The only exceptions appear to be BAV MS lat. 4072 and Mantua MS A. III. I.

6. As in Oxford, Corpus Christi MS 184; BnF MS lat. 3390; BnF MS 6064; BnF MS 14503; and Troyes MS 1235.

7. See, for example, Oxford, Corpus Christi MS 184; and BnF MS lat. 3390.

8. Rouse and Rouse, "*Statim invenire*," 205–9. On Hugh, see Saenger, "Reading in the Later Middle Ages," 121.

9. Only Mantua MS A. III. I (the sixteenth-century manuscript) appears to lack such ruling entirely, while BnF MS 6064 and Troyes MS 1235 appear to have ruling for only some of the notes.

10. On this manuscript (including a photograph of one page), see my "Polemic, Philology, and Ambivalence," 202–4.

11. For examples, see Bodleian MS Selden Supra 31, fols. 33v, 34v.

12. "nocte uero tota non cessent comedere, bibere, et concumbere" (ibid., 38v, lm).

13. Ibid. For another example of bracketed annotations in this manuscript, see 40v, lm.

14. See, e.g., ibid., 36r, rm; 38r, rm.

15. See, for example, Copeland, *Rhetoric, Hermeneutics, and Translation in the Middle Ages*, 92, 147–49. A similar way of reading informed the later medieval creation of a lengthy table of contents for Robert's Latin Qur'ān. This analytic *tabula*, which we will examine below, describes the contents of the Qur'ān at vast length, and often simply incorporates material from the Latin marginal annotations right into its entries. For example, among the contents of surah 22, it points out, is Abraham's building of the "temple of Mecca." Robert's text, however, had said here that Abraham had established the "temple of *Haran*" (*Haran* transliterating *al-ḥarām*: "the sacred temple"). It was a later, philological note that had clarified that this temple was in Mecca ("id est Mecce," [Annotator, fol. 89va]). As in many other cases, the maker of this table of contents made no distinction, then, between the Qur'ān and the annotations that so often accompanied it in Latin manuscripts: both were a single authoritative unit.

16. The phrase is from Chartier, *The Order of Books*, x.

17. An excellent description of this manuscript can be found in Bibliothèque Nationale, *Catalogue général des manuscrits latins*, 6.487–89. My comments on the

physical features of this manuscript depend on this catalogue and on my own examination of the manuscript.

18. Major initials at the beginning of surahs, for example, have been drawn in red or blue with flourishes in the alternate color. While these initials are not enormous (usually just slightly larger than two lines high), the flourishes generally cascade gracefully along the column's edge, extending in many cases along the whole length of the written space and often into the lower margin. Flourished initials of just this sort are common in pocket Bibles. See Christopher de Hamel, *The Book: A History of the Bible* (London, 2001), 116. We have a hierarchy of initials as well, with medium-sized initials at the beginning of important subsections appearing in alternating red and blue as well. These subsection divisions do correspond to those in the Arsenal manuscript, but the unique paragraph sign designed for it and perpetuated in many other manuscripts only appears here irregularly (e.g., on fol. 49r).

19. This appears on fol. 1: "[Liber] monasterii Sancti Adalberti in Wrat[islava] ordinis fratrum Predicatorum." It has been carefully erased but is clearly visible under ultraviolet light, as the *Catalogue général des manuscrits latins*, 6.489 points out. This must, by the way, be the manuscript of Robert's version that Widmanstetter (on whom, see below in this chapter) referred to in 1543 as existing "Vratislauaie . . . apud Praedicatorii ordinis Fratres, ante annos triginta." See his letter to Johannes Otto in Johann Albrecht von Widmanstetter, ed., *Mahometis Abdallae filii theologia dialogo explicata Hermanno Nellingaunense interprete; Alcorani epitome, Roberto Ketense anglo interprete* . . . (Nuremburg, 1543), fols. aiiiV–aivR.

20. BnF MS lat. 3668, fol. 4v.

21. Manuscripts with a height of 200 mm or less are considered "pocket" books. See Dahan, *L'exégèse chrétienne*, 11n1. Its script is not as small as that found in many pocket Bibles, which is often less than 2 mm. high. The script of this pocket Qur'ān is 3.5 mm. high. The Qur'ān, however, is a much shorter book than the Bible, making such minute script unnecessary.

22. Ibid., 11.

23. For a thorough discussion of the characteristic features of the pocket Bibles, see Laura Light, "Versions et révisions du texte biblique," in *Le Moyen Âge et la Bible*, ed. Pierre Riché and Guy Lobrichon, Bible de tous les temps, vol. 4 (Paris, 1984), 55–93 at 79, 84–89; see also de Hamel, *The Book*, 114–39; and Gibson, *The Bible in the Latin West*, 11–12.

24. See Light, "Versions et révisions," 89; Barbara A. Shailor, *The Medieval Book* (Toronto, 1991), 79; and de Hamel, *The Book*, 130–31.

25. BnF MS lat. 3668, fols. 28r–150v, passim. The marginal corrections nearly always correspond perfectly with the text in the Arsenal manuscript, though, intriguingly enough, there are a series of corrections that are one step out of place. The passage that the corrector says should be entered into the text on 31v, lm (at 2:130–31: "impressit moysen rursum dei nutu uobis uacarum"), for example, is the same as the correction suggested correctly for two folios earlier on 29v, lm, which is why the corrected passage on 31v makes no sense. The next recommended correcting insertion on 32r, rm (at 2:144: "confessus est se in deum tocius mundi regem credere") belongs on 31v. Eventually things are put to rights, so that later on 32r, rm (at 2:164) the proper correction is given in the margin (i.e., that "sapientibus"

should be added). This is interesting evidence of how such textual correction worked: obviously one person has read carefully through the text, discovered the lacunae, and then made a list of the passages that need to be inserted; he handed the list over to a copyist, who did not always follow it carefully.

26. On the thirteenth-century *Correctiones* that so often circulated in pocket Bibles, and on the pocket Bibles in general, see de Hamel's recent *The Book*, especially ch. 5, "Portable Bibles of the Thirteenth Century," 122, 133. See also Heinrich Denifle, "Die Handschriften der Bible-Correctorien des 13. Jahrhunderts," *Archiv für Literatur- und Kirchen-Geschichte des Mittelalters* 4 (1888):263–311, 471–601.

27. Lesley Smith, *Masters of the Sacred Page: Manuscripts of Theology in the Latin West to 1274* (Notre Dame, Ind., 2001), 61. See also Dahan, *L'exégèse chrétienne*, 11, nn. 2, 4.

28. See Rouse and Rouse, "La naissance," 97–98, 100–8; id., *Preachers, Florilegia and Sermons: Studies on the Manipulus florum of Thomas of Ireland* (Toronto, 1979), 6–7; and Parkes, "The Influence of the Concepts of *ordinatio* and *compilatio*," 137.

29. The lack of the twelfth-century annotations in the manuscript is paralleled by the lack of the *Glossa ordinaria* in pocket Bibles. They were simply too small to accommodate it. Manuscripts in this period that contained Bible and gloss were much larger. On this see de Hamel, *The Book*, 118.

30. BnF MS lat. 3668, fol. 151v.

31. "Quod peccata sunt a deo et quod deus excecat homines . . . item quod in paradiso erit vinum lac et mel" (ibid.).

32. "Item de cibo paradisi. Item de potu paradisi" (ibid.).

33. Ibid.

34. "Asserunt item quidam universitatis creatorem . . . filium sumpsisse. quibus nequaquam ueritas consonat" (ibid., 31r).

35. This is the manuscript with the immediately following shelf mark (Paris, BnF, MS lat. 3669) . It will be discussed further just below.

36. This is Paris, BnF, MS ar. 384, fols. 1v–2r, on which see François Déroche, *Catalogue des manuscrits arabes*. Deuxième partie: *Manuscrits musulmans*, vol. 1: *Les manuscrits du Coran. 2. Du Maghreb à l'Insulinde* (Paris, 1985), 53.

37. The new gathering itself runs, as the catalogue description makes clear, from fols. 152–59. See *Catalogue général des manuscrits latins*, t. 4, p. 489.

38. Rouse and Rouse, "*Statim invenire*," 210–12; de Hamel, *The Book*, 133.

39. The widely available index to the Vulgate known as *Aaz apprehendens*, for example, was much longer. In one thirteenth-century copy now in Paris (BnF MS lat. 28), this index occupies fully forty folios, and the manuscript is in a much larger format than the pocket Qur'ān now under consideration. See Dahan, *L'exégèse chrétienne*, 10.

40. BnF MS lat. 3668, fol. 152ra. The corresponding passages in Robert's translation in this MS are as follows. 4.d (31r, ll. 31ff.): "Ipsi quoque Abrahe Hismahelique . . . postea nos orationis domum proponentes ut eam mundatam et ornatam . . . efficerent iniunximus . . . ;" 5.c (32r, ll. 1ff): "templumque . . . quod abraham primo fundauit;" 13.a (39v, ll. 19–20): "qui [i.e., Abraham] . . . primam orationis

domum Mecham . . . primo fundauit;" 54.b (80v, ll. 26–30): "templum haran edificatum in terra ;" 71.d (98r, ll. 23–24): "abrahe quidem hoc templum fundare . . ."

41. Ibid., fol. 152ra ("Adam qualiter creatur"), 153vb ("Ione historia"), 153vc ("Ihesus miracula fecit").

42. Ibid., fol. 156va ("Christus"), 153va ("Ieiunium").

43. Ibid., fols. 152vb, 154vb.

44. See for example ibid., 152vc, where "[D]ubitantem in lege mittit ad libros antecessorum. 45. a." is added at the end of a column in smaller script and lacks the rubricated initial that we find in other cases.

45. See Laura Light, "The New Thirteenth-Century Bible and the Challenge of Heresy," *Viator* 18 (1987):275–88 at 276.

46. "Errare homines deus facit" (BnF MS lat. 3668, fol. 153ra).

47. "Ihesus passus non est" (ibid., fol. 153vc).

48. "Machmet nescit futura" (ibid., fol. 154rc).

49. "Uxores quot licitum est habere" (ibid., fol. 156rc).

50. See Daniel, *Islam and the West*, 88–93, 118–25, 181–85, 190–97.

51. "Euangelium et testamentum rectas vias docent" (BnF MS lat. 3668, fol. 153ra).

52. "Ihesus miracula fecit" (ibid., 153vc).

53. "Ihesus dei spiritus et uerbum" (ibid., fol. 153vc).

54. "Christus omnium prophetarum supremus" (ibid., fol. 156va).

55. "Christus viam recta[m] docuit" (ibid., fol. 156va).

56. See Daniel, *Islam and the West*, 70–71, 190–200.

57. BnF MS lat. 3668, fol. 152ra–b.

58. Ibid., 152va, 153ra, 153rb, 153rc, 155va.

59. There may have been further study aids in the manuscript as well. On 151r and 159r–v, there are texts that have been erased, and which are in general not legible *in situ* even under black light, but in which the same reference system seems to have figured. On 159r, in what would have been the first of three columns, for example, the following citation can be made out following an illegible word: "16c. item 23. d."

60. See Bibliothèque Nationale, *Catalogue général des manuscrits latins*, 6.489.

61. BnF MS lat. 3668, fols. 28v, 97v.

62. See, for example, Martí's *Explanatio simboli apostolorum ad institutione fidelium a fratre R[aymundo] Martini de Ordine Predicatorum edita*, ed. J. March in his "En Ramón Martí y la seva 'Explanatio simboli apostolorum,'" *Anuari de l'Institut d'Estudis Catalans* (1908):443–96 at 450–96; and Riccoldo's *Contra legem Sarracenorum*, ed. J.-M. Mérigoux in his "L'ouvrage d'un frère prêcheur florentin en Orient à la fin du XIIIe siècle. Le 'Contra legem sarracenorum' de Riccoldo da Monte di Croce," in *Fede e controversi nel '300 e '500*, Memorie Domenicane, NS 17 (1986):1–144 at 60–144.

63. See Light, "The New Thirteenth-Century Bible," 280–88, and ead., "Versions et révisions," 89.

64. See Light, "The New Thirteenth-Century Bible," 280–81.

65. This is Paris, BnF, MS lat. 16,558, on which see Léopold Delisle, *Le cabinet*

des manuscrits de la Bibliothèque impériale, 3 vols. (Paris, 1868–81), 2.167–69, who points out that it was owned by Pierre de Limoges. See also the following footnote.

66. The phrase is Isidore Loeb's, from his "La controverse de 1240 sur le Talmud," *Revue des études juives* 1 (1880):247–61, 2 (1881):248–70, and 3 (1882):39–57 at 1:248–49. For more on this compilation, see Gilbert Dahan, "Les traductions latines de Thibaud de Sézanne," in *Le brûlement du Talmud à Paris, 1242–44*, ed. Gilbert Dahan (Paris, 1999), 95–120, esp. 95, 97, and, for a list of the contents of this remarkable manuscript, 118–20. Dahan was struck by "l'aspect scientifique" of this manuscript—its searchable, scholarly design. See ibid. 97.

67. See, for example, BnF MS lat. 16,558, fol. 39rb, rm ("eze. xxiiiio") or fol. 158rb, rm ("exo. xx.").

68. Saint Petersburg, National Library of Russia, MS lat. Q. I. 345. On this manuscript, see d'Alverny, "Quelques manuscrits," 216; for more on the Zaluski collection of manuscripts brought from Poland in the eighteenth century that it was originally part of (the greater part of which were returned to Poland after World War I and later destroyed in World War II), see Paul Oskar Kristeller, *Iter Italicum: A Finding List of Uncatalogued or Incompletely Catalogued Humanistic Manuscripts of the Renaissance in Italian and Other Libraries*, 7 vols. in 9 (Leiden, 1963–97), 5.177–78. The polemical index, followed by the list of "Errores alcoran," both largely identical to those in BnF MS lat. 3668, appear respectively on pp. [*sic*] 423–32, and 433. The manuscript also reproduces the greater part of the corrections to the surah titles that were made for the Parisian manuscript. It is slightly larger than the Paris codex, however (228 x 165 mm), and is not otherwise as expensively produced, there being only one color of ink used throughout, and very little ornamentation.

69. Paris, BnF, MS lat. 3669. The list of Qur'ānic errors (*Errores legis mahumeti*) is on fols. 213r–220v; the poem is on 3v, and was added by a slightly later hand. The errors are written in the same hand as the Qur'ān itself, and begin in the same gathering in which the Qur'ānic text ends. The errors are grouped by topic, the list seeming in many ways like the lists of Cathar errors frequently found in pocket Bibles, on which see above in this chapter. On this manuscript in general, see Bibliothèque Nationale, *Catalogue général des manuscrits latins*, 6.489–91, and d'Alverny, "Deux traductions," 112.

70. Rouse and Rouse, "*Statim invenire*," 212.

71. BnF MS lat. 3668, fols.153ra–b, 152ra, 152va, and 155va respectively.

72. Other than Paris, BnF MS lat. 3670, dated 1515, which also has no polemical notes, but does have a remarkable illuminated frontispiece for Robert's translation. But because of its intriguing thematic connections with manuscripts of Flavius Mithridates' new Qur'ān translation, I will discuss it briefly at the end of the following chapter.

73. On this manuscript and its contents, see Franz Schnorr von Carolsfeld and Ludwig Schmidt, *Katalog der Handschriften der Königl. öffentlichen Bibliothek zu Dresden*, vol. 1 (Leipzig, 1882), 55–56. On the inclusion of Riccoldo's treatise in manuscripts of Robert's version, see Piemontese, "Il Corano latino," 241–43, 245–46. A feature of this manuscript that von Carolsfeld did not mention is that while Robert's Latin Qur'ān begins on fol. 73v, a gathering ends on 80v (part of a catchword clearly survives here—"Dies pe-"—despite later edge trimming), and the rest

of this copy of that translation appears to have gone missing. Since 80v is quite worn and soiled, this gathering appears to have passed some substantial amount of time without anything bound after it. On 81r, furthermore, Robert's Latin Qur'ān begins all over again, this page also being more worn than the pages that follow it. It seems almost certain, therefore, that this second copy of Robert's translation had itself become disconnected from the manuscript which it had originally been part of and that, at some later point, these two partial manuscripts were bound together. Moreover, both copies of Robert's version share unusual similarities (both, for example, have a note, which I have seen in no other manuscript, next to 2:17–23: "Similitudo. Lex. Tenebre. Uerum. Falsum. Tonitruus. Nubes. . . ." [see 73v and 81r], and the layout of both is quite similar). All this suggests, then, that both these partial manuscripts were originally produced in the same scriptorium.

74. The few that survive have usually been copied in bright red ink. Examples: fols. 73v ("Iudeos hostes uocat . . ." cf. Annotator, Bodleian MS Selden Supra 31, fol. 33r, rm), 150r ("Christianos legum uariatores appellant uolens dicere illos euangelium corrupisse et ad suum libitum comutasse," cf. Annotator, Arsenal MS 1162, fol. 89rb, rm), 204v–205r (cf. Annotator, ibid., fols. 137r–138r). There are also a number of later notes that have been added among these from the Annotator.

75. At least in this form. Transformed into an abridged version of the Qur'ān, it does exist in several other manuscripts. See below in this chapter.

76. This being the date of the earliest datable manuscript, Paris, BnF, lat. 3671, that contains it, though in a reworked form that will be discussed in the following section of this chapter. For more on this important manuscript, including evidence as to its dating, see Chapter 5.

77. Dresden MS 120b, fols. 37r–73r. This study aid, therefore, is something like the *Aaz apprehendens* and other extensive biblical study aids in amplitude. See above in this chapter.

78. Rouse and Rouse, "La naissance," 98; Parkes, "The Influence of the Concepts of *ordinatio* and *compilatio*," 123.

79. Parkes, "The Influence of the Concepts of *ordinatio* and *compilatio*," 123.

80. In the entry for verse 22:47a in the Dresden manuscript, we have "Homines ad Maumetum sunt promptiores" (Dresden MS 120b, fol. 58r), whereas the version published by Johann Albrecht von Widmanstetter has "homines ad malum sunt promptiores" (Widmanstetter, ed., *Epitome Alcorani* in *Mahometis Abdallae filii theologia dialogo*, fol. i iiiR—on this work, including complete bibliography, see just below). The latter reading is correct since Robert's text here read "plures ad malum sint promptiores" (Robert of Ketton, *Lex Mahumet*, fol. 90ra; Bibliander, *Alcoran* 1550, 1.108). Likewise, the entry that describes verses 91:1–10 includes the phrase, in the Dresden manuscript, "ditauit animam ipsam bonum et Maumetum edocens" (fol. 72r), whereas the printed version has "ditauit animam ipsam bonum et malum edocens" (Widmanstetter, ed., *Epitome alcorani*, fol. miV), which once again conforms to what Robert's translation had: "ditauit animam. ipsam malum et bonum edocens" (Robert of Ketton, *Lex Mahumet*, fol. 136vb; Bibliander, *Alcoran* 1550, 1.185). Note also that the text of Robert's translation itself in the Dresden manuscript conforms at these passages both to what the *Epitome* and the earliest manuscript and printed edition of Robert's translation have (see Dresden MS 120b,

fols. 151r, 204r). This state of affairs can only be explained by assuming that the Dresden text is a corrupt copy of an earlier exemplar of the the *tabula* which had the correct readings, those readings also finding their way into Widmanstetter's edition.

81. "Capitulo. Tertio.
[J]esus filius marie cui spiritus diuine auxilium et testimonium extitit.
Salomon bonus magicam ab angelis didicit; quam iudei didicerunt postea in babillone a malis angelis scilicet Arot et Marot
Spiritus in quem uult et quo uult et quando spirat.
Nemo sine deo anime sue prodesse potest.
Deus qui secreta cordium introspicit suum cuique rependet meritum.
Christiani et Iudei ambo legis latores bonos habuerunt: sed utrique ab ipsis deuii sunt.
Cum dei sit oriens et occidens, uersus quanlibet partem orationes fundens, deum inuenit.
Dei pietas nullo loco circumscribitur.
Dei sapientia cuncta complectitur." (Dresden MS 120b, fols. 37v–38r)

82. Bobzin, while not aware that this text began life as a table of contents, had much to say, as we will see below, about it in its reworked form as an abridged Qur'ān. In his *Der Koran*, 337–43, 348–49, he discussed the summarizing method that generated it and speculated on who may have been responsible.

83. "Secta Maumet promittit summum bonum id est deum dicens quod diuitie nostre erunt ipse deus" (Dresden MS 120b, fol. 37r).

84. Daniel, *Islam and the West*, 172–76.

85. Dresden MS 120b, fol. 37r.

86. "[L]ex Maumetis est confirmatio legum priscarum scilicet Moysi. Christi. reliquorumque prophetarum" (ibid., 38r).

87. "Qui deum habere filium dicunt, inscii sunt" (ibid., fol. 38r).

88. "qui nec genuit, nec est genitus, nec habet quemquam sibi similem" (ibid., fol. 72v; cf. Robert of Ketton, *Lex Mahumet*, fol. 138rb; Bibliander, *Alcoran* 1550, 1.188, which reads "generatus" rather than "genitus").

89. "Multi sunt boni recto calle gradientes: mali autem plures" (Dresden MS 120b, fol. 37r).

90. "Improbus sibi ipse supplicium est" (ibid., fol. 37r).

91. "Virtutis opera sicut prauis molesta et grauia sunt, sic bonis leuia atque iocunda" (ibid., 37v).

92. "Deus omnia uerbo iussuque perficit" (ibid., fol. 38r). Other examples: "Nulla lex bona est nisi creatoris" (ibid., fol. 38r—Q. 2:120a); "Qui sciens ueritatem tacet eam peccat" (ibid., fol. 38r—Q. 2:140b); "In bonis uiris deus inhabitat, illis propitius suam concedans gratiam" (ibid., fol. 38r—Q. 2:153).

93. Ibid, fol. 62v. The entries here under "chapter 81" and "chapter 82," beginning with "Vxorum Maumet diligentia et modestia et uerba dei ad eas," and continuing through "Deus e[s]t angeli propter prophetam orant," summarize verses 33:28–43 (see Bibliander, *Alcoran* 1550, 1.132–33). There is no reference to verse 37 and the matter of Zayd and Zaynab (which appears in Bibliander's edition at 1.132, ll. 33–38). In fact, most of the larger context of this passage concerns the proper actions of Muhammad's wives (vv. 28–52), yet the compiler is remarkably

restrained in general, even though Muhammad's polygamy is explicitly under discussion. The most strident formulation, in fact, is for 33:50 ("Diligentia et licentia magna circa uxores prophete," Dresden MS 120b, fol. 61v), which is aggressive, but not nearly on the level of the typical Christian attacks on the presumed licentiousness of Muhammad and Islam. On 33:37 and its role in anti-Islamic polemic, see Daniel, *Islam and the West*, 119–20.

94. "Hoc dicit propter se ipsum. introducens deum sibi loquentem. ut cuiusdam uxorem quam ualde amabat liuenter stupraret et postea sibi eam uxorem acciperet. quasi ex precepto dei dantis sibi licentiam" (Annotator, fol. 105vb, lm).

95. "Sequitur de deo et adam et angelis et diabolo fabula stultissima. quam nescio ubi repererit" (ibid., fol. 26rb, rm).

96. "Creatio ade et preceptum ad eum" (Dresden MS 120b, fol. 37r).

97. "Multa deus scit que ignorant angeli" (ibid., fol. 37v).

98. "Nota ridiculum quod deus iactauerit se scire quod angeli nesciebant" (Annotator, fol. 26rb, rm).

99. "Omnis recte uiuens scilicet deum adorans, bonique gestor, siue iudeus, siue christianus, seu lege sua relicta in aliam tendat, proculdubio diuinum amorem consequetur" (Dresden MS 120b, fol. 37v; for Robert's version, see Chapter 2 above, note 20).

100. "Hic omnino sibi contrarius est. nam postea pene ubique asserit sine lege sua nullum esse saluandum" (Annotator, fol. 27rb, rm).

101. See just above in this chapter.

102. "Et haec est summa totius heresis huius. ut deus filium nunquam habuisse credatur. quod sepe iste diabolus repetit" (Annotator, fol. 28va, lm).

103. This is the title it bears in at least two of the five manuscripts containing it: BnF MS lat. 3671, fols. 28v–65r (this MS can be dated to sometime before 1537); and Milan, BA, MS R 113 sup, fols. 213r–232v. These two manuscripts, which also contain Flavius Mithridates' Qur'ān translation, will be discussed in greater detail in the following chapter.

104. "Tabula
Capitulo primo
Oratio arabum.
In deo iram et misericordiam ponunt.
Quod in se ipsum uerum est, solis puris quale est uidetur.
Quos deus obdurauit, nemo molliet aut instruet.
Qui ore non opere uirtutem laudant, se ipsos decipiunt, nihil aliud nisi detrimentum anime sue lucrantes" (Dresden MS 120b, fol. 37r).

105. "Compendium Alcorani, id est legis saracenorum.
"Oratio Arabum. In deo iram et misericordiam ponunt. Quod in se ipsum uerum est, solis puris quale est uidetur. Quos deus obdurauit, nemo molliet: aut instruet. Qui ore non opere uirtutem laudant, se ipsos decipiunt, nihil aliud nisi detrimentum anime sue lucrantes" (BnF MS lat. 3671, fol. 28v).

106. "Prę̧cepta dei ad homines. Inferi paradisi uoluptates" (ibid., fol. 29r).

107. Ibid., fols. 33v, l. 5 ("Deus est ex essentia et anima . . .) to 35v, l. 3 (". . . ab angelis potatum"); see also BA MS R 113 sup, fols. 215r, l. 30 to 216r, l. 30.

108. Bobzin has demonstrated this in his discussion of Widmanstetter's printed version of this text. See his *Der Koran*, 347–48.

109. It is possible that the interpolation might have come from a floralegium of extracts from these works but see Bobzin's helpful comments in his *Der Koran*, 348.

110. See Dresden MS 120b, fol. 41v. The interpolation (see n. 107 above) appears in the manuscripts of the abridgment between "Vita hec omnia mundana fortuita sunt" and "Suorum factorum ostentatores . . ." In this manuscript these phrases are (properly) separated only by the basmalah ("Misericordi pioque") and a heading for a new chapter of the table of contents.

111. See Jacqueline Hamesse, "The Scholastic Model of Reading," 107, 111, 114, 117.

112. See Daniel, *Islam and the West*, 77–88.

113. Bobzin has very little to say about the purpose of this abridgment, but see his *Der Koran*, 349.

114. The biographical details to follow are based on Bobzin's exhaustive account in his *Der Koran*, 282–95, but also on Secret's short discussion in *Les kabbalistes chrétiens*, 121–23. On Widmanstetter's relations with other Arabists and Orientalists, see Josée Balagna, *L'imprimerie arabe en Occident: XVe, XVIIe, XVIIIe siècles* (Paris, 1984), 29, and Dannenfeldt, "The Renaissance Humanists and the Knowledge of Arabic," 108–9.

115. Bobzin, *Der Koran*, 295.

116. Ibid., 279–80.

117. Ibid., 308–11.

118. Ibid., 280, 294, 318. Alastair Hamilton has referred to it as a "major contribution to Biblical scholarship'": see his "Humanists and the Bible," *The Cambridge Companion to Renaissance Humanism*, ed. Jill Kraye (Cambridge, England, 1996), 100–117 at 108. See also Hamilton's "Eastern Churches and Western Scholarship," in *Rome Reborn: The Vatican Library and Renaissance Culture*, ed. Anthony Grafton (Washington and New Haven, Conn., 1993), 225–49 at 238, which includes a photograph of the title page.

119. Bobzin, *Der Koran*, 290–91, 356–57 discusses this supposed Latin Qur'ān translation and contemporaries who claim to have seen it.

120. Balagna, *L'imprimerie arabe en Occident*, 29.

121. Bobzin, *Der Koran*, 282, 292, 323–36.

122. Ibid., 295–96, 351–52.

123. Widmanstetter, *Mahometis theologia, 1543*.

124. Widmanstetter, *Mahometis theologia*, fols. aiiR–aiiiR.

125. Ibid., fols. aiiiV–aivR. Bobzin transcribes the whole letter in *Der Koran*, 325–26.

126. Ibid., fols. biR–divV; see Bobzin, *Der Koran*, 332–34 for Bibliander's reworking of it.

127. Ibid., fols. divV–miiR. As Bobzin points out, this abridgment is divided into four divisions, each called an *Oratio*. On these odd divisions and their relation to a different fourfold division that Widmanstetter referred to in his marginal notes on an Arabic manuscript, see Bobzin, *Der Koran*, 343–47.

128. Widmanstetter, *Mahometis theologia*, fols. niR–oiiR (*uariarum impiarumque opinionum Mahometis, quae in Dialogo occurunt, Notationes*), and oiiV–oiiiV (*Mahometis vita*), respectively. Bobzin suggests that Juan Andres's *Confusione delle setta Machometana* is the principal source for this work; see Bobzin, *Der Koran*, 353.

129. In Widmanstetter, *Mahometis theologia*, fols. oiiiV–qiiR. A manuscript in Milan (BA MS R 113 sup.) may contain an earlier version of these notes and those on the *Theology of Muhammad*. See Chapter 5 below, n. 130.

130. My discussion of the contents of these annotations follows and builds on Bobzin's insightful observations in *Der Koran*, 349–53.

131. *Uariarum rerum, impiarumque opinionum, quae in Alcorani Epitome occurrunt, Notationes* (Widmanstetter, *Mahometis theologia*, fol. oiiiV, cited hereafter as *Notationes*).

132. "II. Qui Deum habere) Hic negat Christum Dei filium esse, cum alibi eum et uerbum Dei adpellet, et spiritum" (Widmanstetter, *Notationes*, fol. oivV).

133. See Daniel, *Islam and the West*, 84–88.

134. See note XXXII, Widmanstetter, *Notationes*, fol. piiV. Cf. Daniel, *Islam and the West*, 93–97.

135. Note XXXIX/LX, Widmanstetter, *Notationes*, fol. piiiV.

136. Note LII, Widmanstetter, *Notationes*, fol pivV. Cf. Daniel, *Islam and the West*, 118–25.

137. As in note XIII: ". . . insolentes Iudaei, quorum uestigia insequitur Mahometes" (Widmanstetter, *Notationes*, fol. piR). For other examples, see notes I, XII, XXX (ibid., fols. oiiiV, piR, piiV).

138. "XVI. Principium omnium aqua) Mundum clementia Dei creatum esse sacrae literae docent, clementiam [*sic*] uero aquarum seueritatem uini appellatione contineri Cabalistae testantur. Vnde ad ueteres Graecorum philosophos, è quorum numero Thales Milesius fuit, opinio celebris allata fuit, aquam rerum omnium primam materiam extitisse, quos Aristoteles maiore studio reprehendere, quàm intelligere uelle uidetur" (ibid., fols. piR–V).

139. Note VIII, with its lengthy discussion of various peoples' views on how long the world will endure, is another example of the same thing (see ibid., fols. oivR–V).

140. See ibid., fols. oivV, piiV, piiiR, piiiV.

141. "X. Lex Dei est fides) Iosephus Albo scribit, fidem omnia Iudaicae religionis capita complecti" (ibid., fol. piR).

142. See notes III, XVI, XVII, XXI, XXII, XXXIII, ibid., oivR, piR–piiR, piiiR. Other notes mention Kabbalist doctrines, such as the sefiroth (*numerationes*). See, for example, note XVIIII (ibid., fol. piV) and the previous note. See also Bobzin, *Der Koran*, 349–50. For *numeratio* as the translation for the Hebrew *sefira*, see S. A. Farmer, *Syncretism in the West: Pico's 900 Theses (1486)* (Tempe, Ariz., 1998), 520–21, with my thanks to Harvey Hames for his advice on this and other matters Kabbalistic.

143. "XVII. Tres ordines stellarum) De iisdem stellarum ordinibus . . . eadem ferè à Cabalistis commemorantur" (ibid., fol. piV). Another example: "XVIIII. Hierusalem terrae medium) Hoc Iudaei referunt ad septimam numerationem

[=sefira], quam Hierusalem diuinam, et coelestam adpellent" (Widmanstetter, *Notationes*, fol. piV).

144. "XXII. Christi pulchritudo) Imprudente, et inuito Mahomete, ueritas manifestatur. Nam et Cabalistae Messiae sedem in pulchritudinis numeratione, quae ipsa est diuinitas secundum eos, constituerunt. Quapropter Messiam filium Dei esse hoc loco diserte conitetur" (ibid., fol. piiR). See also Secret, *Les Kabbalistes*, 122.

145. "XXXIII. Omne genus animantium [. . . ad Deum redibit]) . . . Itaque intellegi à nonnullis [Cabalistis], animantium omni generi spem salutis propositam esse. Haec idcirco commemoraui, ut i[n]dicarem, ex hac Iudęorum Caballa infinita opinionum portenta, ueluti ex equo Troiano educta, impetum in Christi ecclesia fecisse" (Widmanstetter, *Notationes*, fols. piiV–piiiR). On the sources of this passage, see Gershom Scholem, "The Beginnings of the Christian Kabbalah," in *The Christian Kabbalah: Jewish Mystical Books and the Christian Interpreters: A Symposium* (Cambridge, Mass., 1997), 17–51 at 18–20. See also Bobzin, *Der Koran*, 301n157, and Secret, *Les Kabbalistes*, 121.

146. On this widespread view, see Joseph Dan, "The Kabbalah of Johannes Reuchlin and its Historical Significance," in Joseph Dan, ed., *The Christian Kabbalah: Jewish Mystical Books and the Christian Interpreters* (Cambridge, Mass., 1997), 60; and also Scholem, "The Beginnings of the Christian Kabbalah," 17.

147. See Secret, *Les kabbalistes*, 121–23.

148. "III. Sed saluantur omnes) Haeretici nonnulli Cabalistas sequuti, affirmant, omnes tandem salutis aeternę participes fore. . . . Sed Cabalistaę de reuersione quadam, non de salute loquuntur" (Widmanstetter, *Notationes*, fol. oivR); "XVIII. Mundus fuit multis seculis ante hominis generationem) Cabalistae obtusiores dicunt infinitos mundos . . . extructos à Deo, rursumque destructos fuisse. Quod acutiores de infinitis aeternae mentis contemplationibus . . . interpretantur . . ." (ibid., fol. piV).

149. *Epitome Alcorani*, in Widmanstetter, *Mahometis theologia*, fol. giiV.

150. Christian Kabbalists frequently traced the primeval philosophy that so interested them from the Jews first and then to the Greeks, especially Pythagorus and Plato. See, among many other works, Joseph Leon Blau, *The Christian Interpretation of the Cabala in the Renaissance* (Port Washington, N.Y., 1944, 1965), 54–55; and Fabrizio Lelli, "*Prisca philosophia* and *Docta religio*: The Boundaries of Rational Knowledge in Jewish and Christian Humanist Thought," *Jewish Quarterly Review* 91 (2000):53–99 at 53–61.

151. XXXVIII. Intermedii). . . . Caeterum cum Christianorum mores uitiis in dies adeo corrumperentur, ut passim ab omnibus remedia potius ad restinguendum purgationis ignem quaererentur, quàm contra uitiorum tyrannidem auxilia, periít ignis Purgatoríí ratio, cum utilis Ecclesiae tam necessaria, apud eos etiam â quibus conseruari uel maxime debuisset" (Widmansetter, *Notationes*, fol. piiiR–V).

152. See Euan Cameron, *The European Reformation* (Oxford, 1991), 127, 134; and Bruce Gordon, *The Swiss Reformation* (Manchester, England, 2002), 273–75.

153. "XLII. [Quos Deus] corde sigillauit, [ineuitabiliter errabunt]) De prędestinatione multa in utranque partem disputata sunt à doctissimis uiris, quę in hunc

locum non sine fastidio referrentur" (Widmanstetter, *Notationes*, fol. pivR, cf. *Epitome Alcorani*, in Widmanstetter, *Mahometis theologia*, fol. hiR).

154. "Si qui sunt, quos Cabalistae doctrinae frequens memoria in hisce notationibus meis offendat, hi sciant me sola necessitate impulsum, ex istorum libris reconditis delibasse nonnulla, quae Iudeorum fraudes, Christianorum è gremio Ecclesiae dilapsorum leuitatem, & Mahometis inconstantiam, atque scelerum atrocitatem commostrarent" (Widmanstetter, *Notationes*, fol. qiiR). See also Bobzin, *Der Koran*, 349n377, and Secret, *Les Kabbalistes*, 122.

155. See Bobzin, *Der Koran*, 287–91, 302–11.

156. Ibid., 352–56.

157. Most of these Kabbalistic sources remain unidentified, though Gershom Scholem showed that note 33, with its lengthy discussion of a Kabbalist teaching on the "vital seeds" (*semina vitalia*), is based on the views of Joseph Shalom Askenazi of Barcelona (fl. 1300–1325). In this case, Widmanstetter tells us where he learned these ideas: "XXXIII. Omne genus animantium) . . . Dattylus Pici Mirandulani praeceptor, quem ego iam decrepitum menses aliquot audiui, dicere solebat, Semina quaedam uitalia in uisceribus terrare . . ." (Widmanstetter, *Notationes*, fol. piiV). As Scholem made clear, this Dattilo was a fairly well-known Jewish Kabbalist. See Scholem, "The Beginnings of the Christian Kabbalah," 18–20.

158. Widmanstetter's notes on the *Mahumetis Theologia* are very similar to his notes on the *Epitome Alcorani*. Many contain standard anti-Islamic polemic (numbers 7, 35, 46, 47), but many refer to Talmudists (25, 37, 43), and the Kabbalah, which he even more explicitly describes as the origin of certain Qur'ānic teachings (6, 11, 14 ["Cabalistae, à quibus doctrinae suae ineptias acceperat Mahometes . . ."], 18, 22, 23, 25, 30 ["Et hoc quoque à peruersis Cabalistis accepit . . ."], 37, 42, 44, 45). See *Uariarum impiarumque opinionum, quae in Dialogo occurunt, Notationes*, in Widmanstetter, *Mahometis theologia*, fols. nR–oiiR. Secret pointed out that this mistrust for the Kabbalah shows up in certain notes to his edition of the Syriac New Testament as well. See his *Les Kabbalistes*, 122, and Bobzin, *Der Koran*, 335.

159. For a thorough, recent treatment of Bibliander's life, thought, and works, with abundant bibliography, see Bobzin, *Der Koran*, 159–80.

160. Ibid., 337.

161. On all this, see Bobzin, *Der Koran*, pp. 359–63. Among the few known readers is Arrivabene; see Secret, "Guillaume Postel et les études arabes," 23–24, note 5.

162. There are, for example, five copies in Oxford alone: three in the Bodleian, one each in Magdalen and Balliol Colleges. On the many later readers of Bibliander's edition, see especially Bobzin, *Der Koran*, 262–75.

163. See most recently Bobzin, *Der Koran*, 181–209, and Katya Vehlow, "The Swiss Reformers Zwingli, Bullinger and Bibliander and Their Attitude to Islam (1520–1560)," *Islam and Christian-Muslim Relations* 6 (1995):229–54. See also Victor Segesvary, *L'Islam et la Réforme: Étude sur l'attitude des Réformateurs zuruchois envers l'Islam, 1510–1550* (Bethesda, Md., 1998), *passim*, esp. 161–99; Harry Clark, "The Publication of the Qur'ān in Latin: A Reformation Dilemma," *Sixteenth-Century Journal* 15 (1984):3–12.

164. Melanchthon, for example, asserts that "Vt abominamur Aegyptias

superstitiones . . . : sic Mahometi deliria abominanda sunt" (*Philippi Melanchthonis praemonitio ad lectorem*, in Bibliander, *Alcoran* 1550 11, fol. a2r); while Bibliander observes that by his edition (*hoc uolumen*), "mortifera uenena draconis istius magni et rubentis sanguine humano, quae per Machumetem infudit miseris mortalibus, fide optima indicantur"(*Christiano lectori Theodorus Bibliander S.*, ibid., fol. a3r).

165. Luther, for example, observes in good Protestant fashion that "Quare ut aegyptiorum opiniones, qui feles, Arabum, qui canes colebant, constanter repudias, ita Mahometi figmentum detesteris, quia palam fatetur ipse, se non amplecti prophetarum et Apostolorum doctrinam" ("Martini Lutheri . . . in Alcoranum praefatio," in *D. Martin Luthers Werke*, vol. 53 [Weimar, 1920], 569–72 at 571). This preface (on which, see Bobzin, *Der Koran*, 153–56) appears on two folios, marked "y1" and "y2," inserted in some copies between Bibliander's apologia and Peter the Venerable's letter to St. Bernard in the 1543 edition. In still other copies, Melanchthon's "Praemonitio" is ascribed to Luther, but Luther's own preface is lacking. On these variant versions of the 1543 edition, see Segesvary, *L'Islam et la Réforme*, 165–66; and Bobzin, *Der Koran*, 209–15.

166. For a full account of the contents of the three volumes, see Segesvary, *L'Islam et la Réforme*, 166–75, 271–272; and Bobzin, *Der Koran*, 215–21.

167. "doctrina Machumetis . . . non edatur in publicum ipsa sola, uerùm cum acie ualidissima scriptorum, qui non tam confutant eam et refellunt, quàm iugulant atque conficiunt" (Bibliander, *Apologia pro editione Alcorani*, in Bibliander, *Alcoran* 1550, 1, fol. a3v).

168. For an overview of the controversy over the publication of Bibliander's edition, see works listed in note 163 above. Bibliander nicely summarizes his argument that his edition will "not harm, but help" (*non laedit, sed iuuat*) the church (Bibliander, *Apologia pro editione Alcorani*, fol. b5v) in the final paragraph of the work (ibid., fol. b6r).

169. Ibid., fol. b4r–b5v.

170. "Vnde nomophylaces, qui hodie Turcarum dialecto uocantur lescherchadii, potestatem habent retractandi sententias per imperatorem latas, si legibus Machumetis repugnent" (ibid. fol. b4v).

171. "Adhaec perspectus Alcoran mirifice monstrat, quàm faciant imprudenter illi magistratus, qui prohibendo Euangelii praedicationem, conantur . . . confirmare suam potestatem uel tyrannidem, et prohibere motus atque novationes rerum" (ibid.). There are other criticisms of Catholicism in this section; see fol. b5v.

172. "Habet etiam aetas nostra exemplum recens & uiuidum in regno Monasteriensi anabaptistarum" (ibid., fol. b5r). Seeing Islam and the Münster Anabaptists as equally erroneous was something of a commonplace among the Reformers. See Luther's "In Alcoranum praefatio," 572, and Segesvary, *L'Islam et la Réforme*, 143.

173. Both Protestants and Catholics habitually accused each other of being similar to and in league with Islam in the Reformation period. See Segesvary, *L'Islam et la Réforme*, 95.

174. Bibliander, *Apologia pro editione Alcorani*, fol. b4r.

175. See above in this chapter.

176. He described this exemplar as "deprauatissimum" in the introduction to his textual annotations on the text (in Bibliander, *Alcoran* 1550, 1.230; on these an-

notations, see just below). See also Bobzin, *Der Koran*, 222–23, and d'Alverny, "Deux traductions," 104.

177. Segesvary, *L'Islam et la Réforme*, 167; Bobzin, *Der Koran*, 230–31. On the remarkable history of the one Arabic Qur'ān manuscript that we do know that he used (Basel, Universitätsbibliothek, MS A III 19), see Bobzin, *Der Koran*, 237–50 (among other things, it was sent a century earlier to Ayton, where Juan de Segovia himself made use of it).

178. See, for example, the following note at surah 91: "Exemplar alterum transposuerat haec duo capita, hoc nempe et praecedens" (Bibliander, *Alcoran* 1550, 1.185; see also Bobzin, *Der Koran*, 230n454).

179. "Annotationes uariae lectionis diversorum quatuor exemplarium" (ibid., 230–39 [231–39 are unpaginated]). These were suppressed in the 1550 edition, though some of the variants in this apparatus were worked into the text of that later edition. See Bobzin, *Der Koran*, 230–31.

180. "annunt al[iás] amminutis" (Bibliander, *Alcoran* 1543, 1.231).

181. E.g., this note referring to p. 37, l. 3: "Sibi suisque nostris uel nil agerent. Haec verba sex desunt alias" (ibid., 232).

182. [Referring to p. 9, l. 24] "Sin autem pro sin minus, subinde ponit interpres" (ibid., 231). Other examples: [Referring to p. 17, l. 1 (v. 2:216), which begins "Litium actum . . . iniunximums"]: "Litium por bello subinde ponit suo more" (ibid.); [referring to p. 17, l. 5 (v. 2:217)]: "Guerra, gallicum uocabulum pro bello" (ibid.); [referring to p. 11, l. 7]: "annotesceret leg[itur?] innotesceret" (ibid.). *Annotesco* means something like "to begin to be recorded or registered" while *innotesco* means "to become known." The latter meaning clearly suits the passage in question better.

183. See Bobzin, *Der Koran*, 170–76, but also J. Fück, *Die arabischen Studien in Europa bis in den Anfang des 20. Jahrhunderts* (Leipzig, 1955), 6.

184. Bibliander, *Alcoran* 1543, 1.100, 234. See also Bobzin, *Der Koran*, 256. Bibliander used Hebrew characters for lack of Arabic type—a common solution to a common problem in this period. See Bobzin, *Der Koran*, 254. Bobzin discusses, at considerable length, the annotations that discuss Arabic terms, reproducing all of them, in fact. See ibid., 254–62. On whether Bibliander used just one Arabic manuscript or perhaps more, see ibid., 237–39.

185. "Christiani. Arab. *Rūm* populus Romanus. Sic enim Imperator Constantinopolitanus tum vocabatur" (Bibliander, *Alcoran* 1543, 1.127, 235).

186. "In Arabico incipit, In nomine dei pii & misericordis" (ibid., 21).

187. "Non omnia hic ponuntur quae sunt in Arabico" (ibid., 187). See also Bobzin, *Der Koran*, 251–54.

188. See Bobzin, *Der Koran*, 230–31.

189. See Bibliander, *Alcoran* 1550, 1.8. See also Bobzin, *Der Koran*, 235.

190. See Bobzin, *Der Koran*, 235–36.

191. "Stultitiarum, et fabularum, atque impietatum plenissima" (Bibliander, *Alcoran* 1550, 1.225b).

192. Ibid., 224a.

193. Bobzin, *Der Koran*, 231. In this Bibliander's notes are rather like the notes

in the copy of Mark of Toledo's translation in the Mazarine library in Paris (MS 708), on which see Chapter 5 below.

194. "Quid conferat liber Alcoran, et quales requirat discipulos" (Bibliander, *Alcoran* 1550, 1.8).

195. "Similitudo de iis qui deserunt sectam, quam similauerant" (ibid., 9).

196. "Paradisus" (ibid.).

197. "A Deo Resurrectio mortuorum. Coeli septem creati" (ibid.; the note has "adeo").

198. "Postulat ab aliis demonstrationem, quam ipse non exhibet" (ibid., 12).

199. See Daniel, *Islam and the West*, 88–89, 93–98, 148–49, 304–5.

200. "Non desinit negare filium Dei" (Bibliander, *Alcoran* 1550 1.188); cf. "Negat dei filium" (ibid., 12).

201. "Resurrectio per fabulas hic abstruitur" (ibid., 19).

202. "fabula Iudaica absurdissima de sabato uiolato" (ibid., 58, this concerning verse 58:12; see Bobzin, *Der Koran*, 232n466).

203. "Precepta Dei uiribus humanis praestari posse, subinde dicit cum Pelagio" (Bibliander, *Alcoran* 1550, 1.21).

204. See Daniel, *Islam and the West*, 209–13.

205. Some of these notes speak directly to Muhammad, as at 2:253 where the soul of God is said to have been conferred on Christ: "Christo prophetarum excellentissimo anima dei collata. Cur igitur negas filium Dei?" (Bibliander, *Alcoran* 1550, 1.19). See also ibid.: "Nemo ui cogendus ad religionem. At quoties tui oblitus Machomet, iubes contrarium?"

206. Cameron, *The European Reformation*, 137. This concern to evaluate Islam in a thoroughly biblical light was, not surprisingly, common among the Swiss and other Reformers. See Segesvary, *L'Islam et la Réforme*, 94.

207. Bobzin, *Der Koran*, 231.

208. Such as his one-word note, *manna*, next to 2:57, which describes the gift of manna to the Israelites. Bibliander, *Alcoran* 1550, 1.10.

209. As at 2:246–47: "I. Reg. II" (ibid., 18).

210. "Matrimonium sit inter consortes religionis. Deut. 7." (ibid., 17). Some notes list multiple biblical parallels, e.g., at 2:275: "Contra usuras. Deu. 25. Eze. 19. Psal. 14." (ibid., 20).

211. Bobzin, *Der Koran*, 232n464.

212. "Commiscet duas historias. Exod. 15. & 17. Historia Exo. 16. deprauata." (Bibliander, *Alcoran* 1550, 1.10).

213. "Praecipue innuit uaccam rusam Nu. 29. sed fabulosa admiscet, nimirum ex iudeorum traditionibus." (ibid., 11). Cf. at 2:249: "Videtur Gedionis historiam admiscere. Iudic. 7." (ibid., 18).

214. Two examples: at 22:17, he has a note saying "Christiani leges uariantes. Accusat enim quanquam falso, ut scripturae sanctae falsarios" (ibid., 107); cf. a twelfth-century note on the same passage: "Christianos legum uariatores appellat. uolens dicere illos euangelium corrupisse. et ad suum libitum commutasse" (Annotator, fol. 89rb rm). At 43:77, Bibliander identifies the transliterated term *Melich* (i.e., *malak*, "angel") as the "angelus mortis" (Bibliander, *Alcoran* 1550, 1.153); cf.

the twelfth-century note on the same passage: "angelus mortis" (Annotator, fol. 118vb lm).

215. See Anthony Grafton and Lisa Jardine, *From Humanism to the Humanities: Education and the Liberal Arts in Fifteenth- and Sixteenth-Century Europe* (Cambridge, Mass., and London, 1986), 16–17, 147.

216. *Collectiones aliquot ex alcorano turcarum fide*, Güssing, Franziskanerkloster, MS 1/35, fol. 234r. On this library, including further bibliography, see Donald Yates, *Descriptive Inventories of Manuscripts Microfilmed for the Hill Monastic Manuscript Library*, vol. 1: *Austrian Libraries* (Collegeville, Minn., 1981), 11–12; Maria Mairold, *Die datierten Handschriften in der Steiermark ausserhalb der Universitätsbibliothek Graz bis zum Jahre 1600*, 2 vols., Katalog der datierten Handschriften in lateinischer Schrift in Österreich 7 (Vienna, 1988), 1.16–17; and especially Theodor Tabernigg, "Die Bibliothek des Franziskanerklosters in Güssing," *Biblos: Österreichische Zeitschrift für Buch- und Bibliothekswesen, Dokumentation, Bibliographie und Bibliophilie* 21 (1972):167–75. On this MS itself, see Yates, *Descriptive Inventories*, 27–28; and Mairold, *Die datierten Handschriften*, 1.97–98 (#150).

217. Yates, *Descriptive Inventories*, 27–28.

218. On Bunderius, see Jacques Quétif and Jacques Echard, *Scriptores Ordinis Praedicatorum recensiti, notisque historicis et criticis*, 2 vols. in 4 (Paris, 1719–23, rpt. New York, 1959), 2.1.160–61.

219. *Confutationes modernarum et veterum heresum per Joannem Bunderium*, Güssing, Austria, Franziskanerkloster, 1/35, fols. 19r–121r.

220. Ibid., fols. 151v–154v.

221. These appear in two sections, suggesting that the gatherings of the manuscript have become disordered in later bindings: surahs 10 to 114 (Azoaras 20–124), fols. 122r–142v; surahs 1 to 10 (Azoaras 1–20), fols. 234r–246v.

222. Ibid., fols. 143r–151r.

223. The convent in Güssing where the MS resides at present was not founded till the 1640s, so it could not have been produced there. The content, however, strongly suggests that this compilation must have been made somewhere in the vicinity. See Yates, *Descriptive Inventories*, I, 11; and Tabernigg, "Die Bibliothek des Franziskanerklosters in Güssing," 168.

224. The work by Bunderius was copied, the incipit tells us, in 1557, while the dominical sermons were copied in 1560. See Yates, *Descriptive Inventories* I, 27–28; and Mairold, *Die datierten Handschriften*, 1.97–98, and see also ibid., 2.252 (figure 358) for a photograph of fol. 151v.

225. See Güssing MS 1/35, fols. 236v–237r where *azoara tertia* and *azoara quarta* figure as key divisions of the compilation.

226. "obsecra Deum, ut ab ominibus diabolicis suggestionibus te protegat, et eas a te proiiciat" (Güssing MS 1/35, fol. 127r, ll. 9–10, here quoting Bibliander, *Alcoran* 1550, 1.111). For other examples of similarly abrupt quotations, see Güssing MS 1/35, fol. 234v, ll. 23–26, which quote Bibliander, *Alcoran* 1550, 1.11: "Omnis autem peccator culpae culpas . . . aeterne fruetur"; and Güssing MS 1/35, fol. 127v, l. 8 which quotes Bibliander, *Alcoran* 1550 1.111: "Huius amor saeculi a nemine bono queratur."

227. The compiler adopts much the same layout for his extracts from the other works excerpted in this manuscript (such as Cusa's *Cribratio*).

228. "Quibus benefacieri" (Güssing MS 1/35, fol. 127v, l. 1; the relevant passage is in Bibliander, *Alcoran* 1550, 1.112).

229. "NON CONCUPISCENDA UXOR ALIENA" (Güssing MS 1/35, fol. 126r, l. 1).

230. Bibliander, *Alcoran* 1550, 1.104 lm.

231. "NEC IUDEI NEC CHRISTIANI. In hac azoara scribit quod ante Mahumet neque iudei neque christiani quicquam sciuerunt. Eius tamen adventu, dissensio est orta" (Güssing MS 1/35, fol. 142r; cf. Bibliander's note: "Ante Machumetem neque Iudei neque Christiani quicquam sciverunt. Eius tamen aduentu dissensio est orta." Bibliander, *Alcoran* 1550, 1.186 lm).

232. "Azoara 114 QUI DAMNANTUR. Precipue fraudatores, detractores, auaros, in feruentissimis comburi dicit." (Güssing MS 1/35, fol. 142r; cf. Biblander's note: "Qui damnandi, praecipue fraudatores, detrectatores, auari." Bibliander, *Alcoran* 1550, 1.187 rm; the relevant Qurʾānic text upon which the paraphrased portions are based is: ". . . obtrector . . . atque . . . coaceruator auarus . . . igne feruente . . . comburente . . . damnabitur." Ibid.)

233. "DEUS UBIQUE EST. Cum dei sit oriens et occidens, versus quamlibet partem orationem fundens deum invenit; sua namque pietas nullo loco circumscribitur, eius sapientia cuncta complectitur" (Güssing MS 1/35, fol. 235r; cf. Bibliander, *Alcoran* 1550, 1.12).

234. See, for example, the conclusion below, note 87. Another, similarly nonpolemical, extract (at surah 113): "Azoara 123 QUID ORANDUM [this rubric quotes Bibliander's note]. In nomine dei domini circuli uisibilis, te sanctifica, postulans ipsum, ut ab opere pessimo, malisque tenebris noctis, magorum et inuidorum et fascinantium nocumentis te proteget" (Güssing MS 1/35, fol. 142v; cf. Bibliander, *Alcoran* 1550, 1.188).

235. "In templis nullus sit cum mulieribus coitus. Die tota ieiunantes, nocte ieiunium soluite, tunc commedentes et bibentes quantum libuerit, fere usque ad principium horae quae solis ortum antecedit" (Güssing MS 1/35, fols. 235v–236r; cf. Bibliander, *Alcoran* 1550, 1.15).

236. Another example (at 23:91): "DEUS FILIUM NON HABET. . . . Deus nequaquam filum seu participem sumsit, Deum alium" (Güssing MS 1/35, fol. 127r; cf. Bibliander, *Alcoran* 1550, 1.111).

237. "Omnium . . . mulierum optimae . . . nostram animam insufflauimus et illam filiumque suum manifestum miraculum gentibus posuimus" (Güssing MS 1/35, fol. 126r, ll. 13–17; Bibliander, *Alcoran* 1550, 1.106).

238. See just above.

239. "Veri adorantes ubique exaudiuntur. Ioan. 4" (Bibliander, *Alcoran* 1550, 1.12. Another example is at 2:62, "OMNES SALUABUNTUR" (Güssing MS 1/35, fol. 234v; cf. Bibliander's note: "Omnes Deum timentes cuiuscumque professionis saluabuntur. Act. 20." Bibliander, *Alcoran* 1550, 1.10).

240. See above in this chapter.

241. For Bibliander's notes on surah 2, see his *Alcoran* 1550, 1.8–21.

Chapter 5

1. There are six complete and one partial manuscript of Mark of Toledo's version (see just below); six copies of Mithridates' translation of two Qur'ānic surahs (see the second half of this chapter); and two copies of the translation made for Egidio da Viterbo (see Chapter 6).

2. See Chapter 3 above, pp. 64–65.

3. On these manuscripts, see d'Alverny, "Marc de Tolède," 49–59, and most recently Petrus, "Marcos de Toledo y la segunda traducción del Corán," 90–91, who does not discuss the fragmentary copy in Milan, BA R 113 sup., on which see following note.

4. See Milan, BA, MS L 1 sup., fols. 3v, 4r (*Liber alcorani id est legis maurorum*); Paris, BnF, MS lat. 3394, fol. 1r (*Liber alchorani machometi*); Paris, Bibliothèque Mazarine, MS 708, fol. 3ra (*Liber alchorani*); Paris, BnF, MS lat. 14503, fol. 217va (*Liber alchorani machometi*, in colophon—the text is acephalous); Vienna, Öster. Nationalbibliothek, MS 4297, fol. 1r (*Alchorani Machometi liber*); and Turin, Biblioteca Nazionale Universitaria, MS F. V. 35, fol. 1ra (*Liber alchorani machameti*). In Milan, BA, MS R 113 sup. the work (fols. 191r–204v) lacks a title, though this fragmentary copy does include the first, second, and part of the third surahs. These folios, by the way, are of smaller format than the rest of this manuscript (29 cm high rather than 32) and clearly were originally separate from it.

5. With the exception of surah 1 entitled *Prohemium*. See Vienna MS 4297, fols. 1r and ff. The Milan fragment of Mark's translation does not even have this much. None of the three surahs preserved here is preceded by any title. See Milan MS R 113 sup, fols. 191r, 202r.

6. "Hud. C.XXI. periodi" (Milan MS L 1 sup., fol. 51v).

7. "prophecia hud cxxi peryodorum" (BnF, MS lat. 14503, fol. 166va), but see next note.

8. See, for example, Paris, BnF, ar. 384, passim. For bibliography on this late twelfth- or early thirteenth-century manuscript, see above Chapter 4 note 36.

9. Though surah 4 is referred to as "Tractatus mulierum" (Milan MS L 1 sup., fol. 20r).

10. After surahs 2 through 4 are identified by title in the Milan manuscript, the next five have no titles; many of the remainder have titles again until well into the manuscript when, on folio 95v, surah titles give out altogether. See, for example, ibid., fols. 26v, 31r, 36v, 42r, 44r, 48v, 51v, 75v. The Paris manuscript, which lacks the first five surahs entirely and begins partway into the sixth, preserves most of the surah titles, but there are notable gaps. See BnF MS lat. 14503, fols. 177vb, 178vb, 189vb, 211ra, etc. There is a further peculiarity here as well. The original copyist of this Paris manuscript left space for surah titles to be filled in by a later rubricator, but these were never added. Rather, the titles are preserved only in what seem to be marginal notes written in tiny script, presumably to indicate to the rubricator what he ought to write. But it is conceivable that they were written in by some later reader who was copying them from another manuscript. There are some remarkably learned notes added by a later hand, including Arabic words, but these are

doubtless the work of the seventeenth-century annotator mentioned by d'Alverny in her "Deux traductions," 111.

11. Turin MS F. V. 35, dated to the fifteenth century, has essentially the same titles as the thirteenth-century Paris manuscript (e.g., at surah 6: *prophetia animalium brutorum clxxxvii miracula*, fol. 16vb), though surahs 3–5 lack titles, and the titles give out entirely after folio 35, even though there is space left for the rubricator to add them. The late sixteenth-century Parisian manuscript has much the same set of titles, but in addition to calling the surahs "prophecies," also refers to them as *azoaras*: *Azoara XXXII. Prophetia Prophetarum* (see BnF MS lat. 3394, fol. 125v). This addition of *azoara* imitates Robert's Latin Qur'ān, and the surah numbers in this copy of Mark's version eventually also come to parallel Robert's eccentric redivision, the final surah, for example, being numbered "124" as it is in later MSS of Robert's version (and in Bibliander's edition): *Azoara CXXIIII. Prophetia hominum* (ibid., fol. 237r).

12. Mazarine MS 708, fols. 42ra, 46vb. For bibliography on this manuscript, see below in this chapter.

13. "Curat de formicis" (i.e., the Surah [27] of the Ants [al-Naml]), ibid., fol. 67ra; "Curat de alfourqan" (i.e., the Surah [25] of the Criterion [al-Furqān]), ibid., fol. 63va. There are errors, as well, such as *Curat Abraham* for surah 3 (ibid., fol. 11rb), a misreading of *alimran*, the name of this surah in transliteration (*Āl ʿImrān*), as *Abraham*. We find this title similarly garbled in Milan MS L 1 sup. fol. 14v.

14. "Curat prohemii libri septem verborum vel versum" (Mazarine MS 708, fol. 3ra).

15. "Curat mense almeyda co. v." (ibid., fol. 20vb).

16. Daniel comments on this as well in *Islam and the West*, 44–45.

17. Milan MS L 1 sup., fols. 4v, lm; 5v, lm; and 8v, lm. This may be a case of the sort of periodic polemical mistranslation that, as I argue in Chapter 1, occurs from time to time, but is in general rather rare in the Latin translations.

18. "quod neque debet sequi iudeos neque christianos" (Milan MS L 1 sup., fol. 7v, rm); the identical note appears in the Mazarine manuscript (Mazarine MS 708, fol. 6ra, lm).

19. "dyabolus" (BA MS L 1 sup., fol. 5r, rm); "dyabolus decepit adam" (Mazarine MS 708, fol. 4ra, lm).

20. Milan MS L 1 sup., fol. 13v, lm; Mazarine MS 708, fol. 10vb, rm. Another example, at 2:219: "de uino et aleis" (Milan MS L 1 sup., fol. 11r, rm) becomes "de uino eis prohibito et aleis" (Mazarine MS 708, fol. 8vb, rm).

21. "quod deus docuit ad[am] omnia nomina et i[pse] narrauit ea angelis"/ "quod nocte ieiunii licitum est eis delectari cum mulieribus" (Mazarine MS 708, fols. 3vb, rm; 7vb, rm).

22. "Quando dixit ei creator suus offerte ait oblatus sum creatori gencium" (Mark of Toledo, *Liber Alchorani*, Mazarine MS 708, fol. 6rb). *Creator* here translates, somewhat oddly, the Arabic *rabb* (= lord), something we find throughout Mark's translation.

23. Ibid. The manuscript actually has *alzam* for the first verb, but this is doubtless the error of a copyist who did not know Arabic himself.

24. Mark's translation: "sumus ei oblati." The adjoining note: "Muzlimuna

id est sarraceni" (ibid.). The manuscript actually has *ymuzlimuna*, another obvious copy error.

25. See above, Chapter 2, note 109.

26. "Et si repudiauit<ur> eam" (ibid., fol. 9ra). On Robert's and Mark's translations of these verses, see my "Exclusion or Concealment," 190–93.

27. "quod repudiata tercio non est licita redire ad virum donec alius contrahat cum ea" (Mazarine MS 708, 9ra).

28. And it is worth pointing out that one note, very likely by this same later learned commentator, seems to have been inserted by the copyist of this manuscript directly into the text of Mark's translation, this note likewise relying on knowledge of the Arabic version. At 2:132, where the Qur'ān says, "Do not die other than as men who have surrendered (*Muslimūn*)," Mark originally gave us *nolite priusquam mori sitis oblati* (as the Mazarine text has it; see also Turin MS F. V. 35, fol. 3rb). But just before this passage, a new version of this sentence has been inserted in the text of the Mazarine manuscript: *non moremini priusquam sitis ysmaelite uel muzlimuna*—"do not die until you are Ishmaelites or Muslims." In this case, the word *muslimuna* actually has been written in the vivid vermilion ink in which the glosses on this manuscript are written. See Mazarine MS 708, fol. 6rb.

29. The large number of marginal notes (which I have just discussed) written in vivid red ink add to the colorfulness of this manuscript.

30. On which, see the beginning of Chapter 4 above.

31. Surah titles are red, as are key initials which have blue flourishes; the folios have been ruled for the text but not for the notes.

32. BnF, MS lat. 14503 has red or blue initials at the beginnings of surahs, and red or blue paraphs before each *basmalah*, but no other ornamentation (Mark's translation—incomplete here—occupies folios 155r–217v). Turin MS F. V. 35 has red titles and large initials in red, smaller initials with a red stroke, but all rubrication ends partway into the text on fol. 36v. In Vienna MS 4297, the surah titles and numbers are in red ink throughout, as is the large initial that begins each surah, but other than this there is no other ornamentation. The fragmentary sixteenth-century copy, BA MS R 113 sup., fols. 191r–204v, has no ornamentation at all. See *Inventario Ceruti dei manoscritti della Biblioteca Ambrosiana*, 5 vols. (Terrazano sul Naviglio, 1973–79), 4.711, and Adolfo Rivolta, *Catalogo dei Codici Pinelliani dell'Ambrosiana* (Milan, 1933), no. 144, pp. 110–13. Rivolta's entry is fuller, though neither contains a complete manuscript description.

33. De Hamel, *A History of Illumintated Manuscripts*, 248–49.

34. It also contains a *questio* attributed to Nicholas of Lira on whether it is possible to prove on the basis of the Jewish scriptures whether "our savior was God and man" (*utrum ex scripturis receptis a judeis possit efficaciter probari saluatorem nostrum fuit deum et hominem*), fols. 144ra–154ra. The Milan manuscript (R 113. sup.) containing the fragmentary copy of Mark's version places it in a similar, though slightly less obviously polemical and apologetic context, though this was done late in the sixteenth century. In this case, what is clearly a gathering from an earlier manuscript of Mark's *Liber Alchorani* has been bound in among works on the origins of the Turks (180r–86r); the life of Muhammad (fols. 187v–r) that Widmanstetter included in his *Machumeti Theologia* (see Chapter 4 above); the *Doctrina*

Machumeti (205r–233v), but under the title *Theologia Machumeti* as it appears in Widmanstetter's edition; Mithridates' translation of surahs 21 and 22, and a genealogy of Muhammad (fols. 286r–v, this being a real genealogy, not the work from the *Collectio Toletana* with that name), as well as a genealogy of the Turkish noble families (fol. 311r), both of these included among a large series of genealogies of European worthies. This vast manuscript miscellany (it contains some 368 folios) also contains a whole range of works having nothing to do with Islam or religious disputation. In general, this framing for Mark's Latin Qur'ān, then, is much less obviously polemical or apologetical than that found in Paris, BN, lat. 14503.

35. Mazarine MS 708. The preface is on folios 1ra–3ra, the Qur'ān on 3ra–108va. On this manuscript, see August Molinier, *Catalogue des Manuscrits de la Bibliothèque Mazarine*, 4 vols. (Paris, 1885–98), 1.377–78, and Petrus, "Marcos de Toledo y la segunda traducción del Corán," 90. For a thorough discussion of the translations and manuscript, see d'Alverny and Vajda, "Marc de Tolède, traducteur d'Ibn Tūmart," and also Marie-Thérèse d'Alverny, "Marc de Tolède," esp. 49–52.

36. Mazarine MS 708, fols. 108va–113rb. These are edited and commented on by d'Alverny and Vajda, "Marc de Tolède, traducteur," 268–307.

37. See Dominique Urvoy, *Ibn Rushd, Averroes*, trans. Olivia Stewart (London, 1991), 18–19, 81; and Madeleine Fletcher, "The Almohad Tawhīd: Theology which Relies on Logic," *Numen* 38 (1991):110–28.

38. These are on fols. 115ra–151va, and 151va–157ra, respectively. On these and the other accounts of Alexander's life that circulated in the medieval West, see D. J. A. Ross, *Illustrated Medieval Alexander-Books in Germany and the Netherlands* (Cambridge, England, 1971), 1–3; id., *Alexander Historiatus: A Guide to Medieval Illustrated Alexander Literature* (London, 1963), 5–65; and G. Cary, *The Medieval Alexander*, ed. D. J. A. Ross (Cambridge, England, 1956) 9–16, 24–61. On the Alexander legend in poetic form, see Maura K. Lafferty, *Walter of Châtillon's Alexandreis: Epic and the Problem of Historical Understanding* (Turnhout, 1998).

39. Christopher de Hamel, *A History of Illuminated Manuscripts*, 2nd ed. (London, 1994), 142.

40. D'Alverny and Vajda, "Marc de Tolède, traducteur," 103ff.

41. The Qur'ānic text ends abruptly at verse 39:74, as d'Alverny points out in her "Quelques manuscrits," 216. It is intriguing to notice, however, that the final folio on which this last line occurs (fol. 101) appears to be a singleton added to the previous gathering, and that the text ends at the end of a sentence, in the middle of the page, as if this had been all the text that was available for copying.

42. On this manuscript, see *Tabulae codicum manu scriptorum praeter Graecos et Orientales in Biblioteca Palatina Vindobonensi asseveratorum*, 11 vols. (Vienna, 1864–1912), 3.232, and Tarif al-Samman and Otto Mazal, *Die arabische Welt und Europa: Ausstellung der Handschriften- und Inkunabelsammlung der Österreichischen Nationalbibliothek: Handbuch und Katalog* (Graz, 1988), 133.

43. The prophecy (*prophecia*) reads as follows (fol. 209v):

"Demonum frater non possum vobis
prodesse et ita nescio an sit prope
ypocritarum principio ypocrite menciuntur

laudis medio quis nos prohibuit
Arenar [*sic*] nescio quid fiet
Aurore inueni te in errore
Diei veneris quamuis fuissent in errore manifesto
Sabe dic deus nescio si ego vel
vos sumus in directione." (Vienna MS 4297, fol. 209v)

[I read this as a dialogue between three speakers—pagan deities or spiritual beings perhaps:

"*Brother of the demons*: I am not able to benefit you
and thus I do not know whether it be near to the
origin of the hypocrites [that] hypocrites lie.
In the midst of praise, who prohibited us?
Arenar: I do not know what will happen
for the dawn. I found you in the error
of the Day of Venus, although they had been in obvious error.
Sabe: Speak, God. I do not know if I or
you are in right guidance."]

The use of *dic* here mimics the frequent command to "speak" in the Qur'ān, translated usually by Mark as *dic*; *in directione* follows Mark's somewhat awkward translation of the Qur'ānic *ʿalá hudan* ("in right guidance"), as in v. 2:5—cf. ibid., fol. 1r. For Muhammad being associated with the sins of Venus, see Daniel, *Islam and the West*, 168, 215, 238, 341. On Islam as polytheistic in popular culture, see Norman Daniel, *Heroes and Saracens: An Interpretation of the Chansons de geste* (Edinburgh, 1984). I know of no source for this "prophecy," though an almost identical version of it appears in at least one other manuscript of Mark's translation, BnF MS lat. 14503, likewise at just the end of the text (fol. 217vb).

44. This manuscript (Vienna MS 4297) has gatherings of ten leaves, the folios marked in the bottom right-hand corner with gathering numbers (a1, a2, a3 . . . b1, b2, b3 . . .) and new gatherings also signaled by catchwords (see, e.g., fol. 10v). Mark's Latin Qur'ān begins at the top of the folio numbered "a1."

45. On this manuscript, see F. Cosentini, *Inventari dei manoscritti delle biblioteche d'Italia* 28, ed. G. Mazzatinti and A. Sorbelli (Florence, 1922–24), 97. This manuscript consists of gatherings of twelve leaves, each marked by a catchword. Mark's translation begins at the top of the first column of the recto side of folio 1 of the first gathering, and ends on the recto side of the last folio of the final gathering (fol. 84), which begins on 73r. On this and on the Vienna manuscript in which Mark's Latin Qur'ān appears with little or no other accompaniment, see also Petrus, "Marcos de Toledo y la segunda traducción del Corán," 90–91.

46. See above, Chapter 4, note 167.

47. Such as when he rightly inserts *non* before *possumus* in v. 2:61. Vienna MS 4297, fol. 3v.

48. At 2:83 he surmises from the context, presumably, that a word meaning "agreement" or "treaty" is missing between *suscepimus* and *filiorum* and so adds *pactum* in the margin (ibid., fol. 5r). His surmise was correct: other manuscripts have *fedus* here. See Turin MS F. V. 35, fol. 2rb.

49. Vienna MS 4297, fols. 6v–7r, 5r ("de ihesu"), 7r.

50. Turin MS F. V. 35, fol. 1ra, l. 33.

51. Another example, at 2:24: above *timete* we have *cavete* (ibid., fol. 1rb, l. 16).

52. "id est faciet oberrare" (ibid., 1rb, l. 27).

53. See, for example, al-Ṭabarī on 2:67 (1.378) and especially on 2:93 (1.466) and 2:124–25 (1.580); and also al-Ṭabarsī on 2:124–125, 1.200, 203.

54. Turin MS F. V. 35, fol. 2ra, l. 10; 2rb, l. 22; 2va, l. 17; 3ra, l. 30; 3ra, l. 33.

55. "et uiuificat terram post mortem suam" (ibid., 3vb; Mark's Latin version follows the Arabic closely and accurately).

56. "ay fa-ʿamara bi-hi al-arḍ baʿda kharābihā li-anna al-arḍ idhā waqaʿa ʿalayhā al-maṭar anbatat wa-idhā lam yaṣubbhā al-maṭar lam tanbut . . . fa-kānat min hādhā al-wajh ka-al-mayyit" (al-Ṭabarsī on 2:164, 1.246; cf. al-Ṭabarī on 2:164, 2.68–69).

57. Another example of a note that depends on direct knowledge of the Arabic text of the Qurʾān, though not necessarily of the traditional exegesis of it, occurs at verse 2:30. Here Mark had translated the Arabic *khalīfah* quite acceptably as *uicarium*, but the annotator writes *id est successorem* above it since this word captures with full precision, in a way that *uicarium* does not, the etymological origins of the Arabic term in the verb *khalafa*, "to follow after, to be the successor of." See Turin MS F. V. 35, fol. 1rb, l. 36.

58. The fragment that appears in this manuscript (fols. 191r–204v) seems to be a single gathering, originally part of another manuscript (the text ends on 204v, partway through surah 3 in mid-sentence, a catchphrase appearing in the bottom margin). Mark's Latin Qurʾān begins at the very top of the recto side of the first leaf of this gathering, this perhaps having been, therefore, the first folio of the original manuscript, the Qurʾān thus appearing, as in the Turin and Venice manuscripts, without Mark's hostile preface to introduce it. There are a number of notes in these folios, written, it would seem, by the copyist of the text. Some of them are related to or derive, in fact, from those in the Turin manuscript. At both 2:63 and 2:125 (fols. 192v and 194v), we have notes that tell us, in conformity with the Muslim exegetical tradition, to insert *mementote* between *et* and *quando* ("subintellige mementote," and "mementote semper supple" respectively), just as in the Turin manuscript (see just above), and both sets of notes urge readers to supply the word "occiditur" in 2:178 (see Turin MS F. V. 35, fol. 4ra, l. 37; and BA MS R 113 sup., fol. 196v). But a number of the notes are unrelated to the Turin notes, and many of these are preoccupied with polemical and apologetic concerns (for example, "nota de fide Christi" on R 113 sup., fol. 193r at 2:87; and "nota trinitatem" on ibid., fol.195r at 2:133).

59. On all this, see Chapter 1 above, pp. 17–18.

60. "Piemontese, "Il Corano latino," 259. On this manuscript in general, see ibid., 258–63, and Cosimus Stornajolo, *Codices Urbinates latini*, 3 vols. (Rome, 1902–21), 3.296–98. See also Kristen Lippincott and David Pingree, "Ibn al-Ḥātim on the Talismans of the Lunar Mansions," *Journal of the Warburg and Courtauld Institutes* 50 (1987):57–81.

61. See Chapter 1 above, pp. 18–19.

62. Flavius Mithridates, preface to his Qur'ān edition, ed. Hartmut Bobzin in his *Der Koran*, 81–82; on Cibò, see ibid., 81n268.

63. "Denique unusquisque sermo in sua columna collocabitur. At dictiones notissimae apud eos quae multum equiuocationis continent: ut in Arabico proferuntur. ita in traductione qualibet ponuntur: et in calce operis declarantur" (Mithridates, preface, ibid.).

64. See "al-Ḳur'ān," EI2 5:400–32 at 431 [art. A. T. Welch and J. D. Pearson] and "Translations of the Qur'ān," EQ 5:340–58 at 344–48 [art. Hartmut Bobzin].

65. Origen's *Hexapla* (third century) set forth the Hebrew Bible alongside a Greek transliteration and four Greek translations (see Dahan, *L'exégèse chretienne*, 161n1); on the later Latin-Hebrew bilingual Psalters, see ibid., 123; on the trilingual Psalter (Latin, Greek, and Arabic) of Sicily, dated 1153, see Piemontese, "Il Corano latino," 231, and Henry Houben, *Roger II of Sicily: A Ruler Between East and West*, trans. Graham A. Loud and Diane Milburn (Cambridge, England, 2001), 109n27.

66. See, for example, Jaroslav Pelikan with Valerie Hotchkiss and David Price, *The Reformation of the Bible, the Bible of the Reformation* (New Haven, Conn., 1996), 19–20, 109–13.

67. Jerry Bentley, *Humanists and Holy Writ*, 74.

68. See below, Chapter 6, note 5.

69. See above, Chapter 1, pp. 24–26.

70. See above, Chapter 1, note 49.

71. And there are other signs of general hastiness in laying out the texts of this edition that might be mentioned as well. The title at the beginning of surah 21 (fol. 65r), which identifies it as *surathilhagi* ("Surah of the Ḥajj"), is wrong; this is the title of the following surah (beginning fol. 75v), which in this manuscript has no title at all. Having forgotten to include the introductory invocation of God as "the clement the merciful" (*In nomine dei clementis et misericordis*) at the beginning of surah 21, the Latin copyist wrote it in the outer margin next to the beginning of the Latin text, thereby taking up the space where the corresponding Arabic should appear but therefore cannot. (At the beginning of surah 22 all is set to rights, however, Arabic and Latin invocations appearing properly side by side.)

72. On both these works, see Stornajolo, *Codices Urbinates latini*, 3.296–97. On the first in particular, see Lippincott and Pingree, "Ibn al-Ḥātim on the Talismans of the Lunar Mansions," 57–81, which contains a translation of the Arabic text and an edition of the Latin; see also Kristen Lippincott, "More on Ibn al-Ḥātim," *Journal of the Warburg and Courtauld Institutes* 51 (1988):188–90.

73. He clearly was otherwise interested otherwise in interreligious disputation and apologia, however, as his sermon on the passion suggests (see Wirszubzski's introduction to his edition of *Flavius Mithridates: Sermo de passione domini* [Jerusalem, 1963]) and his disputation with the contemporary Jew, Elijah Delmedigo, makes clear (see Hames, "Elijah Delmedigo," 42).

74. See BAV MS urb. lat. 1384, fols. 68v (v. 21:36) and 74v (v. 21:105).

75. No new gathering begins here, so the merging of these two different reference works happened before the copying of this deluxe manuscript. Most of the entries after 88ra are not from the two relevant surahs, and the explanations are now short, simple definitions: *Gibha* (*jabhah*, "forehead"), for example, is glossed

correctly as *frons*, and *Asarub* (*al-sharāb*, "a drink, potion,") as *potatio suauis*, neither term occurring in these surahs (BAV MS urb. lat. 1384, fol. 88ra). See also Stornajolo, *Codices Vrbinates latini*, 3.297, who came to the same conclusion.

76. Later copyists also considered them one work. See, for example, BA MS R 113 sup., fols. 238v–239v, and BnF MS lat. 3671, fols. 11v–14r.

77. And of course the presence of the annexed Arabic-Latin glossary emphasizes this same philological orientation.

78. "*Al. Il. Vl.* Articuli sunt. sicut in uulgari nostro *lo. la.* et aliquando secundum uariationem uocalium precedentium sonat in prolatione *il.* aliquando *ul.* cum ipsi arabes non habeant nisi tres uocales *a. i. u.* hebrei uero duos tantum habeant articulos. scilicet *ha.* et <lacuna> et Caldei unum tantum scilicet *yath*" (Mithridates, *Latin-Arabic Qur'ān*, BAV MS urb. lat. 1384, fol. 86va).

79. "*Baith*: id est domus uel templum: unde *baith il macdas* id est templum sanctuarii" (ibid.).

80. *Baith* appears in the phrase *baith al-hatic*, "the Ancient House" (vv. 22:29, 34, fols. 79vb, 80ra).

81. Without going into detail about this, Giorgio Levi della Vida commented many years ago on Mithridates' lack of familiarity with "la tradizione scolastica araba." See his *Ricerche*, 94.

82. E.g.: "*Harami* [= ḥarām] id est uetitum: uel anathema. *Hatic* [= ʿatīq] id est antiqui: unde et templum mahomethi quod est in meccha uocatur: *baithil hatic.* quasi templum antiquum" (BAV MS urb. lat. 1384, fol. 87rb). See also his illuminating and accurate discussions of *ʿushr* (*haxra*), *ḥizb* (*hisbi*), Muhammad, and mosque (*misgid*), ibid., fols. 87rb–vb.

83. "*Muslimin* idem est quod salui et sunt omnes qui credunt in mahometum: quia secundum eos omnes qui seruant legem illam sunt salui" (ibid., fol. 87vb).

84. "*Chifli*: est nomen religionis in secta mahometti [*sic*]: eorum qui patiuntur multum pro deuotione sua in ipso" (ibid., fol. 86va; for his translation of the verse, see ibid., fol. 72vb).

85. See "dhū al-kifl," EI2 2:242 [G. Vajda]. Al-Zamakhsharī, for example, says that Dhū al-Kifl is said to refer to Elijah (*Ilyās*) or Zakariah or Joshua Son of Nun, "just as if he were called this because he is a possessor of wealth/property (*ḥaẓẓ*)" (al-Zamakhsharī on 21:85, 3.128). See also al-Qurṭubī on 21:85, 11.216–17.

86. "*musrafin*: est nomen secte quam dicunt fuisse tempore noe: quae non credebat paradysum neque infernum: et dicebat animam esse mortalem: et nihil post mortem: sicut epycuri apud graecos" (BAV MS urb. lat. 1384, fol. 87va; for Mithridates' translation of the relevant passage, see ibid., fol. 66ra; for the views of commentators on this term, see al-Ṭabarī on 21:9, 9.8; al-Ṭabarsī on 21:9, 4.40; Ibn ʿAṭīyah on 21:9, 10.129).

87. "*Gog et Magog* . . . et dicunt arabes ipsos esse homines parue stature: ita quod non excedunt quantitatem unius brachii" (BAV MS urb. lat. 1384, fol. 86vb–87ra; for a similar view, see Ibn ʿAṭīyah on 18:92–95, 9.402, and see "Gog and Magog," EQ 2:331–33 [art. Keith Lewinstein]).

88. "Gehennam acceperunt arabes ab hebreis: sicut et nos: et significat in hebraeo uallis ecce sunt. quod de inferno intelligitur et alio modo uocatur gebenhinnom: et est locus in hierusalem: ubi sepeliebantur mortui antiquitus. et

significat uallis in qua ecce sunt" (BAV MS urb. lat. 1384, fol. 86vb). This has connections both with what modern scholars say about the word's etymology, though it is far from perfect (see *Encyclopedia Judaica*, 7:357), and with ideas that circulated in Christian circles in the Middle Ages (see, for example, Jerome, *Liber interpretationis hebraicorum nominum*, CCSL 72:136; and the *Glossa ordinaria* on Matthew 5:30, PL 114:95). On the Islamic traditions about and interpretations of *jahannam*, see Jane Idleman Smith and Yvonne Yazbeck Haddad, *The Islamic Understanding of Death and Resurrection* (Albany, N.Y., 1981), 85–86; and also "Hell and Hellfire," EQ 2:414–20 [art. Rosalind W. Gwynne].

89. "Idrisa: est nomen prophete quem dicit mahomet fuisse tempore abrahe: sed abubhachar dicit fuisse iesum unctum" (BAV MS urb. lat. 1384, fol. 87rb). For an overview of the Islamic ideas about Idrīs, see "Idrīs," EI2 3:1030–31 [art. G. Vajda]; and "Idrīs," EQ 2:484–86 [art. Yoram Erder].

90. See al-Ṭabarī on 7:68–69, 5.524–28; and Ibn ʿAṭīyah on 7:69–70, 5.551–54. See also "Ād," EI2 1:169 and "Ād," EQ 1:21–22 [art. Roberto Tottoli].

91. "*Iadus.* inueni in libris cabala iudeorum quod iadus fuit quidam Symeon iustus filius iehosadac pontificis maximi qui uixit multo tempore post magnam sẙnodum tempore hesdre conuentam. In cuius diebus uenit Alexander macedo ad diruendam hierosolimam et exiuit iste Symeon obuiam ei: quem cum uidit Alexander prostrauit se in terram et adorauit: et concessit ei: quecunque petiit: et admirabantur: serui illius cur hoc faceret: quibus dixit nolite admirari imaginem huius semper uidi in bello et superaui" (BAV MS urb. lat. 1384, fol. 87rb–87va).

92. Seder Moʿed, Yoma, *The Babylonian Talmud*, trans. I. Epstein and L. Jung (London, 1938), 325.

93. Mithridates' explanation of *furqān* is another example of his use of Jewish tradition. Islamic exegetes insist that it means "the criterion, the separator of right and wrong," this definition arising from its Qurʾānic usage and from its relation to the Arabic verb FRQ ("to divide, split"). Modern scholars, however, agree that it was borrowed from the Jewish-Aramaic *purqān* or the Syriac *purqāna*, both meaning "deliverance, redemption, liberation" (see Jeffery, *The Foreign Vocabulary of the Quran*, 225–29; "furḳān," EI2 2:949–50 [art. R. Paret]). Mithridates perceived *furqān*'s relationship with the Aramaic and Syriac terms, for he glosses it "*Furcani* id est liberans et significat duos libros unum qui decem precepta que data sunt moyse continet alium eum quem dicit mahometh habuisse a Gabriele archangelo: et uocantur liberantes: quoniam secundum arabes qui precepta contenta in eis seruat: liberatur a penis inferni" (BAV MS urb. lat. 1384, fol. 86va). He rightly understood from context that it often was used of earlier revelations such as the Torah, and could refer to the Qurʾān as well. But his explanation of its meaning reflects his Jewish roots rather than any knowledge of Islamic exegesis.

94. See Flavius Mithridates, *Sermo de passione Domini*, ed. Chaim Wirszubski in his *Flavius Mithridates: Sermo de passione Domini*, 93–94; see also the editor's introduction, 35.

95. Chaim Wirszubski, *Pico della Mirandola's Encounter with Jewish Mysticism* (Cambridge, Mass., 1989), 69–70, 114. His translations, as Wirszubski makes clear, are by no means perfect, but "all his shortcomings notwithstanding," Mithridates "was a remarkable translator [of Hebrew] in an age of remarkable translators" (114).

See also Harvey Hames, "Jewish Magic with a Christian Text: A Hebrew Translation of Ramon Llull's *Ars brevis*," *Traditio* 54 (1999):283–300 at 291 for Mithridates' possibly translating from Latin into Hebrew as well.

96. As Lippincott and Pingree imply, "Ibn al-Ḥātim on the Talismans."

97. Vatican City, BAV MS ebr. 357, fol. 156r. For a full description, with a photograph of one folio, of this manuscript, see Piemontese, "Il Corano latino," 264–72.

98. See above in this chapter.

99. See note 97.

100. As Piemontese has pointed out. See his "Il Corano latino," 270.

101. "Hum al-kāfirūn wa-al-muʿminūn akhtaṣamū fī rabbihim" (al-Ṭabarī on 22:19, 9.124). See also al-Ṭabarsī on 22:19; 4.77.

102. "duo scilicet fideles [et] increduli" (BAV MS ebr. 357, fol. 107v, l. 14).

103. BAV MS urb. lat. 1384, fol. 76r; BAV MS ebr. 357, fol. 107r, l. 24; 107r, l. 1.

104. Levi della Vida, unaware that these copious notes in BAV MS ebr. 357 may well have been written by Mithridates, simply concluded that while Mithridates knew some colloquial Arabic from his homeland, "la sua conoscenza di questa lingua era tutt'altro che perfetta," and that there was little evidence that he had "molta famigliarità colla tradizione scolastica araba" (see his *Ricerche*, 96, 94). As we will see below, however, there is other evidence that Mithridates did not always work with complete scholarly integrity—some of it provided by Levi della Vida himself.

105. See above in this chapter.

106. BAV MS urb. lat. 1384., fol. i verso. See Albert Derolez, "Le livre manuscrit de la Renaissance," in *El libro antiguo español: Actas del Segundo Coloquio Internacional (Madrid)*, ed. María Luisa López-Vidriero and Pedro M. Cátedra (Madrid, 1992), 177–92 at 182, 188. Note that even in this beautiful title medallion, the title of Mithridates' Qur'ān translation is sloppily misspelled: "Alchoramī [*sic*] Mahometi."

107. For the contents of this manuscript, see Stornajolo, *Codices Urbinates latini*, 3:296–8; and also Bobzin, "Latin Translations of the Koran," 201–2; Piemontese, "Le iscrizioni arabe," 205, 213–14; id., "Il Corano latino," 258–63; and Giorgio Levi della Vida, *Ricerche*, 92–97.

108. BAV MS urb. lat. 1384, fol. 1r. See Derolez, "Le livre manuscrit de la Renaissance," 182, 188.

109. BAV MS urb. lat. 1384, fols. 1r, 63v, 65r, 75r.

110. Piemontese, "Il Corano latino," 259.

111. De Hamel, *A History of Illuminated Manuscripts*, 246.

112. Cecil H. Clough, "Federigo da Montefeltro's Artistic Patronage" (Selwyn Brinton Lecture for 1978), *Journal of the Royal Society of Arts* 126 (1978):718–34 at 719. See also id., "Federigo da Montefeltro's Patronage of the Arts, 1468–82," *Journal of the Warburg and Courtauld Institutes* 36 (1973):129–44 at 130–31, 138.

113. Clough, "Federigo da Montefelto's Artistic Patronage," 248–49.

114. Cecil H. Clough, "The Library of the Dukes of Urbino," *Librarium: Revue de la société des bibliophiles suisses* 9 (1966):101–5 at 101. See also Anthony Grafton, "The Vatican and Its Library," in *Rome Reborn: The Vatican Library and Renaissance*

Culture, ed. Anthony Grafton (Washington and New Haven, Conn., 1993), 3–46 at 5; and Richard A. Goldthwaite, *Wealth and the Demand for Art in Italy, 1300–1600* (Baltimore, 1993), 4–6, 243–50.

115. Rosalind Mack, *Bazaar to Piazza: Islamic Trade and Italian Art, 1300–1600* (Berkeley, Calif., 2002), 6.

116. Ibid., 12, 22, and Giordana Mariani Canova, "The Italian Renaissance Miniature," in *The Painted Page: Italian Renaissance Book Illumination, 1450–1550*, ed. Jonathan J. G. Alexander (London and Munich, 1994), 21–34 at 21.

117. For this and many other examples, see Maria Vittoria Fontana, "Byzantine Mediation of Epigraphic Characters of Islamic Derivation in the Wall Paintings of Some Churches in Southern Italy," in *Islam and the Italian Renaissance*, ed. Burnett and Contadini, 61–75, esp. 64, 72.

118. Mack, *Bazaar to Piazza*, 51; for the Italian love of Islamic goods in general, see ibid., passim, esp. 1, 5–6, 13; and also Anna Contadini, "Artistic Contacts: Current Scholarship and Future Tasks," in *Islam and the Italian Renaissance*, ed. Burnett and Contadini, 1–67 at 4–16.

119. On this see Clough, "The Library of the Dukes of Urbino," 102.

120. The phrase is de Hamel's, in his *History of Illuminated Manuscripts*, 234.

121. Alastair Hamilton, *The Apocryphal Apocalypse: The Reception of the Second Book of Esdras (4 Ezra) from the Renaissance to the Enlightenment* (Oxford, 1999), 33. See especially Levi della Vida's discussion of Mithridates' apparent involvement with the drawing up of one of the early Vatican Library catalogues of Arabic manuscripts, some of the entries of which suggest that Mithridates, "abbia inventato di sana pianta . . . quei titoli che gli parevano adatti a suscitare maggior interesse" (see his *Ricerche*, 97). See also Grafton, *Commerce*, 107–8.

122. The phrase once again is de Hamel's, in his *A History of Illuminated Manuscripts*, 236.

123. The discussion that follows is based on my own examination of the manuscript together with the description of it in Bibliothèque Nationale, *Catalogue général des manuscrits latins* (Paris, 1975), 6.492–93. A letter of dedication suggests the dating (fol. 1) of the manuscript, for it is written by Gabriel Venetus (usually called Gabriele della Volta), an Augustinian friar who died in that year (see David Aurelius Perini, *Bibliographia Augustiniana*, 4 vols. [Florence, 1929–38], 2:22–23 [available at web.tiscali.it/ghirardacci/perini/perini.htm]; he was the friend and confrere of another Qur'ān scholar, Egidio da Viterbo; see O'Malley, *Giles of Viterbo*, 49n3, 70n2, 87, 99n4, 151n4, 158n4, 159, 195, and Francis Martin, *Friar, Reformer*, 14.) Dedicated to Antonio Giustiniani, one-time senator of Venice (d. 1565), this manuscript contains, in addition to Mithridates' translation and notes (fols. 2r–14r), the *Doctrina Machumeti* (fols. 15r–28v—here under the title *Theologia Maumethis*) and the *Compendium Alchorani* (fols. 28v–65r), the abridgment of the Qur'ān that I discussed in the last chapter. That both these works appeared also in Johann Albrecht von Widmanstetter's *Mahometis Abdallae filii theologia* of 1543 suggests that his edition is derived from this or a similar manuscript. The last few folios contain a summary of Jewish law called *Leges Mosis* (*sic*, fols. 65v–66v) and a surprisingly irenic summary of Islamic beliefs (fols. 66v–67v). On three other manuscripts with much the same content (Padua, Biblioteca Antoniana, MS 207

Scaff. X; Venice, Biblioteca Nazionale Marciana, MS lat. XIV.123 [4662]; and Vienna, Öster. Nationalbibliothek, MS 11879), see Piemontese, "Il Corano latino," 263–64. On a fourth, BA MS R 113 sup., see just below.

124. Paris, BnF, MS lat. 3671, fol. 3r. On this family, see Michel Hochmann, *Peintres et commanditaires à Venise (1540–1628)* (Rome, 1992), 246. On coats of arms in Renaissance manuscripts, see Jonathan J. G. Alexander, "Patrons, Libraries and Illuminators in the Italian Renaissance," in *The Painted Page*, ed. Alexander, 11–20 at 11–13; see also the catalogue in this volume, 63. For a manuscript rather similar to this one in decorative scheme and relative sumptuousness, see MS J. A. 3160 of the Major J. R. Abbey collection. Containing the vernacular works of Petrarch, this manuscript has the same somewhat restrained ornamentation, the facetted, illuminated initials, and the cursive humanist script. It was the property of Alfonso, Duke of Calabria, whose coat of arms it contains. See J[onathan] J. G. Alexander and A. C. de la Mare in their *The Italian Manuscripts in the Library of Major J. R. Abbey* (London, 1969), 82–83.

125. See Albert Derolez, *Codicologie des manuscrits en écriture humanistique sur parchemin*, 2 vols. (Turhout, 1984), 1:66–68; Martin Davies, "Humanism in Script and Print in the Fifteenth Century," in *The Cambridge Companion to Renaissance Humanism*, ed. Jill Kraye (Cambridge, England, 1996), 49–51; and Alexander, "Patrons, Libraries, and Illuminators," 15.

126. See, for example, Canova, "The Italian Renaissance Miniature," 21.

127. "Atque ideo dies noctesque uersanti animo quo nam modo aliquid gratitudinis indicium ostentarem, quo me ab ingratorum numero procul eximerem illud occurrit nullum quo rarius eo etiam gratius posse sapienti munus offerri quam quod ab impuro nefarioque Mahumethe opus impium irreligiosumque de eius perditissima superstitione uersutissime conscriptum est" (BnF MS lat. 3671, fol. 1r).

128. For another striking example, see Paris, BnF, MS lat. 3670 (on which see *Catalogue général des manuscrits latins*, vol. 6 (Paris, 1975), 491–92, and d'Alverny, "Deux traductions," 112), which contains Robert of Ketton's Latin Qur'ān. Unusually, that text begins on fol. 1r (rather than being preceded by other works from the Collectio Toletana), this manuscript having many of the hallmarks of a deluxe Florentine manuscript of the same period (it is dated 1515): the top border of 1r features *bianchi girari*; the right-hand and bottom borders have white leaf scrolls and illuminated roundels, the one at the bottom of the page featuring a seemingly irenic author portrait of Muhammad. On Florentine manuscripts, see Derolez, "Le livre manuscrit de la Renaissance," 182; J[onathan] J. G. Alexander, *The Painted Page*, 12–13; Canova, "The Italian Renaissance Miniature," 21–22.

129. It is worth observing that this manuscript communicates an intriguing ambivalence about Islam. On the one hand, Gabriele della Volta comments in his dedicatory letter that "Quo perlecto, tu . . . dignosceres quantis quamque tenebricosis mortalium plurimi hoc Basilisco praeeunte detineantur erroribus, quamque deploranda sit miserorum conditio qui ludibiria pseudo prophetę sectati morte pereunt duplici" (BnF MS lat. 3671, fol. 1r), and urges Antonio Giustiniani to hand it over to learned scholars so that its teachings might be *explodenda exsibilandaque* (ibid., fol. 1v). But on the other, the summary of Islamic teachings at the end is thoroughly irenic: "Viri multi fide digni diu cum Mahumeticis [MS:

Mathematicis] conuersati, et quidam etiam Turci, confirmant quę in Alchorano hoc scribuntur teneri hodie ab illis omnibus, pręsertim quod Maumeth fuit princeps Arabię, et quod Christus fuit flatus Dei et virgine natus: vltimus hebreorum propheta: multa miracula operatus: non mortuus, sed assumptus in cęlum: Relicto in manibus hebreorum christi simulachro. . . . Si quis Judeus fieri uult Maumethista, cogitur prius credere Christo: ubi narrant illi breuiter: credisne Christum fuisse flatum Dei? ex Virgine natum? prophetam ultimum hebreorum? Quo concesso fit Maumethista. Habent bibliam et euangelia[m.] quędam oratio eorum solemnis est: quę apud nos pater noster etiam" (ibid., fols. 66v–67r). To my knowledge, this remarkable text has received no scholarly attention.

130. See BA MS R 113 sup., fols. 233r–39v. For bibliography on this manuscript, which is very clearly an amalgamation of a series of gatherings many of which originally circulated separately, see note 32 above. These folios, moveover, are part of a larger discrete unit (fols. 205–44) that is written on four gatherings by several hands, which are, like BnF MS lat. 3671 as well, connected to Widmanstetter's edition of the *Epitome of the Qur'ān* (on which see Chapter 4 above). Not only does the *Compendium Alchorani* also appear here alongside the *Doctrina Machumeti*, but someone has added a set of notes on the former (fols. 241v–244r) and the latter (fols. 240r–241v) that, while fewer in number in both cases, are largely identical with those added by Widmanstetter to his edition of these texts. There are forty-five notes on the *Compendium*, rather than seventy-three as in the edition, and thirty-six on the *Doctrina Machumeti*, rather than forty-five, and the notes seem to be added by a different hand than that which copied the works themselves. It is possible, therefore, that we have here an earlier version of Widmanstetter's notes, to which he later added further notes when he produced his edition. This is a question that clearly merits further study. On these notes see Chapter 4 above.

131. See note 128 just above.

Chapter 6

1. On Colville, see D. M. Dunlop, "David Colville, a Successor to Michael Scot," *Bulletin of Hispanic Studies* 28 (1951):38–42; and also Marie-Thérèse Urvoy, ed., *Le psautier mozarabe de Hafs le Goth* (Toulouse, 1994), iii–v.

2. This preface is found in a flyleaf attached to the beginning of the Milan manuscript; this has been transcribed by Enrico Galbiati, whose typescript accompanies the manuscript and is also reprinted in Oscar Löfgren and Renato Traini, *Catalogue of the Arabic Manuscripts in the Biblioteca Ambrosiana*, 3 vols. (Vicenza, 1975–95), 1:41–43.

3. David Colville, preface, in Löfgren and Traini, *Arabic Manuscripts*, 1:41–42.

4. See Davis, *Trickster Travels*, 241, 367, citing Ernesto Utrillas Valero, "Los Mudéjares Turolenses: Los primeros cristianos nuevos de la Corona de Aragón," in *Actas del VIII Simposio Internacional de Mudejarismo*, 820, 823.

5. All this is described at much greater length in Thomas E. Burman, "Cambridge University Library MS Mm. v. 26 and the History of the Study of the Qur'ān in Medieval and Early Modern Europe," in *Religion, Text, and Society in Medieval Spain and Northern Europe: Essays in Honor of J. N. Hillgarth*, ed. Thomas E. Burman, Mark D. Meyerson, and Leah Shopkow (Toronto, 2002), 335–63, esp. 337–46.

6. "Alcorani liber primus" (Cambridge, Cambridge University Library, MS Mm. v. 26, fol. 1r).

7. "Fātiḥat al-kitāb wa-hiya Makkīyah wa-fīhā sabʿat [*sic*] āyāt" (BA MS D 100 inf., fol. 3r).

8. Ibid., fol. 1v.

9. The Arabic *fātiḥah*, "opening," is mistaken for the cognate form *miftāḥ*, "key" (*clauis*). The first of the two later readers of this translation, the remarkable Leo Africanus, was quite critical of Iohannes' translation and, as we will see, went to great efforts to correct it (see below in this chapter). Errors like this make us understand Leo's criticisms, though I think his criticisms excessive overall.

10. This continues to the last surah: "Sūrat al-nās Madanīyah fīhā sitt āyāt/ Caput de hominibus almedina in eo sex uersus" (ibid., fols. 608v–609r).

11. E.g., *Azoara prima Vacca*—"The First Surah, the Cow"—or the corresponding Arabic, *al-Sūrah al-ūlá al-Baqarah*, ibid., fols. 3v ff. The Surah of the Cow is not, of course, the first surah, but rather the second, and the stipulation here that it is results from the fact that Egidio and his translator treat the short *Fātiḥah* as a sort of preface to the Qur'ān, thus throwing off by one the numbering of the surahs, but then, as we will see presently, the numbering system for the Qur'ān adopted here is unusual in other ways as well, though the surahs are never divided up or given new names as they are in Robert of Ketton's Latin Qur'ān. In the Latin running heads, the surahs are called *Azoaras*, the centuries-old Latin version of *al-sūrah*, though in the surah titles themselves, they are normally called chapters (*caput*).

12. See Bobzin, *Der Koran*, 343–44, who cites Ibn Abī Dāwūd, *Kitāb al-Maṣāḥif*, ed. Arthur Jeffery, in his *Materials for the History of the Text of the Qur'ān: The Old Codices* (Leiden, 1937), 119–20 ff. (Arabic).

13. "Azoara 11.a Joseph. seu .6.a lib. 2 . . . Azoara 116. de hominibus seu 72 lib. 4" (BA MS D 100 inf., fols. 216v, 608v). From the beginning of the second volume of the edition, which in Colville's copy is not a separate codex but is simply identified as "tomus II" where it begins on fols. 284v/285r, the Arabic running heads cease, though the Latin ones continue throughout.

14. At the beginning of surah 38, for example, we find "Explicit liber tertius. Incipit liber quartus," this at just the point where the fourth book begins in the Milan manuscript (see Cambridge MS Mm. v. 26, fol. 249rb). In the Milan manuscript, the numbering for the Arabic verses ceases after folio 227, and for the Latin verses ceases after folio 530; in the Cambridge codex, only the Latin verses are numbered.

15. The paper on which they are written appears to be the same as that used in the manuscript itself.

16. Though not always: the third leaf, for example, now at the beginning of

the second surah, has notes on 2:260 and 2:270; the seventh leaf, now near the end of surah 2, has notes on 2:65–112.

17. These leaves, normally foliated in sequence with the rest of the manuscript, are folios 5 (unbound), 14bis, 17, 20, 28, 32, 40, 43, 51, 52, 54, 68 (unbound), 71 (unbound), 78, 81, 89, 103, 311bis, 448, 449, 455, 458, and 598bis. Folio 182bis (unbound), also a leaf later bound into the manuscript, is simply a textual correction.

18. BA MS D 100 inf., fol. 5. See also a similar heading on one of the last leaves: *glossae lib. 4*, the glosses, that is, on Book 4 of his Qur'ān edition (ibid., fol. 448v). Colville also occasionally suggests that he is copying notes written by another. In a note on 2:55–56, he parenthetically observes "ut loquitur glossa ea qua ista desumpsi," after the phrase *septuaginta barones*, "seventy barons," the latter word (which translates the Arabic *shuyūkh*) being essentially Spanish rather than Latin (see ibid., fol. 5).

19. A comment in the note on 2:53 implies such abbreviation: "the gloss from which I have taken these things." See previous note.

20. For example, "pro uersu 49," ibid., fol. 5. On later leaves, a lemma is often provided as well. See fols. 448–49.

21. "pro uersu 122. dicunt quod Abraham et Israel fabricauerunt Mecham, et quod Deus praecepit eis ut mundarent illud ut esset oratorium piis" (ibid., fol. 20r).

22. E.g., "pro versu 116. dicunt interpretes quod Coraxistae petierunt a Machometo ut faceret miracula, sicut Moyses et alii nuncii dei" (ibid., fol. 20v).

23. "item dicit Azamachxheri quod arbor illa quae fuit uetita illis erat ficus" (ibid., fol. 5). See al-Zamakhsharī on 2:35, 1.131; see also Ibn ʿAṭīyah on 2:35, 1.252.

24. "pro 28 uersu. dicit Azamachzeri super alcoranum liber 4 capitulum 4 num. 10 quod deus primum creauit terram et fecit accendere ignem super illam et creauit caelos ex uaporibus terrae qui ascenderunt" (BA MS D 100 inf., fol. 5).

25. "Mauri habent quinque orationes: prima dicitur in aurora diciturque acobhe [= *al-ṣubḥ*] et in ea dicunt orationem istam septem uersuum bis. 2a in medio die et dicitur adular [= *al-ẓuhr*] et in ea repetunt hanc orationem quater. 3a ad uesperas diciturque adhacur [= *al-ʿaṣr*] similiterque dicunt hanc orationem quater. 4a est autem completorium dicuntque [eam] ter tantum, diciturque oratio niqub [= *al-maghrib*]. 5a est in lecto diciturque alatamar [= *al-ʿatamah*] dicuntque hanc orationem quater" (ibid.). The explanation of the number of times the *Fātiḥah* is said in each of the prayers is correct.

26. "pro uersu 64. ubi incipit historia de vacca a qua azoara ista appellatur *baqarah*" (this last word in Arabic script) (ibid., fol. 40v).

27. "maledic[tor]es exponunt iudaeos et errantes uocant christianos glossatores eorum Abuasia, Azamachshari et Zemawi" (ibid., fol. 5). The text on which this note expounds reads as follows: "dirige nos per uiam beatorum: et illorum qui a te gratias acceperant: et non per uiam maledictorum neque errantium" (ibid., fol. 1v).

28. "wa-qīla al-maghḍūb ʿalayhim hum al-yahūd . . . wa-al-ḍāllūn hum al-naṣārá" (al-Zamakhsharī on 1:7, 1.26; cf. Ibn ʿAṭīyah on 1:7, 1.126).

29. "tres illae literae [alif, lām, mīm written in Arabic characters] A. L. M. varie a variis mauris declarari solent, communiter tamen dicunt aleph significare alla [Allāh in Arabic characters], et lamed Gabrielem et mem melac, angelum, quia

putant Gabrielem detulisse ad machometum scripturam hanc de caelis et a deo, si diis utique placet" (BA MS D 100 inf., fol. 5). (The contemptuous final three words here may be the addition of Colville, or may represent something of the undercurrent of polemic that these philological notes may contain; I will say more about this issue below.) Cf., for example, al-Bayḍāwī on 2:1, 1.12 who suggests, among other interpretations, that "the alif is from Allāh and the lām is from Jabrīl and the mīm is from Muhammad, that is the Qur'ān was sent down from God by the tongue of Jabrīl to Muhammad."

30. "pro uersu 136. dicit Azamachxeri quod sincharolla [= *ṣibghat Allāh*] est baptismus Christianorum" (BA MS D 100 inf., fol. 20r). Cf. al-Zamakhsharī on 2:138, 1.195: "wa-al-maʿná: taṭhīr Allāh . . . wa-al-aṣl fīhi anna al-Naṣārá kānū yaghmisūna awlādahum fī mā' aṣfar yusammūnahu al-maʿmūdīyah."

31. "wa-qīla iltaqá fīhā Ādam wa-Ḥawwā' fa-taʿārafā" (al-Zamakhsharī on 2:198, 1.243; see also Ibn ʿAṭīyah on 2:198, 2.174).

32. "pro uersu 195. dicunt Adam et Eua postquam eiecti fuerunt e paradiso . . . ambo conuenerunt in Monte Araffa" (BA MS D 100 inf., fol. 28v).

33. "pro uersu 100. de angelis illis Herot et Merot, ita fabulantur interpretes Alcorani, quod deus misit istos duos angelos in terra ut uiderent quod agerent homines . . . cumque hoc diu egessent, tandem Deus interrogauit eos an ipsi similiter male agerent si reliqueret eos uiuere in terris, promiseruntque se non facturos talia qualia homines facere consueuerunt; sic deus eos transmisit in Babylonem, ubi . . . amore capti formosissimae cuiusdam mulieris cum qua post tantum conuicium dormierunt, et cum quidam eos uidisset, [eum] interfecerunt, unde tria peccata commisisse dicunt, gulam, luxuriam et homocidam. . . . sed propter peccata ista, aiunt, deum detulisse eos in cisternam in qua stant usque ad diem iudicii; in qua docent Babylonios artem necromantis, ut illi dicunt, et inter caetera, quod mariti possint deserere uxores. et de his omnibus loquitur uersus ille 100" (ibid., fol. 40v). Most of the details included here can be found in hadiths typically quoted to explain this verse. See the representative sample in al-Ṭabarsī on 2:102, 1.175–76.

34. Two further examples, the first relating to the phrase "they say God has taken a son," at 2:116. Ibn ʿAṭīyah observed: "wa-ukhtulifa ʿalá man yaʿūdu al-ḍamīr fī *qālū* fa-qīla ʿalá al-Naṣārá li-annahum qālū 'al-masīh ibn Allāh' . . . wa-qīla ʿalá al-Yahūd li-annahum qālū "Uzayr ibn Allāh' wa-qīla ʿalá kafarat al-ʿArab li-annahum qālū 'al-malā'ikah banāt Allāh" (Ibn ʿAṭīyah on 2:116, 1.460). Others said that the phrase referred to all three mentioned here (see al-Zamakhsharī on 2:116, 1.180). Cf. the Latin note: "dicunt interpretes quod erant tres nationes, sectas dicere deberent, qui putassent deum habuisse filium, primo sunt christiani, secundo sunt iudei qui dicunt Eleazar [et] Esdram esse filios dei, tertio sunt Çeiles qui dixerunt angelos esse filios dei" (BA MS D 100 inf., fol. 20v). See also the note on 2:140: "ibidem dicunt quod Iudei et Christiani abscondiderunt nomen Machometi et delerunt illud e scripturis suis et hic est quod dicit 'abscondere testimonium'" (ibid., fol. 32v); cf., for example, al-Zamakhsharī on 2:140, 2.196.

35. For example, in a note on 2:196: "almarate significat uisitationem quam faciunt omnes ad templum Meche extra illud templum in mense de Heia" (BA MS D 100 inf., fol. 28v), *almarate* being the transliteration of *al-ʿumrah* (the "minor

Hajj," on which see "ʿumra," EI2 10:864–66 [art. R. Paret-E. Chaumont]; but Iohannes translated this term (*uisitatio*) in this verse.

36. For these views, see Ibn ʿAṭīyah on 2:104, 1.425–26, and al-Zamakhsharī on 2:104, 1.174.

37. "pro versu 102. dixit author annotationum illorum quod *rāʿinā* [in Arabic characters] quod scribit literis latinis hoc modo, rahine, est uox arabica et hebraica et in lingua arabica significat aspice nos et in hebraica, maledictionem, ac proinde quando Mauri dicebant Machometi rahine significabant salue et aliquid aliud: quando uero hebrae illud dicabant significabat deus te perdat, ac proinde inquit mandauit Machometus ut iudei non amplius proferrent uocem" (BA MS D 100 inf., fols. 40v–r). As will be obvious here, David Colville, the copyist of this manuscript, is drawing attention to the fact that he is copying notes written by someone else. In this case, he also quarrels with the note's contents, arguing that the Hebrew root in question does not mean what the note claims, and commenting that the author of the notes was "leniter uersatus in arabica ut iure dubitare possimus quantum uersatus fuerit in hebraica" (ibid., fol. 40r). Colville clearly does not understand that Iohannes Gabriel, the probable author of these notes, was following Muslim commentaries here.

38. See, for example, al-Ṭabarī on 2:55–56, 1.331.

39. "pro uersu 53. dicunt interpretes, quod erant septuaginta barones (ut loquitur glossa ea qua ista desumpsi) qui non credebant Moysi si non uiderent deum clare, quos fulmen descendens ex caelo interemit, sed postea Moyses precibus suis eos a mortuis resuscitauit; et de hac resuscitatione hic loquitur" (BA MS D 100 inf., fol. 5).

40. See above, note 18.

41. See, for example, Ibn ʿAṭīyah on 2:55, 1.299–301.

42. See, e.g., the note on 2:65 ("Be you monkeys, despised and rejected"). Here commentators explained that certain Israelites transgressed Sabbath law by fishing causing God eventually to curse them by turning them into monkeys. See al-Zamakhsharī on 2:65, 1.149; Ibn ʿAṭīyah on 2:65, 1.334–36. Cf. the Latin note: "pro uersu 62. dicunt interpretes quod quidam Iudei cuiusdam urbis quia piscati sunt in Sabbato, conuersi fuerunt in simias" (BA MS D 100 inf., fol. 40v).

43. The only other work that I know of that does this in the period this book covers is Ramon Martí's *De secta Machometi o de origine, progressu, et fine Machometi et quadruplici reprobatione prophetiae eius*, ed. and trans. into Spanish, Josep Hernando i Delgado, *Acta historica et archeologica medievalia* 4 (1983):9–51, on which see my *Religious Polemic*, 205–6 (where I refer to the work as *Quadruplex reprobatio*).

44. As in this comment, "maledic<tor>es exponunt iudaeos et errantes uocant christianos glossatores eorum Abuasis, Azamachxeri et Zewawi" (BA MS D 100 inf., fol. 5), in which the identity of the second "glossator" is clear enough—the great al-Zamakhsharī—but the identities of other two, *Abū ʿAzīz*, presumably, and *al-Zawāwī*, are uncertain. The same three seem to be cited together elsewhere: "pro uersu 138. dicunt tres interpretes illi quod . . ." (BA MS D 100 inf., 32v).

45. See, for example, the previous note.

46. See the notes on 2:215 [211] and 2:158 [155], ibid., fols. 28r, 32r.

47. *Al-Muḥarrar al-wajīz fī tafsīr al-kitāb al-ʿazīz.* For bibliographic information, see list of short titles under "Ibn ʿAṭīyah." Despite the regard that this commentary earned in the premodern world, it has received little attention from modern scholars. See Ḥajjī Khalīfah (Kātib Çelebi), *Kashf al-ẓunūn ʿān asāmī al-kutub wa-al-funūn*, ed. and trans. Gustav Fluegel as *Lexicon bibliographicum et encyclopaedicum a Mustafa ben Abdallah Katib Jelebi dicto et nomine Haji Khalifa celebrato compositum*, 7 vols. (Leipzig and London, 1835–58, rpt. New York and London, 1964) 5:421; Carl Brockelmann, *Geschichte der arabischen Literatur*, Supplementband 1 (Leiden, 1996), 732; Anwar G. Chejne, *Muslim Spain: Its History and Culture* (Minneapolis, 1974), 295; and İsmail Albayrak, "Isrāʾīliyyāt and Classical Exegetes' Comments on the Calf with a Hollow Sound Q.20:83–98/ 7:147–155 with Special Reference to Ibn ʿAṭiyya," *Journal of Semitic Studies* 47 (2002):39–65.

48. See, for example, notes 31 and 36.

49. See McAuliffe, *Qurʾānic Christians*, 53.

50. See, for example, the note on the meaning of the term *ṣibghah* (2:138), above, note 30.

51. "ibidem idem fecit obiectionem contra se: quomodo daemon potuerit tentare Adam in caelo ubi erat Paradisus, si iam daemon ejectus fuit e caelo, quia noluit ut, inquiunt illi, adorare Adam. Respondet more suo, quod daemon assumpsit os serpentis et sic decepit angelos custodes paradisi, et ingressus est et tentare potuit eos" (BA MS D 100 inf., fol. 5).

52. See McAuliffe, *Qurʾānic Christians*, 53.

53. "fa-in qulta 'kayfa tawaṣṣala ilá izlālihimā wa-waswasatihi la-humā baʿdamā qīla la-hu 'ikhraj minhā fa-innaka rajīm'? [al-Ḥijr 34] . . . wa-qīla: 'qāma ʿinda al-bāb fa-nādá, wa-ruwiya annahu arāda al-dukhūl fa-manaʿathu al-khazanah, fa-dakhala fī fam al-ḥayyah ḥattá dakhalat bi-hi wa-hum lā yashʿurūna' " (al-Zamakhsharī on 2:36, 1.131–32).

54. "dicit azamachxeri, quod sunt quidam uersus alcorani qui mutati fuerunt et penitus deleti ex alcorano, ut ille qui erat in cap. 6. lib. 3. in capite huius, in quo quidem uersu proscribebatur lapidare adulteros et adulteras" (BA MS D 100 inf., fol. 40r). This appears to be a reference to one or some of the several verses in surah 24 that related to adultery (vv. 2–11). See al-Zamakhsharī on 2:106, 1.175.

55. David Colville in BA MS D 100 inf., fol. 448v., though his tone is rather snide in this note which, of considerable interest for several reasons, is worth quoting in its entirety: "glossae istae iam per multa stadia [?] defecere hic iterum incipiunt in lib. 4. sed parum duratura, et lubentiss[im]o animo eas [?] scribo, quia in multis azoaris iam praeteritis, haerebam cum [?] non intelligabam, suspicabar latere aliquid mysterium, hic eodem modo haesitabam et legi commentarium istum quod illa explicabat quae non intelligabam, et laetabat me non intellexisse ea, quia non erant intellegibilia, et nunquam quidpiam transcripsi maiori gusto quam glossas istas, quibus intellexi me quae non intelligebam, intelligere et uere sapere cum putabam me non sapere." The beginning of book 4 is the Surah [38] of Ṣad, though referred to here as the Surah of David.

56. Bentley, *Humanists and Holy Writ*, 70–117; Pelikan with Hotchkiss and Price, *The Reformation of the Bible*, 20, 111–13; Hamilton, "Eastern Churches and Western Scholarship," 236.

57. See note 37 above.

58. See ibid.

59. "CIV. *Ne dicatis: Intuere nos*] Arabicè *rāʿinā* et *unẓurnā* (both in Arabic characters) idem ferè signficant, nempe: *respice nos*, vel *intuere nos*. Cur autem Mahumetus noluerit salutari à suis per *rāʿinā* sed per *unzhurnā*, ita explicat Gelal. (In Arabic characters:) Wa-kānū yaqūlūna la-hu dhālika wa-hiya bi-lughat al-Yahūd sabb min al-ruʿūnah fa-sarrū bi-dhālika wa-khāṭabū bi-hā al-nabī fa-nahá al-mu'minīn ʿanhā. *Salutabant eum hac uoce, quae in lingua Hebraica sonat Conuicium: irresoriè autem Judaie alloquebantur illa Mahumetum: quamobrem hic prohibuit suos asseclas ab usu illius*" (Ludovico Marracci, *Alcorani textus*, 2:44). As we have seen before, Marracci refers to al-Suyūṭī by his first name, "Gelal" (=*Jalāl*); he quotes him here with complete accuracy. See al-Suyūṭī, *Tafsīr*, on 2:104, p. 19.

60. Further examples: On 2:106: see above, note 54, and Marracci, *Alcorani textus*, 2:46–47; on 2:198: see above, note 32, and Marracci, *Alcorani textus*, 2:78a.

61. See Marracci, *Alcorani textus*, 1, passim.

62. "Otiosè omninò ponuntur tres illi characteres solitarii in principio hujus Surae . . . si eorum cognitio Deo tantùm reservatur, neque ab hominibus possunt intelligi" (Marracci, *Alcorani textus*, 2:13).

63. Ibid., 2:13–20. See also, for example, his refutations of surah 22, which contain a great deal of traditional polemic: "Omnia, quae Mahumetus praecipit suis circa Peregrinationem Meccanam, desumpta ferè sunt ab antiqua Ethnicorum Arabum superstitione. . . . Promittit Impostor suis asseclis Paradisum, qui consistit in hortis, fluminibus, vestibus sericis. . . . Certum est autem etiam apud veteres Philosophos, non posse in his bonis . . . veram hominum felicitatem sitam esse. . . . Turpiter sibi contradicit Impostor. Cùm enim superiùs semel dixit, Deum mittere legatos suos, non Angelos, sed homines: hìc oppositum affirmat" (ibid., 2:467–68).

64. David Colville, preface, in Löfgren and Traini, *Arabic Manuscripts*, 41.

65. "Correctiones autem illas edidit Iohannes Leo Granatinus" (ibid., 42).

66. On Leo Africanus, see Natalie Zemon Davis's recent *Trickster Travels*, passim. I thank Professor Davis for kindly allowing me to read this remarkable work in page proofs.

67. "Coranum, quod antea contrarium et oppositum aliquibis locis et in quibusdam totaliter obscurus (sic ad literam scriptum erat) extiterat, nunc autem . . . apertus est; ego uero totum posse meum in eius correctione imposui et quod possibile fuerat ad verbum traducere traduxi, et quod non fuerat possibile aliam pro alia dictione convenientiore commutavi" (David Colville, quoting Leo Africanus, in preface, Löfgren and Traini, *Arabic Manuscripts*, 43).

68. "qui [i.e., Leo Africanus] dicit se scripsisse ista anno 1525 Viterbii" (ibid., 43).

69. "Translationem Latinam tertiae columnae una cum emendationibus eodem modo transcribere coactus sum quo ibidem reperi" (ibid., 42).

70. Perhaps the notes as they stand in the Milan manuscript might be the result of Leo Africanus and Egidio da Viterbo himself, working together (see Bobzin, *Der Koran*, 87; id., "Latin Koran Translations," 201). A clearer idea of the relationship between the two sets of notes might be gained by a fuller analysis of them than I have been able to undertake here.

71. "declara eis sua nomina" in the Milan codex (BA MS D 100 inf., fol. 7r); "declara tu illis nomina eorum" in the Cambridge codex (Cambridge MS Mm. v. 26, fol. 4r). As I observed above in this chapter, the two manuscripts preserved two slightly different recensions of the same translation.

72. "nuncia scilicet angelis nomina eorum scilicet rerum" (BA MS D 100 inf., ibid.); "angelis scilicet omnium rerum" (Cambridge MS Mm. v. 26, ibid).

73. "quod uos scilicet angeli manifestatis et absconditis" (BA MS D 100 inf., ibid.); "angeli" (Cambridge MS Mm. v. 26, fol. 5r)

74. "scilicet Adam, Eva, demon" (BA MS D 100 inf. ibid.); "adam et eua et demon" (Cambridge MS Mm. v. 26, fol. 5r).

75. Al-Ṭabarī on 2:38, 1.284.

76. Ibn ʿAṭīyah on 2:38, 1.263: "wa-ukhtulifa fī al-maqṣūd bi-hādhā al-khiṭāb, fa-qīla Ādam, wa-Ḥawwā', wa-Iblīs wa-dhurrīyatihim." See also Ibn Kathīr on 2:38, 1.79.

77. See my "Cambridge University Library MS Mm. v. 26," 350–54.

78. Over the letters written in Roman script (*A. L. M.*), we have "alla, gibril, machoma" (BA MS D 100 inf., fol. 1v; see above, pp. 70–71).

79. See Lane, *Arabic-English Lexicon* 2.2594.

80. "fa-qāla baʿḍuhum: huwa nahr fī al-jannah" (al-Ṭabarī on 108:1, 12.716; see also Ibn ʿAṭīyah on 108:1, 15.584). Leo's note reads "id est flumen paradisi" (BA MS D 100 inf. fol. 606v). Further examples of notes only in the Milan manuscript are interlinear glosses at 1:7 ("those with whom God is angry and those who have gone astray," *maledictorum* and *errantium* in Iohannes' version): *id est judeorum* and *id est christianorum* (ibid., fol. 1v), these conforming to the Muslim exegesis (see note 28 above). Another gloss improves the translation of the latter: "illorum super quos iratus est <super eos>" (ibid.).

81. "qui uocabatur Abdaghir [?] qui factus est Maurus" (Cambridge MS Mm. v. 26, fol. 269rb).

82. See al-Ṭabarī on 46:10, 11.279, and Ibn Kathīr on 46:10, 4.158–59. A further example of a commentary-inspired note that only appears in the Cambridge manuscript: Iohannes's version of 46:27 reads, "Et destruximus ciuitates qui erant apud vos," this glossed as "Sodamam et alios" (ibid., fol. 279rb). Cf. "ka-ḥijr Thamūḍ wa-arḍ Sadhūm, wa-Ma'rib, wa-naḥwahā" (al-Ṭabarī on 46:27, 11.295; see also Ibn ʿAṭīyah on 46:27, 13.365). On the first city mentioned here, see F. S. Vidal, "al-ḥ*idj*r," EI2, 3:365–66; on the third, see W. W. Müller, "Mārib," EI2, 6:559–67 at 564–66.

83. This dating is suggested by the connection of the notes to William Tyndale, on which see below.

84. The lacunae are at 28r/29r, where we move from the the middle of verse 2:129 ("Mitte illis unum nuncium ex-") to the middle of 2:164 ("et in aquam quam deus defundere fecit"), and at 38r/39r, where we pass from 2:196 ("est satisfactio") to 2:230 ("invicem, si putauerunt seruare mandata dei").

85. Cambridge MS Mm. v. 26, fol. 8r.

86. At 2:85, Iohannes Gabriel's version confusingly reads, "et si uenient uobis captiui, redimitis illos, quod est prohibitum uobis" (Cambridge MS Mm. v. 26, fol.

17r). This annotator rightly inserts "ejicere eos" at the end, corresponding to the Qur'ān's *wa-huwa muḥarram ʿalaykum ikhrājuhum.*

87. Ibid., fol. 32r.

88. Ibid., fol. 8r.

89. Ibid., fol. 39r. Other examples: at 2:61 (*wa-ḍuribat ʿalayhim al-ḍillah wa-al-maskanah*; Iohannes's translation: "super quos uenit confusio et calamitas;" the correcting note: "et percussum est super eos" [ibid., fol. 11r]); at 2:85 (*anfusakum*; Iohannes wrote, "illi qui occidimini adinuicem"; the corrector: "illi qui occidimini animas vestras" [ibid., 17r]); at 2:174 (*yawm al-qiyāmah*; Iohannes's version: "dies iudicii"; the corrector's: "dies resurrectionis" [ibid., fol. 31r]).

90. He was also examining a second Arabic manuscript of the Qur'ān, as will become apparent below.

91. Ibid., fol. 7r. Other examples: at 2:58 (*ḥiṭṭatun* in Arabic next to Iohannes's commentary-inspired paraphrase ("aufer nostras culpas") of this Arabic term (ibid., fol. 9r); at 2:112 (*balá* in Arabic over "certe," *li-lāh* in Arabic [written with an extra lām] corresponding to "deo" in both Iohannes's version and the corrector's adjoining reformulation, and *salima* in Arabic, the first form of the verb which, in its fourth form, is used in this verse [ibid., fol. 24r]); sometimes the Arabic words appear in Roman script, as at 2:111 (*haud* over "Iudeus" and *Nasara* over "Christianus" [ibid.]).

92. Here Iohannes had written "et introiuit vetulas in corda eorum." The humanist reader gives a new verb in the singular rather than the plural, and changes the number of the object as well: "et imbiberunt vitulam in corda eorum." The Greek/Latin note appears just next to all this in the empty right column. His adjustments correspond closely with the Arabic, the main verb here being *ushribū* ("they were made to drink") and the object—*al-ʿijl* ("the cow")—being singular. See ibid., fol. 19r. For other uses of this expression, see ibid., fols. 11r, 12r, 14r, 19r, 20r, and 26r. I thank my learned friends Peter E. Pormann and Maura K. Lafferty for their assistance in deciphering and translating this and other Greek terms in these notes.

93. Ibid., fols. 24r–25r. He uses ἀντί in a similar way at 2:74 on 14r, on which note 95 below.

94. Ibid., fol. 22.

95. His "bibere fecit" for *istasqá* at 2:60 is quite incorrect, and Iohannes' "postulauit aquam" was just right (ibid., fol. 10r); at 2:74, where Iohannes had correctly written *Deus non ignorat quod facitis*, we have this misleading note: "et non est Deus in tegente (ἀντί non tectum ei est) ab eo quod facitis φράσις Arabicus," apparently misreading GhFL as QFL ("to lock, to close up"), though at 2:85 he read this verb quite rightly: "[non] est in ignorante . . ." (ibid., fols. 14r, 17r).

96. "*tattakhidhunā* f. d. *akhadha* forma *iftaʿala*" (ibid., fol. 12r). Another example at 2:178 discusses how a different pointing of a single letter of *takhfīf* ("lightening, mitigation, alleviation") makes for a very different word. The note observes that "alio libro sine punctu super *khā'*. hoc est constrictio." The resulting word, *taḥfīf*, can indeed mean something like "enclosing, encompassing, surrounding." It then offers a corresponding retranslation: "hoc est et haec est res [?] qua astrinxit Deus" (ibid., fol. 33r).

97. "hoc est Alcoranum" (ibid., fol. 19r). Ibn ʿAṭīyah (on 2:91, 1.394), for ex-

ample, pointed out that early interpreters had suggested that "what was after it" (*mā warā'ahu*) meant the Qur'ān (*ya'nī bi-hi al-Qur'ān*).

98. "aḍāfa dhunūbahum wa-ajrāmahum ilá al-aydin" (Ibn 'Aṭīyah on 2:95; 1.402). See also al-Ṭabarī on 2:95, 1.471–72.

99. Cambridge MS Mm. v. 26, fol. 20r.

100. "wa-ghayr [Allāh]: al-murād mā dhubiḥa lil-anṣāb wa-al-awthān" (Ibn 'Aṭīyah on 2:173, 2.70; see also al-Zamakhsharī on 2:173, 1.213).

101. Iohannes wrote, "quae fuerunt oblata idolis," which the annotator changed to "et in quo iubilato [?] in aliis quam Deo" (Cambridge MS Mm. v. 26, fol. 31r), this puzzling retranslation embodying the mistaken reading of HLL IV, which here means "to offer a sacrifice," as HLL II, which means "to rejoice, jubilate."

102. See Burman, "Cambridge University Library MS Mm. v. 26," 338.

103. On Tyndale's knowledge of Hebrew, see Gareth Lloyd-Jones, *The Discovery of Hebrew in Sixteenth-Century England: A Third Language* (Manchester, England, 1983), 116–23; for other evidence of his knowledge of Arabic, see David Daniell, ed., *Tyndale's Old Testament* (New Haven, Conn., 1992), xvi–xvii.

104. See Robert Wakefield, *Oratio de laudibus et utilitate trium linguarum Arabicae, Chaldaicae et Hebraicae*, in *On the Three Languages*, ed. and trans. Gareth Lloyd Jones (Binghamton, N.Y., 1989). On Wakefield, see most recently G. Lloyd Jones, "Robert Wakefield (d. 1537): The Father of English Hebraists?" in *Hebrew Study from Ezra to Ben-Yahuda*, ed. William Horbury (Edinburgh, 1999), 234–48. On the value of studying Arabic in this period, see Karl H. Dannenfeldt, "The Renaissance Humanists and the Study of Arabic," *Studies in the Renaissance* 2 (1955):96–117; Angelo Michele Piemontese, "Le iscrizioni arabe," 200–207; and my "Polemic, Philology, and Ambivalence," 186–87.

105. See above, Chapter 1.

106. For a brief discussion of the modern scholarship on this philological achievement, see Anthony Grafton, "Renaissance Readers and Ancient Texts," in his *Defenders of the Text: The Traditions of Scholarship in an Age of Science, 1450–1800* (Cambridge, Mass., 1991), 27.

107. Ibid., 33. See also Moss, *Ovid in Renaissance France*, 44–53, whose work Grafton ("Renaissance Readers," 31) rightly sees as fruitfully demonstrating the complexities of Renaissance reading.

108. See above, note 28.

109. See al-Ṭabarī on 1:1, 1.90; Ibn 'Aṭīyah on 1:1, 1.99.

110. Ibn 'Aṭīyah on 1:1, 1.102: "*al-'ālamin* jam' 'ālam wa-huwa kull mawjūd siwá Allāh . . . yuqālu li-jumlatihi 'ālam wa-li-ajzā'ihi min al-ins wa-al-jinn wa-ghayr dhālika 'ālam 'ālam." See also al-Ṭabarī on 1:1, 1.92.

111. See al-Ṭabarī on 1:5, 1.103–6; and Ibn 'Aṭīyah on 1:5, 1.120.

112. See Chapter 2, pp. 41–42 above.

113. BA MS D 100 inf., fol. 1v.

114. See Ibn 'Aṭīyah on 2:3, 1.145–46; and also al-Ṭabarī on 2:3, 1.133–34.

115. "al-maraḍ 'ibārah musta'ārah lil-fasād alladhī fī 'aqā'id ha'ulā'i al-munāfiqīn," Ibn 'Aṭīyah on 2:10, 1.164–65; see also al-Ṭabarī on 2:10, 1.154–55.

116. See al-Ṭabarī on 2:19, 1.184–88; and Ibn 'Aṭīyah on 2:19, 1.190–92.

117. See al-Zamakhsharī on 2:26, 1.120–21; Ibn ʿAṭīyah on 2:26, 1.215; al-Ṭabarī on 2:26, 1.216–17.

118. BA MS D 100 inf., fol. 4v.

119. See above, Chapter 2, notes 100–101.

120. D 100 inf., fol. 5.

121. See above in this chapter. On God teaching Adam the properties of things, see al-Ṭabarī on 2:33, 1.258–59; al-Ṭabarsī on 2:33, 1.76–77.

122. See Daniel, *Islam and the West*, 67–88, 145–50.

123. "pro uersu 113" [2:115], BA MS D 100 inf., fol. 20r; "pro uersu 139" [2:141], ibid., fol. 32v; "pro uersu 142" [2:144], ibid., fol. 32v.

124. "pro uersu 119" [2:21], ibid., fol. 20r; "pro uersu 138" [2:140], ibid., fol. 32v; "pro uersu 144" [2:146], ibid., fol. 32r.

125. "pro uersu 190" [2:193], ibid., fol. 28v; "pro uersu 211" [2:215], ibid., fol. 28r; "pro uersu 150" [2:153], ibid., fol. 32r.

126. "pro uersu 155" [2:158], ibid., fol. 30r.

127. "pro uersu 100" [2:102], ibid., fol. 40v.

128. "pro uersu 104" [2:106], ibid., fol. 40r.

129. See Daniel, *Islam and the West*, passim.

Conclusion

1. The former event inspired Riccoldo da Monte di Croce's remarkable *Epistolae V de perditione Acconis, 1291*, ed. R. Röhricht, *Archives de l'orient latin* 2 (1884):258–96 (on which, see most recently Tolan, *Saracens*, 245–47), while the latter inspired a host of despondent reactions in the West (on these, see Nancy Bisaha, *Creating East and West: Renaissance Humanists and the Ottoman Turks* [Philadelphia, 2004], 62–69, 127–29).

2. Darío Cabanelas Rodríguez described his efforts as a "verdadera cadena de titánicos esfuerzos." See his *Juan de Segovia y el problema islámico* (Madrid, 1952), 129; see also 155.

3. For the most thorough and recent account of Juan's life, see Anne Marie Wolf, "Juan de Segovia and Western Perspectives on Islam in the Fifteenth Century," Ph.D. dissertation (University of Minnesota, 2003). On his family background, see ibid., 10–34.

4. Ibid., 59.

5. Ibid., 137–38.

6. On these, see ibid., 111. See also Gerard Wiegers, *Islamic Literature in Spanish and Aljamiado: Yça of Segovia (fl. 1450), His Antecedents and Successors* (Leiden, 1994), 69.

7. Cabanelas, *Juan de Segovia y el problema islámico*, 100–107; Wolf, "Juan de Segovia," 129–34.

8. Wolf, "Juan de Segovia," 181; Wiegers, *Islamic Literature*, 70–71.

9. Wolf, "Juan de Segovia," 188.

10. See R. W. Southern, *Western Views of Islam in the Middle Ages* (Cambridge, Mass., 1962), 86–94, 98–103.

11. See Jesse Mann, "Truth and Consequences: Juan de Segovia on Islam and Christianity," *Medieval Encounters* 8 (2002):79–90 at 84–85; and Wolf, "Juan de Segovia," 119, 188–97.

12. See Wolf, "Juan de Segovia," 204–9, 211–19.

13. His plan is described at great length by Cabanelas, *Juan de Segovia*, 108–27, but see recently Wolf, "Juan de Segovia," 226–31.

14. Mann, "Truth and Consequences," 86, 89; see also Wolf, "Juan de Segovia," 226n175 for his use of the word *contraferentia*.

15. Nicholas Cusanus, *Cribratio alkorani*, ed. Ludwig Hagemann [Nicolai de cusa opera omnia, iussu et auctoritate academiae litterarum Heidelbergensis, 9] (Hamburg, 1986).

16. This is Bernkastel-Kues, Hospital zu Cues, MS 108, on which, see J. Marx, *Verzeichnis der Handschriften-Sammlung des Hospitals zu Cues bei Bernkastel a./Mosel* (Trier, 1905), 107–8; James E. Biechler, "Three Manuscripts on Islam from the Library of Nicholas of Cusa," *Manuscripta* 27 (1983):91–100; and id., "Nicholas of Cusa and Muhammad: A Fifteenth-Century Encounter," *The Downside Review* 101 (1983):50–59.

17. Wolf speaks of "Juan's propensity for long-windedness" and describes him as "never one for brevity." See her "Juan de Segovia," 132, 174–75.

18. Wiegers has argued in his *Islamic Literature*, 112–14, that a manuscript in the Municipal Library of Toledo (MS 235) contains Iça's Castilian translation by itself, but see Consuelo López-Morillas's very cogently expressed doubts about this attribution in her "Lost and Found?"

19. These are the twin concerns of the preface: "Expositio autem . . . notificat in quibus prima [translatio] deficeret, et quod translatio hec conformis omnino sit substantie stiloque arabici ydeomatis" (Juan de Segovia, "Prefatio . . . in translationem," ll. 12–14). On this prologue, see most recently Martínez's introduction in his edition of it in Martínez, "El prólogo de Juan de Segobia," and id., "Las traducciones latinas medievales del Corán," 498–502.

20. Juan de Segovia, "Prefatio . . . in translationem," ll. 104–8.

21. Bentley, *Humanists and Holy Writ*, 8.

22. "Desiderium quoque translatoris prefati minime adimpletum esse dignoscitur, libro ipso Alchurani parum et omnino fere non deducto in communem christianorum notionem" (Juan de Segovia, "Prefatio . . . in translationem," ll. 160–62).

23. "Sed de hoc certissimum perhibere queo testimonium, translationem predictam in quam plurimis deviare a textus Arabici continentia" (ibid., ll. 168–70).

24. "Quo uero amplius inspiciebam prefate translationis stilum procedendique modum et ordinem ac substantialia libri, eo magis suspicio se ingerebat non esse ueram, quod ipse agnoui accepto ex Hyspania testimonio, uisis ibidem certis, quas mandaueram, Alchurani membranas [*sic*]" (ibid., ll. 218–21).

25. On Iça's background, collaboration with Juan, and other achievements, see Cabanelas, *Juan de Segovia*, 145–53; Wolf, "Juan de Segovia," 97–98, 107–9; L. P. Harvey, *Islamic Spain, 1250–1500* (Chicago, 1990), 78–97; and Wiegers, *Islamic Literature*, 71, 142–50, and passim. It is Wiegers who has intriguingly argued that Iça may have been a member of the al-Shādhilī order, this term being the source, perhaps, of the name "Gidelli" by which he was often known. See Wiegers, *Islamic Literature*,

145. On the learned culture of Mudejars in fifteenth-century Iberia, see especially Kathryn Miller's fascinating forthcoming study, *Guardians of Islam.*

26. Juan de Segovia, "Prefatio . . . in translationem," ll. 240–45.

27. "Utque translationem facere posset, secum adduxit suorum libros doctorum Alchuranum exponentes" (ibid., ll. 275–76). For an intriguing reflection on the broader significance of the collaboration of Juan and Iça for the history of Christian-Muslim relations, see Leyla Rouhi's recent "A Fifteenth-Century Salamancan's Pursuit of Islamic Studies," in *Under the Influence: Questioning the Comparative in Medieval Castile*, ed. Cynthia Robinson and Leyla Rouhi (Leiden, 2005), 21–42.

28. On this sort of two-handed translation, see especially Marie-Thérèse d'Alverny, "Les traductions à deux interprètes."

29. "Unde oportuit . . . uni intendere cure, quatenus magister ipse, opus . . . impleret, translationem facturus libri Alchurani Arabico ydeomati et textui conformem, absque glosis, limitationibus, expositionibus quoque insertis textui, sed et quasdam breues certe admodum rarasque in marginibus addidit pro quorumdam uocabulorum annotatione" (Juan de Segovia, "Prefatio . . . in translationem," ll. 246–51). On this passage, see also Martínez, "Las traducciones latinas medievales del Corán," 502. Both Wiegers and López-Morillas take "absque" here to mean "apart from," a translation that I think unlikely in medieval Latin in the first place, but which is made even less plausible by the presence of the adversative "sed" which begins the following clause: "without" strikes me as making far better sense of the whole passage. As is apparent from my translation, furthermore, I fully share López-Morillas's serious reservations (see her "Lost and Found?" 282–83) about Wiegers's translation of "limitationibus" in this passage as "slashes separating the glosses from the translated text" (see Wiegers, *Islamic Literature*, 112). That Iça also understood his job in this way can be seen in comments he made in a letter to Juan just before he left Spain. See Cabanelas's edition in his *Juan de Segovia*, 273.

30. "Interpretatus est in vulgari Hyspanico, translationem etiam ipsam propria describens manu" (Juan de Segovia, "Prefatio . . . in translationem," ll. 270–71).

31. Ibid., ll. 252–55.

32. Ibid., ll. 285–86.

33. "uelut sillabicando legere incipiebam, agnitis literis, nec tamen signis aut caracteribus omnibus accentum tantumue significantibus uel in alium sensum trahentibus dictiones" (ibid., ll. 309–12).

34. Ibid., ll. 257–63. The Arabic alphabet actually contains twenty-eight letters, so Juan may be including one of the many other signs that are used in Arabic writing, or we may have a scribal error here.

35. Ibid., ll. 471–75, 485–92.

36. "Est preterea in Alchurano decurtatus ualde loquendi modus, nominatiuis et ablatiuis absolutis positis . . ." (ibid., ll. 507–8).

37. Juan's discussion of Arabic vowels is misleading as well. He seems to have assumed that Arabic necessarily had to have five vowels, just as Latin does, so he points out that three of the vowels, "a," "i," and "u," are indicated by small marks (*titellis*) over the adjoining consonants. This is all quite correct. But he then explains that "o" is indicated by doubling the mark used for "u," while "e" is designated by

marks in black or red (see ll. 252–68). The former describes the marking for the indefinite nominative ending "-un," while the latter could describe a number of different signs used to mark vowels or other aspects of the text. He has clearly not understood entirely either the Arabic vowel system or the orthographic conventions for marking vowels in Qur'an manuscripts.

38. Ibid., ll. 265–68. On one Arabic MS of the Qur'ān that Juan is known to have used (Basel Universitätsbibliothek, MS A III 19), see Bobzin, *Der Koran*, 239–50.

39. "et huiusmodi casuum designationes reperi attentius obseruatas in uno libro Alchurani empto michi antiquissimo certe et, ut dicitur, in regno scriptum Granate, quam in nouo penes me edito" (Juan de Segovia, "Prefatio . . . in translationem," ll. 475–77).

40. Ibid., ll. 361–63.

41. "psalmorum singulus pauciores continet versus, ita ut ex ultimis psalmis, qui VI, qui V, qui IV contineat; ex prioribus (primo excepto qui sat paruus est reputatur oratio substantialis omnium aliorum . . .), alii psalmi sunt in uersibus abundantes, secundo CCLXXXV continente, tertio CC . . ." (ibid., ll. 373–78).

42. Ibid., ll. 367–69.

43. "Et sunt duo nominata loca, Tribola . . . et Meca, domus ab eis reputata sanctorum sancta" (ibid., ll. 383–85).

44. ". . . sed primum psalmi materia [*sic*] de qua tractat ab eis reputatam principalem" (ibid., ll. 378–80).

45. "Sciatis quod vester alumpnus fecit me intelligere vestrum bonum desiderium sciendi et fundandi omnia et specialiter unum Alchoranum interpretatum in Romancio . . . sine accidente ullo et si possibile foret post conversum in Romancium habere gratiam sciendi a suo Romanciatore intenciones et declarationes cualibet [*sic*] textuum eius" (Iça Gedilli to Juan de Segovia, 24 April 1454, in Wiegers, *Islamic Literature*, 230–32). On this letter, written originally in Arabic, and Juan's dual charge, see ibid., 75, 101.

46. "Quo tempore, ille . . . permultum laborauit quatenus literas discerem arabicas. Summarium etiam intelligentie super quolibet psalmorum Alchurani, quod Yspanie pro me inchoauerat, hic completum communicauit. Similiter et articulos XIII fidei mahumetice, rationibus, iuxta intellectum ipsorum, ad illorum probationem exaratis habunde. Et quod singularissimum arbitror . . . in scriptura translationis per eum facte designauit CCXXVII articulos revocatos, quasi aliis uersibus Alchurani detrahentes ac repugnantes; uitam quoque et genealogiam Mahumeti . . . scripsit . . . Sed et magno rogatu meo, causas quare dictorum versuum fieret revocatio . . . [explanauit]" (Juan de Segovia, "Prefatio . . . in translationem," ll. 285–96). On the nature and authorship (whether by Iça or others) of these various and largely nonextant treatises, see Wiegers, *Islamic Literature*, 75–76, 92–99, 114. Juan was carefully studying at least the first two works soon after. See ibid., 73.

47. See above, note 27.

48. Iça explicitly pointed out elsewhere that he translated the Qur'an into Castilian "with the *tafsīr* [i.e., commentary] in front of him" ("tiniendo el atasçir delante"). See his prologue to his later Castilian treatise on Islamic law, *Brevario sunni*, in Wiegers, *Islamic Literature*, 236–39 at 237 (see also 106). Harvey has co-

gently argued that the first part of this prologue, including the cited passage, must originally have been a separate preface to Iça's Castilian Qur'an translation which later was mistakenly affixed to the preface of the legal work in question. See Harvey, *Islamic Spain*, 83. "Vidi preterea quod multos haberet libros scriptos absque uocalibus et presertim doctores suos, quos dicebat Alchurani expositores, et quos, ubi putabat dubitare, inspiciebat" (Juan de Segovia, "Prefatio . . . in translationem," ll. 498–500).

49. "quoniam in quam multis passibus, uelut commentans, sensum explicat Sarracenorum, uix ex arabicis literis aperientem, quem sensum magister ille fatebatur" (ibid., ll. 426–28).

50. Juan and Iça remained in contact, however, carrying on discussions by correspondence. See Wolf, "Juan de Segovia," 185–86, and Wiegers, *Islamic Literature*, 74–75.

51. Juan de Segovia, "Prefatio . . . in translationem," ll. 279–84. See also Cabanelas, *Juan de Segovia*, 142–45, 153.

52. Juan de Segovia, "Prefatio . . . in translationem," ll. 343–48.

53. L. P. Harvey has rightly observed that Juan's goal in his Latin translation was to create "a close linguistic calque" of the Arabic version of the Qur'an. See Harvey, *Islamic Spain*, 83.

54. Juan de Segovia, "Prefatio . . . in translationem," ll. 442–43.

55. "Arabicum magis quam Hyspanum seruare uolui loquendi modum" (ibid., ll. 469–70). On this passage, see also Martínez, "Las traducciones latinas medievales del Coran," 502.

56. "quod apud Latinos uerbum deponens commune est uel neutrum aut neutropassiuum, prout Arabicum exprimebat ydeoma, in uerbum conuertans actiuum; et pro datiuo ponens accusatiuum" (Juan de Segovia, "Prefatio . . . in translationem," ll. 446–49).

57. "Utitur preterea, ubi de suitate mentionem facit . . . adiectiuo pluralis, singularis numeri substantiuo sistente, pro quo a principio, ut incongruitatem uitarem, utebar pronomine alio, dicendo *ipsorum* uel *eorum* quandoque etiam suitate in plurali expressa. At quando fixe intuitus sum differentiam Arabice locutionis, crebro magis pronomine *suus, sua, suum* quam aliis utentis, duobus ut pluralis designaretur numerus adieci, dicendo *sussuus*, et sic in aliis casibus, ita ubi duplicatur indicat plurale esse in ydeomate Arabico" (ibid., ll. 453–60).

58. "Aliis etiam aut nouitatibus aut incongruitatibus usus fui, latina uerba, quamuis alia suppeterent, iuxta hyspanum ydeoma componens, propterea quod reperi in Alchurano multa uocabula que pro uulgari habet Hyspanum ydeoma; occupauerunt namque diu magnam Hyspanie partem, et assuetudine ydeoma coalescit" (ibid., ll. 461–65).

59. This apt description is by G. M. Wickens in his *Arabic Grammar: A First Workbook* (Cambridge, England, 1980), 45.

60. "Interpres igitur ille, ut intelligibilem magis suum laborem redderet, uerba addidit substantiua nominatiuis absolute positis . . . quoniam ydeoma Hyspanum . . . hiis non utitur absolutis, quod etiam ab initio seruaui ego; sed in processu malui Latinam interpretationem Arabico quam Hyspano loquendi modo fieri conformem, positis nominatiuis absolutis quoque absque uerbo" (Juan de Segovia,

"Prefatio . . . in translationem," ll. 513–18). I have read "substantiua" where the edition has "substantiam."

61. "mimime dubitaui uerberare Priscianum, admodum incongrua persepe usus Latinitate" (ibid., ll. 444–45).

62. Harvey, *Islamic Spain*, 84.

63. There are four brief quotations of the Qurʾān in Latin quoted and discussed by Wiegers in his *Islamic Literature*, 112–14, including two in the preface to the trilingual Qurʾān (verses 8:65–66, 2:279, ll. 76–80). In the inventory of books that Juan gave to the University of Salamanca, for example, he quotes the incipit of his Latin Qurʾān: "et illis qui credunt cum eo quod misi tibi" (2:4). Here he translates the Arabic *bi-*, normally meaning "with," as *cum*, which also normally means "with," even though in this case *bi-* really should be translated *in*—a case, then, of making his Latin conform to "the Arabic way of speaking."

64. Juan de Segovia, "Prefatio . . . in translationem," ll. 277–84.

65. Ibid., ll. 277–84, 538–41.

66. Ibid., ll. 541–42. See also Martínez, "Las traducciones latinas medievales del Corán," 502.

67. We know he did so because the document recording the donation of his books to the University of Salamanca describes the manuscript thoroughly. See Wiegers, *Islamic Literature*, 98–99, and 72–73, esp. n. 13, where he quotes in its entirety the relevant passage, and see also Benigno Hernández Montes, *Biblioteca de Juan de Segovia: Edición y comentario de su escritura de donación* (Madrid, 1984), 107–8, 285–87.

68. "ut per illud trium peritis linguarum innotescat quid secta Mahamudonis contineat, tenore monstrante suo quam facile Christiani docti Sarracenos ex secta sua conuincere ualeant et quam illis compatiendum sit pereuntibus ignorantia, inscientia cecitateue" (Juan de Segovia, "Prefatio . . . in translationem," ll. 541–45).

69. See Dahan, *L'exégèse chrétienne*, 31, 38, 73.

70. See above, Chapter 3, notes 66–71, and Chapter 4, notes 184–87.

71. See above, Chapter 4, note 61.

72. See above, Chapter 6, notes 7–9.

73. See above, Chapter 5, notes 54–58.

74. See above, Chapter 4, notes 77 and ff.

75. The most notable of such manuscripts were those of Egidio da Viterbo's 1518 bilingual Qur'an, though, as we have seen, this did not necessarily mean that this edition did not perhaps contain veiled polemical preoccupations as well. See above, Chapter 6. See also, on certain nearly "frameless" manuscripts of Mark of Toledo's Latin Qur'an, above, Chapter 5, notes 42–46 and ff.

76. On these readers, see above, Chapter 4, notes 11–15, 216, and ff.

77. See Bobzin, *Der Koran*, v–vi, 296.

78. See above, Chapter 4, notes 138, 142–58.

79. Chartier, *The Order of Books*, vii–xi; see also Jean-François Gilmont, "Protestant Reformations and Reading," in *A History of Reading in the West*, ed. Cavallo and Chartier, 232–33; and Anthony Grafton, "The Humanist as Reader," 205–6.

80. See Chapter 4, notes 17–28 and ff.

81. See above, Chapter 4, notes 129–58.

82. Other scholars have also observed this. See Richard and Mary Rouse, "*Statim invenire*," 212; Gilmont, "Protestant Reformations and Reading," 228.

83. For interesting reflections on how the concerns of other translators—this time Greek-to-Arabic and Syriac-to-Arabic scientific translators in the early Middle Ages—likewise gradually grew far beyond what was strictly practical, see Goodman, "The Translation of Greek Materials into Arabic," 482–83, 490.

84. Benjamin A. Elman, *From Philosophy to Philology: Intellectual and Social Aspects of Change in Late Imperial China*, 2nd ed., rev. (Los Angeles, 2001), 69.

85. This is not particularly unusual. Anthony Grafton has argued that along with the needs of pedagogy and prosody, polemic is one of the "great stimulators of historical research" (see his "Renaissance Readers and Ancient Texts," in his *Defenders of the Text*, 42). See also Robert Schwoebel's discussion of how the needs for accurate information about the Turks to ensure effective military campaigns against them led the French king to transform "the Burgundian court into a seminar for Turkish studies" in Schwoebel, *The Shadow of the Crescent: The Renaissance Image of the Turk (1453–1517)* (Nieuwkoop, 1967), 98.

86. Glick, "My Master, the Jew," 158–61, 166–68, 173, 181.

87. Paris, BnF MS lat. 3669, fol. 18r, rm.

88. See above, Chapter 3, notes 11, 12.

89. See above, Chapter 6, note 55.

90. See, for example, Dannenfeldt, "The Renaissance Humanists and the Study of Arabic," 106–8, and Alastair Hamilton, *William Bedwell, the Arabist (1563–1632)* (Leiden, 1985), 8, 31, 71.

91. The earliest such Arabic copy of the Qur'ān that I know of is Paris, BnF ar. 384, copied in Egypt or Syria and containing abundant Latin marginalia from the late thirteenth or early fourteenth centuries. For bibliography on it, see above, Chapter 4, note 36.

92. See above, Chapter 6, notes 83 and ff.

93. Anthony Grafton, "In No Man's Land" [review of Adam Sutcliffe, *Judaism and Enlightenment* (Cambridge, England, 2003) and Maurice Olender, *The Languages of Paradise: Aryans and Semites, a Match Made in Heaven*, trans. Arthur Goldhammer (New York, 2003)], *The New York Review of Books* 51.3 (February 26, 2004):34–37 at 34.

94. See above, Chapter 5, notes 91–92; Chapter 4, notes 145–50; Chapter 1, note 35.

95. Angelo Michele Piemontese, "Il Corano latino," 231–32, 235, and Victor Segesvary, *L'Islam et la Réforme*, 27, 57–60, 92, for example, stress the innovativeness of Renaissance humanist Qur'ān scholarship in Europe, the latter quoting with approval Renan's view that "le Moyen Âge a eu des philosophes, des savants, des poètes, mais n'a pas eu des philologues" (27; see Ernst Renan, *L'avenir de la science* [Paris, 1890], 138–39, 141). Edward Said, on the other hand, asserted that it was only in the eighteenth century that Europeans finally began "to let Muslim commentators on the [Qur'ān] speak for themselves" (see Said, *Orientalism* [London and New York, 1978], 117).

96. See Daniel, *Islam and the West*, 321–22.

97. This gradual emergence of modern scholarly approaches to studying the Qur'ān might be seen as paralleling the gradual emergence of modern Western attitudes toward Islam that Nancy Bisaha has argued for in her recent *Creating East and West.* She emphasizes that Renaissance humanists, while turning to new classical sources that provided some new models for understanding Islam, nevertheless frequently perpetuated medieval conceptions of Islam. See, for example, 13–14, 79–80, 135.

98. Ibid., 25–30.

Appendix

1. Apprantly a transliteration of "sa'īr" = "fire, hell."

2. Note that Leo Africanus corrects this to "ut non," which makes more sense and conforms better to the Arabic.

Selected Bibliography

Primary Sources in Latin and Other Western Languages

Anonymous. *Alcorán: Traducción castellana de un morisco anónimo del año 1606*. Ed. Lluís Roqué Figuls with introduction by Joan Vernet Ginés. Barcelona, 2001.

———. Twelfth-century annotations on Robert of Ketton's *Lex Mahumet*. Paris, BnF, MS Arsenal 1162, fols. 26–140 and several other manuscripts.

———. *Collectiones aliquot ex alcorano turcarum fide* [extracts from Bibliander's edition of Robert of Ketton's Qur'an translation, c. 1550–60]. Güssing, Franziskanerkloster, MS 1/35.

———. *Compendium Alcorani* [a minimally revised version of the *Tabula* presented as an abridgment of Robert of Ketton's Qur'ān translation, late fifteenth or early sixteenth century]. Paris, BnF MS 3671, fols. 28v–65r, and four other manuscripts.

———. *Tabula* [analytical table of contents for Robert of Ketton's Qur'ān translation, late fifteenth or early sixteenth century]. Dresden, Sächsiche Landesbibliothek, MS 120b, fols. 37r–73r.

Bibliander, Theodore, ed. *Machumetis Saracenorum principis, eiusque successorum vitae, doctrina ac ipse Alcoran . . .* Basel, 1543.

———, ed. *Machumetis Saracenorum principis, eiusque successorum vitae, doctrina ac ipse Alcoran . . .* Basel, 1550.

Colville, David. Prefatory note to his manuscript copy of Iohannes Gabriel Terrolensis's translation of the Qur'ān transcribed in *Catalogue of the Arabic Manuscripts in the Biblioteca Ambrosiana*, ed. Oscar Löfgren and Renato Traini. 2 vols. Vicenza, 1975, vol. 1, 41–43.

Dominicus Germanus de Silesia. *Interpretatio literalis Alcorani* [mid-seventeenth-century edition and Latin translation of the Qur'ān]. El Escorial, Real Biblioteca de El Escorial, MS ar. 1624.

Iohannes Gabriel Terrolensis. *Alcoranus* [Latin translation and edition of the Qur'ān completed under Egidio da Viterbo's auspices, 1518]. Milan, BA, MS D 100 inf.; Cambridge, Cambridge University Library, MS Mm. v. 26.

Juan de Segovia. "Prefatio . . . in translationem nouiter editam ex Arabico in Latinum uulgareque Hyspanum libri Alchorani." In Martínez Gázquez, "El prólogo de Juan de Segobia," 389–410.

Mark of Toledo, trans. *Liber Alchorani* [Latin translation of the Qur'ān (c. 1210–11)]. Turin, Biblioteca Nazionale Universitaria, MS F. v. 35 and other manuscripts.

———. "Préface à la traduction du Coran." In d'Alverny and Vajda, "Marc de Tolède, traducteur d'Ibn Tūmart," 260–68.

Marracci, Ludovico. *Alcorani textus universus . . . his omnibus praemissus est Prodromus*. Padua, 1698.

Mithridates, Flavius. Edition and translation of surahs 21 and 22 (c. 1480–81). Vatican City, BAV MS urb. lat. 1384, fols. 65–88, and other manuscripts.

Robert of Ketton, trans. *Lex Mahumet pseudo-prophete que arabice Alchoran, id est, collectio preceptorum vocatur* [Latin translation of the Qur'ān, 1142–43]. Paris, BnF, MS Arsenal 1162, fols. 26–140 and many other manuscripts. Published by Bibliander in his two editions of *Machumetis Saracenorum principis, eiusque successorum vitae, doctrina ac ipse Alcoran*, 8–189.

———. "Praefatio Roberti tractatoris ad Dominum Petrum Cluniacensem Abbatem in Libro legis sarracenorum quem Alchoran vocant." Ed. David Howlett. In Howlett, *Insular Inscriptions*. Dublin, 2003, 168–75.

Widmanstetter, Johann Albrecht von, ed. *Mahometis Abdallae filii theologia dialogo explicata Hermanno Nellingaunense interprete: Alcorani epitome, Roberto Ketense anglo interprete . . .* Nuremberg, 1543.

Primary Sources in Arabic

Al-Bayḍāwī, ʿAbd Allāh ibn ʿUmar. *Anwār al-tanzīl wa-asrār al-ta'wīl*. In *Beidhawii commentarius in Coranum*, ed. H. O. Fleischer. 2 vols. Osnabrück, 1968 [reprint of Leipzig edition of 1846–48].

Ibn ʿAṭīyah al-Andalusī, Abū Muḥammad ʿAbd al-Ḥaqq. *Al-Muḥarrar al-wajīz fī tafsīr al-kitāb al-ʿazīz*. Ed. al-Raḥḥālī al-Fārūq et al. 15 vols. Doha, 1977–91.

Ibn Kathīr, Abū al-Fidā' Ismā'īl. *Tafsīr al-Qur'ān al-ʿAẓīm*. 4 vols. Beirut, 1990.

Al-Qurṭubī, Abū ʿAbd Allāh Muḥammad ibn Aḥmad al-Anṣārī. *Al-Jāmiʿ li-aḥkām al-Qur'ān*. 21 vols. in 11. Beirut, 1993.

Al-Suyūṭī, Jalāl al-Dīn ʿAbd al-Raḥmān ibn Abū Bakr. *Al-Itqān fī ʿulūm al-Qur'ān*. Beirut, n.d.

———. *Tafsīr al-Qur'ān al-Karīm* [his continuation of Jalāl al-Dīn Muḥammad ibn Aḥmad al-Muḥallī's *Tafsīr al-Qur'ān al-Karīm*]. Cairo, 1966.

Al-Ṭabarī, Abū Jaʿfar Muḥammad ibn Jarīr. *Jāmiʿ al-bayān ʿfī ta'wīl āy al-Qur'ān*. 12 vols. Beirut, 1997.

Al-Ṭabarsī, Abū ʿAlī al-Faḍl ibn al-Ḥasan. *Majmaʿ al-bayān fī tafsīr al-Qur'ān*. 5 vols. Qum, 1983.

Al-Zamakhsharī, Abū al-Qāsim Jār Allāh Maḥmūd ibn ʿUmar. *Al-Kashshāf ʿan ḥaqā'iq ghawāmiḍ al-tanzīl wa-ʿuyūn al-aqāwīl fī wujūh al-ta'wīl*. Ed. Muḥammad ʿAbd al-Salām Shāhīn. 4 vols. Beirut, 1995.

Secondary Literature

Abel, Armand. "L'Apologie d'Al-Kindi et sa place dans la polémique Islamo-chrétienne." In *Atti del convegno internazionale sul tema L'Oriente cristiana nella storia della civiltà: Roma 31 marzo–3 aprile 1963, Firenze 4 aprile 1963*, 501–23. Rome, 1964.

Adang, Camilla. *Muslim Writers on Judaism and the Hebrew Bible: From Ibn Rabban to Ibn Hazm*. Leiden, 1996.

Alexander, Jonathan J. G. *Italian Renaissance Illuminations*. New York, 1977.

———. "Patrons, Libraries and Illuminators in the Italian Renaissance." In Alexander, *The Painted Page: Italian Renaissance Book Illumination, 1450–1550*, 11–20.

Alexander, Jonathan J. G., ed. *The Painted Page: Italian Renaissance Book Illumination, 1440–1550*. London and Munich, 1994.

Alexander, Jonathan J. G. and A. C. de la Mare. *The Italian Manuscripts in the Library of Major J. R. Abbey*. London, 1969.

D'Alverny, Marie-Thérèse. "La connaissance de l'Islam en Occident du IXe au milieu du XIIe siècle." In *L'occidente e l'Islam nell'alto medioevo*. Vol. 2: *Settimane di studio del Centro italiano di studi sull'alto mediovo* 12. Spoleto, 1965, 577–602.

———. "Deux traductions latines du Coran au Moyen Âge." *Archives d'histoire doctrinale et littéraire du Moyen Âge* 22–23 (1947–48):69–131.

———. "Marc de Tolède." In *Estudios sobre Alfonso VI y la reconquista de Toledo: Actas del II Congreso Internacional de Estudios Mozárabes (Toledo, 20–26 Mayo 1985)*. Vol. 3. Toledo, 1992, 25–59.

———. "Quelques manuscrits de la «Collectio Toletana»." In *Petrus Venerabilis, 1156–1956: Studies and Texts Commemorating the Eighth Centenary of His Death*, Studia Anselmia 40, ed. Giles Constable and James Kritzeck. Rome, 1956, 202–18.

———. "Les traductions à deux interprètes, d'arabe en langue vernaculaire et de langue vernaculaire en latin." In *Traduction et traducteur au Moyen Âge: Actes du colloque international du CNRS organisé à Paris, Institut de recherche et d'histoire des textes, les 26–28 mai 1986*, ed. Geneviève Contamine. Paris, 1989, 193–206. [Reprinted in ead., *La transmission des textes philosophiques et scientifiques au moyen âge*, ed. Charles S. F. Burnett. Aldershot, England and Brookfield, Vt., 1994.]

———. "Translations and Translators," In Benson and Constable, *Renaissance and Renewal in the Twelfth Century*, 421–62.

D'Alverny, Marie-Thérèse, and Georges Vajda. "Marc de Tolède, traducteur d'Ibn Tūmart." *Al-Andalus* 16 (1951):99–140, 259–307, and 17 (1952):1–56.

Anonymous. "Inventaire des manuscrits latins de Saint-Victor conservés à la Bibliothèque Impériale sous les numéros 14232–15175." *Bibliothèque de l'École des Chartes* 6th series, 5 (1869): 1–79.

———. *World Bibliography of Translations of the Holy Qur'ān in Manuscript Form*. Istanbul, 2000.

Antolín, Guillermo. *Catálogo de los códices latinos de la Real Biblioteca del Escorial*. 5 vols. Madrid, 1910–23.

Balagna, Josée. *L'imprimerie arabe en Occident: XVe, XVIIe, XVIIIe siècles*. Paris, 1984.

Barceló, Miquel, and José Martínez Gázquez, eds. *Musulmanes y cristianos en Hispania durante las conquistas de los siglos XII y XIII*. Barcelona, 2005.

Baswell, Christopher. *Virgil in Medieval England: Figuring the Aeneid from the Twelfth Century to Chaucer.* Cambridge, England, 1995.

Benson, Robert L., and Giles Constable, eds. *Renaissance and Renewal in the Twelfth Century.* Cambridge, Mass., 1982.

Bentley, Jerry. *Humanists and Holy Writ: New Testament Scholarship in the Renaissance.* Princeton, N.J., 1983.

Biechler, James E. "Nicholas of Cusa and Muhammad: A Fifteenth-Century Encounter." *Downside Review* 101 (1983):50–59.

———. "Three Manuscripts on Islam from the Library of Nicholas of Cusa." *Manuscripta* 27 (1983):91–100.

Bisaha, Nancy. *Creating East and West: Renaissance Humanists and the Ottoman Turks.* Philadelphia, 2004.

Blau, Joseph Leon. *The Christian Interpretation of the Cabala in the Renaissance.* Port Washington, N.Y., 1944, 1965.

Bobzin, Hartmut. *Der Koran im Zeitalter der Reformation: Studien zur Frühgeschichte der Arabistik und Islamkunde in Europa.* Beirut and Stuttgart, 1995.

———. "Ein oberschlesischer Korangelehrter: Dominicus Germanus de Silesia, O.F.M. (1588–1670)." In *Die oberschlesische Literaturlandschaft im 17. Jahrhundert*, ed. Gerhard Kossek, 221–31. Bielefield, 2001.

———. "Geschichte der arabischen Philologie in Europa bis zum Ausgang des achtzehnten Jahrhunderts." In *Grundriss der Arabischen Philologie*, Band 3: *Supplement*, ed. Wolfdietrich Fischer. Wiesbaden, 1992, 155–87.

———. "Latin Koran Translations: A Short Overview." *Der Islam* 70 (1993):193–206.

———. "Pre-1800 Preoccupations of Qur'anic Studies." EQ 4:235–53.

———. "Translations of the Qur'an." EQ 5:340–58.

Burman, Thomas E. "Cambridge University Library MS Mm v. 26 and the History of the Study of the Qur'ān in Medieval and Early Modern Europe." In *Religion, Text, and Society in Medieval Spain and Northern Europe: Essays in Honor of J. N. Hillgarth*, ed. Thomas E. Burman, Mark D. Meyerson, and Leah Shopkow. Toronto, 2002, 335–63.

———. "Exclusion or Concealment: Approaches to Traditional Arabic Exegesis in Medieval-Latin Translations of the Qur'ān." *Scripta mediterranea* 19–20 (1998–99):181–97.

———. "The Latin-Arabic Qur'ān Edition of Egidio da Viterbo and the Latin Qur'āns of Robert of Ketton and Mark of Toledo." In Barceló and Martínez Gázquez, *Musulmanes y cristianos en Hispania*, 103–17.

———. "Polemic, Philology, and Ambivalence: Reading the Qur'ān in Latin Christendom." *Journal of Islamic Studies* 15 (2004):181–209.

———. *Religious Polemic and the Intellectual History of the Mozarabs, c. 1050–1200.* Leiden, 1994.

———. "*Tafsīr* and Translation: Traditional Qur'ān Exegesis and the Latin Qur'āns of Robert of Ketton and Mark of Toledo." *Speculum* 73 (1998):703–32.

Burman, Thomas E., and Thomas J. Heffernan, eds. *Scripture and Pluralism: Reading the Bible in the Religiously Plural Worlds of the Middle Ages and Renaissance.* Leiden, 2005.

Burnett, Charles S. F. "The Coherence of the Arabic-Latin Translation Program in Toledo." *Science in Context* 14 (2001):249–88.

———. "A Group of Arabic-Latin Translators Working in Northern Spain in the Mid-12th Century." *Journal of the Royal Asiatic Society* (1977):62–70.

———. "Ketton, Robert of (fl. 1141–57)." *Oxford Dictionary of National Biography* 31:465–67.

———. "Al-Kindī on Judicial Astrology: 'The Forty Chapters.'" *Arabic Science and Philosophy* 3 (1993):77–117.

———. "Some Comments on the Translating of Works from Arabic into Latin in the Mid-Twelfth Century." In Zimmerman and Craemer-Ruegenberg, *Orientalische Kultur und Europäisches Mittelalter*, 161–71.

———. "The Translating Activity in Medieval Spain." In Jayyusi, *The Legacy of Muslim Spain*, 1036–58.

Burnett, Charles S. F., and Gerrit Bos, eds. *Scientific Weather Forecasting in the Middle Ages: The Writings of al-Kindī. Studies, Editions, and Translations of the Arabic, Hebrew and Latin Texts.* London, 2000.

Burnett, Charles S. F., and Anna Contadini, eds. *Islam and the Italian Renaissance.* London, 1999.

Burnett, Charles S. F., Keiji Yamamoto, and Michio Yano. "Al-Kindī on Finding Buried Treasure." *Arabic Science and Philosophy* 7 (1997):57–90.

Burnett, Stephen G. "Reassessing the 'Basel-Wittenberg Conflict': Dimensions of the Reformation-Era Discussion of Hebrew Scholarship." In Coudert and Shoulson, *Hebraica Veritas?*, 181–201.

Cabanelas Rodríguez, Darío. "Juan de Segovia y el primer Alcorán trilingüe." *Al-Andalus* 14 (1949):149–73.

———. *Juan de Segovia y el problema islámico.* Madrid, 1952.

Cahn, Walter B. "The 'Portrait' of Muhammad in the Toledan Collection." In *Reading Medieval Images: The Art Historian and the Object*, ed. Elizabeth Sears and Thelma K. Thomas. Ann Arbor, Mich., 2002, 51–60.

Cameron, Euan. *The European Reformation.* Oxford, 1991.

Canova, Giordana Mariani. "The Italian Renaissance Miniature." In Alexander, *The Painted Page*, 21–34.

Cary, George. *The Medieval Alexander.* Ed. D. J. A. Ross. Cambridge, 1956.

Caspar, Robert. "Textes de la tradition musulmane concernant le *taḥrīf* (falsification) des écritures." *Islamochristiana* 6 (1981):61–104.

Castells i Criballés, Margarita. Review of *Alcorán: Traducción castellana de un morisco anónimo. Al-Qantara* 23 (2002):550–54.

Cavallo, Guglielmo, and Roger Chartier, eds. *A History of Reading in the West.* Trans. Lydia G. Cochrane. Amherst, Mass., 1999.

Chartier, Roger. *The Order of Books: Readers, Authors, and Libraries in Europe between the Fourteenth and Eighteenth Centuries.* Trans. Lydia G. Cochrane. Stanford, Calif., 1994.

———. "Reading Matter and 'Popular' Reading: From the Renaissance to the Seventeenth Century." In Cavallo and Chartier, *A History of Reading in the West*, 269–83.

Clark, Harry. "The Publication of the Qur'ān in Latin: A Reformation Dilemma," *Sixteenth-Century Journal* 15 (1984):3–12.

Clough, Cecil H. "Federigo da Montefeltro's Artistic Patronage" (Selwyn Brinton Lecture for 1978). *Journal of the Royal Society of Arts* 126 (1978):718–34.

———. "Federigo da Montefeltro's Patronage of the Arts, 1468–82." *Journal of the Warburg and Courtauld Institutes* 36 (1973):129–44.

———. "The Library of the Dukes of Urbino." *Librarium: Revue de la société des bibliophiles suisses* 9 (1966):101–5.

Cohen, Jeremy. "The Muslim Connection or On the Changing Role of the Jew in High Medieval Theology." In *From Witness to Witchcraft: Jews and Judaism in Medieval Christian Thought*, ed. Jeremy Cohen. Wiesbaden, 1996, 141–62.

Contadini, Anna. "Artistic Contacts: Current Scholarship and Future Tasks." In Burnett and Contadini, *Islam and the Italian Renaissance*, 1–60.

Copeland, Rita. *Rhetoric, Hermeneutics, and Translation in the Middle Ages: Academic Traditions and Vernacular Texts*, Cambridge Studies in Medieval Literature 11. Cambridge, England, 1991.

Coudert, Allison P., and Jeffrey S. Shoulson, eds. *Hebraica Veritas? Christian Hebraists and the Study of Judaism in Early Modern Europe*. Philadelphia, 2004.

Dahan, Gilbert. "L'enseignement de l'hébreu en Occident médiéval (XIIe-XIVe siècles)." *Histoire de l'éducation* 57 (1993):3–22.

———. *L'exégèse chrétienne de la Bible en Occident médiéval, XIIe-XIVe siècle*. Paris, 1999.

———. *Les intellectuels chrétiens et les juifs au Moyen Âge*. Paris, 1990.

———. "Les traductions latines de Thibaud de Sézanne." In *Le brûlement du Talmud à Paris, 1242–44*, ed. Gilbert Dahan. Paris, 1999, 95–120.

Dan, Joseph, ed. *The Christian Kabbalah: Jewish Mystical Books and Their Christian Interpreters: A Symposium*. Cambridge, Mass., 1997.

———. "The Kabbalah of Johannes Reuchlin and Its Historical Signficance." In Dan, *The Christian Kabbalah*, 55–95.

Daniel, Norman. *Islam and the West: The Making of an Image*. Rev. ed. Oxford, 1993.

Daniell, David, ed. *Tyndale's Old Testament*. New Haven, Conn., 1992.

Dannenfeldt, Karl H. "The Renaissance Humanists and the Knowledge of Arabic." *Studies in the Renaissance* 2 (1955):96–117.

Davies, Martin. "Humanism in Script and Print in the Fifteenth Century." In Kraye, *The Cambridge Companion to Renaissance Humanism*, 47–62.

Davis, Natalie Zemon. *Trickster Travels: A Sixteenth-Century Muslim Between Worlds*. New York, 2006.

De Frede, Carlo. *La prima traduzione italiana del Corano sullo sfondo dei rapporti tra Cristianità e Islam nel Cinquecento*. Naples, 1967.

De Hamel, Christopher. *The Book: A History of the Bible*. London and New York, 2001.

———. *Glossed Books of the Bible and the Origins of the Paris Booktrade*. Woodbridge, Suffolk, 1984.

———. *A History of Illuminated Manuscripts*. 2nd ed. London, 1994.

De la Cruz Palma, Oscar. "La trascendencia de la primera traducción del Corán

(Robert de Keton, 1142)." *Collatio* 7 (2002):21–28 [http://www.hottopos.com/collat7/oscar.htm].

Delisle, Léopold. *Le cabinet des manuscrits de la Bibliothèque impériale*. 3 vols. Paris, 1868–81.

Denifle, Heinrich. "Die Handschriften der Bibel-Correctorien des 13. Jahrhunderts." *Archiv für Literatur- und Kirchen-Geschichte des Mittelalters* 4 (1888):263–311, 471–601.

Déroche, François. *Catalogue des manuscrits arabes*. Deuxième partie: *Manuscrits musulmans*. Vol. 1: *Les manuscrits du Coran. 2. Du Maghreb à l'Insulinde*. Paris, 1985.

Derolez, Albert. *Codicologie des manuscrits en écriture humanistique sur parchemin*. 2 vols. Turnhout, 1984.

———. "Le livre manuscrit de la Renaissance." In *El libro antiguo español: Actas del Segundo Coloquio Internacional (Madrid)*, ed. María Luisa López-Vidriero and Pedro M. Cátedra. Madrid, 1992, 177–92.

Devic, Marcel. "Une traduction inédite du Coran." *Journal asiatique*, 8th series, 1 (1883):343–406.

Dunlop, D. M. "David Colville, a Successor to Michael Scot." *Bulletin of Hispanic Studies* 28 (1951):38–42.

Elman, Benjamin A. *From Philosophy to Philology: Intellectual and Social Aspects of Change in Late Imperial China*. 2nd ed. rev. Los Angeles, 2001.

D'Esneval, Amaury. "La division de la Vulgate latine en chapitres dans l'édition Parisienne du XIIIe siècle." *Revue des sciences philosophiques et théologiques* 62 (1978):559–68.

Faral, Edmond. *Les arts poétiques du XIIe et du XIIIe siècle: Recherches et documents sur la technique littéraire du moyen âge*. Paris, 1924.

Fontana, Maria Vittoria. "Byzantine Mediation of Epigraphic Characters of Islamic Derivation in the Wall Paintings of Some Churches in Southern Italy." In Burnett and Contadini, *Islam and the Italian Renaissance*, 61–75.

Fück, Johann. *Die arabischen Studien in Europa bis in den Anfang des 20. Jahrhunderts*. Leipzig, 1955.

Gibson, Margaret T. *The Bible in the Latin West*. Notre Dame, Ind., 1993.

———. "The Twelfth-Century Glossed Bible." *Studia patristica* 33 (1989):232–44.

Gilmont, Jean-François. "Protestant Reformations and Reading." In Cavallo and Chartier, *A History of Reading in the West*, 213–37.

Glick, Thomas F. "My Master, the Jew: Observations on Interfaith Scholarly Interaction in the Middle Ages." In *Jews, Muslims, and Christians in and around the Medieval Crown of Aragon: Studies in Honor of Elena Lourie*, ed. Harvey Hames. Leiden, 2004, 157–82.

Goddard, Hugh. *A History of Christian-Muslim Relations*. Chicago, 2000.

Goldthwaite, Richard A. *Wealth and the Demand for Art in Italy, 1300–1600*. Baltimore, 1993.

González Muñoz, Fernando, ed. and trans. *Exposición y refutación del Islam: La versión latina de las epístolas de al-Hāšimī y al-Kindī*. A Coruña, Spain, 2005.

———. "*Liber Nycholay*. La leyenda de Mahoma y el Cardenal Nicolás." *Al-Qantara* 25 (2004):5–43.

———. "La versión latina de la *Apología de al-Kindī* y su tradición textual." In Barceló and Martínez Gázquez, *Musulmanes y cristianos en Hispania*, 25–40.

Goodman, L. E. "The Translation of Greek Materials into Arabic." In *Religion, Learning and Science in the ʿAbbasid Period*, ed. M. J. L. Young, J. D. Latham, and R. B. Serjeant. Cambridge, 1990, 477–97.

Gordon, Bruce. *The Swiss Reformation*. Manchester, England, 2002.

Grafton, Anthony. *Defenders of the Text: The Traditions of Scholarship in an Age of Science, 1450–1800*. Cambridge, Mass., 1991.

———. "The Humanist as Reader." In Cavallo and Chartier, *A History of Reading in the West*, 179–212.

———. "In No Man's Land" [review of Adam Sutcliffe. *Judaism and Enlightenment*. Cambridge, England, 2003; and Maurice Olender. *The Languages of Paradise: Aryans and Semites, a Match Made in Heaven*. Trans. Arthur Goldhammer. New York, 2003], *New York Review of Books* 51.3 (February 26, 2004):34–37.

———. *Joseph Scaliger: A Study in the History of Classical Scholarship*. 2 vols. Oxford, 1983–93.

———. *New Worlds, Ancient Texts: The Power of Tradition and the Shock of Discovery*. Cambridge, Mass., 1992.

———, ed. *Rome Reborn: The Vatican Library and Renaissance Culture*. Washington and New Haven, Conn., 1993.

Grafton, Anthony, and Lisa Jardine. *From Humanism to the Humanities: Education and the Liberal Arts in Fifteenth- and Sixteenth-Century Europe*. Cambridge, Mass., and London, 1986.

Griffith, Sidney. "The First *Summa Theologiae* in Arabic: Christian *Kalām* in Ninth-Century Palestine." In *Conversion and Continuity: Indigenous Christian Communities in Islamic Lands, Eighth to Eighteenth Centuries*, ed. Michael Gervers and Ramzi Jibran Bikhazi. Toronto, 1990, 15–31.

Gutas, Dimitri. *Greek Thought, Arabic Culture: The Graeco-Arabic Translation Movement in Baghdad and Early ʿAbbāsid Society (2nd–4th/8th–10th Centuries)*. London and New York, 1998.

Hagemann, Ludwig. "Die erste lateinische Koranübersetzung—Mittel zur Verständigung zwischen Christen und Muslimen im Mittelalter?" In Zimmerman and Craemer-Ruegenberg, *Orientalische Kultur und europäisches Mittelalter*, 45–58.

———. *Der Ḳurʾān in Verständnis und Kritik bei Nikolaus von Kues: Ein Beitrag zur Erhellung islāmisch-christlicher Geschichte*. Frankfurt, 1976.

Hames, Harvey. "Elijah Delmedigo: An Archetype of Halakhic Man?" In *Cultural Intermediaries: Jewish Intellectuals in Early Modern Italy*, ed. David B. Ruderman and Giuseppe Veltri. Philadelphia, 2004, 39–54.

———. "Jewish Magic with a Christian Text: A Hebrew Translation of Ramon Llull's *Ars brevis*." *Traditio* 54 (1999):283–300.

Hamesse, Jacqueline. "The Scholastic Model of Reading." In Cavallo and Chartier, *A History of Reading in the West*, 103–19.

Hamilton, Alastair. *The Apocryphal Apocalypse: The Reception of the Second Book of Esdras (4 Ezra) from the Renaissance to the Enlightenment*. Oxford, 1999.

———. "Eastern Churches and Western Scholarship." In Grafton, *Rome Reborn: The Vatican Library and Renaissance Culture*, 225–49.

———. "Humanists and the Bible." In Kraye, *The Cambridge Companion to Renaissance Humanism*, 100–117.

———. "A Lutheran Translator for the Quran: A Late Seventeenth-Century Quest." In *The Republic of Letters and the Levant*, ed. Alastair Hamilton, Maurits H. Van Den Boogert, and Bart Westerweel. Leiden, 2005, 197–221.

———. "The Study of Islam in Early Modern Europe." *Archiv für Religionsgeschichte* 3 (2001):169–82.

———. *William Bedwell, the Arabist (1563–1632)*. Leiden, 1985.

Hamilton, Alastair, and Francis Richard. *André du Ryer and Oriental Studies in Seventeenth-Century France*. London and Oxford, 2004.

Hankins, James. *Plato in the Italian Renaissance*. 2 vols. Leiden, 1990.

Häring, Nikolaus. "Commentary and Hermeneutics." In Benson and Constable, *Renaissance and Renewal*, 173–200.

Harvey, L. P. *Islamic Spain, 1250–1500*. Chicago, 1990.

Henderson, John B. *Scripture, Canon, and Commentary: A Comparison of Confucian and Western Exegesis*. Princeton, N.J, 1991.

Hernández Montes, Benigno. *Biblioteca de Juan de Segovia: Edición y comentario de su escritura de donación*. Madrid, 1984.

Howlett, David. *Insular Inscriptions*. Dublin, 2005.

Illich, Ivan. *In the Vineyard of the Text: A Commentary of Hugh's Didascalicon*. Chicago, 1993.

Irvine, Martin. *The Making of Textual Culture: 'Grammatica' and Literary Theory, 350–1100*. Cambridge, England, 1994.

Jayyusi, Salma Khadra. *The Legacy of Muslim Spain*. Leiden, 1992.

Jeffery, Arthur. *The Foreign Vocabulary of the Qur'ān*. Baroda, 1938.

Jensen, Kurt Villads. "Christian Reading of the Quran Before and After 1300." In *Rapports entre Juifs, Chrétiens et Musulmans: Eine Sammlung von Forschungsbeiträgen*, ed. Johannes Irmscher. Amsterdam, 1995, 173–78.

Kelly, L. G. *The True Interpreter: A History of Translation Theory and Practice in the West*. Oxford, 1979.

Kraye, Jill, ed. *The Cambridge Companion to Renaissance Humanism*. Cambridge, England, 1996.

Kritzeck, James. *Peter the Venerable and Islam*. Princeton, N.J., 1964.

Lafferty, Maura K. *Walter of Châtillon's Alexandreis: Epic and the Problem of Historical Understanding*. Turnhout, 1998.

Lazarus-Yafeh, Hava. *Intertwined Worlds: Medieval Islam and Bible Criticism*. Princeton, N.J., 1992.

Lelli, Fabrizio. "*Prisca philosophia* and *Docta religio*: The Boundaries of Rational Knowledge in Jewish and Christian Humanist Thought." *Jewish Quarterly Review* 91 (2000):53–99.

Levi della Vida, Giorgio. "Ludovico Marracci e la sua opera negli studi islamici." In Giorgio Levi della Vida, *Aneddoti e svaghi arabi e non arabi*. Milan and Naples, 1959, 193–210.

———. *Ricerche sulla formazione del più antico fondo dei manoscritti orientali della Biblioteca Vaticana*. Vatican City, 1939.

Lévi-Provençal, Evariste. *Manuscrits arabes de l'Escurial, décrits par Hartwig Derenbourg*. Vol. 3: *Théologie—géographie—histoire*. Paris, 1928.

Light, Laura. "The New Thirteenth-Century Bible and the Challenge of Heresy." *Viator* 18 (1987):275–88.

———. "Versions et révisions du texte biblique." In *Le Moyen Âge et la Bible*, ed. Pierre Riché and Guy Lobrichon. Bible de tous les temps 4. Paris, 1984, 55–93.

Limor, Ora, and Israel Jacob Yuval. "Skepticism and Conversion: Jews, Christians, and Doubters in *Sefer ha-Nizzahon*." In Coudert and Shoulson, *Hebraica Veritas?*, 159–80.

Lippincott, Kristen. "More on Ibn al-Ḥātim." *Journal of the Warburg and Courtauld Institutes* 51 (1988):188–90.

Lippincott, Kristen, and David Pingree. "Ibn al-Ḥātim on the Talismans of the Lunar Mansions." *Journal of the Warburg and Courtauld Institutes* 50 (1987):56–81.

Lloyd-Jones, Gareth. *The Discovery of Hebrew in Sixteenth-Century England: A Third Language*. Manchester, England, 1983.

———. "Robert Wakefield (d. 1537): The Father of English Hebraists?" In *Hebrew Study from Ezra to Ben-Yahuda*, ed. William Horbury. Edinburgh, 1999, 234–48.

Loeb, Isidore. "La controverse de 1240 sur le Talmud." *Revue des études juives* 1 (1880):247–61, 2 (1881):248–70, and 3 (1882):39–57.

Löfgren, Oscar, and Renato Traini. *Catalogue of the Arabic Manuscripts in the Biblioteca Ambrosiana*. 3 vols. Vicenza, 1975–95.

López-Morillas, Consuelo. "Lost and Found? Yça of Segovia and the Qur'ān among the Mudejars and Moriscos." *Journal of Islamic Studies* 10 (1999):277–92.

———. *The Qur'ān in Sixteenth-Century Spain: Six Morisco Versions of Sūra 79*. London, 1982.

Lozovsky, Natalia. *"The Earth Is Our Book": Geographical Knowledge in the Latin West, ca. 400–1000*. Ann Arbor, Mich., 2000.

Mack, Rosalind. *Bazaar to Piazza: Islamic Trade and Italian Art, 1300–1600*. Berkeley, Calif., 2002.

Mairold, Maria. *Die datierten Handschriften in der Steiermark ausserhalb der Universitätsbibliothek Graz bis zum Jahre 1600*. 2 vols. Katalog der datierten Handschriften in lateinischer Schrift in Österreich 7. Vienna, 1988.

Mann, Jesse D. "Truth and Consequences: Juan de Segovia on Islam and Conciliarism." *Medieval Encounters* 8 (2002):79–90.

Martin, Francis X., O.S.A. *Friar, Reformer, and Renaissance Scholar: Life and Work of Giles of Viterbo, 1469–1532*. Villanova, Pa., 1992.

———. "The Problem of Giles of Viterbo: A Historiographical Survey." *Augustiniana* 9 (1959):357–79 and 10 (1960):43–60.

Martin, H. *Catalogue des manuscrits de la Bibliothèque de l'Arsenal*. 9 vols. Paris, 1885–92.

Martin, Henri-Jean, and Jean Vezin, eds. *Mise en page et mise en texte du livre manuscrit*. Paris, 1990.

Martin, Janet. "Classicism and Style in Latin Literature." In Benson and Constable, *Renaissance and Renewal in the Twelfth Century*, 537–68.

Martínez Gázquez, José. "Finalidad de la primera traducción latina del Corán." In Barceló and Martínez, *Musulmanes y cristianos en Hispania*, 71–77.

———. "El lenguaje de la violencia en el prólogo de la traducción latina del Corán impulsada por Pedro el Venerable." *Cahiers d'études hispaniques médiévales* 28 (2005):243–52

———. "Observaciones a la traducción latina del Corán (Qur'ān) de Robert de Ketene." In *Les traducteurs au travail: Leurs manuscrits et leurs méthodes*, ed. Jacqueline Hamesse. Turnhout, 2001, 115–27.

———. "Los primeros nombres de Allāh en la traducción latina del *Alchoran* de Robert de Ketton." *Euphrosyne* 33 (2005):303–13.

———. "El prólogo de Juan de Segobia al Corán (*Qur'ān*) trilingüe (1456)." *Mittellateinisches Jahrbuch* 38 (2003):389–410.

———. "Las traducciones latinas medievales del Corán: Pedro de Venerable-Robert de Ketton, Marcos de Toledo, y Juan de Segobia." *Euphrosyne* 31 (2003):491–503.

Martínez Gázquez, José, and Óscar de la Cruz Palma. "Las traducciones árabe-latinas impulsadas por Pedro el Venerable." In *Las órdenes militares: Realidad e imaginario*, ed. M. D. Burdeus, E. Real, and J. M. Verdegal. Castellón de la Plana, 2000, 285–95.

Marx, J. *Verzeichnis der Handschriften-Sammlung des Hospitals zu Cues bei Bernkastel a./Mosel.* Trier, 1905.

McAuliffe, Jane Damen. *Qur'ānic Christians: An Analysis of Classical and Modern Exegesis.* Cambridge, England, 1991.

Metlitzki, Dorothee. *The Matter of Araby in Medieval England.* New Haven and London, 1977.

Meyerson, Mark D. *The Muslims of Valencia in the Age of Fernando and Isabel: Between Coexistence and Crusade.* Berkeley, Calif., 1991.

Miller, Kathryn. *Guardians of Islam: Muslim Minorities in Medieval Aragon.* New York, forthcoming.

Minnis, A. J., and A. B. Scott, with David Wallace. *Medieval Literary Theory and Criticism, c. 1100–1375: The Commentary Tradition.* Oxford, 1988.

Monfrin, Jacques. "Préface." In Martin and Vezin, *Mise en page et mise en texte du livre manuscrit*, 9–16.

Monneret de Villard, Ugo. *Lo studio dell'Islam in Europa nel XII e nel XIII secolo.* Vatican City, 1944.

Morey, James H. "Peter Comestor, Biblical Paraphrase, and the Medieval Popular Bible." *Speculum* 68 (1993):6–35.

Moss, Ann. *Ovid in Renaissance France: A Survey of the Latin Editions of Ovid and Commentaries Printed in France Before 1600.* London, 1982.

Munk-Olsen, Birger. "L'humanisme de Jean de Salisbury, un Cicéronien au 12e siècle." In *Entretiens sur la renaissance du 12e siècle*, Maurice de Gandiallace and Édouard Jeauneau. Paris, 1968, 53–69.

Nallino, Carlo Alfonso. "Le fonti arabe manoscritte dell'opera di Ludovico Marracci sul Corano." In Carlo Alfonso Nallino, *Raccolta di scritti editi e inediti.* Vol. 2:

L'Islām: Dogmatica—Ṣūfismo—Confraternite, ed. Maria Nallino. Rome, 1940, 90–134.

O'Malley, John W. *Giles of Viterbo on Church Reform: A Study in Renaissance Thought*. Leiden, 1968.

Ouy, Gilbert, et al. *Le catalogue de la bibliothèque de l'abbaye de Saint-Victor de Paris de Claude de Grandrue, 1514*. Paris, 1983.

Parrinder, Geoffrey. *Jesus in the Qur'an*. New York, 1977.

Parkes, Malcolm B. "The Influence of the Concepts of *ordinatio* and *compilatio* in the Development of the Book." In *Medieval Learning and Literature: Essays Presented to Richard William Hunt*, ed. J. J. G. Alexander and M. T. Gibson. Oxford, 1976, 115–41.

———. "Reading, Copying and Interpreting a Text in the Early Middle Ages." In Cavallo and Chartier, *A History of Reading in the West*, 90–102.

Pelikan, Jaroslav, with Valerie Hotchkiss, and David Price. *The Reformation of the Bible, the Bible of the Reformation*. New Haven, Conn., 1996.

Petrus i Pons, Nàdia. "Marcos de Toledo y la segunda traducción latina del Corán." In Barceló and Martínez, *Musulmanes y cristianos en Hispania*, 87–94.

Pick, Lucy. *Conflict and Coexistence: Archbishop Rodrigo and the Muslims and Jews of Medieval Spain*. Ann Arbor, Mich., 2004.

Piemontese, Angelo Michele. "Il Corano latino di Ficino e i Corani arabi di Pico e Monchates." *Rinascimento: Rivista dell'Instituto Nazionale di Studi sul Rinascimento*, 2nd series, 36 (1996):227–73.

———. "Le iscrizioni arabe nella *Poliphili Hypnerotomachia*." In Burnett and Contadini, *Islam and the Italian Renaissance*, 199–220.

Quillen, Carol Everhart. *Rereading the Renaissance: Petrarch, Augustine, and the Language of Humanism*. Ann Arbor, Mich., 1998.

Reeve, Michael D. "Classical Scholarship." In Kraye, *The Cambridge Companion to Renaissance Humanism*, 20–46.

Reynolds, Suzanne. *Medieval Reading: Grammar, Rhetoric and the Classical Text*. Cambridge, England and New York, 1996.

Richard, F. "Le Franciscain Dominicus Germanus de Silesie, grammairien et auteur d'apologie en Persan." *Islamochristiana* 10 (1984):91–107.

Rippin, Andrew. "Lexicographical Texts and the Qur'ān." In *Approaches to the History of the Interpretation of the Qur'ān*, ed. Andrew Rippin. Oxford, 1988, 158–74.

Rivolta, Adolfo. *Catalogo dei Codice Pinelliani dell'Ambrosiana*. Milan, 1933.

Robinson, Neal. *Discovering the Qur'ān: A Contemporary Approach to a Veiled Text*, London, 1996.

Rodinson, Maxime. *Europe and the Mystique of Islam*. Trans. Roger Veinus. Seattle, 1987.

Ross, D. J. A. *Alexander Historiatus: A Guide to Medieval Illustrated Alexander Literature*. London, 1963.

———. *Illustrated Medieval Alexander-Books in Germany and the Netherlands*. Cambridge, 1971.

Ross, E. Dennison. "Ludovico Marracci." *Bulletin of the School of Oriental and African Studies* 2 (1921–23):117–23.

Rouse, Richard H. and Mary A. Rouse. "Layout as a Finding Device of the Schools." In *Authentic Witnesses: Approaches to Medieval Texts and Manuscripts*, ed. Richard H. Rouse and Mary A. Rouse. Notre Dame, Ind., 1991.

———. "La naissance des index." In *Histoire de l'édition française*, ed. Henri-Jean Martin and Roger Chartier. Vol. 1: *Le livre conquérant*, 77–85, Paris, 1983.

———. *Preachers, Florilegia and Sermons: Studies on the Manipulus florum of Thomas of Ireland*. Toronto, 1979.

———. "*Statim invenire*: Schools, Preachers and New Attitudes to the Page." In Benson and Constable, *Renaissance and Renewal*, 201–25.

Ruderman, David B. "The Italian Renaissance and Jewish Thought." In *Humanism: Foundations, Form, and Legacy*, ed. Albert J. Rabil. Vol. 1: *Humanism in Italy*. Philadelphia, 1988, 382–433.

Saenger, Paul. "Reading in the Later Middle Ages." In Cavallo and Chartier, *A History of Reading in the West*, 120–48.

Said, Edward W. *Orientalism*. London and New York, 1978.

Al-Samman, Tarif, and Otto Mazal. *Die arabische Welt und Europa: Ausstellung der Handschriften- und Inkunabelsammlung der Österreichischen Nationalbibliothek: Handbuch und Katalog*. Graz, 1988.

Schnorr von Carolsfeld, Franz, and Ludwig Schmidt. *Katalog der Handschriften der Königl. öffentlichen Bibliothek zu Dresden*. 4 vols. Leipzig, 1882–1923.

Scholem, Gershom. "The Beginnings of the Christian Kabbalah." In Dan, *The Christian Kabbalah*, 17–51.

Schwoebel, Robert. *The Shadow of the Crescent: The Renaissance Image of the Turk (1453–1517)*. Nieuwkoop, 1967.

Secret, François. "Guillaume Postel et les études arabes à la Renaissance." *Arabica* 9 (1962):21–36.

———. *Les Kabbalistes chrétiens de la Renaissance*. Paris, 1964.

Segesvary, Victor. *L'Islam et la Réforme: Étude sur l'attitude des Réformateurs zurichois envers l'Islam, 1510–1550*. Bethesda, Md., 1998.

Setton, Kenneth. *Western Hostility to Islam and the Prophecies of Doom*. Philadelphia, 1992.

Shahīd, Irfan. "*Fawātiḥ al-suwār*, The Mysterious Letters of the Qur'an." In *Literary Structures of Religious Meaning in the Qur'ān*, ed. Issa J. Boullata. Richmond, Surrey, 2000, 125–39.

Shailor, Barbara A. *The Medieval Book*. Toronto, 1991.

Shuger, Debora Kuller. *The Renaissance Bible: Scholarship, Sacrifice, and Subjectivity*. Berkeley, Calif., 1994.

Signer, Michael. "Consolation and Confrontation: Jewish and Christian Interpretation of the Prophetic Books." In Burman and Heffernan, *Scripture and Pluralism*, 77–94.

Smalley, Beryl. *The Study of the Bible in the Middle Ages*. 3rd ed. Notre Dame, Ind., 1983.

Smith, Jane Idleman and Yvonne Yazbeck Haddad. *The Islamic Understanding of Death and Resurrection*. Albany, N.Y., 1981.

Smith, Lesley. *Masters of the Sacred Page: Manuscripts of Theology in the Latin West to 1274*. Notre Dame, Ind., 2001.

———, trans. *Medieval Exegesis in Translation: Commentaries on the Book of Ruth.* Kalamazoo, Mich., 1996.

Southern, R. *Scholastic Humanism and the Unification of Europe.* 2 vols. Oxford, 1995–2001.

———. *Western Views of Islam in the Middle Ages.* Cambridge, Mass., 1962.

Steiner, George. *After Babel: Aspects of Language and Translation.* 2nd ed. Oxford, 1992.

Stornajolo, Cosimus. *Codices Urbinates latini.* 3 vols. Rome, 1902–21.

Tabernigg, Theodor. "Die Bibliothek des Franziskanerklosters in Güssing." *Biblos: Österreichische Zeitschrift für Buch- und Bibliothekswesen, Dokumentation, Bibliographie und Bibliophilie* 21 (1972):167–75.

Tolan, John V. "Peter the Venerable and the 'Diabolic Heresy of the Saracens.'" In *The Devil, Heresy, and Witchcraft in the Middle Ages: Essays in Honor of Jeffrey Burton Russell*, ed. Alberto Ferreiro. Leiden, 1998, 345–67.

———. *Saracens: Islam in the Medieval European Imagination.* New York, 2002.

———. "Las traducciones y la ideología de reconquista: Marcos de Toledo." In Barceló and Martínez, *Musulmanes y cristianos en Hispania*, 79–85.

Van Liere, Frans. "Andrew of St. Victor, Jerome, and the Jews: Biblical Scholarship in the Twelfth-Century Renaissance." In Burman and Heffernan, *Scripture and Pluralism*, 59–76.

Vehlow, Katya. "The Swiss Reformers Zwingli, Bullinger and Bibliander and Their Attitude to Islam (1520–1560)." *Islam and Christian-Muslim Relations* 6 (1995):229–54.

Versteegh, Kees. "Greek Translations of the Qur'ān in Christian Polemics (9th-Century A.D.)." *Zeitschrift der Deutschen morgenländischen Gesellschaft* 141 (1991):52–68.

Watt, W. Montgomery. *Bell's Introduction to the Qur'ān.* Edinburgh, 1970.

Wiegers, Gerard. "'Īsà de Ŷābir and the Origins of Aljamiado Literature." *Al-Qantara* 11 (1990):155–91.

———. *Islamic Literature in Spanish and Aljamiado: Yça of Segovia (fl. 1450), His Antecedents and Successors.* Leiden, 1994.

Wirszubski, Chaim, ed. *Flavius Mithridates: Sermo de passione domini.* Jerusalem, 1963.

———. *Pico della Mirandola's Encounter with Jewish Mysticism.* Cambridge, Mass., 1989.

Wolf, Anne Marie. "Juan de Segovia and Western Perspectives on Islam in the Fifteenth Century." Ph.D. dissertation, University of Minnesota, 2003.

Yates, Donald. *Descriptive Inventories of Manuscripts Microfilmed for the Hill Monastic Manuscript Library.* Vol. 1: *Austrian Libraries.* Collegeville, Minn., 1981.

Zimmerman, Albert, and Ingrid Craemer-Ruegenberg, eds. *Orientalische Kultur and Europäisches Mittelalter.* Miscellanea Mediaevalia 17. Berlin and New York, 1985.

Index of Qur'ānic References

Index of Manuscripts

Index of Persons and Subjects

Acknowledgments

I have been helped by so many people and institutions as I worked on this book that it is hard to know where to begin expressing my gratitude. But perhaps I should first say thanks to the libraries that welcomed me and gave me access to the many medieval manuscripts and old books that are the basis of this study: the Cambridge University Library; the Bodleian Library and Corpus Christi College Library in Oxford; the Bibliothèque nationale, the Bibliothèque Mazarine, and the Bibliothèque de l'Arsenal in Paris; the Sächsiche Landesbibliothek in Dresden; the Franziskanerkloster in Güssing (Austria); the Österreichische Nationalbibliothek in Vienna; the Biblioteca Nazionale Universitaria in Turin; the Biblioteca Ambrosiana in Milan; the Biblioteca Apostolica Vaticana in Vatican City; and the Real Biblioteca de San Lorenzo de El Escorial (Spain).

My research was generously underwritten by the University of Tennessee in the form of a series of Professional Development Awards that allowed me to travel to many marvelous European cities to do research. Together with a grant from the American Philosophical Society, those awards also underwrote the acquisition of a large number of essential microfilms. During the year 2002–3 I had the great fortune of holding a fellowship from the National Endowment for the Humanities, which gave me a year off from teaching to write the first draft of this book. During that year, I also held the Abdul Aziz Al-Mutawa Fellowship at the Oxford Centre for Islamic Studies. I cannot thank the Centre enough for providing me an office in the heart of Oxford where I wrote that initial draft. Especial thanks are due to Farhan Nizami, the Centre's director, and to James Piscatori, Yahya Michot, Basil Mustafa, and—by no means least—Afifi al-Kiti for making me feel so much at home there. Nor can I properly express my gratitude to Harris Manchester College, Oxford, and especially its Senior Tutor, Lesley Smith, for welcoming me as a visiting fellow during that year.

What seem like countless friends and colleagues have offered their expertise and insight during the course of this research and writing. Paul Barrette, Salvatore DiMaria, Jeff Mellor, Consuelo López-Morillas, Vejas

Liulevicius, Natalie Zemon Davis, David Daniell, Peter Pormann, Fernando González Muñoz, and José Martínez Gázquez all came through with essential help when I needed it most. Scott Hendrix was an excellent research assistant in the summer of 2004. Lesley Smith kindly smoothed my way in Oxford and astutely critiqued important sections of the book. Harvey Hames, Anne Marie Wolf, J. N. Hillgarth, and Alastair Hamilton each also read key parts of the manuscript. Ahmet Karamustafa, Charles Lohr, and Blake Beattie all read the whole book and improved it enormously with their wise comments. Several colleagues here at the University of Tennessee—Robert J. Bast, Palmira Brummett, Michael Kulikowski, and Rosalind Gwynne—also graciously read the whole manuscript at different points in its development and likewise are responsible for innumerable improvements. The history department at this university has been a fine professional home and a stimulating scholarly community for the fifteen years that I have been a part of it: many thanks to colleagues there, especially to Todd Diacon, a fine friend and an excellent department head, who has been unfailingly encouraging. The growing Marco Instutitue for Medieval and Renaissance Studies has become a marvelous second scholarly home on this campus, thanks in large part to the hard work of Bob Bast, its first director, and its energy and intellectual fervor have been a great stimulus to my work. My biggest scholarly debt, though, is surely to another fine friend, Maura K. Lafferty (now, blessedly enough, a colleague at my own university), with whom I have discussed every aspect of this book as I worked on it over the last decade and who also read the whole manuscript, some parts of it twice.

I initially tried out many of the ideas that form the core of this study in a series of invited lectures. I am grateful both to those institutions and to the scholars who brought me to those campuses: the Catholic University of America (Uta-Renate Blumenthal), Tulane University (F. Thomas Luongo), Yale University (María Rosa Menocal), the University of Chicago (Cornell Fleischer), the Warburg Institute in London (Charles S. F. Burnett), the University of North Carolina, Chapel Hill (Maura Lafferty), and the University of Pennsylvania (Jerome Singerman). Some portions of Chapter 2 appeared earlier in my article "*Tafsīr* and Translation: Traditional Qur'ān Exegesis and the Latin Qur'āns of Robert of Ketton and Mark of Toledo," *Speculum* 73 (1998): 703–32. An earlier version of Chapter 6 appeared under the title "The Latin-Arabic Qur'ān Edition of Egidio da Viterbo and the Latin Qur'āns of Robert of Ketton and Mark of Toledo," in *Musulmanes y cristianos en Hispania durante las conquistas de los siglos XII y XIII*, ed. Miquel Barceló and José Martínez Gázquez (Barcelona, 2005), 103–17.

I cannot imagine a better acquisitions editor than Jerry Singerman. He and the rest of the staff at the University of Pennsylvania Press, especially Mariana Martínez and Erica Ginsburg, have been a delight to work with. I owe a special word of thanks to Marie Deer, the astounding copyeditor whom the Press assigned to my book. All authors should be so lucky as to have her work her magic on their manuscripts.

Three members of my family died while I worked on this book. Each of them, I like to think, left the imprint of his character both on me and on the book itself. My eldest brother, James Robert Burman (1953–95), loved, and was a deeply learned scholar of, linguistics and the problems of translation; my younger brother, Edward Ide Burman (1963–98), incarnated both honest seriousness about religion and humble charity toward the religiously other; my father, Robert D. Burman (1925–2003), modeled in the most gracious and goodhearted way imaginable the life of the university professor. *Corpora ipsorum in pace sepulta sunt, et nomen eorum vivit in generationem et generationem* (Ecclesiasticus 44:14). I hope that I have lived up to their examples. I dedicate the book to their memory but also, and equally, to my wife, Elizabeth, and children, David and Erin, three rare gifts whom I do not deserve. I could in no way have brought this project to a close without their support, good cheer, and well-deserved teasing (or Elizabeth's wise advice on matters of both content and style). They have all put up with me and my book for many years now; I suspect that they will each soon write much better ones.

Breinigsville, PA USA
05 January 2011
252709BV00002B/90/P

9 780812 220629